TRANSNATIONAL FRENCH STUDIES

Postcolonialism and *Littérature-monde*

FRANCOPHONE POSTCOLONIAL STUDIES

The annual publication of the Society for Francophone Postcolonial Studies
New Series, Vol. 1

Francophone Postcolonial Studies

New Series, Vol. 1, 2010

The annual publication of the Society for Francophone Postcolonial Studies

The Society for Francophone Postcolonial Studies (SFPS) is an international association which exists in order to promote, facilitate and otherwise support the work of all scholars and researchers working on colonial/postcolonial studies in the French-speaking world. SFPS was created in 2002 with the aim of continuing and developing the pioneering work of its predecessor organization, the Association for the Study of Caribbean and African Literature in French (ASCALF). SFPS does not seek to impose a monolithic understanding of the 'postcolonial' and it consciously aims to appeal to as diverse a range of members as possible, in order to engage in wide-ranging debate on the nature and legacy of colonialism in and beyond the French-speaking world. SFPS encourages work of a transcultural, transhistorical, comparative and interdisciplinary nature. It implicitly seeks to decolonize the term Francophone, emphasizing that it should refer to all cultures where French is spoken (including, of course, France itself), and it encourages a critical reflection on the nature of the cognate disciplines of French Studies, on the one hand, and Anglophone Postcolonial Studies, on the other.

Our vision for this new publication with Liverpool University Press is that each volume will constitute a sort of *état present* on a significant topic embracing various expressions of Francophone Postcolonial Cultures (e.g., literature, film, music, history), in relation to pertinent geographical areas (e.g., France/Belgium, the Caribbean, Africa, the Indian Ocean, Asia, Polynesia) and different periods (slavery, colonialism, the post-colonial era, etc.): above all, we are looking to publish research that will help to set new research agendas across our field. The editorial board of *Francophone Postcolonial Studies* invites proposals for edited volumes touching on any of the areas listed above: proposals should be sent to Professor David Murphy: d.f.murphy@stir.ac.uk. Fur further details, visit: www.sfps.ac.uk.

TRANSNATIONAL FRENCH STUDIES

Postcolonialism and *Littérature-monde*

Edited by
Alec G. Hargreaves,
Charles Forsdick
and David Murphy

Editorial Assistant:
Nora Hertel

Liverpool University Press

First published 2010 by
Liverpool University Press
4 Cambridge Street
Liverpool
L69 7ZU

British Library Cataloguing-in-Publication data
A British Library CIP record is available

ISBN 978-1-84631-483-4 cased

Typeset by Carnegie Book Production, Lancaster
Printed and bound by CPI Antony Rowe, Chippenham and Eastbourne

Contents

Acknowledgements

Among the many people whom the editors would like to thank for the ideas and assistance they contributed in the preparation of this volume, we wish especially to acknowledge Nora Hertel, Office Manager from 2008 to 2010 at the Winthrop-King Institute for Contemporary French and Francophone Studies, who provided outstanding support both as administrative coordinator of the conference from which many of the chapters are drawn and as editorial assistant in the preparation of the manuscript. During the conference, held at Florida State University (FSU) in February 2009 in association with the Society for Francophone Postcolonial Studies (SFPS), Nora was very ably assisted by Ashley Garrigus. William J. Cloonan and other colleagues in the French Division at FSU helped to foster a stimulating intellectual environment for the conference debates. Our two translators, Teresa Bridgeman and Aedín Ní Loingsigh, provided skilful renderings of texts originally written in French, and Emily Harding deserves great praise for her cover illustration which gives brilliant visual form to debates essentially concerned with words and literature. We are also grateful to the editors of *World Literature Today* for their permission to reproduce Daniel Simon's translation of the *littérature-monde* manifesto.

We are particularly grateful to Anthony Cond of Liverpool University Press for his commitment to this project, and for his willingness to develop the collaborative venture with the Society for Francophone Postcolonial Studies of which the present volume marks the first published output.

Finally, we acknowledge the support of our friends and colleagues in Tallahassee, Liverpool, Stirling, on the Executive Committee of SFPS and elsewhere, and would like to extend a warm tribute to our contributors, whose innovative and scholarly work made it such a pleasure to prepare this volume.

Introduction:
What Does *Littérature-monde* Mean for French, Francophone and Postcolonial Studies?

Alec G. Hargreaves, Charles Forsdick and David Murphy

The 2007 manifesto in favour of a 'littérature-monde en français' has generated wide-ranging debate both within French/Francophone Studies and in literary studies more generally. Praised by some for breaking down the hierarchical division between 'French' and 'Francophone' literatures, the manifesto has been criticized by others for recreating that division through an exoticizing vision that continues to privilege the publishing industry of the metropolitan centre of the former empire. For scholars working at the intersection of 'French', 'Francophone' and 'postcolonial' studies, the nomenclature, ambition and bravado of the manifesto make it impossible to ignore, and it has prompted a series of probing questions about the nature, shape and evolution of French-language literary studies. Does the declaration of a *littérature-monde* signal the advent of a new critical paradigm destined to render obsolescent those of 'French', 'Francophone' and/or 'postcolonial' studies? Or is it simply a passing fad, a glitzy but ephemeral publicity stunt generated and promoted by writers and publishing executives from whom scholars and critics should maintain a sceptical distance? Despite – or perhaps because of – its polemical tone, might it serve as a catalyst for new thinking leading beyond current impasses in the theoretical and institutional practices of teaching and research on literatures of French expression? These are among the key questions raised by the manifesto and the debates to which it has given rise.

We do not wish to suggest that these debates are entirely new. The meaning and pertinence of the distinction between 'French' and 'Francophone' studies have already been at the heart of much critical work over the past two decades.

1

To cite just a few of the most prominent examples, a series of special issues
of major journals have sought to explore and evaluate the evolving status of
French Studies as a transnational field of study. For instance, the titles of two
landmark special issues of *Yale French Studies* – 'Post/Colonial Conditions:
Exiles, Migrations, Nomadisms' (Lionnet and Scharfman, 1993) and 'French
and Francophone: The Challenge of Expanding Horizons' (Laroussi and
Miller, 2003) – clearly illustrate that questions of travel and mobility have
been at the heart of a desire on the part of many French/Francophone studies
scholars to de-centre a model of French studies that was focused exclusively
on the hexagon. The scholarly debates launched by the publication of the
littérature-monde manifesto might thus be seen to constitute the latest
phase in what Françoise Lionnet has termed – in her introduction to yet
another prominent journal special issue, co-edited with Dominic Thomas in
Modern Language Notes – 'the "becoming-transnational" of French Studies'
(Lionnet, 2003: 784). If, as the manifesto claims, French is no longer the sole
possession of France, it prompts us to ask: have we finally reached a stage
where the 'and' in 'French and Francophone Studies' unambiguously denotes
equality and complementarity rather than the optional extra that it has often
appeared to signal?

Central to this 'becoming-transnational' of French studies has been a
profound engagement, over the past decade, with a hitherto predominantly
Anglophone postcolonial studies (see Britton and Syrotinski, 2001; Forsdick
and Murphy, 2003 and 2009; Murdoch and Donadey, 2005). The aim of such
work has not been simply to 'import' Anglophone postcolonial theory in
order to render French/Francophone work somehow more nuanced or more
complex. On the contrary, work in this area has sought to open a critical
dialogue with the two existing fields that it straddles. As one of the authors
of the present lines has written previously: 'The persistent assertion of
Francophone Postcolonial Studies as a field of enquiry in its own right reflects
a constructively critical strategy emerging from dissatisfaction with both the
monolingual emphases of postcolonial criticism [...] and the monocultural,
essentially metropolitan biases of French Studies' (Forsdick, 2003: 36). The
emergence of a Francophone postcolonial field has thus taken as a given the
need to question a monocultural vision of French literature, and equally of
French Studies more generally, while it has also insisted upon the need to
embrace a multilingual approach to our postcolonial world.

In many respects, the development of Francophone postcolonial studies
would appear to echo some of the key demands of the *littérature-monde*
manifesto: the challenging of a perceived neo-colonial relationship between
France and its former colonies via the institutions of *Francophonie*; the
demand that French be recognized as a world language that has permanently

escaped from metropolitan control; the celebration of rhizomatic hybridity and mobility over rooted national identities. However, in reality, the relationship between *littérature-monde* and the postcolonial field has been anything but clear cut. For a start, the hostility of Michel Le Bris towards postcolonial approaches to literature has long been documented: he famously denounced Edward Said's *Orientalism* (1978) as 'l'hystérisation de toute pensée, le refus de toute complexité, de toute nuance' [the hystericization of all thought, the refusal of any complexity or nuance] (1995: 197).[1] The manifesto may decry the persistence of colonial mentalities, but its call is for the creation of an egalitarian (and utopian) world literature in French, and not for a more finely attuned historical and political engagement with the legacies of imperialism.

For their part, most scholars active in the field of Francophone postcolonial studies have responded cautiously to the vision of French-language literary studies that has been opened up by the manifesto. While they have acknowledged a shared desire to challenge the Francocentrism of *les lettres françaises*, most of the scholars who have thus far entered the debate have been critical of the manifesto's blind spots and what has generally been perceived as its excessive utopianism. For example, Kathryn Kleppinger's scathing critique of Le Bris *et al.* is evident from the disparaging title of her article 'What's Wrong with the Littérature-Monde Manifesto?' (2010). Kleppinger decries the lack of self-awareness of the contributors to the manifesto, as well as the subsequent volume edited by Le Bris and Rouaud, regarding their own conflicting relationships to the French language; she identifies the ambiguity of the manifesto's seeming challenge to a French universalism that it in other ways appears to reassert; and she is particularly critical of the notion that emerges from the essays by Le Bris and Rouaud that a *littérature-monde* will help to 'save' French literature. Other commentators have perhaps been more measured in their critiques, but a consistent refrain has insisted upon the dangers of simply announcing the end of the French/Francophone dichotomy without taking into account the complex historical and cultural challenge that has been posed by the development of a field called Francophone studies (see Thomas 2010), which intersects in important ways with considerations of the still potent legacy of empire. So, in the light of these debates, does *littérature-monde* offer an all-embracing transnational vista leading beyond the confines of postcolonialism, or reintroduce an incipient form of neo-colonialism even while proclaiming the end of the centre/periphery divide? This is the main

---

[1] Unless otherwise indicated, all translations from French into English are by the authors of this Introduction.

question posed by this collection of essays and our contributors seek to answer it in many different ways.

In order to understand fully the questions outlined above and to set out the rationale for the sections of the volume that follow, there is a need to explore the genealogy of the *littérature-monde* manifesto and the circumstances of its emergence. As contributions to the first two sections of this collection by Deborah Jenson, Typhaine Leservot and Jane Hiddleston make clear, the concept, modes of cultural circulation and loosely defined textual corpus variously gathered under the term 'world-literature in French' are all to be situated in an international context of cosmopolitanism and humanism, and more particularly of historical and contemporary attempts to define a transcultural literary corpus that challenges or ignores the boundaries of the nation state. Such a project emerged clearly in the work of Herder and Goethe in the early nineteenth century (Menges, 2009; Stich, 1949), when the term *Weltliteratur* was coined, and these foundational efforts have been followed by subsequent explorations – in particular by English- and French-language scholars – to sketch out 'world literature' as an academic field (Damrosch, 2003) or the 'république mondiale des lettres' [world republic of letters] as a system of global literary production (Casanova, 2005). The revelation of links between the 2007 text on *littérature-monde en français* and this wider context often depends, however, more on the work of careful reading to which contributors to this collection apply themselves than to any explicit references in the manifesto itself. For the overwhelmingly presentist tone of the manifesto does not situate itself in relation to global or historical debates regarding world literature, and seems implicitly to be more directly in debt to contemporary Francophone thinkers such as Édouard Glissant (whose concept of the *Tout-monde* is closely linked to the hyphenated *littérature-monde*).

The choice of the manifesto form was somewhat surprising given the decline of the form in France since its early twentieth-century Modernist heyday (Caws, 2001), but, as David Murphy, Laura Reeck and Michael Syrotinski make clear in their contributions to this volume, 'Pour une "littérature-monde" en français' forms part of – and is perhaps more importantly to be illuminated by – a network of early twenty-first-century manifesto-style texts that engage in questions of history, culture and identity in the postcolonial French-speaking world. Moreover, this particular manifesto did not itself emerge *ex nihilo*, but represents – as its content and in particular its privileging of travel literature make clear – the latest stage in a series of literary events and phenomena associated with a group of authors loosely associated with Michel Le Bris and the Etonnants Voyageurs literary festival held annually in Saint-Malo, Brittany. Launched in 1990 along with the journal *Gulliver*, the festival was dominated at the outset by a number of travel writers (and other authors, such as Kenneth White, with an interest in the poetics of space) who published in 1992 a *livre-manifeste* entitled *Pour une littérature voyageuse* [For a travelling literature]. In this volume and a series of associated publications, Le Bris set an agenda for what he saw as a new literary movement that, on the one hand, reconnected with the adventure novel of the later nineteenth and early twentieth centuries and that, on the other hand, rejected what were seen as the experimental or theoretical tendencies of post-war French literature (and in particular Structuralism, the New Novel and *autofiction*). The contributions to the *livre-manifeste* were eclectic, ranging from the colonial nostalgia of Jean-Luc Coatalem to the more subtle poetics of disappearance of Nicolas Bouvier, but what united them was the 'guild' identity of contemporary French-language travel writers, an aspect that had many similarities with their English-language equivalents associated in the 1980s with the journal *Granta*. The contributors to *Pour une littérature voyageuse* were exclusively white, metropolitan and male. Any leaning towards such identitarian homogeneity was offset, nevertheless, by the evolution of the festival with which the movement was so closely associated as well as by the bibliography by which the collection of essays that constituted their manifesto concluded.

The Saint-Malo event rapidly evolved to include postcolonial authors from a range of language traditions, although most notably from Francophone Sub-Saharan Africa and the Francophone Caribbean. At the same time, there was a clear diversification of the genres on which the festival focused, with a growing prominence of *bandes dessinées* and detective fiction. From a clear emphasis on travel writing, the *Pour une littérature voyageuse* movement shifted its focus towards an inclusive but hazily neo-realist notion of what, in an often repeated slogan, was described as 'une littérature qui dise le monde' [a literature that recounts the world]. The signatories of the 2007 manifesto include several of the travel writers originally associated with the earlier grouping – most notably Le Bris himself, as well as Alain Borer, Alain Dugrand and Gilles Lapouge – but there is a clear movement away from any earlier metropolitan and even Gallocentric emphases in order to underline the genuinely transnational production of contemporary literature in French. In such a manoeuvre, world literature becomes monolingual, and at the same time seemingly averts the location of *littérature-monde* in a context that is clearly – without adopting the term – postcolonial. David Murphy situates the manifesto in this wider field, suggesting that a reading of the 2007 text in the light of a series of other, often more politicized contemporary statements regarding identity and colonial history reveals the silences and blind spots of a 'world-literature in French' that eclipses the postcolonial dimensions of contemporary literary production and elides any residual distinctiveness of metropolitan and non-metropolitan literary traditions by suggesting that *littérature-monde* does not have a complex 'Francophone' genealogy but is instead a contemporary phenomenon that has emerged from Western travel writing.

It is with such unspoken assumptions and conceptual sleights of hand that many chapters in the present volume engage, accordingly developing some of the immediate – and largely negative – reactions to the manifesto that appeared in the French press. Even President Nicolas Sarkozy entered the debate, outlining in an article in *Le Figaro* (22 March 2007) his frustration over what he saw as the greater prominence achieved by 'Francophone' writers in American, as compared with French, institutions of higher education, but it was Abdou Diouf, general secretary of the Organisation internationale de la Francophonie, who took particular exception to the celebration of the decline of the institution of which he was the head. Diouf (2007) accused the authors of the manifesto of confusing Francocentrism with *Francophonie*, and of conflating a new notion of 'cultural diversity' with the cultural exceptionalism of the past. Diouf's article – and his intervention in debates about world-literature in French at the Saint-Malo festival in May 2007 – could not escape the overtones of an official intervention that their author's status inevitably granted them, and might even counterpro-ductively have granted additional credibility to the manifesto's contrarian stance. What Diouf's shrill defence of *Francophonie* lacked was the histori-cizing and contextualizing approach evident in a further response, that of Amadou Lamine Sall and Lilyan Kesteloot (2007), who focused on what they saw as a striking flaw in the manifesto, its overt emphasis on the contem-porary, and its unwillingness to acknowledge the important traditions of non-metropolitan literature in French to which – rather than to post-war travel writing – a number of its signatories were heir. Sall and Kesteloot spared few punches. They presented the *littérature-monde* movement as a barely veiled act of marketing contemporary literary works, and criticized its principal signatories for what they saw as ignorance of an earlier generation of authors – including diverse key figures such as Jacques Roumain, Jacques Stephen Alexis, Mongo Beti, Ferdinand Oyono, Jean Métellus, Joseph Zobel, Sembène Ousmane, Bernard Dadié, Cheikh Hamidou Kane, Olympe Bhély-Quenum, Bertène Juminer – who had, since the interwar period, expressed a very similar critique regarding the neo-colonial assumptions of the French metropolitan literary establishment and the persistence of centre-periphery relations on which this depended.

Jean-Pierre Cavaillé, in another early article on the manifesto (2007), had underlined what he saw as the latent Gallocentrism of *littérature-monde*, which failed to acknowledge the oxymoronic contradictions of a phenomenon that purports to have a global reach but retains a stubbornly monolingual definition. Cavaillé's short piece in *Libération* – 'Francophones, l'écriture est polyglotte' – suggests that the *littérature-monde* manifesto ends up performing the very agenda it seeks to challenge. 'World-literature in French' is seen to be closely associated with the French and Francophone publishing circuits centred on Paris itself, and ultimately reveals traces of the conservatism detected by Dominic Thomas in his study, in this volume, of often perplexed French reactions to Marie NDiaye's 2009 Goncourt prize, or of the exoticism detected by Jean-Xavier Ridon who sees in the concept of *littérature-monde* a reheating of metropolitan strategies of cultural domestication. As Cavaillé concludes:

> En fait, il s'agissait simplement de simuler sa propre crise, de jouer le décentrement pour se réimposer comme centre; centre de légitimité et de légitimation non plus des littératures du monde (la chose n'est visiblement plus possible), mais des littératures d'expression française dans le monde. De cette opération, l'idéologie de la francophonie ne sort pas vaincue, contrairement à la tonitruante proclamation, mais triomphante.[2]

No less significantly, as Thomas Spear signals in his chapter, the manifesto ignores the fact that Francophone literary production in sites such as Montreal and Port-au-Prince is evolving progressively and is increasingly distancing itself from the need for such neo-colonial legitimacy and legitimization.

Since the publication in 2008 of Camille de Toledo's mordant study of the concept of *littérature-monde*, criticizing the loose notion of realism on which the subject of the manifesto – as well as its predecessor, *littérature voyageuse* – appears to be based, the ripples initially caused by the manifesto within the hexagon have largely subsided. Notwithstanding a further flurry of media attention for *littérature-monde* signatories who in 2010 coined the related notion of 'identité-monde' (Le Bris and Rouaud, 2010) as a rejoinder to the recent political debate on French national identity, considered as a whole the main impact of the *littérature-monde* manifesto appears to have been outside France and even beyond the parameters of the French-speaking world. In his autobiography, Le Bris lists the numerous colloquia and special

---

[2] In fact it was simply a matter of feigning their own crisis, of adopting the rhetoric of decentring in order to reimpose themselves as centre: the centre of legitimacy and legitimization not of the world's literature (patently not possible), but of literatures in French across the world. In this way, far from being vanquished (as the manifesto noisily proclaims), the ideology of *francophonie* emerges triumphant.

issues of journals devoted to *littérature-monde* (2009: 354–56),[3] presenting this external attention and French metropolitan indifference as proof of the continued centripetalism of the Parisian literary establishment, and of the persistent hierarchization of 'French' and 'Francophone' literatures this supposedly betokens.

In the light of this situation, the future of *littérature-monde en français* – as historical phenomenon still under construction, *état présent* of contemporary literary production, or project yet to be realized – remains uncertain, for although the concept remains central to the rationale (and programming) of the Saint-Malo festival, the illustrative journal promised as part of the 'Convention de Saint-Malo' (Le Bris, Mabanckou, Rouaud and Waberi, 2007) has not yet seen the light of day. The genealogies of the term – and the often contradictory conceptual resonances with associated notions – continue to attract scholarly attention, as the chapters in this volume by Mounia Benalil and Typhaine Leservot make particularly clear. At the same time, 'world-literature in French' serves as a vehicle for disciplinary debates – or, perhaps more accurately, as an amplifier and at times catalyst for pre-existing debates – about the appropriate ways to study the cultural production of France and the French-speaking world. Charles Forsdick's chapter, providing a Francophone spin to issues first raised in Ngũgĩ's 1972 text 'On the Abolition of the English Department', suggests that *littérature-monde* in many ways echoes and confirms post-national shifts evident in French studies for some decades, whilst Lydie Moudileno counsels against the erosion of a distinctive field of 'Francophone studies' that the potentially apolitical levelling of the notion enacts. Several other contributors to this volume suggest concrete directions in which the concept might be drawn, to expand its reach or illuminate its current limits. Jacqueline Dutton accordingly engages with the mobility that appears to underpin *littérature-monde* to posit a more concrete emphasis on literatures of migration, focusing on a zone largely if not entirely ignored in the manifesto, that of Australasia. Michelle Keown similarly focuses on the Pacific, but to suggest the ways in which a reading of *littérature-monde* in the light of French-language literary production of the region raises questions of classification whose implications are much more than taxonomic.

---

[3] These include the international conference on '*Littérature-monde*: New Wave or New Hype?' hosted in February 2009 by Florida State University's Winthrop-King Institute for Contemporary French and Francophone Studies, from which selected papers are included here together with others commissioned for the present volume. For other papers from the Winthrop-King Institute conference, see Célestin, Cloonan, DalMolin and Hargreaves (2010).

In future considerations of *littérature-monde*, particularly in those inspired by postcolonial criticism and by a more general engagement with questions of translation and transcultural exchange, it is likely, however, that two issues will predominate. The first is the importance of politics, and not simply cultural politics, in matters of contemporary literary interpretation and cultural circulation, an aspect foregrounded by Chris Bongie in his polemical engagement with Édouard Glissant's and Lyonel Trouillot's roles as signatories of the manifesto and as scribes of the post-politics that, in Bongie's view, the document represents. Bongie represents *in extremis* a position adopted by a number of contributors to this volume, namely that the celebratory, hybridizing, universalizing ambitions of *littérature-monde* risk replicating – rather than questioning, let alone critiquing – the globalizing, entropic tendencies of contemporary cultural production. The more recent notion of *identité-monde*, explored in a further collection of essays edited by Le Bris and Rouaud, would undoubtedly benefit from interrogation along these lines, for it too depends on the coupling of distinct terms by a hyphen that at once globalizes and undermines distinctiveness, presenting as universalized what is more accurately 'worlded'. Central to such an interpretation are persistent discussions of the universal and the translatable, debates that Peter Hallward has himself articulated in the light of a distinction between the 'singular' and the 'specific' (2001). In the current volume, Jeanne Garane interrogates *littérature-monde* through translation theory and the question of the specific locations of literary production, and this is the second area to which critiques of 'world-literature in French', and 'world literature' more generally, are likely to contribute. These are not, or are not only, questions of language, although the 'en français' coupled with 'littérature-monde' makes the concept by turns enabling and disabling, inclusive and exclusive. They touch instead – as Emily Apter's comments in the Afterword to this volume make clear – on wider philosophical issues of translatability, untranslatability and the politics of cultural relationality, and lead us to engage anew with the linkages, connections and disjunctions between the two terms maintained in tension by the hyphen of 'littérature-monde'.

Works Cited

Britton, Celia, and Michael Syrotinski (eds). 2001. *Paragraph* 24.3. [Special issue: 'Francophone Texts and Postcolonial Theory'.]

Casanova, Pascale. 2005. *The World Republic of Letters*. Trans. by M. B. DeBevoise. Cambridge, MA: Harvard University Press.

Cavaillé, Jean-Pierre. 2007. 'Francophones, l'écriture est polyglotte'. *Libération* 30 March.

Caws, Mary Ann (ed.). 2001. *Manifesto: A Century of Isms*. Lincoln and London: University of Nebraska Press.

Célestin, Roger, William J. Cloonan, Eliane DalMolin and Alec G. Hargreaves (eds). 2010. *Contemporary French and Francophone Studies: Sites* 14.1 [Special issue: '*Littérature-Monde*: New Wave or New Hype?']

Damrosch, David. 2003. *What is World Literature?* Princeton, NJ and Oxford: Princeton University Press.

Diouf, Abdou. 2007. 'La francophonie, une réalité oubliée'. *Le Monde* 20 March.

Forsdick, Charles. 2003. 'Challenging the Monolingual, Subverting the Monocultural: The Strategic Purposes of Francophone Postcolonial Studies'. *Francophone Postcolonial Studies* 1.1: 33–41.

Forsdick, Charles, and David Murphy (eds). 2003. *Francophone Postcolonial Studies: A Critical Introduction*. London: Arnold.

—. (eds). 2009. *Postcolonial Thought in the French-Speaking World*. Liverpool: Liverpool University Press.

Hallward, Peter. 2001. *Absolutely Postcolonial: Writing Between the Singular and the Specific*. Manchester: Manchester University Press.

Kleppinger, Kathryn. 2010. 'What's Wrong with the Littérature-Monde Manifesto?'. *Contemporary French and Francophone Studies: Sites* 14.1: 77–84. [Special issue: Roger Célestin, William J. Cloonan, Eliane DalMolin and Alec G. Hargreaves (eds). '*Littérature-Monde*: New Wave or New Hype?']

Laroussi, Farid, and Christopher L. Miller (eds). 2003. *Yale French Studies* 103. [Special issue: 'French and Francophone: The Challenge of Expanding Horizons'.]

Le Bris, Michel. 1995. *Fragments du royaume*. Vénisseux: Paroles d'Aube.

—. 2009. *Nous ne sommes pas d'ici: autobiographie*. Paris: Grasset.

Le Bris, Michel, and Jean Rouaud (eds). 2010. *Je est un autre: pour une identité-monde*. Paris: Gallimard.

Le Bris, Michel, Alain Mabanckou, Jean Rouaud and Abdourahman Waberi. 2007. 'Convention de Saint-Malo "Pour une littérature-monde en français"' Etonnants-voyageurs. 16 March. <http://www.etonnants-voyageurs.com/spip.php?article1575>. Consulted on 12 April 2009.

Lionnet, Françoise. 2003. 'Introduction'. *Modern Language Notes* 118.4: 783–86. [Special issue: 'Francophone Studies: New Landscapes', edited by Françoise Lionnet and Dominic Thomas.]

Lionnet, Françoise and Ronnie Scharfman (eds). 1993. *Yale French Studies* 82–83. [Special issues: 'Post/Colonial Conditions: Exiles, Migrations, Nomadisms'.]

Menges, K. 2009. 'Particular Universals: Herder on National Literature, Popular Literature and World Literature'. In H. Adler and W. Koepke (eds), *A Companion to the Work of Johann Gottfried Herder*. Rochester, NY: Camden House: 189–213.

Murdoch, H. Adlai, and Anne Donadey (eds). 2005. *Postcolonial Theory and Francophone Literary Studies*. Gainesville: University Press of Florida.

Ngũgĩ Wa Thiong'o. 1995. 'On the Abolition of the English Department'. In Bill Ashcroft, Gareth Griffiths and Helen Tiffin (eds), *The Postcolonial Studies Reader*. London: Routledge: 438–42. [First published in *Homecoming: Essays on African and Caribbean Literature, Culture and Politics*. New York: Lawrence Hill and Co. (1972).]

Said, Edward W. 1978. *Orientalism: Western Conceptions of the Orient*. London: Routledge and Kegan Paul.

Sall, Amadou Lamine, and Lilyan Kesteloot. 2007. 'Un peu de mémoire, s'il vous plaît!'. *Le Monde* 6 April.

Sarkozy, Nicolas. 2007. 'Pour une francophonie vivante et populaire'. *Le Figaro* 22 March.

Stich, F. 1949. *Goethe and World Literature*. Trans. by C. A. M. Sym. London: Routledge and Kegan Paul.

Thomas, Dominic. 2010. 'Decolonizing France: From National Literatures to World Literatures'. *Contemporary French and Francophone Studies: Sites* 14.1: 47–55. [Special issue: William J. Cloonan and Alec G. Hargreaves (eds), '*Littérature-Monde*: New Wave or New Hype?']

Toledo, Camille de. 2008. *Visiter le Flurkistan, ou les illusions de la littérature monde*. Paris: Presses Universitaires de France.

From World Literature
to *Littérature-monde*:
Genre, History and
the Globalization of Literature

Francophone World Literature (*Littérature-monde*), Cosmopolitanism and Decadence: 'Citizen of the World' without the Citizen?

Deborah Jenson

'I, too, am a translated man'

Salman Rushdie, *Shame* (1983)

The resurgence of cosmopolitanism as a 'wedge issue' in the 2008 US presidential election following Barack Obama's reference to 'citizen of the world' (one occurrence), 'people of the world' (six occurrences), and 'world' *tout court* (a stunning thirty occurrences) in his 24 July 2008 Berlin speech, is a reminder that cosmopolitanism is a powerful precedent for any 'world' philosophy, whether related to law, politics, economy or letters. The candidate Obama's oratorical 'worldliness' led to George F. Will's column 'The Cosmopolitan', in which Will associated the expressions 'citizen of the world' and 'global citizenship' with the elevation of 'narcissism to a political philosophy'. To be a citizen of the world is an oxymoron, Will argued, since 'Citizenship is defined by legal and loyalty attachments to a particular political entity with a distinctive regime and culture. Neither the world nor the globe is such an entity' (Will, 2008). This preceded Rudy Giuliani's Republican convention line, 'I'm sorry that Barack Obama feels that [Sarah Palin's] hometown isn't cosmopolitan enough' (Giuliani, 2008), which was abbreviated in sound bites to the curt jeer, 'Not Cosmopolitan Enough for You?'[1]

---

[1] The election blogosphere was filled with repetitions of this line. Some blog commentators seemed to relish the drama of pointing to themselves while asking Barack Obama himself this question, as in the case of Ronnie, on 16 October

15

The 'world' has been creeping into the place occupied by the term 'French' or 'Francophone' in descriptions of the increasingly transnational field of literature studied by *vingtièmistes* in the French field: the French-language or Francophone linguistic basis of *littérature-monde* is simply designated through the language of the term describing the targeted corpus. This construct of 'World Literature' in the French-speaking world is fundamentally based on recognition of the transnational nature of *francophonie*, outside of now outdated and over-determined colonial coordinates. As Alain Mabanckou put it in an article published in 2006: 'La littérature francophone est un grand ensemble dont les tentacules enlacent plusieurs continents',[2] whereas 'La littérature française est une littérature nationale. C'est à elle d'entrer dans ce grand ensemble francophone'.[3] The philosophically corrective stance of *littérature-monde*, as we approach the fiftieth anniversary of the postcolonial era, not only towards the colonial architecture of *francophonie*, but towards the much older (even transhistorical)[4] cosmopolitical paradigm, highlights the omnipresent fault-lines within cosmopolitanism of unprivileged transnational migration.

In this chapter I will relate those suppressed fault-lines of migrant rather than citizen cosmopolitanism, as they are revalorized in the post-colonization

---

2008, on hotair.com: 'I'm going to the next Obama rally anywhere near me, and I WILL get my question answered if I have to take a bullhorn. "What's wrong, Obama? Plumbers not cosmopolitan enough for you?"'

 [2] 'Francophone literature is a large organism whose tentacles stretch across several continents'. Unless otherwise indicated, all translations from French into English are by the author of this chapter.

 [3] 'French literature is a national literature. It has to become part of this vast Francophone ensemble'.

 [4] The specific form of universalism within cosmopolitanism, established around the universality of translocal political institutions, debts and commitments, has to be coordinated with inevitably local social existence. The fragile equilibrium between these two spheres can be conceptualized in psychoanalytic terms as the problematic relation of the collective to the individual ego, with the bourgeois family mediating the alienating space between them. It also extends to the problematic relation between currently living populations and the historical and future existence of other life. Although 'transhistoricism' generally has a bad rap within the research sphere, as a marker of globalized identifications and lack of attention to historical detail, it presents the same potentially ideal but fraught universalism as the transnational or any other form of the translocal. The work of Edmund Burke on the rights of deceased generations in the 1790 *Reflections on the Revolution in France* epitomizes the problematic rather than ideal form of this would-be universalism through its anti-Semitism and anti-progressivism.

framework of *littérature-monde*, to the troubled and troubling forms of cosmopolitanism whose polycultural dissonance inspired the nineteenth-century literary and artistic movement of decadence. The positioning of French-language literature with regard to a transregional polis, even if it is one in which the *citizen* is no longer the key political emblem of the human in the world, replaced by the plurality of the Rushdian category of *hommes traduits*[5] as embraced by Michel Le Bris and Jean Rouaud in the spring 2007 *littérature-monde* manifesto, invokes the history of debates about (and aesthetics derived from) cosmopolitanism's relationship to slaves, workers, migrants and diasporas.

This is a cosmopolitanism remapped over the sprawling and often disorienting linguistic and cultural encounters of a moment of globalization in which Western imperialist hegemonies are themselves becoming the translational vehicles of a larger and inconsistently ideological economic hegemony.[6] Economic globalization challenges Stuart Hall's Gramscian observation in 1988 that 'Ruling or dominant conceptions of the world [may] not directly prescribe the mental content of [...] the heads of the dominated classes. But the circle of dominant ideas *does* accumulate the symbolic power to map or classify the world for others' (Hall, 1988: 44). It is not clear that the US or France or Great Britain continue to hold the power to classify the world for others to the same degree, not so much because of autonomous resistance to Euro-American hegemony, but because the very factors that reinforce the wealth of Western nations are increasingly disassociated from political selfhood. (What one might categorize as an extreme rendition of *laissez-faire* liberal agency may in effect be a waning of the historically delimited and almost magical status of the nation state in the modern era.) Ideological hegemony, as '*a condition in process* in which a dominant class (in alliance with other classes or class fractions) does not merely *rule* a society but

---

[5] The adoption of Salman Rushdie's expression 'translated man' [hommes traduits] is one of the more expressive aspects of the 'Pour une "littérature-monde" en français' manifesto by Michel Le Bris and Jean Rouaud, signed by forty-two additional writers.

[6] The epistemological challenge in the humanities and social sciences of moving from structural assumptions about 'hegemonic control over peripheral material and human resources – colonial control during the era of British hegemony, monopoly control during U.S. hegemony, transnational control in the contemporary period of capitalist restructuring' to awareness of 'transnational integration of networks of finance, production, and trace' makes 'reformulation of our inherited categories of analysis imperative' according to R. A. Palat (2000: 66–67).

leads it through the exercise of *"moral and intellectual leadership"'* (Storey, 2006: 63–64)[7] is circumstantially rather than politically undermined by globalized market and migrant dynamics which surpass, in their power to shape societies mimetically, the power of exclusive identities. In this translational and vehicular phase of now antipodal economic imperialisms (China as well as the US, or new economic 'couplings' such as Africa and China), they continue to arbitrate social entry and socioeconomic status, but they no longer directly aspire to or succeed in imposing ontologies of worlding. In the words of Ken Surin, 'the absolute spatial division between exploiters and exploited posited by more conventional Marxism has effectively been eliminated – the exploiters are everywhere and so are the exploited' (Surin, 1997: 208). (This is, without question, a highly contested area of political theory. Is globalization simply a myth fostered by American hegemony, as scholars including G. John Ikenberry (2007: 41–61) have suggested? Is what we may think of as globalization really a form of hegemony exercised from something other than 'a hegemon or seat of empire', as John A. Agnew (2005: 13) argues?)

Le Bris, later joined by Rouaud and other like-minded individuals in the Etonnants Voyageurs literary festival organization, originally sought out 'the world' not in relation to a postcolonial project but as a refuge from the social dominance in French intellectual circles of the semiotic paradigm. Like pilgrims fleeing the intricate rituals of the Roman-influenced Anglican Church, they hoped that, in Le Bris's words, 'après des décennies d'asservissement au Signe-Roi' [after decades of subjugation to the Sign-King] literature would be able to *'retrouver le monde'* [rediscover the world] (Le Bris, 2007: 28). However, 'Francophone' literary co-signatories of the manifesto saw in the 'world' trope not a way around the problem of the socially and intellectually impenetrable relegation of the world to the *hors-texte*, but a new form of literary potential at the intersection of the postcolonial and the cosmopolitan, with which *littérature-monde* has become decisively associated. Le Bris and Rouaud opportunistically embraced this post-*francophonie* identity, no matter how philosophically incompatible with their own flight from an ultra-cosmopolitan academic metropole, dominated by the likes of the Algerian-French philosopher Jacques Derrida, Lithuanian-French philosopher Emmanuel Levinas, Algerian-French Marxist theorist Louis

---

[7] John Storey also notes that 'Hegemony involves a specific kind of consensus: a social group seeks to present its particular interests as the interests of society as a whole', yielding 'a society in which subordinate groups and classes appear to actively support and subscribe to values, ideals, objectives [which] "incorporate" them into the prevailing structures of power' (Storey, 2006: 63–64).

Althusser, Algerian-French writer Hélène Cixous and the Bulgarian-French intellectuals Julia Kristeva and Tzevtan Todorov (not to mention the transnational origins of many writers at the heart of the twentieth-century French canon, from Guillaume Apollinaire, Albert Camus, Natalie Sarraute and Claude Simon to Michel Houellebecq). Tossing out decades of exploration of the politics of translation among *hommes [et femmes] traduits* in the academic world, and the brilliant earlier engagement of some among their own ranks, notably Édouard Glissant, with the dreaded Sign-King, not to mention the firm entrenchment of many of their co-signatories, such as Mabanckou, in academia, Le Bris and Rouaud advanced directly to a new millennial French-language movement that would parallel the Anglophone postcolonial and World Literature traditions. Thus perceived, Francophone writers 'étaient moins les produits de la décolonisation que les premiers acteurs d'une nouvelle vague internationale, et transculturelle' (Pico Iyer paraphrased by Le Bris, 2007: 33).[8]

As Le Bris convincingly notes, the internationalism and transculturalism of a cosmopolitan-identified World Literature (as distinct from the 'world literature' from all ages and places outside of the Western canons taught in primary and secondary school curricula in the US) had been primarily identified as the provenance of the Anglophone world: 'Limité d'abord aux villes-mondes anglo-saxonnes,[9] le mouvement était désormais mondial, témoin d'un gigantesque toho-bohu planétaire' (2007: 38).[10]

Even against that dominant Anglophone/World Literature alignment, the non-alignment of *francophonie* with cosmopolitanism is not intuitive, and it arguably took *littérature-monde* to make their disjuncture more salient. *Francophonie* as a transregional French-language world and literature originated within the French colonial project and has long had a relation to French colonial and neo-colonial ambitions, as Jean-Marc Moura suggests (2007: 163). The coercive nature of the colonial project, combined with the racial hierarchies that undermine the ostensibly universalist aspirations of

---

8 'were not so much products of decolonization as the first actors in a new wave of internationalism and transculturalism'.

9 Anglo-Saxon is a misnomer in this formulation; the World Literature of the Anglophone world cannot be Anglo-Saxon, even if the Anglophone publishing arena previously had been associated with Anglo-Saxon ethnic identity. In this connection, Le Bris pertinently notes Rushdie's genealogy of an Anglophone heritage for World Literature as 'l'histoire de l'immigration en Grande-Bretagne' [the history of immigration to Britain] (Le Bris, 2007: 36).

10 'Initially limited to Anglo-Saxon global cities, the movement then became globalized, in a testament to a gigantic planetary reshuffling'

its *mission civilisatrice,* made colonialism as a political system incompatible with the political theory of cosmopolitanism. Whether the mixing of populations and cultures and the transregional world experience of even subjugated colonial demographics fit the cosmopolitical model is a much more complex problem. Charles Forsdick contends that 'Despite the intention to "de-colonize" the epithet "Francophone" and to redeploy it inclusively', especially at the intersection between 'new intercultural or translational dynamics', the colonial implications of '*La Francophonie* as a political project persist' (Forsdick, 2005: 526). Achille Mbembe argues that today no major black intellectuals continue to locate their 'world politics' at the crossroads of *francité* and the critically cosmopolitan ethos of *négritude* because of the historical baggage of *francophonie* (Mbembe, 2007).[11] The 'world' of Anglophone World Literature has not shown itself to be particularly aligned with the African diaspora, however, and the potential shifting of African and African diasporan French-language writers from the Francophone rubric to the *littérature-monde* rubric only partially addresses potential needs for the strategic representation of arguably majoritarian African/African diasporan stakeholders in the literary group formerly identified as 'Francophone'.[12]

---

[11] 'Il n'y a plus, aujourd'hui, un seul grand intellectuel noir disposé à célébrer sans façons les noces de la "négritude" et de la "francité", comme n'hésitait pas à le faire, récemment encore, Léopold Sédar Senghor.' [Today not a single leading black intellectual is willing unequivocally to celebrate the marriage of *négritude* and *francité*, as Léopold Sédar Senghor continued to do until recently.]

[12] *Francophonie,* despite earnest attempts by interested scholars to encompass the French-language literature of Western European nations such as Belgium and Switzerland into its 'canon', remains stubbornly associated in US academic practice with Africa, the African diaspora (notably in the Caribbean), and other regions formerly colonized by Western European nations in the context of triangular trade. Theories related to race-based identity politics, and literary content related to the history of slavery in colonialism, are widely represented in the 'Francophone' field. In Francophone World Literature, one can see a side effect of displacement of African/African diasporan authors from majority status among the 'Francophone' authors studied in US French departments, in the list of co-signatories on the *littérature-monde* manifesto. It includes slightly less than half African (including North African) and African diasporan (notably Caribbean) authors; and yet, if the group had been defined as 'Francophone', with French writers related to another category, the African/African diasporan group would have represented the large majority, surrounded by a relatively small contingent of Asian, Eastern European and Quebecois authors. On a strategic level, however, registering in the twentieth- and twenty-first-century fields, rather than being compartmentalized in a category implicitly related

Littérature-monde as a willed identity implies that what I will call the decadent cosmopolitanism of the new millennium legitimately edges voice and aesthetics away from identity politics, especially those derived from the particular modern monumentality of colonial triangular trade, and towards a universalism born of the migrant trajectories of globalization.

Cosmopolitanism and Diaspora

The Greek trope of the *kosmopolites* or 'citizen of the world' came into use in the early third century BCE, a time when the role of the citizen had a clear counterpoint in the role of the slave. In a globalized third millennium, the question of what it might mean to be a citizen of a world polis rather than a national, state, city or republican polis remains hotly contested on the diverse possible levels of political, economic, ethical or literary cosmopolitan identity and action. Cosmopolitanism, as Sheldon Pollock, Homi Bhabha, Carol A. Breckenridge, and Dipesh Chakrabarty note, is one of 'today's most challenging problems of academic analysis and political practice, especially when analysis and practice are seen [...] as a conjoint activity' (2002: 1). Diaspora, an even more ancient term, may not be a conjoint activity of academic analysis and political practice, but it does span academic analysis and social reality. Jana Evans Braziel and Anita Mannur describe that social reality in the following terms: 'Diaspora can perhaps be seen as a naming of the other which has historically referred to displaced communities of people who have been dislocated from their native homelands through the movements of migration, immigration, or exile' (Braziel and Manur, 2003:1). Yet if diaspora studies and cosmopolitan studies today elbow one another for room in the humanities, it may well be because diaspora in our time is associated with not just academic analysis and a social reality, but a social practice – a social practice involving the maintenance and empowerment of an ethnic or cultural identity and community that have been threatened through dislocation. This social practice in turn often becomes a political practice.

Some scholars are actively pursuing the confluence of diaspora and political practice. Kim Butler writes:

Narratives of diaspora once focused on oppression and displacement; today they focus on diaspora as a potential strategy of empowerment.

---

to colonialism, has been embraced by Mabanckou and others. The tendency to move from a grouping influenced by identity politics to a more universally defined thematic categorization can be seen in numerous other fields, such as the trajectory in many departments from Women's Studies to Gender Studies.

The ability to harness that potential varies greatly from one diaspora to the next, and these differences are evident between different branches of single diasporas as well. [...] As a multi-layered diaspora, the African example illuminates the vast difference in political options for recent emigrants from nation-states versus the slave-era dispersals from a generic continental homeland. To what extent is it possible to coordinate multiple types of strategies towards a collective transnational political agenda? (Butler, 2007: 19–20)

There is arguably a significant internal split between the political narrative of diaspora as dislocation – the *hors-polis* – and the political narrative of empowerment in diasporan communities as one small transnational polis in a larger network of transnational diasporan communities. In Butler's terms, this would represent a 'meta-diaspora'; this latter development is far closer to cosmopolitanism as traditionally conceived.

Ostensibly, cosmopolitanism involves an avoidance of any political engagement that is based on restrictive identity claims – even those that one might find in a diasporan community. The French histories of colonial and postcolonial literature, and of literatures in other languages associated with the histories of French (post)colonialism such as creole (*kreyòl*), are marked by their difference from the potentially universalizing linguistic embrace of Anglophone World Literature, in which one feature of 'world' status, as Rebecca Walkowitz has demonstrated, is simply the translation and dissemination of literatures from other languages into English within the Anglophone literary marketplace (Walkowitz, 2006: 1–32). A field of Francophone World Literature implicitly invokes the paradox of non-universal 'worlds', such as the universalism of pan-Africanist *négritude*, and of diasporan cosmopolitanism.

Cosmopolitanism involves recognition of all cosmos-dwellers as fellow members of a shared entity with civic and political responsibilities such as those that align with the privileges of citizenship ('citizen of the world'). Although cosmopolitanism does not exclude what Will, in his column on cosmopolitanism as narcissism, cited as the 'legal and loyalty attachments to a particular political entity with a distinctive regime and culture' (Will, 2008), it nevertheless strongly encourages what Amanda Anderson calls 'reflective distance from one's own cultural affiliations, a broad understanding of other cultures and customs, and a belief in universal humanity and structures that exceed the boundaries of the local' (Anderson, 1998: 267).

Pollock, Bhabha, Breckenridge and Chakrabarty contend that '[a]s a historical category, the cosmopolitan should be considered entirely open, and not pregiven or foreclosed by the definition of any particular society or discourse' (2002: 1). Yet, as Chakrabarty separately notes, 'we "world" this earth' in diverse ways, all belying 'universalistic assumptions about history or human nature' (Chakrabarty, 2002: 82); there is no purely constructionist cosmopolitan openness that is devoid of all essentialist affiliations. In fact, the historic moments and geopolitical sites of maximum interest in cosmopolitanism, notably the ancient republics and the European Enlightenment, have tended to project commitment to the world from a position of cultural panopticism and privileged clairvoyance. Humanist philosophies of cosmopolitanism can, in their most uncharitable interpretation, seem like synecdoches of 'worlding', with the privileged part standing in for the whole, rather than combining strategies with the whole – if we can apprehend the whole at all.

Writers have critiqued cosmopolitanism since the nineteenth century for a polyvalent liberal or neoliberal blindness to the ways that capital and labour organize individuals' access to the infrastructural field of this cosmopolitical openness. While Marx and Engels (1848) acknowledged the 'cosmopolitan' dissolution of national economic cultures in modernity, and even the yielding of 'national and local literature' into 'world literature',[13] they did so without sanctioning the implicit pluralism of a cosmic political identification as a legitimate instantiation of the communist international. Marx viewed cosmopolitanism as a kind of trick played by international money on the identity of the commodity owner, who finds himself newly minted as a cosmopolitan through his possession of circulating commodities and his relations to other commodity owners: 'As money develops into international money, so the commodity-owner becomes a cosmopolitan. The cosmopolitan relations of men to one another originally comprise only their relations as commodity-owners. Commodities as such are indifferent to all religious, political, national and linguistic barriers' (Marx, 1858). Engels cited Ludwig Börne's perception of cosmopolitanism as effete in its non-applicability to the world of *main d'œuvre*, working hands; he wrote of the 'shame of cosmopolitanism, which merely had impotent, more pious wishes' (Engels, 1841). Engels also noted Börne's critique of cosmopolitanism

---

13 'The bourgeoisie has through its exploitation of the world market given a cosmopolitan character to production and consumption in every country. All old-established national industries have been destroyed [...]. And as in material, so also in intellectual production. The intellectual creations of individual nations become common property. National one-sidedness and narrow-mindedness become more and more impossible, and from the numerous national and local literatures, there arises a world literature' (Marx and Engels, 1848).

with 'the words of the Cid: *Lengua sin manos, cuemo osas fablar?* (Tongue without hands, how dare you speak?)' (Engels, 1841).

The modern Western use of the term cosmopolitan as a synonym for the metropolitan sophisticate has created connotations, like those invoked in the Sarah Palin anti-cosmopolitan identification, of cosmopolitans' circulation in the world with the possession of a 'ticket to ride', not with slave holds or cattle cars or illegal immigration. The classical cosmopolitan circulates as a free and individual agent in world spaces, analogous to tourists or international students or expatriates. Logically, however, many urbane cosmopolitans, or their parents, must have entered transcultural spaces through unprivileged diasporan migration.

There is in fact a discursive tradition of associating slaves, diasporas and migrants with cosmopolitanism, but this unpassported cosmopolitan experience of transculturality generally has been framed pejoratively. Stalin denounced critics of the Soviet state as *bezrodnye kosmopolity*, 'rootless cosmopolitans', a term which came to connote Jewish intellectuals.[14] African slaves in the New World were sometimes called cosmopolitans, as in this 1802 newspaper editorial about 'Negro cosmopolites' of the Haitian Revolution: 'If LeClerc has an ill opinion of the Cosmopolites, he is much mistaken; they will baffle all his skill, they will not attack him by day, but at night, and then they are in a state of nudity in the bushes; consequently they possess every advantage over the whites'.[15] Such negative applications of the generally idealistic term 'cosmopolitan' show the threat to dominant subject positions of accepting that those who have been forcibly 'dispersed' in the world have in the process received an important education about the larger world, via their transcultural and polyglot experiences.

If the philosophical discourse of cosmopolitanism has been critiqued for an unintentionally blithe relationship to citizenship, commodity ownership and free crossing of borders, does this suggest that cosmopolitanism colludes with imperialist power? Ultimately, the relationship of cosmopolitanism to imperialism is a vexed one. The Roman Empire often has been viewed as an example, even if failed, of a cosmopolis. Eric Brown and Pauline Kleingeld write that the idea of the cosmopolis was popularized during the Roman Empire: 'Empire made the doctrine [of cosmopolitanism] very easy for many Romans by identifying the Roman *patria* with the cosmopolis itself. [...]

---

[14] See Herman Ermolaev (1997: 100) on the history of the rootless cosmopolitan trope under Stalin.

[15] Extract of a letter, received by the ship Lydia, via Philadelphia, from 'a gentleman in St. Domingo', to his correspondent in this city, dated 'Cape François, 20 February 1802' in the *Gazette of the United States* 20 March 1802.

[T]he rise of the Roman Empire united the whole of the Mediterranean under one political power' (Brown and Kleingeld, 2002). Clearly, this origin has the potential to frame cosmopolis as a veiled analogy for empire, but it is important to note that cosmopolitanism began to be articulated as a philosophical discourse and ideal in ancient Greece and the Roman Republic, *prior* to the assimilation of Greece into the Roman Empire. Kleingeld and Brown emphasize that cosmopolitanism cannot be viewed as a sequel to either the rise or fall of Rome, both because the discourse pre-dated the Empire, and also because Rome continued to foster important forms of local political and cultural engagement after its imperial genesis. Nevertheless, they note, 'there is no doubting that the empires under which Stoicism developed and flourished made many people more receptive to the cosmopolitan ideal and thus contributed greatly to the widespread influence of Stoic cosmopolitanism' (Brown and Kleingeld, 2002).

For Sheldon Pollock, the spread of the Latin language under Rome serves at once as an example of linguistic cosmopolitanism, and as a means of distinguishing between the spread of empire and true cosmopolis. If one can define cosmopolitanism as literary communication 'that travels far, indeed, without obstruction from any boundaries', it was demonstrated by the spread of *Latinitas* 'in places as diverse as Gallia, Lusitania, Tripolitana, Egypt, Cappadocia, and Syria', just as linguistic cosmopolitanism was demonstrated by the spread of Sanskrit in an area extending from 'today's Afghanistan to Java and from Sri Lanka to Nepal' (Pollock, 2002: 22). But Pollock qualifies linguistic Romanization as 'a sort of decapitation of the conquered culture' (25), whereas he affirms that 'the Sanskrit cosmopolis' was not an action of a 'conquest state' (26). He does note that in the Roman Empire, 'in other areas of life, such as religious practices, there seems to be evidence of a general indifference to the cultural diversity of conquered peoples' (25), rather than evidence of an interest in suppressing diversity in the name of Empire. A firm historical distinction between the imperial and the voluntaristic spread of a dominant power's language may be elusive, a question of degree rather than a binary, just as a firm distinction between globalization and cosmopolis cannot be found in Kwame Anthony Appiah's 2006 *Cosmopolitanism: Ethics in a World of Strangers,* which in turn recalls the tension between Immanuel Kant's interest in colonial mercantile investment and his ideal of perpetual peace.

The point at which cosmopolitanism and imperialism fail to align, and where cautionary allegories against the cosmopolitical underpinnings of the 'world' in *littérature-monde* begin to come apart at the seams, is precisely the transition in the Roman Empire from imperialist cosmopolis to decadent multiculturalism.

Rome as Decadent 'cratère des villes-mondes'[16]

The French Enlightenment philosopher and historian Charles de Secondat Montesquieu viewed the Roman Empire as a key example of what we might think of as failure in the *worlding* of this earth. In Montesquieu's 1721 *Considerations on the Causes of the Grandeur and Decadence of the Romans*, the term 'world' recurs with great frequency. Rome is, quoting Livy, the polis that 'all the world failed to contain' (Montesquieu, 1896: 28). People were 'nothing in the world' (95) if they were not Roman citizens. Much of the world, west and east, 'became' Rome. In Montesquieu's narrative, once those ever-multiplying populations had seen that to be a Roman citizen was to have a key to the world-polis, they began rebelling against their conqueror until they were granted citizenship also. But once subjugated populations had gained citizenship they brought to Rome 'their particular genius, their self-interest, and their dependence on some great protector' (96). This proliferation of cultural codes through the migration of conquered ethnicities to the metropolitan centre of Rome led to a city that 'no longer formed a whole; and as one was only a citizen of it through a kind of fiction, one no longer had the same magistrates, the same ramparts, the same gods, the same temples, the same tombs, one no longer saw Rome with the same eyes' (96–97). Rome, 'mistress of the world' (176), had become 'not a monarchy or a republic', but 'the head of the body formed by all the peoples of the world' (76).

What we see in this hapless sociological cosmopolitanism is a simultaneous gravitation towards the polis that is a synecdoche for the cosmos, and a retention of local identity, community and custom, now monstrously imbricated with a host of other subjugated civic organisms. Montesquieu also linked the variety of coexistent cultures in Rome with the decadence of the Roman Empire. This decadence, which one might call a diasporan decadence, in that cosmopolis remained organized around a hybrid assemblage of mobile but partly preserved cultures, turns out to be a profoundly contradictory construct.

It should be noted that 'decadence' and 'fall' are often used interchangeably in histories of Rome. But the fall of the Roman Empire, as analysed notably by Edward Gibbon in the 1788 *Decline and Fall of the Roman Empire*, is a late phenomenon, when it is admitted to have occurred at all: it does not

---

[16] Globalized cities, such as those studied by Pascale Casanova (1999), have become the hosts of 'World' literary production and consecration: Le Bris refers to 'le cratère furieux des villes-mondes où se brassaient les identités et les cultures' [the furious craters of city-worlds fomenting mixed identities and cultures] (2007: 38).

pre-date the Third century CE. And yet the *decadence* of the Roman Empire (as portrayed by Monty Python, for example) is popularly associated with the era of the emperors who presided over the apogee of the Roman Empire, such as Caligula. Caligula lived in the time of Jesus of Nazareth; he is thought to have been born in 12 CE, and to have died in 41 CE, whereas the dates ascribed by some historians to Jesus are 7–2 BCE to 26–36 CE. Someone like Petronius, the 'arbiter of elegance' in the court of Nero, who committed suicide slowly over the course of a final lavish party, may appear to be an emblem of Roman decadence. However, even Nero, the emperor who played the lyre while Rome burned, long precedes the period of Roman decadence *per se*, if that decadence is interpreted as coinciding with the fall of the Roman Empire.

Interestingly, Montesquieu associated the kind of diasporan proliferation of conquered but active cultures both with that popular view of Roman decadence *and* with the fall of Rome: and he also obliquely defends decadence as a successful part of Roman strategy or at least adaptation to the logistical problems of empire. Thus the fall of Rome is described as a period when 'there was no longer anything foreign in Rome' (Montesquieu, 1896: 176) precisely because *everything* was foreign. Rome 'was no longer mistress of the world, but accepted the laws of all the nations' (176). Instead of one emperor, Rome now accommodated a host of defeated emperors, each of whom 'carried with him to the capital something peculiar to his own land, in the form of manner, or morals, or police, or worship' (176). Decadence ultimately becomes a feature of a cosmopolitan or diasporan proliferation of cultures within imperial 'worlding', and appears simultaneously linked to imperial success and failure.

These paradoxes of an imperialist cosmopolitan era that remains marked by unfathomable differences of particular and often diasporan conquered cultures is forcefully represented in the nineteenth-century French and English decadent movement in literature and art. Decadent writers showed a fascination with post-imperial cultural hybridity through representations of Salomé and the religious dissonance surrounding Herod's court in the Roman Empire in the time of Jesus, creating an aesthetics based on the morbid social potential of proliferating cultural systems.

Decadent Rome as Aesthetic

For Humanities scholars, the dominant model of decadence has long been, not Rome, but the nineteenth-century Decadent literary and artistic style in Europe, featuring such iconic figures of cultural modernity as Charles Baudelaire, Aubrey Beardsley, Friedrich Nietzsche and Oscar Wilde. The nineteenth-century discourse on decadence was primarily generated around an experimental modality that the scholar Charles Bernheimer described as a 'stimulant that bends thought out of shape, deforming traditional conceptual molds' (2002: 5). Scholarly appreciation of philosophical innovations in nineteenth-century decadent work has arguably led from post-structuralism onwards to an identification with the decadent movement as a precursor to critical theory. This identification with the positive valences of decadence as an experimental movement may help to explain academic resistance to integrating the currently widespread and influential Islamic critique of Western decadence into study of the larger discourse of decadence. Condemnations of decadence, however interesting in gender studies and the investigation of circum-Mediterranean tensions, are difficult to align with nineteenth-century decadence.

Nineteenth-century literature and art in the decadent style are obsessed with subject matter from the Middle East and North Africa, albeit from the pre-Islamic Roman Empire. The omnipresent representations of Salomé's dance of veils by Gustave Moreau, Joris-Karl Huysmans, Stéphane Mallarmé and others, beg the question of the significance of this decadent affinity for the Roman imperial Middle East. Many of these texts, as in the story 'Herodias' by Flaubert, seemed to focus on a baroque cataloguing of multiple ethnic groups, languages, religions, histories, traditions and styles in the early Roman Empire.

The texts present such a cacophony of systems of classification and values that it becomes literally difficult to follow the storylines, and I will argue that this opacity is not only intentional, it is the 'point' of these texts, in a creative development of the cultural potential and pathology of an imperial cosmopolis of post-conquest migrants. Consider this reflection by Flaubert's main character, the Tetrarch Herod Antipas, on his complex political affiliations with the Roman administration, the Jews, the Arabs and the Parthians:

> Agrippa, sans doute, l'avait ruiné chez l'Empereur? Philippe, son troisième frère, souverain de la Batanée, s'armait clandestinement. Les Juifs ne voulaient plus de ses mœurs idolâtres, tous les autres de sa domination; si bien qu'il hésitait entre deux projets: adoucir les Arabes ou conclure une alliance avec les Parthes [...].[17] (Flaubert, 1986: 110).

Oscar Wilde's play *Salomé* extends this theme of the glut of potentially

---

[17] 'Agrippa, he thought, had probably discredited him with the [Roman] Emperor. His third brother, Philip, sovereign of Batanea, was secretly arming. The Jews had had enough of his idolatrous ways, and everyone else of his rule,

hostile and yet intricately related cultures in the early Roman Empire to general confusion about the cultural origins and meanings of things and events. Everyone in the play refers to the wild breaching of cultural norms. When a Nubian soldier refers to his gods' lust for human lives, a Cappadocian soldier responds mournfully:

> In my country there are no gods left. The Romans have driven them out. There are some who say that they have hidden themselves in the mountains, but I do not believe it. Three nights I have been on the mountains, seeking them everywhere. I did not find them. And at last I called them by their names, and they did not come. I think they are dead' (Wilde, 1907: 1).

The first soldier tries to reassure him. 'The Jews worship a God one cannot see'. Says the Cappadocian: 'I cannot understand that'. First Soldier: 'In fact, they only believe in things one cannot see' – a comment that suddenly frames Judeo-Christian warnings against and interdictions of material idolatry as a freakish counter-empiricism (Wilde, 1907: 1).

This cosmopolitan disorientation in the polycultural crater of the Roman world is remarkably consistent throughout the Salomé texts. Amidst the continuously confounding array of cultural differences, the greatest common-alities in Wilde's text are metonymic. The moon excites great commentary; Salomé, moon-like, excites great commentary. Both prefigure the death of Iokaanan (spelled differently than in the Flaubert text) or John the Baptist. Following that sacrifice, which is both erotic (Salomé) and self-preserving (Herodias), Iokaanan's death is doubled by the death of Salomé herself, the wan white princess who has learned to love the bearded, medusa-like prisoner in a hole beneath the stage. In Flaubert's narrative, Iaokanann's accusations and curses reawaken for his listeners in Herod's court the memories of their own cultural catastrophes and forced immigration: 'Le peuple revoyait les jours de son exil, toutes les catastrophes de son histoire' (Flaubert, 1986: 124).[18] These catastrophes are the traumatic legacy of imperial diasporas, involving the cadavers of their mothers, jackals gnawing on bones in the former public squares, and their virgins playing the sitar at the foreigner's feasts.

In Wilde's play, when a dead body is found in the court prior to Salomé's dance, the Tetrarch automatically scrolls mentally through the possible meanings of cadavers in ceremonies in an array of different cultural contexts.

---

so that he was hesitating between two possible courses: to conciliate the Arabs or to conclude an alliance with the Parthians [...]'.

[18] 'The people saw before their eyes the days of their exile, with all the catastrophes of their history'.

> HEROD And this body, what does this body here? Think you that I am like the King of Egypt, who gives no feast to his guests but that he shows them a corpse? (Wilde, 1907: 15).

Or later:

> HEROD I thought it was but the Roman philosophers who slew themselves. Is it not true, Tigellinus, that the philosophers at Rome slay themselves? (Wilde, 1907: 15).

Egyptian exhibiters of death, Roman suicidal philosophers ... For Herod, a dead body is a hieroglyphic of cultural semiotics.

Ultimately, this hybridity comes to a decadent end in the Salomé texts. In Wilde's play, Salomé bites the mouth of the severed head of Iokaanan like a pomegranate, and notes that it tastes like blood. The soldiers from many lands rush forward to crush her beneath their shields. In Flaubert's text, 'la tête entra' [the head [of John the Baptist] entered] (Flaubert, 1986: 142) on a platter, and comes to govern all the other competing semiotic systems, in a foreshadowing of an epistemic shift to Christianity.

Is cosmopolitanism the unacknowledged apogee of imperial eras in which conquered diasporas are allowed, for pragmatic reasons, to coexist with imperialist powers to the point of producing either significant cultural cacophony and 'decadence' or major shifts of episteme? The beauty of the decadent representations of diasporan dissonance in the regions Rome had appropriated as its world is their implication that diaspora and cosmopolis are mutually constitutive. How can the world be accessible as world unless empire or technology or belief have shaped it and labelled it as the world? How can the world's peoples be manifest in the world unless they have migrated through the subject's phenomenological spaces? How can conquered worlds survive in the imperial world that has imposed its law as the boundaries of the world, making life outside of that world simultaneously unlivable except as past? This is a space in which the emperor, or at least the tetrarch, is fully as confused as the slave or the soldier. And it is a world that had drawn itinerant philosophers to the Stoic cosmopolitical movement along complex trajectories. Epictetus, who proclaimed, 'Each human being is primarily a citizen of his own commonwealth; but he is also a member of the great city of gods and men, whereof the city political is only a copy' ('Stoicism'), is thought to have been born a slave in what is now Turkey, and to have lived in Rome only until his exile to Greece. Panaetius, from Rhodes, engaged in diplomatic roles in North Africa with kings of Asia and Egypt. Posidonius travelled through and beyond the Roman world. Cosmopolitan agents, they must have articulated their ethos of world fidelity through witnessing, as in the nineteenth-century decadent Salomé texts, the ceaseless shifts of people and power through Mediterranean spaces, learning to recognize identities and ruptures of identity all along the way.

Literary representations of cosmopolitanism in the form of the decadent encounter with a mosaic of conquered and conquering identities converge with a stylistic core of Anglophone World Literature and also of *littérature-monde*. In *littérature-monde*, we see writers like Dai Sijie subsuming the history of French as the language of a conquest state to its attractiveness both for access to global literary markets or 'republics of letters', and also to its charms as a monumental space of reinvention of the linguistic and literary self, outside of the contingent determinations of birth and nation. This can yield a picaresque space of unsuccessful self-invention, as in the criminal failure to copy pathological genius in Mabanckou's 2003 *African Psycho*. In the Anglophone domain, Kazuo Ishiguro's unadorned first-person narration of a clone's banal discovery of her future as an organ donor or counsellor to organ donor clones in the 2005 *Never Let Me Go* exemplifies a refusal of drama in World Literature, an ability, as opposed to a Kafkaesque inability, to believe in a world so complex that the ego only suspiciously, nostalgically and privately guides the individual. J. M. Coetzee's characters similarly put up with conditions of disgrace or disability as part and parcel of the organicity of a dysfunctional historical moment that frames their ego as a relic of a simpler time, a neuronal imprint, a lost limb. The eponymous hero of the 1983 *Life & Times of Michael K.* cannot understand, or accept, why his extreme refusal to eat makes people want to know his story: the entire novel is an anorexic protest against having to have a story, despite the fact that that story is food. And yet we bond in literary community with his battered wisp of a South African body and its resistance to story, and this is a phenomenon that is arguably key to the mimetic form and content of World Literature.

In our own era, it is hard to resist the conclusion that the politics of world citizenship have become especially epistemologically fraught in at least three contexts: the counter-utopian valences of labour and capital under globalization; the ecological reframing of human cosmos-dwellers as something more like parasites than legislators; and the ever more complex rearticulation in the domain of physics of what the world or worlds may be in the first place – potentially starkly incompatible with an extended 'polis' model. In *littérature-monde*, readers chart the arrival of a multicultural confluence of group cultural actors in a post-imperialized world. This blurring of cosmopolitanism with diasporan or migrant agency creates a new decadence to be valorized as a critical opportunity to crack open the hard nuts of universalist pieties. Cosmopolis in World Literature is not 'true cosmopolis' as opposed to conquest cosmopolis. It is not affiliated with the active moments of imperialism's reshaping of the world, and with the individual stories that on some level mirror, in their coherent and generally dissenting subjective worlds, the hegemonic coherence of those moments. It is not double; it has instead the plurality of shards in a broken kaleidoscope. Main characters, the migrants Abdourahman Waberi associates with the 'Flâneurs, fugitifs, filibustiers' [Flaneurs, fugitives, pirates] (Waberi, 2007: 71), stray in and out of narrative worlds that openly fail to invest in universal designs. *Littérature-monde* charts the bitterly jubilant trajectory of the *homme traduit* (or *femme traduite*) at the same time that it witnesses, with deadpan affect, the advent of translational hegemony.

Works Cited

Agnew, John A. 2005. *Hegemony: The New Shape of Global Power.* Philadelphia, PA: Temple University Press.

Anderson, Amanda. 1998. 'Cosmopolitanism, Universalism, and the Divided Legacies of Modernity'. In Pheng Cheah and Bruce Robbins (eds), *Cosmopolitics: Thinking and Feeling Beyond the Nation.* Minneapolis: University of Minnesota Press: 265–89.

Appiah, Kwame Anthony. 2006. *Cosmopolitanism: Ethics in a World of Strangers.* London: Allen Lane.

Braziel, Jana Evan, and Anita Mannur. 2003. 'Nation, Migration, Globalization: Points of Contention in Diaspora Studies'. In Jana Evan Braziel and Anita Mannur (eds), *Theorizing Diaspora.* Oxford: Blackwell: 1–22.

Bernheimer, Charles. 2002. *Decadent Subjects: The Idea of Decadence in Art, Literature, Philosophy, and Culture of the Fin de Siècle in Europe.* Ed. by T. Jefferson Kline and Naomi Schor. Baltimore, MD: Johns Hopkins University Press.

Brown, Eric, and Pauline Kleingeld. 2002. 'Cosmopolitanism'. The Stanford Encyclopedia of Philosophy. 23 February. <http://plato.stanford.edu/entries/cosmopolitanism/>. Consulted on 3 August 2008.

Butler, Kim D. 2007. 'Multilayered Politics in the African Diaspora: The Metadiaspora Concept and Minidiaspora Realities'. In Gloria P. Totoricagüena (ed.), *Opportunity Structures in Diaspora Relations: Comparisons in Contemporary Multilevel Politics of Diaspora and Transnational Identity.* Reno: Center for Basque Studies, University of Nevada: 19–51.

Casanova, Pascale. 1999. *La République mondiale des lettres.* Paris: Seuil.

Chakrabarty, Dipesh. 2002. 'Universalism and Belonging in the Logic of Capital'. In Carol A. Breckenridge, Sheldon Pollock, Homi K. Bhabha, and Dipesh Chakrabarty (eds), *Cosmopolitanism.* Durham, NC: Duke University Press: 82–109.

Coetzee, J. M. 1983. *Life & Times of Michael K.* London: Secker & Warburg.

Engels, Frederick (writing under the pseudonym F. Oswald). 1841. 'Ernst Moritz Arndt'. *Telegraphe für Deutschland* nos. 2–5. January. Marx & Engels Internet Archive. <http://www.marxists.org/archive/marx/works/1841/01/arndt.htm>. Consulted on 15 October 2008.

Ermolaev, Herman. 1997. *Censorship in Soviet Literature, 1917–1991.* New York: Rowman & Littlefield.

Flaubert, Gustave. 1986. 'Herodias'. *Trois contes.* Paris: Flammarion: 109–42.

Forsdick, Charles. 2005. 'Between "French" and "Francophone": French Studies and the Postcolonial Turn'. *French Studies* 54.9: 523–30.

Gazette of the United States. 1802. Letter received by the ship, Lydia via Philadelphia, from 'a gentleman in St. Domingo', to his correspondent in this city, dated 'Cape François, 20 February 1802'. 20 March.

Gibbon, Edward. 1783. *The History of the Decline and Fall of the Roman Empire.* London: Printed for W. Strahan and T. Cadell.

Giuliani, Rudy. 2008. 'Wrong Reform & Wrong Reason'. Republican National Convention speech. American Rhetoric Online Speech Bank. 3 September. <http://www.americanrhetoric.com/speeches/convention2008/rudygiuliani2008rnc.htm>. Consulted on 15 October 2008.

Hall, Stuart. 1988. 'The Toad in the Garden: Thatcherism Among the Theorists'. In Cary Nelson and Laurence Grossberg (eds), *Marxism and the Interpretation of Culture.* Urbana: University of Illinois Press: 35–57.

Ikenberry, G. John. 2007. 'Globalization as American Hegemony'. In David Held and Anthony G. McGrew (eds), *Globalization Theory.* Cambridge: Polity Press: 41–61.

Ishiguro, Kazuo. 2005. *Never Let Me Go.* New York : Alfred A. Knopf.

Le Bris, Michel. 2007. 'Pour une littérature-monde en français'. In Michel Le Bris and Jean Rouaud (eds), *Pour une littérature-monde.* Paris: Gallimard: 23–53.

Le Bris, Michel, and Jean Rouaud (eds). 2007. *Pour une littérature-monde.* Paris: Gallimard.

Mabanckou, Alain. 2003. *African Psycho.* Paris: Serpent à plumes.

—. 2006. 'La francophonie, oui, le ghetto: non!'. *Le Monde* 19 March.

—. 2007. 'Le chant de l'oiseau migrateur'. In Michel Le Bris and Jean Rouaud (eds), *Pour une littérature-monde.* Paris: Gallimard: 55–66.

Marx, Karl, and Friedrich Engels. 1848. 'Bourgeois and Proletarians'. *Manifesto of the Communist Party.* Marx & Engels Internet Archive. <http://www.marxists.org/archive/marx/works/1848/communist-manifesto/ch01.htm#007>. Consulted on 15 October 2008.

Marx, Karl. 1858. 'Notebook VII'. *Outlines of the Critique of Political Economy.* Marx & Engels Internet Archive. <http://www.marxists.org/archive/marx/works/1859/critique-pol-economy/ch02_3b.htm>. Consulted on 15 October 2008.

Mbembe, Achille. 2007. 'Francophonie et politique du monde'. Le blog d'Alain Mabanckou. 24 March. <http://congopage.com/Achille-MBEMBE-Francophonie-et>. Consulted on 3 August 2009.

Montesquieu, Charles de Secondat. 1896. *Considérations sur la cause de la grandeur des Romains et de leur décadence*. Paris: Hachette. [First published in 1721.]

Moura, Jean-Marc. 2007. *Littératures francophones et théorie postcoloniale*. 2nd Edn. Paris: Presses Universitaires de France.

Obama, Barack. 2008. 'A World that Stands as One' Speech in Berlin. 24 July. <http://my.barackobama.com/page/content/berlinvideo/>. Consulted on 15 October 2008.

Palat, R. A. 2000. 'Fragmented Visions: Excavating the Future of Area Studies in a Post-American World'. In Neil L. Waters (ed.), *Beyond the Area Studies Wars*. Middlebury, VT: Middlebury College Press: 64–106.

Pollock, Sheldon. 2002. 'Cosmopolitan and Vernacular in History'. In Carol A. Breckenridge, Sheldon Pollock, Homi K. Bhabha, and Dipesh Chakrabarty (eds), *Cosmopolitanism*. Durham, NC: Duke University Press: 15–53.

Pollock, Sheldon, Homi K. Bhabha, Carol A. Breckenridge and Dipesh Chakrabarty. 2002. 'Cosmopolitanisms'. In Carol A. Breckenridge, Sheldon Pollock, Homi K. Bhabha, and Dipesh Chakrabarty (eds), *Cosmopolitanism*. Durham, NC: Duke University Press: 1–14.

'Pour une "littérature-monde" en français'. 2007. *Le Monde* 16 March.

'Ronnie'. 2008. Hot Air. 16 October. <http://hotair.com/archives/2008/10/16/what-we-can-learn-from-the-joe-the-plumber-episode/comment-page-3/>. Consulted on 17 October 2008.

Rushdie, Salman. 1983. *Shame*. New York: Alfred A. Knopf.

Sijie, Dai. 2007. 'La nuit du conteur'. In Michel Le Bris and Jean Rouaud (eds), *Pour une littérature-monde*. Paris: Gallimard: 321–37.

'Stoicism'. NationMaster. <http://www.nationmaster.com/encyclopedia/Stoicism>. Consulted on 3 August 2009.

Storey, John. 2006. *Cultural Theory and Popular Culture: An Introduction*. Athens: University of Georgia Press.

Surin, Kenneth. 1997. 'On Producing the Concept of a Global Culture'. In V. Y. Mudimbe (ed.), *Nations, Identities, Cultures*. Durham: Duke University Press: 199–218.

Waberi, Abdourahman A. 2007. 'Écrivains en position d'entraver'. In Michel Le Bris and Jean Rouaud (eds), *Pour une littérature-monde*. Paris: Gallimard: 67–75

Walkowitz, Rebecca L. 2006. *Cosmopolitan Style: Modernism Beyond the Nation*. New York: Columbia University Press.

Wilde, Oscar. 1907. *Salomé: A Tragedy in One Act*. Boston: J. W. Luce.

Will, George F. 2008. 'The Cosmopolitan'. *Washington Post* 3 August. <http://www. washingtonpost.com/wp-dyn/content/article/2008/08/01/AR2008080102871. html>. Consulted on 15 October 2008.

From *Weltliteratur* to World Literature
to *Littérature-monde*: The History
of a Controversial Concept

Typhaine Leservot

The term *littérature-monde*, proposed by the forty-four signatories of the manifesto which appeared on 16 March 2007 in the journal *Le Monde* to describe a concept further developed in their book published by Gallimard in May of the same year, is not exactly a neologism. Although the term *Francophonie*, against which it sets itself, has a considerable number of problematic connotations, *littérature-monde* is itself just as loaded. Indeed, we should be aware of its associations and should explore the issues raised by them. Although it appears to be a completely new expression in French, the forty-four's concept of *littérature-monde* is actually drawn from three pre-existing concepts or phenomena. The first is the concept of travel literature and world writing developed since 1992 by Michel Le Bris, himself a signatory of the manifesto. For him, *littérature-monde* signifies a literature open to the world or, in other words, a literature which speaks of the real and the lived rather than turning in on itself in a state of narcissistic self-consciousness (2007: 25). The second is the concept of the *Tout-monde*, defined by the Martinican thinker and writer Édouard Glissant as being 'le monde actuel tel qu'il est dans sa diversité et dans son chaos' [today's world as it is in its diversity and chaos][1] (Chanda, 2000).[2] The *Tout-monde* is not a systematic or rationalizing vision of the world, but instead underlines the global spread

---

[1] All translations from French into English are by the translator of this chapter.

[2] Although Glissant began to use the expression *Tout-monde* from 1993 onwards, it is in the many interviews he has given since the publication of

of the concept and practice of creolization, a practice of cultural exchange which rejects unequal power relationships. Glissant's *Tout-monde* links the *littérature-monde* of the forty-four signatories to the hybrid or culturally mixed literatures which are often on the syllabus in Francophone studies in English and North American universities. These Francophone literatures are sometimes the output of migrants or new citizens whose multiple cultural influences encourage a new way of seeing and telling the world. The last of the three is the term 'world literature' which is regularly used in comparative literature studies in Anglo-American universities (Schulz and Rhein, 1973).[3] The very term *littérature-monde* in fact appears to be a literal translation of the Anglo-American term 'world literature', to such an extent that we could not only describe it as an 'Anglo-Americanism', but even go so far as to label it 'Anglo-Americanization'. This aspect of the term has not escaped its critics who, like Pierre Assouline, have seen *littérature-monde* as undoubtedly inspired by the model of 'World Fiction' (2007).[4] Although the link between *littérature-monde*, 'world literature' and Anglo-American universities is emphasized by those who criticize the manifesto, the book which followed the manifesto is not particularly concerned with the term's Anglophone links. By contrast, this same book hides neither its ties to Glissant's concept of the *Tout-monde* (Édouard Glissant himself signed the manifesto and contributed a chapter to the book) nor its debt to Michel Le Bris (the latter is the book's co-editor alongside Jean Rouaud). Since the manifesto and the book make only the briefest of references to the links between the concept

---

his *Traité du Tout-monde* in 1997 that his choice of this term has been fully elucidated.

  [3] The texts chosen by Schulz and Rhein for their anthology of the founding texts of comparative literature confirm that the concepts of 'comparative literature' and 'world literature' are interchangeable in Anglo-American universities, with the translation of an extract from Goethe on the concept of *Weltliteratur*, or 'World-literature', as the opening piece in the collection. The reader of the volume soon understands, however, that 'comparative literature' refers to the method of analysis, while 'world literature' refers to the object of the analysis.

  [4] This reaction is strengthened by the recent impression in France that anything that concerns *Francophonie* in any way is increasingly Americanized. In her report on *Francophonie* submitted to President Nicolas Sarkozy on 20 March 2007, just four days after the publication of the manifesto, Rama Yade, then secretary of state for *Francophonie*, underlined the increasing number of Francophone writers teaching in the United States where there are many chairs in Francophone studies. Sarkozy expressed his indignation at this tendency two days later, speaking of the 'comble' [ultimate irony] of a 'Francophonie sauvée par l'Amérique' [*Francophonie* saved by America] (2007).

of *littérature-monde* and the term 'world literature', the present chapter will explore the history of this concept and the issues it raises in order to achieve a better understanding of both the problems posed by the concept of *littérature-monde* and its potential uses. For what will emerge from the analysis of the history of the concept of 'world literature' is that this term too, like *Francophonie*, has found it hard to escape the hierarchies between nations and cultures which the very concept of *littérature-monde* aims to transcend. Nevertheless, its shared history with comparative literature studies enables *littérature-monde* to encourage the development of a field of comparative studies which would benefit Francophone studies.

Goethe's *Weltliteratur*

Although *littérature-monde* seems to be an exact translation of 'world literature', the connection needs closer analysis. In order to examine the concept of 'world literature' we must first go back to an earlier manifestation of the concept, the German *Weltliteratur*, a term first used by Johann Wolfgang von Goethe on 15 January 1827 (Strich, 1949: 68).[5] We can follow the development of the term from 31 January 1827 thanks to Johann Peter Eckermann, Goethe's young secretary at the time, who first published his *Gespräche mit Goethe* [Conversations with Goethe] in 1836, four years after the writer's death (Eckermann, 1998: 165).[6] During these conversations, Goethe appears to suggest that he understands *Weltliteratur* (literally 'World-literature' or *littérature-monde*) to be a group of contemporary texts praised by either an elite or the masses, and circulating throughout the world as a result of developments in the field of translation. Goethe's term was innovative on a number of levels. First, by specifying contemporary texts, Goethe set himself in opposition to the concept of an immutable classical canon inherited from the ancient world. Second, in describing the global circulation of literature, Goethe emphasized that the circulation of contemporary texts anticipated the imminent obsolescence of national frontiers; the sharing of such texts should, in his view, awaken awareness of a shared

---

[5] This term, as Strich reminds us, was merely the formulation of an idea which had been preoccupying Goethe for some years (1949: 159). Although it has since been discovered that it was probably Christoph Martin Wieland who was the true inventor of this term, some years before Goethe, it is the latter's definition of *Weltliteratur*, not Wieland's, which endures today (Pizer, 2006: 1).

[6] Émile Delerot, translator of Goethe's conversations with Eckermann for the French edition of 1883, chose to translate *Weltliteratur* as 'littérature universelle' [universal literature] (Eckermann, 1883).

humanity which went beyond borders and, even if it did not banish war between nations, would at least help them to understand each other better. Last, in adding that the tastes of the elite and of the people (here, Goethe was employing a vocabulary which was new at the time, as Hendrick Birus (2000: 4) points out) could contribute to the creation of this World-literature, Goethe appears to have avoided all the traps into which *Francophonie* has fallen, obsessed as it is by nationhood and typified by a strong cultural hierarchy. *Weltliteratur* thus seems to be the ideal ancestor for *littérature-monde*, allowing it to avoid the pitfalls encountered by *Francophonie*.

But Goethe's concept is not as clear as all that. His conversations with Eckermann on this topic reveal serious contradictions. Far from being a literary space where the great contemporary works of literature coexisted in harmony, judged purely on merit, Goethe's world literature was still governed by the same hierarchies between nations and cultures which it had hoped to transcend.

From the outset, Goethe's world literature had a particularly problematic relationship with nationhood. Although Goethe saw *Weltliteratur* as the herald for the imminent obsolescence of national borders, he thought, paradoxically, that the inclusion of his own work in the corpus of world literature was a cause for German national pride rather than his own personal pride (Damrosch, 2003: 7). His conversations with Eckermann are also filled with comments on the national characteristics of the French, the English and the Germans in particular, demonstrating how far he failed to throw off national categorizations in his literary discussions. We thus encounter him saying: 'I praise this in the French that their poetry never deserts the firm ground of reality' (Eckermann, 1998: 144). He also comments that 'the English in general appear to have certain advantages over many others' (Eckermann, 1998: 255). But above all we find him asserting on Thursday, 3 May 1827, only a few months after the key date of 15 January 1827 when he first spoke of world literature, that every writer's talent depends above all on his national environment: 'if a talent is to be speedily and happily developed, the great point is that a great deal of intellect and sound culture should be current in a nation' (Eckermann, 1998: 201).

The failure of Goethe's world literature to transcend national barriers reflects how unready Goethe was to see frontiers disappear within his world literature, for he already considered there to be a clear hierarchy between different national literatures. He considered the German literature of his time to be too provincial in nature, and saw France in particular as the central player in the theatrical world (Damrosch, 2003: 8). Paris was, for Goethe, the place where all German plays should aspire to be recognized. In a more general way, he also continually praised the French writers of his period in front of Eckermann: François-René de Chateaubriand, Victor Hugo and Prosper Mérimée in particular. The German precursor of *littérature-monde* was thus already imbued with a certain francocentrism which ties him more closely to *Francophonie* than to the signatories of the *littérature-monde* manifesto.

This hierarchy between contemporary cultures which gives pride of place to Paris is not the only hierarchy to constrain *Weltliteratur* and to cause it to move away from its declared desire to go beyond national frontiers. Indeed, Goethe's World-literature brings with it another contradictory hierarchy: that between the classics of yesterday and contemporary masterpieces. Although Goethe spoke of World-literature as the means to confirm the quality of contemporary writings, he could not resist telling his secretary Eckermann how much the poetry of Ancient Greece was, for him, an unequalled high point in literature: 'if we really want a pattern, we must always return to the ancient Greeks, in whose works the beauty of mankind is constantly represented', he tells us (Eckermann, 1998: 166), before going on to explain that 'we ought rather to admire the period and the nation in which their production was possible than the individual authors' (Eckermann, 1998: 201).

Last, far from accepting the taste of the general populace in a democratic way, Goethe does not conceal his worry at the thought of popular influence over the content of a world literature. In his opinion, readers from the intellectual elite are far better placed to select the 'real' world literature, that is to say the literature which is capable of promoting mankind's true progress (see Birus, 2000: 4). In Eckermann's report of 20 June 1827, accordingly, we learn that the global circulation of ideas gave Goethe a genuine fear of 'nothing but a medley' (Eckermann, 1998: 201) which would lead people to forget the origins of certain works or cultural tendencies.

Despite his initial desire to break up the fixed canon of the classics by daring to suggest that it was possible to admire contemporary authors, Goethe's world literature remains an elitist concept which favours the literary production of certain nations over that of others (France over Germany), of certain periods over others (the ancient world over the modern), of certain genres (poetry rather than the novel) and of certain readers (those from the elite classes rather than from the lower classes). Regardless of the good intentions of its inventor, the hierarchical nature of Goethe's *Weltliteratur* brings it closer to *Francophonie* than to the *littérature-monde* of the forty-four signatories, even though, paradoxically, its initial aims were those of the latter group. The failure of *Weltliteratur* to free itself from the hierarchies it condemned is a warning to us that *littérature-monde* may be no better equipped in reality to overcome these same limitations.

'World literature' and Comparative Literature

While from the outset Goethe's concept of world literature was more problematic than it at first seemed, its subsequent evolution and use during the nineteenth and twentieth centuries have reinforced the confusion which initially surrounded the term. The area of research which has made the greatest use of it, comparative literature, has effectively never succeeded in clarifying the object of its study. We could go so far as to say that it has reinforced the very characteristics which Goethe hoped to transcend. The topic is moreover such a vexed one that it has preoccupied comparative literature experts for a long time. In 2000, the comparatist Marián Gálik provided an overview of the debates concerning the concept of world literature and recorded that the field of comparative literary studies, in which the concept of world literature is a central one, has been writing about the issue since the nineteenth century. According to Gálik, between 1884 and 1982 some 187 essays were written on the subject and the debate has continued since that period (Gálik, 2000: 2). When Charles Bernheimer produced his report on 'comparative literature in the era of multiculturalism', he confirmed that the anxiety typical of this area of study had in no way been conquered during the following decades (1995: 1–17). Although comparative literature and the concept of world literature emerged at almost exactly the same historical moment – comparative literature came into being in France towards 1816, just eleven years before Goethe's concept of world literature was developed – the object of study nevertheless remains unclear. The definition of the concept will accordingly vary depending on which comparatist is speaking to you. Studies by the comparatists Dionyz Durisin (1984) and David Damrosch (2003) between them contain a minimum of five definitions of the concept of world literature as used in the field of comparative studies: (i) a history or vision of the whole of global literature; (ii) a fixed canon bringing together the collection of world classics; (iii) a selection of the greatest works of the literatures of different nations forming a flexible canon which changes over time; (iv) a global literary product which is the sum of national literatures; (v) a view of the world (this last is the same definition as that of *littérature-monde* proposed by the forty-four signatories of the manifesto).

Although they employ a global discourse, the many definitions of world literature to be found in comparative literature have not spared it from accusations of nationalism and Eurocentrism, just as Francophone studies are accused of Francocentrism. These tendencies finally led Gayatri Spivak to declare in 2003 that the discipline of comparative studies was dead. In her book *The Death of a Discipline* she puts forward a strong critique of the concept of world literature as it is used in comparative studies, highlighting in particular the nationalism and Eurocentrism of this discipline. In their manifesto for a *littérature-monde* in French, the forty-four signatories announced another death, that of *Francophonie*, without realizing that the term *littérature-monde*, adopted in preference to it, had itself been killed off in its English-language form by Spivak four years earlier.

From Nation, to Region, to a Global Dimension?

The history of concepts of world literature from Goethe to the Anglo-American theorists and the debates such concepts have provoked are thus important because they not only confirm how hard it is to pin down the meaning of the term *littérature-monde* but also remind us that, through its etymology, this term has greater affinities with *Francophonie* than we might think. How, then, might a concept which has until now been fractured by national, cultural and literary hierarchies, be reborn in a new form free of these same hierarchies?

Despite the problems which beset the concept of *littérature-monde*, its link to comparative studies can also teach us something. In particular, the way in which comparative studies have attempted to address their Eurocentric and nationalist version of a world literature might help French-language *littérature-monde* and/or *Francophonie* (depending on which term comes to be used in practice) to avoid the same pitfalls. In 1995, the Bernheimer report on comparative literature studies suggested that they emerge from their Eurocentrism and nationalism to move towards multiculturalism, abandoning outdated categories based on countries and periods (most often centuries) in favour of a structure founded on regions. But it is essential, adds Bernheimer, for the proposed model to rethink completely the traditional regional model of 'area studies' if it is not to repeat the mistakes of the latter. In effect, 'area studies', created during the cold war, divided third-world countries into areas for study founded on colonial territorial boundaries. Bernheimer therefore suggests that regional studies must be rethought to avoid the colonial trap: 'Still, the area studies model could be reconceptualized [...] to undo [... .] the notion of a stable geographical area' (1995: 14). Bernheimer proposes in particular that the rethinking of the regional model could follow the example of American Studies which, without rejecting the concept of regions, encourages transnational studies (in particular trans-Atlantic and trans-American studies), generating a perpetual destabilization of any given geographical model. In her contribution to the collection of articles edited by Bernheimer, Marie-Louise Pratt summarizes this need in a call to 'globalize, democratize, decolonize' comparative studies and the concept of world literature associated with them (1995: 59).

This reconsideration of the rationale for regional studies in the field of comparative studies, destabilizing as it does the (neo-)colonial boundaries of the former, has the potential to help *Francophonie* to escape the new trap in which it increasingly finds itself. For the growing problem encountered by *Francophonie* – not so much in its institutional form, which retains its focus on France, it is true, but in the academic field of Francophone studies – goes beyond questions of nationalism and language as targeted by the concept of *littérature-monde*, to the issue of regions.

The national identities of *Francophonie* may be a problem for those with a certain vision of France, for some Parisian publishers, for example, who all too often relegate non-French Francophone writers to special collections, thereby contributing to the separation of France from *Francophonie* and ghettoizing Francophone writers in a category of secondary writers.[7] This vision is to be encountered in the Bibliothèque Nationale where the categorization of authors by nationality classifies Maryse Condé as Guadeloupian, whereas Marie Redonnet, from Normandy, is indeed French. But it is not generally a Francophone problem, nor is it one for certain French academics and researchers, for example Charles Bonn, recently retired from the University of Lyon-Lumière, who contributed to the development of Francophone studies in France for many years, nor indeed is it one for those very French writers who signed the manifesto for a *littérature-monde*. It is no longer even a problem for the Fnac bookshop which, since its reorganization a few years ago dividing the French-speaking world into regions (France, Caribbean, North Africa, Middle-East, etc.), no longer includes Maryse Condé, a Frenchwoman from Guadeloupe, in its foreign writers section.

This is not to say that *Francophonie* presents no problem in the academic world, but rather that it poses a different kind of problem: as the reorganization of Francophone literature at the Fnac suggests, the problem of *Francophonie* in contemporary academic practice has increasingly to do with regions rather than nations. Francophone studies as we know them are so eager to divide their research into regions that those working on each region rarely communicate with those working on others. Despite the numerous collections of articles bringing together the work of researchers specializing in different Francophone regions, monographs (or single-authored works) in Francophone studies are rigorously separated into regions, to such a degree that one would be hard pressed to find a collection into which a book comparing several Francophone regions including France could fit.

---

7 Alain Mabanckou, one of the main signatories of the manifesto, is particularly strong in his resistance to the Gallimard collection *Continents noirs* [dark continents].

This regionalization in publishing is noticeable at L'Harmattan and Karthala in France, for example, and is also to be found in Anglo-American journals which might review a researcher's work: the website of the Centre International d'Études Francophones [International Centre for Francophone Studies] (CIEF), for example, asks for works on North Africa or the Maghreb to be sent to one person, those on the Middle East to another, those on sub-Saharan Africa and the Caribbean to another, and so on for the areas of North America and Acadia, North America and Quebec, South Pacific and Tahiti, Indian Ocean, Asia, Central and Eastern Europe, and Western Europe. With this sort of regionalization of the French-speaking world, there is no possibility for an academic covering Quebec, Maghreb and France together in the same work to find a reviewer even if, by a miracle, she or he has managed to find a publisher.

This regionalization does, it is true, have its advantages: in particular, it countered the mistaken impression that a specialist in *Francophonie* was necessarily familiar with all Francophone regions and could, as a consequence, teach as a general *Francophonie* expert. But this same region-alization can become tyrannical if it preserves an outmoded (even colonial) concept of regions and prevents interregional and transregional comparatist studies. For the real problem lies not so much with the regions themselves but rather in the absence of properly comparative studies between them. This critique of the regionalization of Francophone studies is thus not an anti-regional stance, far from it, but is rather an invitation to rethink the way in which we study the Francophone regions. It is here that the link between *littérature-monde* and comparative studies, emphasized above, can be useful, as the latter have encountered the same problem. During the present period of globalization, we need to rethink regions as unstable entities, that is to say in their ongoing relationships with the phenomena of migration, exile, diaspora and/or cultural exchange, following new paths which no longer necessarily trace the postcolonial migratory movements between ex-colonies and ex-colonizers. A specialist in Maghreb studies, for example, can no longer discuss only migratory relationships with France, but must now also take into account the migration of 40,000 Algerians to Montreal since 1992. This migratory movement between Algeria and Quebec requires a dialogue between academic researchers on migration in Quebec, France and the Maghreb. The need to encourage transnational and transregional research is indeed to be found in the manifesto signed by the forty-four writers, who speak of the need to take account of transnational literatures. Although we must be careful not to generalize the process of globalization, and, by extension, experiences of immigration, exile, or diaspora which, although they are increasing in number, do not concern everybody, we should not make the mistake of restricting Francophone studies to relatively fixed geographical regions or to traditional postcolonial migratory routes.

It is not new to encourage such a comparatist dialogue. As early as 2003, Charles Forsdick and David Murphy wrote in favor of the development of comparative studies in their collection of essays on Francophone postcolonial studies: 'The more active promotion of a comparatist dimension in postcolonial criticism is a logical development' (2003: 12). This call itself echoed a similar one sent out four years earlier by Ashok Bery and Patricia Murray in which they spoke of 'dislocation' (1999). In France, Jean-Marc Moura also sees comparative studies as the great source of promise in postcolonial studies (2006). But these repeated calls for comparative studies often envisage comparisons between postcolonial practices drawn from different linguistic traditions (English, French, Spanish, Dutch, etc.) and not, as we understand it here, intercultural comparisons within the same language group. Is this to say that Francophone studies should 'globalize' themselves, a question asked of comparative studies by Giles Gunn and other contributors (including Edward Said) to a special number of *PMLA* (2001)? From one point of view, this call for a transnational and transregional dialogue is indeed a reply to the growing number of polemics on the need to 'globalize' literary studies that increasingly preoccupy the field of comparative literature. But in order to avoid any adherence to a particular creed we would then have to imagine, not how globalization has modified literature, but how literature itself displays, directs, manipulates and even creates, to a certain extent, the phenomenon of globalization. Although inter- or transregional dialogue is desirable, it needs to extend its rethinking from the level of the region to globalization itself.

As a consequence of its link to Goethe's concept of world literature, formulated in the nineteenth century and employed since that time in comparative studies, the *littérature-monde* of the forty-four signatories brings with it a cultural heritage that both runs the risk of preventing the freedom it seeks from *Francophonie* and simultaneously offers Francophone studies the potential benefits of new developments in comparative studies which are no longer bound by outdated notions of the region. While the concept of *littérature-monde* has managed to open up a debate in France on its own relationship with *Francophonie*, it has also remained useful to Anglo-American Francophone studies, who themselves need to rethink their approach to regionality, given that the concept of the region can be as problematic, and leave as powerful a colonial aftertaste, as that of the nation if it remains defined by obsolete borders. To say, therefore, as did many speakers at the conference on *littérature-monde* in February 2009 at Florida State University, that Francophone studies as they are practised in Anglo-American universities have always analysed the *littérature-monde* discussed in the manifesto, when our researchers mostly confine themselves (and are obliged to do so for reasons of access to employment and publication) to a single Francophone region of the world, seems somewhat paradoxical. Each of the two *Francophonies*, that of the academic world just as much as that of Parisian publishers, needs to make an effort to shed both national and regional limitations if it is really to free *Francophonie* from its colonial roots.[8]

Translated by Teresa Bridgeman.

Works Cited

Assouline, Pierre. 2007. 'Quelle "littérature-monde"?'. *La République des livres. Le blog de Pierre Assouline.* 10 June. <http://passouline.blog.lemonde.fr/2007/06/10/ quelle-litterature-monde/>. Consulted on 14 January 2009.

Bernheimer, Charles (ed.). 1995. *Comparative Literature in the Age of Multiculturalism.* Baltimore, MD: Johns Hopkins University Press.

Bery, Ashok, and Patricia Murray (eds). 1999. *Comparing Postcolonial Literatures: Dislocations.* Basingstoke: Macmillan.

Birus, Hendrik. 2000. 'The Goethan Concept of World Literature and Comparative Literature'. *CLCWeb: Histories and Concepts of Comparative Literature* 2.4: 1–8, article 7. <http://docs.lib.purdue.edu/clcweb/vol2/iss4/7/>. Consulted on 22 May 2010.

Centre International d'Études Francophones (CIEF). 'Responsables des Recensions et Comptes rendus'. <http://www.cief.info/nef/responsables.html>. Consulted on 12 January 2009.

Chanda, Tirthankar. 2000. 'The Cultural "Créolization" of the World: Interview with Édouard Glissant'. <http://www.diplomatie.gouv.fr/en/france_159/label-france_2554/label france-issues-2555/label-france-no.-38_4204/feature-together-into-the-21st-century_4285/exchanging_4286/the-cultural-creolization-of-the-world.-interview-with-edouard-glissant_6589.html>. Consulted on 11 October 2010.

---

  [8] I would like to thank those who have made it possible to have such a fruitful discussion following the version of this chapter presented at the conference entitled 'Littérature-monde: New Wave or New Hype?' on 12–14 February 2009, organized by Alec Hargreaves and William Cloonan in Tallahassee, Florida: Dominique Fisher, Stéphanie Bérard, Jane Moss, Jonathan Gosnell, Paul Touré, Benoît Trudel and Keithley Woolward. I would also like to thank Krishna Winston for the information she provided on Wieland's role in the creation of the term *Weltliteratur*.

Damrosh, David. 2003. *What is World Literature?* Princeton, NJ: Princeton University Press.

Dimock, Wai Chee. 2001. 'Literature for the Planet'. *PMLA Special Topic: Globalizing Literary Studies* 116.1: 173–88.

Durisin, Dionyz. 1984. *Theory of Literary Comparatistics*. Bratislava: Veda.

Eckermann, Johann Peter. 1883. *Conversations de Goethe: pendant les dernières années de sa vie, 1822–1832. Recueillies par Eckermann*. Vols I–II. Trans. by Emile Delerot. Intro. by M. Sainte-Beuve. Paris: Bibliothèque Charpentier. [First published as *Gespräche mit Goethe in den letzten Jahren seines Lebens* (1836).]

—. 1998. *Conversations of Goethe*. Trans. by John Oxenford. Cambridge, MA: Da Capo Press. [First published in 1930.]

Forsdick, Charles, and David Murphy (eds). 2003. *Francophone Postcolonial Studies: A Critical Introduction*. London: Arnold.

Gálik, Marián. 2000. 'Concepts of World Literature, Comparative Literature, and a Proposal'. *CLCWeb: Histories and Concepts of Comparative Literature* 2.4: 1–8, article 8. <http://docs.lib.purdue.edu/clcweb/vol2/iss4/8/>. Consulted on 22 May 2010.

Glissant, Édouard. 1993. *Tout-monde*. Paris: Gallimard.

—. 1997. *Traité du Tout-monde (Poétique IV)*. Paris: Gallimard.

Gunn, Giles. 2001. 'Introduction: Globalizing Literary Studies'. *PMLA, Special Topic: Globalizing Literary Studies* 116.1: 16–31.

Le Bris, Michel (ed.). 1992. *Pour une littérature voyageuse*. Brussels: Éditions Complexe.

Le Bris, Michel, and Jean Rouaud (eds). 2007. *Pour une littérature-monde*. Paris: Gallimard.

Loliée, Frédéric. 1903. *Histoire des littératures comparées: Des origines au XXe siècle*. 2nd Edn. Paris: Delagrave.

Moura, Jean-Marc. 2006. 'Postcolonialisme et comparatisme'. *Vox Poetica*. <http://www.vox-poetica.org/sflgc/biblio/moura.html>. Consulted on 28 April 2009.

Pizer, John David. 2006. *The Idea of World Literature: History and Pedagogical Practice*. Baton Rouge: Louisiana State University Press.

'Pour une "littérature-monde" en français'. 2007. *Le Monde* 16 March.

Pratt, Mary-Louise. 1995. 'Comparative Literature and Global Citizenship'. In Charles Brenheimer (ed.), *Comparative Literature in the Age of Multiculturalism*. Baltimore, MD: Johns Hopkins University Press: 48–65.

Said, Edward W. 2001. 'Globalizing Literary Study'. *PMLA* 116.1: 64–68.

Sarkozy, Nicolas. 2007. 'Pour une francophonie vivante et populaire'. *Le Figaro* 22 March.

Schulz, Hans-Joachim, and Phillip H. Rhein (eds). 1973. *Comparative Literature:*

The Early Years. An Anthology of Essays. Chapel Hill: The University of North Carolina Press.

Spivak, Gayatri Chakravorty. 2003. *Death of a Discipline.* The Welleck Library Lectures Series. New York: Columbia University Press.

Strich, Fritz. 1949. *Goethe and World Literature.* London: Routledge and Kegan Paul.

Yade, Rama. 2007. '15 propositions pour une nouvelle francophonie'. Rapport remis au Président Nicolas Sarkozy 20 mars. <http://web.archive.org/web/20070329025336/http://www.u-m-p.org/site/index.php/s_informer/actualites/15_propositions_pour_une_nouvelle_francophonie>. Live link consulted on 23 April 2009. Archived link consulted on 11 October 2010.

Littérature-monde
in the Marketplace of Ideas:
A Theoretical Discussion

Mounia Benalil

Peut-être l'histoire universelle n'est-elle que l'histoire de quelques métaphores. [...] Peut-être l'histoire universelle n'est-elle que l'histoire des diverses *intonations* de quelques métaphores.[1]

Jacques Derrida, *L'Écriture et la différence* (1967), 137.

Over the past two decades, the constant epistemological renewal that has characterized critical discourse in the humanities has given rise to the concept of the 'market' which accords a central role to the notion of globalization. Presented simultaneously as 'paradigm', 'logic', 'mechanism' and 'rhetoric', this concept of the market has also shaped a number of discursive and theoretical positions. For example, critics have debated 'l'invention du marché' [the invention of the market] (Norel, 2004), the 'temps du marché' [era of the market] (Laïdi, 2000: 173), the 'primat de la rationalité marchande' [primacy of market rationality] as a form of modern 'rationalité' [rationality] (Castillo Durante, 2004: 17) and the 'procès de marchandisation' [commodification process] as a 'monde spectral' [spectral world] (Fradin, 2005: 206) that haunts the critical discourse of modernity.[2] It is within this context of

---

[1] 'Perhaps universal history is but the history of several metaphors. [...] Perhaps universal history is but the history of the diverse *intonations* of several metaphors' (Derrida, 1978: 92). Derrida is here citing approvingly from the work of Jorge Luis Borges.

[2] Unless otherwise indicated, all translations from French into English are by the translator of this chapter.

paradigmatic transformation, linked in turn to various manifestations of globalization, that the relevance and validity of certain contemporary critical concepts require closer examination.

Amongst the modish concepts that have generated debate and often contradictory commentary is that of *littérature-monde*, which Michel Le Bris introduced in his 1992 edited volume, *Pour une littérature voyageuse*, and which was then further developed by the forty-four writers who signed the *littérature-monde* manifesto in *Le Monde* on 16 March 2007 (hereafter referred to as the Manifesto). The strategy of these defenders of a French-language *littérature-monde* is tied into a dynamic of rejection of the politics of *Francophonie*, an institution seen as a legacy of colonialism and for a long time dependent on hexagonal France (in turn seen as the site of consecration for all 'peripheral' French-language literature). Although this strategy has its attractions, the Manifesto and the collectively authored volume *Pour une littérature-monde* that followed it leave several questions unanswered. Consequently, this chapter aims to discuss various aspects of *littérature-monde* within the marketplace of new theoretical concepts. For how can we interpret, even if only on a metaphorical level, this extrapolation of the idea of the 'world' when it is so inextricably woven into the literary (and, by implication, the social)? Indeed, as Patrick Marot argues, a metaphor itself 'se voie réglée par un principe d'économie. Elle est par exemple [...] une approximation qui permet de condenser une pensée complexe: sa valeur réside dans son efficacité pragmatique. Dans le [...] cas [...] où la métaphore est porteuse de vérité [...], elle dévoile un rapport jusque-là occulte entre les choses' (2007: 19–20).[3] The ultimate aim of this chapter, then, is to discuss the importance of the Manifesto to critical thought by demonstrating that the challenge arising from the idea of the 'decomposition' of *Francophonie* (in other words 'its demise'), and its replacement with the notion of a French-language *littérature-monde*, is more concerned with the threat of an ideological imperialism arising from a cultural globalization which *Francophonie* is called upon to confront.

Francophonie on Trial: The Logic of Globalization

What does judging *Francophonie* mean? And what fate can we envisage for the novel in the light of this proposal if we accept, along with Mikhaïl

---

[3] 'is regulated by an economic principle. It is for example [...] an approximation that allows the condensing of complex thought: its value resides in its pragmatic effectiveness. In the [...] case [...] where metaphor contains a truth [...], it reveals a hitherto hidden link between things'.

Bakhtin, that of all genres the novel best translates the 'tendances évolutives du monde nouveau et s'avère ainsi le reflet intégral et multiforme de son époque' (1987: 233; 244)?[4] In his recent collection of essays, *Le Roman, le réel et autres essais*, Philippe Forest writes:

> Répondre au réel, répondre du réel, essayer de ne pas trahir son appel dans le simulacre d'une représentation rassurante, tenter de traduire cet appel dans l'espace d'un récit incertain et inquiet, rester fidèle à une éthique proprement moderne où l'écriture a partie liée avec la négativité et un certain exercice critique de la pensée, telle est la morale du roman moderne.[5] (Forest, 2007: 238)

These issues are refracted throughout the collected thinking of the Manifesto: in the signatories' united aim to liberate the French language from 'son pacte avec la nation' [its pact with the nation] (Le Bris, 2007: 47) and in their demand that their works be included within a Francophone literature where hexagonal writing is simply one element among others.

The desire to put *Francophonie* on trial poses an enormous challenge that implies a historical, political and philosophical revision of the term. Indeed, since the end of the Second World War, and the decolonization of France's colonial territories, *Francophonie* has invariably been represented, at least on the level of ideas, as a problematic network, or a site of contradictory and permanently evolving discourses.[6] If we understand globalization as the 'européanisation du monde' [Europeanization of the world], that is to say 'quadrillage de la terre par des liens de toutes sortes, ne se sépar[ant] pas de la diffusion planétaire des références européennes' (Moreau Defarges, 2002: 13)[7] then, from a historical point of view, *Francophonie* can be said to have emerged from globalization. Derrida, in *Foi et savoir*, refers to this historical process as 'mondialatinisation' [globalatinization]

---

[4] 'evolving tendencies of the modern world and thus reveals itself to be the integral and multiformed reflection of its age'.

[5] 'To respond to the real, and from the real, to try to remain faithful to its demand by avoiding the pretence of a reassuring mode of representation, to attempt to convey this demand within the space of a narrative that is uncertain and full of doubt, to remain loyal to a properly modern ethic in which writing goes hand in glove with a negative attitude and a certain critical exercise of thought. Such is the moral of the contemporary novel.'

[6] On this subject, see, for example: Tétu, 1992; Maugey, 1993; Moura, 1999; Beniamino, 1999; Tonnet-Lacroix, 2003; Wolton, 2006; and Roy, 2008.

[7] 'an endless subdivision of the world through all kinds of links, which is inextricably tied to the global diffusion of European references'.

in order to explain the global expansion of 'cette alliance étrange du christianisme, comme expérience de la mort de Dieu, et du capitalisme télé-technoscientifique' (2000: 23).[8] Globalization, in its direct and logical link with colonization, favoured contact between peoples that subsequently gave rise to the decomposition and re-composition of various identities. For example, even if such material institutionalization of the Francophone project (in the form of conferences, heads of state summits, and the creation of organizations and agencies for cooperation) guarantees those declarations of principle – in which anti-imperial criticism and the affirmation of identity are articulated as part of a universal ideal of the unity of all people affected by colonization – more often than not these institutions are concerned with defending the French language against the global rise of Anglo-American culture. For English has become the 'porteur de cette mondialisation et de cette globalisation [...] [contrairement au] français [qui] porte en lui, sans doute depuis la Révolution française, l'idée d'universel' (Sfeir, 2005: 11).[9] The Manifesto signatories also stress the language question, and especially the loaded usage of the term 'Francophone', which, for many, evokes imperialist nostalgia.

The linguistic dimension of *Francophonie* is key. By insisting on a relationship between French-speaking territories based on exchange, Onésime Reclus, the geographer who originally coined the term, accorded it a predominantly linguistic meaning. The defence and promotion of the French language in which Francophone countries participate nonetheless reveal the ambiguity of that which Anne Judge qualifies as 'un certain francocentrisme qui fait penser au passé colonial de la France, même si les paramètres du problème [...] sont tout à fait différents à l'heure actuelle' (1996: 34).[10] To propose the demise of *Francophonie* and its replacement by a French-language *littérature-monde* is, then, one means of envisaging how *Francophonie* might free itself from its imperialist connotations (or, indeed, for some critics, its neo-imperial role). In other words, it means imagining a rupture with a Francocentric and neo-colonial idea of *Francophonie* where the paternalism and dependence that characterize the relationship between certain Francophone countries and hexagonal France persist. This desire for a shift in paradigm and status is akin, on a practical level, to modifying

---

[8] 'this strange alliance of Christianity, as the experience of the death of God, and teleotechnoscientific capitalism'.

[9] 'bearer of this globalization [...] [contrary to] French [which] contains within it, since the French Revolution, the idea of the universal'.

[10] 'a certain Francocentricism that evokes France's colonial past, even if the parameters of the problem have entirely changed today'.

the culture of French institutions (that decide whether a writer from the Francophone periphery is to be accepted or marginalized), modifying the ways in which books circulate within the Francophone space, and laying down a challenge to third-level institutions with regard to the integration or normalization of Francophone literatures within their various critical and institutional discourses.

The clash of all these different elements might explain why the concept of *Francophonie*, in its neo-colonial version, is described in the Manifesto as a Grand Narrative that must be reconfigured, and as a doxa so contentious that it is too politically charged to represent other realities. For this reason, it is no longer capable of taking account of the transcultural and translinguistic phenomena that form the richness and diversity of the Francophone literary space. This richness is also frequently absent from readings that have been, and remain, content to make colonization and anti-colonial resistance the major thematic concerns of Francophone literature, denying in this very process the capacity of these literatures to articulate what Édouard Glissant refers to as 'la totalité-monde contemporaine' [contemporary *totalité-monde*] or, in other words, 'le choc, l'intrication, les répulsions, les attirances, les connivences, les oppositions, [et] les conflits entre les cultures des peuples' (1996: 82).[11] For this reason, the recourse to postcolonial theory as a reading practice that illuminates the Francophone novel needs to be undertaken with care. For if these novels often reflect preoccupations of a postcolonial order, they are not necessarily novels of the post-colony.[12] The hyphen distinguishing 'post-colonial' and 'postcolonial'

> répond aux deux axes suivis par la critique: l'un chronologique, relève d'une évolution colonisation-lutte pour l'indépendance-indépendance et désigne une période (la 'post-indépendance'); l'autre, thématico-formel,

---

[11] 'the shock, complexity, repulsions, attractions, complicities, contrasts, conflicts that exist between human cultures'.

[12] In the case of Francophone Quebecois and Antillean writing, for example, the chronological principle does not apply given that Quebec remains 'in anticipation' of its political independence as do certain Creole regions that are either French overseas departments or territories (Martinique and Guadeloupe). On the other hand, several novels published in Quebec after the 1970s display certain preoccupations of a postcolonial nature. These can include the recourse to linguistic 'tropicality', the search for an aesthetic of resistance and the exploration of the challenge posed by identity and 'Americanness'. On this subject, see, for example, Vautier (1994), who clarifies this question by examining the paradoxes of postmodernity and postcolonialism (or post-Europeanism, to use a term Vautier borrows from Max Dorsinville) of Quebec literature.

détermine un ensemble littéraire doté de qualités identifiables.[13] (Moura, 1997: 62)

Jean-Marc Moura is correct when he affirms in *Littératures francophones et théorie postcoloniale* that

> l'opposition binaire colonial/postcolonial fait du colonialisme le marqueur déterminant de l'histoire. Elle fait retomber l'analyse dans le schéma littéraire du temps propre à l'Europe, marquée par la téléologie du progrès et de la civilisation. Il y aurait là tous les symptômes d'une histoire monolithique qui accorde à toutes les autres littératures un statut prépositionnel et qui déplace la problématique de l'axe du pouvoir (véritable axe de ces études avec l'opposition Centre/Périphérie) à celui du temps.[14] (Moura, 1999: 4)

Any rereading of the Manifesto's various proposals in the light of these comments must follow the same direction. In other words, what criticism must 'correct' in the Manifesto, depends, I believe, on a sustained demonstration of the confusion and slippage that occasionally take place between *Francophonie* and postcolonialism and that risk neutralizing the rich potential of the Manifesto's emphasis on the 'world'.[15]

---

[13] 'corresponds to the two directions followed by critics: the first, chronological, refers to a historical period ('post-independence') concerned with the evolution from colonization to the struggle for independence and finally independence itself. The second is thematic and formal and determines a literary ensemble in which identifiable characteristics are found'.

[14] 'the binary opposition colonial/postcolonial privileges colonialism as a determining historical marker. It reinserts analysis into a temporal literary paradigm that is European and marked by the teleology of "progress" and "civilization". This displays all the symptoms of a monolithic history that accords a prepositional status to other literatures and replaces the question of the axis of power (the true axis of these studies with its opposition between centre and periphery) with a temporal axis'.

[15] Given that this chapter's discussion of the various facets of *Littérature-monde en français* is structured around the concept of the market, it is important to mention another work that is carried out in a similar vein, Graham Huggan's seminal *The Postcolonial Exotic*. Here Huggan highlights the danger for postcolonial literature (or Francophone literature with postcolonial inflections) of becoming an exotic literature within the logic of a commercial rhetoric. For, is the idea of 'World literature in French' not another means of exoticizing the relationship with the Other by means of an over-aestheticization of the complex nature of its representation through the vocabulary of globalization? Similar to Roland Barthes in *Mythologies*, Huggan insists on the idea of 'mystification'

In this way it becomes possible to concur both with the main supporters of the Manifesto and with Louis-Jean Calvet in *Linguistique et colonialisme* in rejecting the idea that *Francophonie* represents the 'dernier état de l'impérialisme culturel français' [final stage of French cultural imperialism] (Calvet 1974: 9) and that Francophone studies are merely the poor relative of French studies, 'minority literatures' (in Deleuze and Guattari's 1975 sense of the term) or even 'colonial sub-cultures', as defined by Aimé Césaire (1956). In his contribution to *Pour une littérature-monde*, Alain Mabanckou argues that the 'procureurs les plus impitoyables regardent la francophonie comme la continuation de la politique étrangère de la France dans ses anciennes colonies!' (2007a: 55) before concluding that '[l]a vérité est là, irréductible: aucune littérature ne peut se contenter d'un rôle d'officier d'ordonnance. On n'écrit pas pour *sauver* une langue, mais justement pour en *créer* une' (59–60).[16]

Nonetheless, the demise of *Francophonie* is announced by the Manifesto within the context of a postmodern condition understood as the reworking of all of these issues. Here, 'le "post" représente la capacité d'aller au-delà de la naïveté d'une épistémologie tentant de renvoyer à des entités stables, qu'il s'agisse d'essences ou d'une conception cartésienne du sujet' (Imbert, 1997: 32).[17] This rewriting, which goes hand in hand with a chronotopic reorganization of *Francophonie*'s axes, confers another sense and status on *Francophonie* by extricating it from the historical frame of colonization. As Dominique Wolton writes in *Demain la francophonie*, 'la mondialisation change la donne de la francophonie. Hier celle-ci était à tort identifiée à la décolonisation. Demain elle devient un des acteurs

---

that underpins exoticist discourse and the new forms it assumes in its symbolic transactions with others. Indeed the quixotic tendency underlying the comments of those who spearhead the Manifesto are symptomatic of what Huggan terms 'strategic exoticism': 'the means by which postcolonial writers/thinkers, working from within exoticist codes of representation, either manage to subvert those codes [...], or succeed in redeploying them for the purposes of uncovering differential relations of power' (2001: 32).

16 'The notion of *francophonie* [...] has been contested by those who have emphasized its political overtones and therefore denounced it as an extension of France's foreign policy in its former colonies' (2009: 144); 'There lies the undoubted truth: no literature can be content with playing the role of an orderly. One does not write to *save* a language, but rather to *create* one' (2009: 146).

17 '"post" refers to a capacity to move beyond a naïve epistemology that attempts to return us to stable entities be they essences or a Cartesian concept of the subject'.

de la diversité culturelle' (2006: 54).[18] The global future of *Francophonie* implies its reconfiguration as it evolves from a neo-colonial to a universalist idea. Confronted with the impressive potential of globalization as well as the latter's disadvantages, *Francophonie* is no longer a vestige of the colonial past but a 'francosphere' (Wolton, 2006: 190), enlarged so as better to partake in contemporary debates regarding globalization's greatest political challenge: cultural diversity. This evolution from 'Francophone literature' to *littérature-monde* indicates the desired-for transformation of *Francophonie* from the point of view of the Manifesto's signatories. It gives rise to what Pierre Ouellet qualifies as '"mutations esthétiques" qui affectent l'expérience perceptive que nous avons de nous-mêmes et des autres, dont l'opposition et la face à face ne sont plus envisageables comme tels' (2008: 173).[19] Developing a certain idea of the Francophone *tout-monde* 'ne relève [pas] d'une simple coquetterie intellectuelle, mais devient une indispensable démarche qui s'articule autour d'une vision' (Sfeir, 2005: 11)[20] of the *œuvre-monde* in which the fictional reality takes into account not only the multiple character of the 'world-reality' but finds all sorts of echoes in a 'rhizome' of irreducible references. This resembles, on a metaphorical level, the famous 'Babel's library' described by Jorge Luis Borges in *Fictions*, except that if the image of totality is the common denominator of Glissant's *totalité-monde* and Borges's total library, their vision of the labyrinth is not the same. For Glissant it is the world, for Borges the archive. But in both cases its function is to destabilize meanings and coincidences.

Meanings and Counter-meanings of *Littérature-monde*

In the light of these ideas the following question arises: how does one define the Francophone *œuvre-monde* within the logic of cultural globalization? In his recent study of the post-exotic work of Antoine Volodine, Lionel Ruffel develops the following idea:

> Peu d'œuvres méritent le nom d'œuvre-monde, mais toutes celles qui le méritent doivent être étudiées car l'étude d'un monde est toujours celle *du* monde. [...] On pourra ainsi vérifier cette assertion: tout, dans cette œuvre, des discours aux structures en passant par les positions énonciatives, tout

---

[18] 'globalization changes the rules of *Francophonie*. Yesterday [*Francophonie*] was wrongly identified with decolonization. Tomorrow it will become a player in cultural diversity'.

[19] '"aesthetic mutations" that affect our experience of how we perceive ourselves and others and in which opposition and conflict can no longer be envisaged'.

[20] 'does not arise from some form of intellectual vanity but becomes an indispensable strategy that is built upon a vision'.

est politique. [...] On comprend qu'elle s'accorde mal avec la brièveté, mais aussi avec une lecture univoque. Elle doit convoquer conjointement les ressources de l'esthétique, de la politique, de l'histoire, de la philosophie, de la stylistique pour tenter non pas d'être exhaustive, car le monde ne s'épuise pas, mais, [...] complète. [...] Celle d'Antoine Volodine, parce qu'elle pense littérairement l'histoire, parce qu'elle pense l'esthétique et la politique, parce qu'elle reconfigure le passé et la représentation d'un avenir, tout en troublant les images du présent, justifie cette méthode labyrinthique et obsessionnelle.[21] (Ruffel, 2007: 12; 13; 11; 9)

Even though Volodine's work avoids the ambiguity of the Francophone and the controversy surrounding *littérature-monde*, it seems, through its 'ambition totalisante' [totalizing ambition] to 'faire monde' [render the world] (99), to correspond to the declared intentions of several of the contributors to the Manifesto. In this regard, Mabanckou asserts:

[Il] ne s'agit pas de proposer une littérature de rêve, encore moins de décréter que la seule création qui vaille est celle qui s'éloigne de son propre univers, exalte un ailleurs lointain pour finir par s'autodétruire à force de ne pas avoir un point d'ancrage. Nous risquerions alors de réveiller les vieux démons de l'exotisme. [...] La littérature-monde est le concert de la multiplicité d'*expériences*, la reconnaissance de la force de l'art dans ce qui apparaît comme le 'désordre de la vie'. [...] Notre tâche est de suivre la marche de cette littérature-monde en langue française, de tracer sommairement ses contours, de la regarder dans un ensemble plus étendu, plus éclaté, plus bruyant, c'est-à-dire *le monde*. (Mabanckou, 2007a: 65; 64; 65)[22]

---

[21] 'Few works deserve the qualification 'œuvre-monde', but all those that do so deserve to be studied because the study of a world is always a study of *the* world. [...] It is possible then to confirm this claim: everything in this work, from the discourses to the structures via enunciative positions, is political. [...] One can understand that it might not sit well with brevity, or with a univocal reading. It must convoke conjointly resources from aesthetics, politics, history, philosophy, stylistics so as to attempt, not to be exhaustive, because the world is never spent, but [...] to be complete. [...] The work of Antoine Volodine, because it literally thinks history, because it thinks aesthetics and politics, because it reconfigures the past and the representation of the future whilst unsettling the images of the present, justifies this labyrinthine and obsessive method.'

[22] The aim is not to propose a literature of dreams, even less to claim that the only worthy literature is that which distances itself from its own universe, exalting in the process a far-off place that finally leads to self-destruction by failing to have any roots. This would run the risk of stirring the old demons of

Could the term 'post-exoticism', if it includes this world, constitute a new poetics capable of imagining and expressing the comic dimension of the 'novel-world' that confronts the residual spectres of the neo-colonial *Francophonie*? Writing about this new poetic procedure, Glissant notes that when

> on essaie de mener une œuvre poétique et non de poésie, c'est-à-dire qu'on essaie de voir ce qui se passe dans le chaos-monde, on a besoin d'avoir une activité qui soit non pas une activité politique au sens littéral du terme, mais une activité d'adaptation de tous les éléments du réel auquel on touche avec tous les éléments de la problématique qu'on a deviné. [23] (Glissant, 2007: 84)

From this, it is possible to understand that instead of levelling out Diversity, *l'œuvre-monde* returns us to the multiple forms that can represent this post-exotic totality. For Ruffel, this universe 'prend au final la forme d'une archive, d'une anthologie, [ou] d'une bibliothèque' [ultimately takes the form of an archive, an anthology [or] a library] (108).

It must be said that if the advocates of *littérature-monde* project their literary universe and its textual materialization in terms of these variations, that is to say through a bold dynamic that denounces at times the neologisms and dated practices of *Francophonie* (in its neo-colonial version) and at times the prevailing trends of global exchange (in its unifying version), it is nonetheless true that their Manifesto is guilty of a lack of cohesion, of fragmented conclusions and fundamental ambiguities.

This arises, in the first instance, from the context in which the controversy surrounding a *littérature-monde en français* arose. In his contribution to the edited volume *Pour une littérature-monde*, Michel Le Bris associates the emergence of the concept of *littérature-monde* with the Étonnants Voyageurs festival in Saint-Malo and the creation of its equivalent in Bamako. 'Il était né, ce festival d'un gigantesque ras-le-bol devant l'état de la littérature française,

---

exoticism. [...] World literature in French is the culmination of a multiplicity of *experiences*, the recognition of the power of art in what appears as the 'disorder of life'. [...] Our task consists in monitoring the progress of this World Literature in French, in delineating its contours, in considering it in a broader, expanded, explosive framework, that is to say *the world*'. (Mabanckou, 2009: 149)

[23] 'one tries to shape and lead a poetic work as opposed to a work of poetry, that is to say when one attempts to see what is happening in the chaos of the world, one needs an activity that is not political in the literal meaning of the term, but an activity capable of adapting to all the elements of the real that one rubs up against with all the elements of the problematic one has identified'.

devenue sourde et aveugle [...] à la course du monde, à force de se croire la seule, l'unique, l'ultime référence' (25).[24] For Le Bris, a new literature is required, one that is adventurous and plurivocal and evokes the 'merveilles' [marvels] of his parents' 'grenier' [attic] where as a child he discovered such masterpieces as Flaubert's *Salammbô*. Yet if Le Bris rejects the accusation that he is promoting an exotic literature, this reference to Flaubert (and writers such as Joseph Conrad and Robert Louis Stevenson) as a literary model for his *littérature-monde* imbues his vision with exotic nostalgia. In his forceful request for recognition, Le Bris only barely manages to avoid the pitfalls of Orientalist discourse, and his programme for a *littérature-monde* in French can be seen as a desire to copy what has gone before. From the 'empire du Signe' [the empire of the Sign] (46) to the 'empire des nuages' [empire of clouds] (51), Le Bris, along with Jean Rouaud, appears to be confirming the 'deuil du récit' [mourning for narrative] (Rouaud, 2007: 18), 'la mort du roman' [the death of the novel] and 'la mort de la France' [the demise of France] (20) as overly rigid symbols that reveal 'le grand texte du monde' [the great text of the world] that is to come (Le Bris, 2007: 49). Furthermore, this concurrence of a debate on *Francophonie* and the organization of festivals raises the issue of the seriousness of this proclamation of a new *littérature-monde*. Of course, this 'festive' quality of the Manifesto is reminiscent of the Bakhtinian notion of carnival as a symbolic location (and mode) of subversion and renaissance. Thus, as Jacques Godbout humorously remarks, 'Les "francophones", n'est-ce pas, seraient une race à part que l'on rencontre en Afrique, en Amérique et dans les territoires périphériques de Belgique ou Suisse. Il n'y en aurait pas en France, sauf quand on les invite, à l'occasion, à chanter aux Francofolies ou à se produire aux Francoffonies du Salon du livre, porte de Versailles' (2007: 105).[25]

Although the idea of *littérature-monde* in French is repeated in the statements of its main original proponents (Le Bris and Rouaud) as an adventure in experimentation, the question remains whether the concept is capable of forming the basis for a rigorous theoretical position. According to Michel Beniamino (1999), one of the problems facing Francophone literatures is precisely both the lack of theoretical developments capable of constructing

---

24 'This festival was born of an enormous sense of frustration at the state of French literature which had become deaf and blind [...] to the ways of the world because it believed itself to be the sole and ultimate reference'.

25 '"Francophones" are seen as a race apart, found in Africa, America and in the peripheral territories of Belgium and Switzerland. There are none in France, apart from occasions when they are invited to sing at the Francofolies or appear at the Francoffonies section of the book festival at the Porte de Versailles'.

a Francophone poetics as well as the difficulty of proposing a typology that could represent the different linguistic and literary realities contained within *Francophonie*. And this even before the question of postcolonial poetics is raised, a theoretical position frequently referred to in the study of Francophone literatures yet one which remains in the main dependent upon intellectual categories originating in the West, in other words, disciplinary notions developed in the West, including the widespread usage amongst academics in the Francophone world of Michel Foucault's concepts on discourse and those of Jacques Derrida on deconstruction.

These issues also beg the question as to why important contemporary writers, and practitioners of *littérature-monde*, such as Yasmina Khadra, Hédi Bouraoui, Abdelkébir Khatibi, Patrick Chamoiseau or Joël Des Rosiers, did not sign (or were not invited to sign) the Manifesto and why others did not hesitate to underline their scepticism. In an interview, Amin Maalouf explains that

> l'idée de littérature-monde n'est pas une notion à laquelle je suis sensible spontanément. Je comprends la vision mondiale d'une littérature en langue française, la relation d'ouverture et d'interaction avec le reste du monde. Dans ce sens j'approuve, mais je ne peux pas définir ce mot car je ne l'aurais pas utilisé moi-même.[26] (Maalouf, 2007)

The other argument that lies at the heart of the notion of *littérature-monde* is the signatories' use of the concept of *Weltliteratur* developed by Goethe in 1827 in order to argue for the acknowledgement and inclusion within European literature of writing from beyond its borders. If *littérature-monde* is not merely a paraphrasing of *Weltliteratur* in a metadiscursive form, could it be seen as a modern rewriting or recycling of a Goethean way of imagining inclusion? In this way, *Francophonie*'s self-reflection conditions its revival. If the signatories of the Manifesto regularly mention their debt to Goethe, they 'se contentent de faire jouer les vieilles et gratifiantes recettes de la littérature [européenne] [...] en les agrémentant d'un coefficient d'ironie prétendument sophistiqué et censé exonérer les auteurs de toute accusation de [répétivité]' (Forest, 2007: 238).[27]

Thirdly, the call for a *littérature-monde* is also linked to the discourse

---

[26] 'the idea of *littérature-monde* is not one to which I immediately warm. I can understand the global vision of a French-language literature and its open and interactive relationship with the rest of the world. In this sense I approve of it, but I cannot define this word as I wouldn't have used it myself'.

[27] 'are content to bring into play the old and gratifying recipes of [European] literature [...] which they flavour with an element of irony that is allegedly sophis-

of the pamphleteer. The rhetoric that defines this form, as Marc Angenot illustrates in *La Parole pamphlétaire* (1982) is characterized by paradox and conflict: 'Forme réactionnelle, souvent tournée vers un passé mythique, le pamphlet est un monde de fausse conscience spécifique à des sociétés en "déstabilisation" idéologique constante' (349).[28] 'Plus tard' [at a later date], as Le Bris writes, echoing the opening words of the Manifesto, 'on dira peut-être que ce fut un moment historique' [it will perhaps be said this was a historic moment] (23). Although a 'vision crépusculaire' [twilight vision] (Angenot, 1982: 345) of the multihued world to come runs through the Manifesto, the text nonetheless remains, by its very nature, 'perméable à un certain pessimisme catastrophique' [permeable to a certain catastrophic pessimism] (345), and its defenders, in their (falsely) sublimated contradictions 'prennent le *contre-pied* de la doxa, ce qui revient à dire qu'ils demeurent dans la mouvance de celle-ci'[29] (339).[30] It is easy to agree with Angenot when he rigorously establishes 'l'homologie de structure' [the structural homology] between 'la position idéologique imaginaire que s'attribue le pamphlétaire et la situation "exotope" du héros du roman, tel que défini par György Lukács et réinterprété par Lucien Goldman' (339).[31] This homology reveals the quixotic attitude of the pamphleteer, 'chercheur

---

ticated and supposed to exonerate them from all accusations that they are being [repetitive].'

[28] 'The pamphlet is a reactive form frequently turned towards a mythical past. It is a world of false consciousness specific to societies experiencing constant ideological "destabilization"'.

[29] 'take the opposing view to generally accepted theory which means they remain within its sphere of influence'.

[30] Where this pessimism is concerned, Jean Rouaud's comment in the Manifesto seems particularly relevant: 'C'est toute une génération qui va porter le deuil de cette disparition de la France, par une sorte de passage au noir, une entreprise d'effacement, de purgation, de renoncement, qui se convainc qu'il n'y a plus de lumière à diffuser, que tous les feux sont éteints, que les seuls qui clignotent sont les dernières braises sous les cendres où se consume la gloire passée. Ce qui se traduira par le deuil du récit' [An entire generation is going to carry the grief resulting from this disappearance of France. It will mean going through a black period, a process of erasure, of atonement and renouncement. For this France is convinced it is no longer radiant, that all its light has been extinguished and the only flickers are the dying embers beneath the ashes of a glorious past. This will mean the death of narrative] (2007: 18).

[31] 'the imaginary ideological position the pamphleteer accords him/herself and the 'exotopic' situation of the novel's hero as defined by György Lukács and reinterpreted by Lucien Goldman'.

errant, nostalgique d'un âge d'or perdu au milieu d'une société dégradée et grand pourfendeur de moulins à vent, [...] prêt à mettre sa plume désinté-ressée au service de nobles causes' (337).[32] Here quite literally is the perfect portrait of a modern Don Quixote (Michel Le Bris) and Sancho Panza (Jean Rouaud) with the former promoting an incoherent and unlimited idealism and the latter, more realistic, reminding us of the imminence of death in various guises: the demise of France, the narrative, the novel and even 'd'une certaine idée' [of a certain idea].

In such a context, can the notion of *littérature-monde*, with the opposition and irresolvable paradoxes it generates, provide a constructive framework for new demands? And to what precisely does *littérature-monde* refer? A generic aberration or makeshift theory? An avant-garde attempt to insert *Francophonie* into the marketplace of disciplinary concepts and ideological disputes? Or does it express a form of resistance with a view to creating an alternative future for *Francophonie*?

These questions also force us to ask why the interrogation of the concept of *Francophonie* has been expressed in terms of a *littérature-monde* and not as a 'post-*Francophonie*'. To my mind, the idea of 'post-*Francophonie*' would allow for engagement with two directions generally followed by critical work on the postcolonial: first, a chronological axis that could trace the development of a neo-colonial *Francophonie* to a universalist one and, secondly, a formal-thematic axis that could identify a literary grouping displaying qualities worthy of a 'world-poetics'. It is in this way that I believe criticism must 'readjust' the orientation of the Manifesto's debate on *littérature-monde* in French. For the debate, as it is currently formulated, is ineffectively engaged with the question of cultural globalization and the challenges it poses for *Francophonie*.

It seems to me that in trying to revise some of the parameters of *Franco-phonie* and '[la] porter à un autre niveau pour tenir compte du changement d'échelle qui découle de la mondialisation de l'espace culturel' (Roy, 2008: 35),[33] the *littérature-monde* project fails to avoid the pitfalls of totalizing (and totalitarian) totality that is the risk that besets all nationalist ideology. The exception here, of course, is that the aspiration towards this totality remains dispersed and also highly unlikely to materialize given that Francophone literatures retain their specificity and cannot be shaped to fit a global model.

---

[32] 'errant adventurer, nostalgic for a golden age lost amidst a corrupt society and great destroyer of windmills [...] ready to use his/her disinterested pen in the service of noble causes'.

[33] 'take it to another level so as to take account of the changes in scale deriving from the globalization of cultural space'.

These literatures depend on individuals with diverse geo-cultural origins and demands. In an opinion column published by *Le Monde* on 19 March 2007, Abdou Diouf refers to the signatories of the Manifesto as 'fossoyeurs de la francophonie' [the gravediggers of *Francophonie*] who in his opinion contibute 'à entretenir le plus grave des contresens sur la francophonie, en confondant francocentrisme et francophonie, en confondant exception culturelle et diversité culturelle'.[34] Here it is perhaps necessary to agree with Boris Cyrulnik (2007) that the process of producing change necessarily implies repetition as a means of overcoming trauma. For the Francophone author has a compulsive need to repeat (in the sense of defend) both the decision to write in French and a sensibility towards this language and all those that pass through it. And there is a need, too, to preserve opaqueness and to differentiate and defer (in the Derridean sense of *différance*) the unifying protocols of reading that see the novel of a Francophone writer not as a world-novel but one whose classification and categorization remain problematic.

Thus, if the claim of newness underpinning the notion of *littérature-monde* is questionable, it seems to me that the main challenge of this entire debate lies elsewhere, and that the militant stance of the Manifesto signatories is of an entirely different nature. In my opinion, what we are dealing with is a utopian desire to democratize the literary object in general and the Francophone literary object in particular. And this democratization refers to the sense of constructing a worldwide French-language literature without borders and capable of placing non-European French-language writers on an equal footing with their European counterparts (see Bonnet, 2003). It means democratizing too in the sense of decommercializing the literary object by refusing to see it as mere consumer object. Finally, it means democratizing in the sense of taking account of the Other's alterity not as savage and uncompromising but as a 'source de savoir sur soi-même' [a source of knowledge of oneself] (Castillo Durante, 1997: 8), that is to say in the spirit of an 'événement anthropologique' [anthropological event] (6). In his contribution to the Manifesto, Tahar Ben Jelloun writes: '[À] partir du moment où la culture n'est pas rentable immédiatement il faut la négliger et chercher du brillant ailleurs. Telle est l'époque. C'est le règne de la valeur marchande' (2007: 16).[35] Raising

---

[34] 'to maintaining the most serious of misunderstandings about *Francophonie* by confusing Francocentrism with *Francophonie* and cultural exceptionalism with cultural diversity'.

[35] '[A]s soon as culture is no longer immediately profitable it must be disregarded and brilliance found elsewhere. This is the era we live in. It is the reign of market value'.

the primacy of profitability that characterizes contemporary culture also means confronting the challenge faced by *Francophonie* and the pivotal role it plays in the third millennium and in the contemporary process of cultural globalization. In *Le Roman de la démocratie*, Nelly Wolf explains that 'On croit que les romans parlent d'amour. Il serait plus juste de dire qu'ils parlent des affaires humaines. L'amour, étranger au monde, antipolitique, est une hypothèse que les romanciers opposent au monde dévoré par la politique, laquelle est devenue, dans les démocraties, l'affaire de tout le monde' (2003: 5).[36] This is, perhaps, a fair measure to use for celebrating the arrival of the French-language world-novel in its 'logique paradoxale' [paradoxical logic]. Because of this paradoxical logic, henceforth it will be up to interpretive communities to decide the shape of future debates on *littérature-monde* and the implications of its multiple possibilities.

Translated by Aedín Ní Loingsigh.

Works Cited

Angenot, Marc. 1982. *La Parole pamphlétaire: contribution à la typologie des discours modernes*. Paris: Payot.

Bakhtin, Mikhaïl. 1987. *Esthétique et théorie du roman*. Paris: Gallimard.

Barthes, Roland. 1957. *Mythologies*. Paris: Seuil.

Ben Jelloun, Tahar. 2007. 'La cave de ma mémoire, le toit de ma maison sont des mots français'. In Michel Le Bris and Jean Rouaud (eds), *Pour une littérature-monde*. Paris: Gallimard: 113–24.

Beniamino, Michel. 1999. *La Francophonie littéraire: essai pour une théorie*. Paris: L'Harmattan.

Bonnet, Véronique, Pierre Zoberman, Jean-Louis Joubert, and Jacques Tramson. 2003. *Frontières de la francophonie; francophonie sans frontières*. Paris: L'Harmattan.

Borges, Jorge Luis. 1994. *Fictions*. Trans. by Nestor Ibarra. Paris: Gallimard. [First published as *Ficciones* (1944).]

Calvet, Louis-Jean. 1974. *Linguistique et colonialisme: petit traité de glottophagie*. Paris: Payot.

Castillo Durante, Daniel. 1997. 'Culture et mondialisation à l'aube d'un nouveau millénium'. *Carrefour* 19.1: 3–30.

---

[36] 'It is believed that novels talk about love. It would be more accurate to say they speak of human affairs. Love, as foreign to the world and anti-political, is a hypothesis that novelists contrast with a world consumed by politics, which in democracies, has become everyone's business'.

—. 2004. 'L'altérité polémique: guerre, *sémiocratie*, exclusion et économies du savoir: de la *Pax Americana* à l'implosion du modèle argentin'. In Daniel Castillo Durante and Patrick Imbert (eds), *L'Interculturel et l'économie à l'œuvre: les marges de la mondialisation*. Ottawa: Les Éditions David: 15–46.

Césaire, Aimé. 1956. 'Culture et colonialisme'. *Présence africaine* 8-9-10: 190–205.

Cyrulnik, Boris. 2007. *Parler d'amour au bord du gouffre*. Paris: Odile Jacob.

Deleuze, Gilles, and Félix Guattari. 1975. *Kafka: Pour une littérature mineure*. Paris: Minuit.

Derrida, Jacques. 1967. *L'Écriture et la différence*. Paris: Seuil.

—. 1978. *Writing and Difference*. Trans. by Alan Bass. London: Routledge and Kegan Paul.

—. 2000. *Foi et savoir* (suivi de) *Le siècle et le pardon*. Paris: Seuil.

Diouf, Abdou. 2007. 'Une nouvelle guerre de cent ans'. *Le Monde* 19 March.

Forest, Philippe. 2007. *Le Roman, le réel et autres essais*. Nantes: Éditions Cécile Defaut.

Fradin, Jacques. 2005. *La Voie pauvre de la rébellion*. Paris: L'Harmattan.

Glissant, Édouard. 1996. *Introduction à une poétique du divers*. Paris: Gallimard.

—. 2007. '"Solitaire et solidaire": Entretien avec Édouard Glissant'. In Michel Le Bris and Jean Rouaud (eds), *Pour une littérature-monde*. Paris: Gallimard: 77–86.

Godbout, Jacques. 2007. 'La Question préalable'. In Michel Le Bris and Jean Rouaud (eds), *Pour une littérature-monde*. Paris: Gallimard: 103–11.

Huggan, Graham. 2001. *The Postcolonial Exotic: Marketing the Margins*. London and New York: Routledge.

Imbert, Patrick. 1997. 'Langages publics et langages spécialisés'. *Carrefour* 19.1: 31–50.

Judge, Anne. 1996. 'La francophonie: mythes, masques et réalités'. In Bridget Jones, Arnauld Miguet and Patrick Corcoran (eds), *Francophonies: mythes, masques et réalités. Enjeux politiques et culturels*. Paris: Publisud: 19–41.

Laïdi, Zaki. 2000. *Le Sacre du présent*. Paris: Flammarion.

Le Bris, Michel (ed.). 1992. *Pour une littérature voyageuse*. Brussels: Éditions Complexe.

—. 2007. 'Pour une littérature-monde en français'. In Michel Le Bris and Jean Rouaud (eds), *Pour une littérature-monde*. Paris: Gallimard: 23–53.

Le Bris, Michel, and Jean Rouaud (eds). 2007. *Pour une littérature-monde*. Paris: Gallimard.

Maalouf, Amin. 2007. 'Conflits d'identité. Interview de Amin Maalouf'. evene. fr. 26 August. <http://www.evene.fr/livres/actualite/interview-amin-maalouf-tanios-origines-identites-meurtrieres-874.php>. Consulted on 1 June 2010.

Mabanckou, Alain. 2007a. 'Le chant de l'oiseau migrateur'. In Michel Le Bris and Jean Rouaud (eds), *Pour une littérature-monde*. Paris: Gallimard: 55–66.

—. 2007b. '"Littérature-monde en français": Abdou Diouf répond aux 44 écrivains qui "choisissent de se poser en fossoyeurs de la Francophonie"'. Blog d'Alain Mabanckou. 21 March. <http://www.congopage.com/article4588.html>. Consulted on 1 June 2010.

—. 2009. '"The Song of the Migrating Bird": For a World Literature in French'. Trans. by Dominic Thomas. *Forum for Modern Language Studies* 45.2: 144–50.

Marot, Patrick. 2007. 'Que nous disent les métaphores littéraires?'. In Jean Bessière (ed.), *Littérature, représentation, fiction*. Paris: Honoré Champion: 16–32.

Maugey, Axel. 1993. *Le Roman de la francophonie*. Montreal: Humanitas.

Moreau Defarge, Philippe. 2002. *La Mondialisation*. Paris: Presses Universitaires de France.

Moura, Jean-Marc. 1997. 'Francophonie et critique postcoloniale'. *Revue de littérature comparée* 1: 59–87.

—. 1999. *Littératures francophones et théorie postcoloniale*. Paris: Presses Universitaires de France.

Norel, Phillipe. 2004. *L'Invention du marché: une histoire économique de la mondialisation*. Paris: Seuil.

Ouellet, Pierre. 2008. *Hors-temps: Poétique de la posthistoire*. Montreal: VLB.

Rouaud, Jean. 2007. 'Mort d'une certaine idée'. In Michel Le Bris and Jean Rouaud (eds), *Pour une littérature-monde*. Paris: Gallimard: 7–22.

Roy, Jean-Louis. 2008. *Quel avenir pour la langue française? Francophonie et concurrence culturelle au XXIᵉ siècle*. Montreal: Éditions Hurtubise.

Ruffel, Lionel. 2007. *Volodine post-exotique*. Nantes: Éditions Cécile Defaut.

Sfeir, Antoine. 2005. 'Préface'. In Yves Montenay, *La Langue française face à la mondialisation*. Paris: Les Belles Lettres: 11–13.

Tétu, Michel. 1992. *La Francophonie: histoire, problématique et perspectives*. Montreal: Guérin.

Tonnet-Lacroix, Éliane. 2003. *La littérature française et francophone de 1945 à l'an 2000*. Paris: L'Harmattan.

Vautier, Marie. 1994. 'Les métarécits, le postmodernisme et le mythe postcolonial au Québec: Un point de vue de la "marge"'. *Études littéraires* 27.1: 43–58.

Wolf, Nelly. 2003. *Le Roman de la démocratie*. Saint-Denis: Presses Universitaires de Vincennes.

Wolton, Dominique. 2006. *Demain la francophonie*. Paris: Flammarion.

The Postcolonial Manifesto:
Partisanship, Criticism and
the Performance of Change

David Murphy

The question of how one moves beyond the problematic legacy of colonialism and race in order to re-imagine collective identities beyond conventional conceptions of nationally defined spaces is at the heart of the *littérature-monde* manifesto. Since it burst on to the literary scene in early 2007, *littérature-monde* as a concept has thus been widely associated with a decentred and seemingly de-nationalized French-speaking world: indeed, the manifesto itself and virtually all of the essays contained in the edited volume that followed specifically reject a metropolitan-centred, 'Francocentric' view of literature (and, of the world, more widely). In essence, these texts imagine France as a country that exists within a transnational space that it cannot define or contain.

Nonetheless, it is my (perhaps paradoxical) contention in this chapter that the manifesto and the subsequent edited volume also pose – and, in turn, through their silences, lead the reader to pose – searching questions about the nature of both French literary culture and French national identity. In particular, I am interested in the ways in which the challenge posed to Frenchness by the *littérature-monde* manifesto overlaps with but also departs from what might collectively be termed a series of postcolonial challenges to received notions of Frenchness over the past decade.[1] The privileged forms

---

[1] Of course, the *littérature-monde* project features several writers who do not have a postcolonial relationship of any kind to France. My aim is not to subsume their concerns into a general postcolonial challenge deemed to be at the heart of the manifesto; rather, I wish to explore the ways in which the *littérature-monde*

taken by this challenge have been *manifestes, appels, pétitions*, all of which involve groups coming together around a collectively authored – or, more accurately, as I will argue below, collectively *signed* – text that outlines a set of demands, grievances and/or a projected solution to the problems identified. The public sphere in France has long been the site of what Marc Angenot (1982) has termed 'la parole pamphlétaire' [the discourse of the pamphleteer],[2] an ideologically charged discourse that is wilfully partisan. However, it was only in the early years of the new millennium that what I here collectively term the 'postcolonial manifesto' (in fact, constituted by *manifestes, appels, pétitions*) became the site of concerns relating to empire and its aftermath.[3] This chapter will thus focus on the period from 2005 to 2010, during which there was an explosion of often rancorous postcolonial debates, which took on a wide range of forms and adopted a wide range of stances. Although perceived in certain quarters as the emergence of a 'communitarian' attack on so-called 'universal' Republican principles, the postcolonial manifesto has in fact emerged, at least in part, as a response to a colonialist nostalgia for France's former imperial 'greatness', which has been driven variously by the government, parliamentarians and/or pressure groups (often linked to southern-based *pied noir* groups).[4] This has led to a situation in which a series of reactionary government measures have been met with counter-manifestos/appeals/petitions that seek to challenge a state-sponsored memory of empire. The historians' petitions against the *loi du 23 février 2005*,[5] like the call 'pour un véritable débat sur l'identité nationale' [for a genuine debate on national identity] (December 2009) countering the Sarkozy government's promotion of a 'grand débat sur l'identité nationale' [major debate on national identity], have sparked a highly charged and sometimes vitriolic public debate. Owing to considerations of space, I will

---

project envisages a post-imperial order in comparison with texts that often explicitly position themselves as postcolonial.

  [2] Unless otherwise indicated, all translations from French into English are by the author of this chapter.

  [3] I am conscious that the term 'postcolonial manifesto' elides some of the 'generic' differences between *manifestes, appels, pétitions*, thereby seeming to assume an absolute correspondence between them. However, my essay will limit its focus to *manifestes* and *appels*, which are in fact very close in form and content: petitions, which are often more narrowly circumscribed in their remit (responding to a specific event, law, etc.), will be omitted from my discussion, in large part due to limitations of space.

  [4] For a discussion of this recent 'postcolonial' history, see Forsdick and Murphy (2007; 2009).

  [5] See 'Liberté pour l'histoire' and 'La pétition des historiens'.

focus here on just three of these postcolonial texts, which will be examined alongside the *littérature-monde* manifesto: 'L'Appel des indigènes de la République' [Appeal of the natives of the Republic] (January 2005); the 'Appel pour une République multiculturelle et postraciale' [Call for a multicultural and post-racial Republic] (January 2010); and the literary *cri du cœur* from the *banlieue* [suburban] authors of the literary manifesto 'Qui fait la France?' [Who makes France/Love France?][6] (2007). The main aim of the chapter is to identify where the primarily literary claims of the *littérature-monde* manifesto sit in relation to other 'partisan' texts that position themselves as radical challenges to 'une certaine idée de la France' [a certain idea of France]. Just how valuable a contribution to the 'decolonization' of France is the *littérature-monde* project?

In the process, I also wish to reflect upon the relationship between these partisan texts and postcolonial scholarship within the academy. Academic scholarship tends to be sceptical about claims of radical change and paradigm shifts, and postcolonial studies as a field of inquiry has rightly underlined the persistence of colonial modes of thought after the formal end of empire: however, this begs the question of how precisely one might ever arrive at a genuinely 'postcolonial France' in which such problems might be widely seen to have been resolved? And how would we know if or when this moment has been reached? Is a critique of the postcolonial manifesto's arguments/ ideology/politics a sufficient response or should we not also explore its political strategies and effectiveness? My argument here overlaps with recent debates within postcolonial studies regarding what Chris Bongie has called the field's 'scribal politics' (Bongie, 2008); for Bongie, postcolonial studies has focused on the 'universal' literary values of its corpus at the expense of a sustained analysis of the ideological positions revealed in such works. My own sense is that the initial critical reaction to the *littérature-monde* project has, in fact, provided a relatively thorough analysis of its 'scribal politics'; however, it is my contention here that this necessary focus on (capital 'P') Politics has not been accompanied by sufficient analysis of the (small 'p') politics involved in any attempt to bring about change. Scholars have been absolutely right to underline the intellectual failings/weaknesses of *littérature-monde* but should we not also take account of what Lydie Moudileno elsewhere in this volume refers to as the 'conditions of possibility of its success'? Critics may find the *littérature-monde* project timid or misguided in its claims but, at the same time, we should recall the specific context from which it emerged and the vitriolic reaction that it received in some quarters (see, for example,

---

6 The title of the collective puns on the words 'Qui fait?" [Who makes?] and the slang term 'kiffer' [to love].

the newspaper articles by Abdou Diouf, Nicolas Sarkozy and Alexandre Najjar). Essentially, then, this essay will seek to explore whether postcolonial scholarship gives sufficient weight to the strategies, compromises and allegiances at play in the postcolonial manifesto.

Theatricality and Performativity in the Manifesto

Before examining the precise claims and strategies of the postcolonial manifesto, it is important to examine the generic features that have defined the modern manifesto more generally. The twentieth century witnessed many artistic manifestos, proclaiming with vehemence the arrival of a new way of perceiving the world (1968 is regularly posited as a high watermark after which the genre beats a retreat from the political and artistic scenes). Whether explicitly artistic in focus or not, the manifesto almost always seeks to define itself in relation to the politics/ideology of its time, as well as aiming to provide a transcendence of the limitations of that political moment, and this extends to the *littérature-monde* manifesto. Seeking to legitimize what are presented as previously marginalized forms of artistic creation, it constitutes a complex engagement with the modernity of a postcolonial world, which attempts to define the role and nature of literature after empire, and although it seeks to situate itself as post-ideological, such a stance, even if taken at face value, is in itself a form of ideological engagement with the world.

The manifesto has existed for many centuries but, as recent studies have shown, it is only since the nineteenth century that it has come to occupy a central position – both in the artistic and political spheres – within the context of the public space created by the emerging nation state.[7] Martin Puchner claims that Marx and Engels' *Communist Manifesto* (1848) created the distinct modern genre of the manifesto through its explicit desire to situate itself as a landmark text marking a decisive break in world history, as well as its self-conscious appeal to the reader to take sides and to act at a defining moment in that history. For Puchner, all manifestos, whether artistic or political in focus, display a profound *theatricality* due to their need to dramatize the importance of their words and of the situation with which they are concerned; equally, they display an almost obsessive *performativity* as they seek, through words alone, to make the outcomes announced appear as though they have been instantaneously willed into action. Through these

---

[7] For a range of discussions of the modern manifesto, see Lyon, 1999; Caws, 2001; Burger, 2002; Somigli, 2003; and Puchner, 2006.

rhetorical strategies, the reader is to be convinced of the need for immediate change:

> Manifestos tend to present themselves as mere means to an end, demanding to be judged not by their rhetorical or literary merits – their poetry – but by their ability to change the world. Marx, however, helps us understand that it is their form, not their particular complaints and demands, that articulates most succinctly the desires and hopes, maneuvers and strategies of modernity: *to create points of no return; to make history; to fashion the future.* (Puchner, 2006: 2; my emphasis)

Essentially, Le Bris, Rouaud and their fellow signatories create *a point of no return* at which the reader has a chance to take sides in the creation of a new artistic and, by analogy, political future.

I have explored elsewhere the specific strategies deployed by the *littérature-monde* manifesto in order to legitimize and persuade, and have sought to relate the text to parallel debates in the Anglophone world that took place in the 1980s (see Murphy, 2010). To summarize the key points of my analysis here, the *littérature-monde* manifesto is highly theatrical from its first paragraph, opening with the statement, 'Plus tard, on dira peut-être que ce fut un moment historique' [In due course, it will perhaps be said that this was a historic moment] ('Toward a "World-Literature" in French', 2009: 54) (referring to the various non-French winners of the big literary prizes in the autumn of 2006), which displays an audacious mixture of coyness and self-assurance about the significance of this turning point in the history of literature in French. The remainder of the paragraph is not so coy in its definition of the sea change that is taking place as nothing less than a 'révolution copernicienne' [Copernican revolution] (54). The announcement of an emergent 'littérature-monde en français' [world-literature in French] performs the change required to overcome a hierarchical system centred on France and fuelled by an imperial nostalgia that is given its most powerful incarnation in the institutions of *Francophonie* which are decried as 'le dernier avatar du colonialisme' [the last avatar of colonialism] (56), while 'l'émergence d'une littérature-monde [...] signe l'acte de décès de la franco-phonie' [the emergence of a world literature [...] signs the death certificate of so-called Francophone literature] (56). Essentially, the manifesto establishes a number of binary oppositions that it brings to an end through its own performance of change: the metropolitan centre (for which we can essentially read Paris) versus the French-speaking world; a (Parisian) literary elite versus 'real' writers, for the most part identified as 'marginal' writers from other French-speaking (or indeed non-French-speaking) spaces; and, finally, I think one can also read into the constant evocation of centre–periphery relations an opposition between Paris and the provinces. (This latter opposition is made far more clearly in the essays by Rouaud and Le Bris which evoke a Jacobinist literary sphere with 'functionaries' and 'little gray men' dispensing centrally ordained rules on how to write literature.)

Manifesto versus Essay?

Having identified the theatrical and performative strategies at work in the *littérature-monde* manifesto, it is necessary to explain why exactly I am focusing on the original text as published in *Le Monde* on 16 March 2007, when it was followed by an edited collection, and the concept of a *littérature-monde* has been further explored in festivals, conferences and other forums since 2007. Although the *littérature-monde* 'project' is often cited as though it constitutes a uniform set of ideas shared by a wide range of writers, the reality of the situation is in fact far more complex. The initial revelation and exposition of *littérature-monde* via the form of the manifesto marked a wilfully belligerent entry into the world of ideas: the text elaborated a shared platform, and set out the values, goals and indeed aesthetics of a new world-literature in French. The subsequent generic shift to the essay in *Pour une littérature-monde*, the collection of texts edited by Le Bris and Rouaud (2007), did not result in the expansion of our critical understanding of a monolithic *littérature-monde*: on the contrary, it revealed the loose coalition of interests that had come together around this concept.[8] The signatories of the manifesto had clearly been willing to allow their collectively authored text to speak for them at that precise juncture but their essays in *Pour une littérature-monde* marked out their differences.[9] In essence, the edited

---

[8] The essay as a genre is renowned for its fluidity and indeterminacy (see Forsdick and Stafford, 2005) but even by general standards *Pour une littérature-monde* is a fragmented and polyphonic collection of texts in which the term *littérature-monde* is deployed as a deliberately vague federating concept rather than as a clearly defined critical concept. The essays range from discursive texts on the literary sphere (Mabanckou, Huston) to experimental explorations of the in-between nature of the work produced by transnational authors of a *littérature-monde* (Waberi, Ben Jelloun) to literary examples of this *littérature-monde* in action, sometimes in the form of work reprinted from earlier publications (Djavann).

[9] The edited Gallimard volume, published in May 2007, contains twenty-seven pieces in total, many of which are by signatories of the 16 March manifesto but others are by new authors not previously associated with the manifesto. Some critics have sought to identify a specific literary politics at work here in terms of the exclusion/inclusion of authors. On the contrary, I see this as another

volume underlined the significance of the manifesto as the lodestar of the *littérature-monde* project, while simultaneously and paradoxically drawing attention to its highly problematic nature. Having read the manifesto in *Le Monde* at the time of its original publication, many readers would have opened a copy of the edited volume a few months later firmly expecting to fall upon a reprint or perhaps an extended version of the text at the start of the volume. However, what they discovered was that the 'manifesto' as a separate text no longer existed within the context of the edited volume: for, instead, the opening essays by Rouaud and Le Bris (in that order) contained significant chunks that had previously featured in the collectively signed manifesto as published in *Le Monde* in March 2007. (The question of which texts were written first – the essays or the manifesto – is an intriguing one for critics.[10]) This is not to claim that Rouaud and Le Bris were the sole authors of the manifesto. For a start, various signatories, including Alain Mabanckou and Abdourahman Waberi have consistently stressed that the text was, in the words of Mabanckou, 'un texte global' [a collective text] ('Ecrivains du monde': 107), with initial drafts sent to signatories and 'soit ils le complétaient, ils ajoutaient, ils disaient ça oui je voudrais ajouter ceci, cela' ('Ecrivains du monde': 107);[11] and a detailed analysis of the manifesto does indeed reveal sections that do not appear in either of the pieces in the edited volume by Le Bris and Rouaud. Nonetheless, it remains the case that the text as it appeared in *Le Monde* on 16 March 2007 appears largely to have been written by a combination of Le Bris and Rouaud, two ethnic majority French metropolitan writers who are (understandably) preoccupied with French national literary debates.[12]

What, then, of the 'representative' nature of the collectively signed

---

illustration of the slightly haphazard, ad hoc conditions in which the manifesto and the edited collection came about. However, conclusions can legitimately be drawn from the list of those included: not least, the aesthetic preferences of Le Bris and Rouaud and the names most readily found in their address books.

[10] We are still awaiting the first detailed textual analysis of the manifesto and its relationship to the essays by Le Bris and Rouaud. A close analysis of this kind will be very useful in helping to trace the development of the various texts and the ways in which they might be seen to diverge/converge.

[11] 'either they would add their own ideas, or they would say yes to this part or for this part I'd like to add this or that'.

[12] I do not want for a moment to suggest that Le Bris and Rouaud are somehow delegitimized because they are white and French: rather, I am seeking to underline and reveal the processes of 'representation' at work in the manifesto as a form. For this slippage between the speculative, idiosyncratic essay and the more aggressive and assertive form of the manifesto illustrates the profound ambiguity

manifesto? To what extent does the text of the *littérature-monde* manifesto represent the views of its forty-four signatories? I am not seeking here to single out Le Bris and Rouaud, for their text is far from unique in revealing the representational ambiguity of the manifesto, which Janet Lyon defines as follows:

> [T]he form is embedded in the contradictions of political representation. On the one hand, the manifesto as we know it from the French Revolution forward is the liberatory genre that narrates in no uncertain terms the incongruous experiences of modernity of those whose needs have been ignored or excluded in a putatively democratic political culture. On the other hand, the manifesto is the genre not of universal liberation but of rigid hierarchical binaries: on this reading, the manifesto participates in a reduced understanding of heterogeneous social fields, creating audiences through a rhetoric of exclusivity, parceling out political identities across a polarized discursive field, claiming for 'us' the moral high ground of revolutionary idealism, and constructing 'them' as ideological tyrants, bankrupt usurpers, or corrupt fools. (Lyon, 1999: 2–3)

Does the *littérature-monde* manifesto fall into this trap, simply replacing old hierarchies and binaries with new ones? And are these binaries ones that are meaningful to all of the signatories of the manifesto? Angenot claims that pamphleteers 'prennent le *contre-pied* de la doxa, ce qui revient à dire qu'ils demeurent dans la mouvance de celle-ci' (1982: 339);[13] do those who engage in polemical public debates through *manifestes, appels, pétitions* remain trapped within the original terms of those oppositions that they are seeking to overcome?

In the next and final section of this essay, I will explore the nature of the oppositions created by my chosen postcolonial manifestos, focusing specifically on their theatrical exposition of French national identity and the ways in which a changed conception of Frenchness is 'performed'. Who is posited as the marginalized 'us' and who is the oppressive 'them'? Are these positions and identifications shared across all of these texts? And do these polemical texts genuinely break with dominant ideologies or are they still trapped within their logic as Angenot claims?

---

of a process whereby the words/ideas of a few key figures are asked to bear the weight of representing the views of a disparate body of authors.

[13] 'take the opposing view to generally accepted theory which means that they remain within its sphere of influence'.

The Postcolonial Manifesto

Qui fait la France?

I will begin with the literary manifesto, 'Qui fait la France?' (first published in the autumn of 2007), for it appears, on the surface at least, to share many of the assumptions of the *littérature-monde* manifesto. 'Qui fait la France?' was the work of a collective of authors who initially announced their existence via the press (*Les Inrockuptibles* and *Le Nouvel Observateur*) before publishing a collection of short stories, *Chroniques d'une société annoncée*, featuring the work of each of the signatories, and prefaced by a republication of the full manifesto (Collectif Qui fait la France?, 2007). Although the manifesto was explicitly labelled a 'collective' endeavour, the group was clearly centred on the personality of Mohamed Razane.[14] The 'Qui fait la France?' manifesto decries a dominant French literature that is categorized as 'égotiste et mesquine, exutoire des humeurs bourgeoises' [egotistical and mean-spirited, an outlet for bourgeois whims], and the authors belonging to the collective situate themselves within an aesthetic focused on 'le réel' [the real]: 'Nous, écrivains en devenir, ancrés dans le réel, nous nous engageons pour une littérature au miroir, réaliste et démocratique, réfléchissant la société et des imaginaires en leur entier' ('Qui fait la France?', 2007).[15]

In other ways, though, 'Qui fait la France?' deploys its theatricality to announce a very different subject position to the *littérature-monde* manifesto in relation to these debates on literature and national identity. The collective is explicitly constituted of those who are 'catalogués écrivains de banlieue, étymologiquement le lieu du ban' [classified as writers of the *banlieue*, etymologically the place of banishment], a group omitted in its entirety from the authors collectively associated with the *littérature-monde* project.[16] 'Qui fait la France?' consistently underlines a united 'we' through the insistent use of a 'nous', defined variously as 'Nous, artistes' [We, artists], 'Nous, enfants d'une France plurielle' [We, children of a plural France], 'Nous, somme d'identités mêlées' [We, the product of mixed identities], 'Nous, citoyens de là et d'ailleurs' [We, citizens of here and elsewhere], 'Nous, fils de France' [We,

---

[14] The other authors associated with the collective are Karim Amellal, Jean-Eric Boulin, Khalid El Bahji, Dembo Goumane, Habiba Mahany, Samir Ouazene, Mabrouk Rachedi and Thomté Ryam.

[15] 'We, emerging writers, anchored in the real, we commit ourselves to a mimetic literature, realist and democratic, and that reflects all of society and its imaginaries.'

[16] This omission has been identified by many critics: see, for example, Célestin, *et al.* (2010).

sons of France]. If this collective 'we' is very different from that proposed by the *littérature-monde* manifesto, then so are the means by which they intend to 'perform' change. In place of the writer as 'traveller', the reader is told of the need for a writing that is 'engageé, combattante et féroce' [committed, combative and ferocious]. The collective explicitly evokes the socio-political sphere as a site of artistic engagement: 'Nous, artistes, décidons de rassembler nos forces et d'œuvrer ensemble pour lutter contre les inégalités et les injustices'.[17] This advocacy of a Sartrean 'littérature engagée' [committed literature] is accompanied by a perhaps unexpected articulation of a belief in a renewed and truly inclusive Republicanism. For the collective are also 'Nous, enfants de la République' [We, children of the Republic] and they write of their desire to 'participer à la force de son message, la puissance de son inspiration et à traduire dans les faits la valeur de ses principes'.[18] From their position confined to the margins, they demand 'l'aspiration légitime à l'universalisme' [the legitimate aspiration to universalism]; and there are several references to France's 'universal mission': 'ce pays, notre pays, a tout pour redevenir exemplaire, à condition qu'il s'accepte comme il est, et non tel qu'il fut';[19] and their struggle is for 'l'égalité des droits et le respect de tous' [equality of rights and respect for all] ('Qui fait la France?', 2007).

The emphasis throughout 'Qui fait la France?' on a revised and reinvigorated Republic is highly significant. For, as we shall see below, none of the postcolonial manifestos analysed here engages in a communitarianism posited as an active rejection of the principles of the Republic. Does this desire for change within the framework of a renewed Republic constitute a genuinely postcolonial challenge to Frenchness or does it signal an ongoing dependence on dominant modes of thought?

L'Appel des indigènes de la République

One of the most contested postcolonial challenges to Frenchness was the one that, in many ways, launched the current period of intense 'pamphleteering', that is 'L'Appel des indigènes de la République', first posted on-line in January 2005. Although at first it received relatively little attention, it came to be seen in the light of the events that followed (the controversy

---

[17] 'We, artists, have decided to pool our resources and to act together in order to fight against inequality and injustice.'

[18] 'participate in the force of its message, its inspirational power and to translate into reality the value of its principles'.

[19] 'this country, our country, has all it needs to become exemplary once more, on condition that it accepts itself as it is today and not as it was'.

surrounding the *loi du 23 février 2005*, requiring high schools to teach the 'positive' role of French colonization, and the riots that shook the *banlieues* of many major French cities in October and November of that year) as the harbinger of a 'postcolonial' crisis. In particular, the harshest critics of the postcolonial debate in France saw in the 'Appel des indigènes' precisely the sort of essentializing communitarianism that the Republic must reject outright.

What, then, is the theatricality of the 'Appel' in its depiction of the socio-political landscape? Throughout the text runs the image of the *banlieue* as the new colonial frontier, a supposedly savage land facing conquest by a domineering, civilizing France. In essence, 'La France a été un Etat colonial ... [...] La France reste un Etat colonial!'[20] The context outlined is one of legislative repression – 'Discriminatoire, sexiste, raciste, la loi anti-foulard est une loi d'exception aux relents coloniaux'[21] – and a neo-conservative turn inspired by the Bush Jr regime, which has led certain intellectuals and media figures to recycle 'la thématique du "choc des civilisations" dans le langage local du conflit entre "République" et "communautarisme"'.[22] However, the 'Appel' seeks to move beyond immediate political concerns in order to challenge the fundamental philosophical underpinnings of the Republic:

> La République de l'Egalité est un mythe. L'Etat et la société doivent opérer un retour critique radical sur leur passé-présent colonial. Il est temps que la France interroge ses Lumières, que l'universalisme égalitaire, affirmé pendant la Révolution Française, refoule ce nationalisme arc-bouté au 'chauvinisme de l'universel', censé 'civiliser' sauvages et sauvageons.[23]

Essentially, the universality of the Republic is deemed a front for a narrow-minded nationalism. France itself needs to be decolonized so that a truly universal Republicanism can emerge, and it is the 'native' – the manifesto builds to a proclamation of this collective identity as 'natives of the Republic' in its final paragraphs – who will save the Republic from itself:

---

[20] 'France was a colonial state ... [...] France remains a colonial state!'

[21] 'Discriminatory, sexist, racist, the law against the [Islamic] headscarf is a law that singles out one part of society and that reeks of colonialism.'

[22] 'the theme of the "clash of civilizations" so that it becomes in the local vocabulary a clash of "Republic" and "communitarianism"'.

[23] 'The Egalitarian Republic is a myth. The state and society must carry out a radical critique of their colonial past–present. It is time for France to reflect critically on its Enlightenment, time for egalitarian universalism, professed during the French Revolution, to reject the cramped nationalism of a "universalising chauvinism" that is supposed to "civilize" savages and wild children.'

NOUS, descendants d'esclaves et de déportés africains, filles et fils de colonisés et d'immigrés, NOUS, Français et non-Français vivants en France, militantes et militants engagées dans les luttes contre l'oppression et les discriminations produites par la République postcoloniale, lançons un appel à celles et ceux qui sont parties prenantes de ces combats à se réunir en Assises de l'anticolonialisme en vue de contribuer à l'émergence d'une dynamique autonome qui interpelle le système politique et ses acteurs, et, au-delà, l'ensemble de la société française, dans la perspective d'un combat commun de tous les opprimés et exploités pour une démocratie sociale véritablement égalitaire et universelle.[24]

Unlike the other manifestos examined here, the 'Appel des indigènes' eschews any form of named authorship; instead, the collective proclaims the right to self-identify as 'natives'. However, this is not a 'separatist' identity; for the struggle to reform Republicanism is cast as a struggle that should unite all Republicans irrespective of their origins. The *indigènes* may be 'descendants of slaves and the colonized' but they are not enclosed within this identity:

Nous sommes leurs héritiers [esclaves, colonisés] comme nous sommes les héritiers de ces Français qui ont résisté à la barbarie nazie et de tous ceux qui sont engagés avec les opprimés, démontrant, par leur engagement et leurs sacrifices, que la lutte anticoloniale est indissociable du combat pour l'égalité sociale, la justice et la citoyenneté.[25]

A postcolonial challenge to Frenchness is here presented not as a 'communitarian' challenge from the margins but rather an attempt to liberate *all* French people from a failed model of Republicanism.

---

[24] 'WE, descendants of slaves and deported Africans, daughters and sons of the colonized and of immigrants, WE, French and non-French living in France, male and female militants engaged in struggles against oppression and discrimination perpetrated by the post-colonial Republic, launch an appeal to all those who wish to partake in these struggles to join together in an anti-colonial union with the aim of contributing to the emergence of an autonomous dynamic that challenges the political system and its actors, and, beyond them, all of French society, as part of a common struggle on behalf of all of the oppressed for a social democracy that is genuinely egalitarian and universal.'

[25] 'We are their heirs [slaves, colonized] just as we are the heirs of those French who resisted the barbarism of the Nazis as well as those who are engaged alongside the oppressed, displaying through their commitment and their sacrifice, that the anti-colonial struggle is inseparable from the struggle for social equality, justice and citizenship'.

Appel pour une République
multiculturelle et postraciale

The most recent of the texts to be analysed, 'Appel pour une République multiculturelle et postraciale', dates from early 2010. Published as a supplement to the 'multicultural' magazine, *Respect Mag*, the 'Appel' clearly situates itself within the highly charged 'postcolonial' landscape that emerged in 2005, and that led to the intellectual contortions of the Sarkozy government's 'débat sur l'identité nationale' in late 2009 to early 2010. The date on which the 'Appel' was launched, 20 January 2010, is given a special significance: on that very day, one year earlier, Barack Obama had been inaugurated as the first black President of the United States, while at the same moment France's overseas territories were convulsed in crisis. The contrast is clear: as the United States symbolically casts off the legacy of slavery, the universal model of Republicanism grinds to a halt: 'la mécanique républicaine se heurte à un défi majeur: comment ouvrir la République à tous les citoyens qui la composent?'[26] However, the crisis lies not in a general inability on the part of 'the French' to come to terms with their postcolonial realities but rather in the very specific failures of a Republican elite: 'La société française, riche de la pluralité de ses talents, s'est profondément renouvelée. Par contraste, les élites – politiques, économiques, culturelles – ne parviennent pas à intégrer ces nouvelles dynamiques.'[27] The 'Appel' is co-signed by five public figures, each from very different walks of life – the footballer Lilian Thuram, historian/activist François Durpaire, comedian/activist Rokhaya Diallo, journalist Marc Cheb Sun, historian Pascal Blanchard – but who as a collective are intended to illustrate precisely the type of diversity heralded by the text (this is clearly indicated by the group photograph on the cover of the booklet featuring all five signatories wearing a *bleu, blanc, rouge* rosette on their lapels). The change they wish to perform in French society is recognizable to anyone familiar with the work of the ACHAC (Association Connaissance de l'histoire de l'Afrique contemporaine) research group (of which Blanchard is a leading figure): they aim to 'réconcilier la France avec son passé' [reconcile France with its past] and 's'approprier une histoire

---

26 'The mechanics of Republicanism face a major challenge: how can the Republic be opened to all of the citizens of which it is composed?' (The 'Appel' has no page numbers, hence the lack of specific page references in the following pages.)

27 'French society has renewed itself thanks to the plurality of its talents. By contrast, the elites – political, economic, cultural – have been unable to integrate these new dynamics.'

commune' [appropriate for ourselves a common history] in order to 'assumer la République multiculturelle' [embrace the multicultural Republic]. Finally, in an innovative development for the idealistic manifesto form, the signatories call upon a range of public figures to suggest what they term 'propositions pluricitoyennes' [pluricitizen proposals] that might help to create the post-racial France they desire to see.

Despite its more reasonable tone and far less highly charged symbolism and rhetoric, the text clearly echoes the 'Appel des indigènes' in decrying the ethnocentrism of a dominant mode of Republican thought. The signatories argue that change is required:

> Parce qu'il n'y a pas de combat plus républicain que celui de dessiner une République non réduite à une seule communauté, fût-elle majoritaire. Et que la République n'est pas une couleur mais toutes nos couleurs, qu'elle n'est pas un héritage, mais la pluralité de nos héritages.[28]

This is not simply a 'return' to universal values somehow betrayed by empire but an attempt to overcome failings that were always there: 'Il apparaîtra alors à tous que cette société – devenue post-racial – sera plus conforme aux idéaux de notre République qu'elle ne le fût jamais.'[29] As with the 'Appel des indigènes', the creation of the postcolonial Republic promises a shift towards a genuinely universal Frenchness in which unspoken ethnic norms are finally overturned.

Pour une 'littérature-monde' en français

The *littérature-monde* manifesto's questioning of the French nation primarily takes the form of a sustained critique of Jacobin centralism. The principal enemy is the 'centre' and its various agents (*les maitres-penseurs, la Francophonie*, etc.), and the literary prize season of autumn 2006 is deemed to have signalled the absolute de-centring of the French literary world. As was illustrated above, the manifesto imagines a shared set of concerns between the margins of France (the provinces) and the margins of the Francophone world:

> Le centre relégué au milieu d'autres centres, c'est à la formation d'une

---

[28] 'Because no combat is more Republican than that of pointing the way to a Republic that is not reduced to a single community, even if constitutes the majority. And because the Republic is not a colour but all of our colours, that is, not a legacy but the plurality of our legacies.'
[29] 'It will then be obvious to all that this society – having become post-racial – will conform more closely to the ideals of our Republic than it has ever done.'

constellation que nous assistons, où la langue libérée de son pacte exclusif avec la nation, libre désormais de tout pouvoir autre que ceux de la poésie et de l'imaginaire, n'aura pour frontières que celle de l'esprit. ('Pour une "littérature-monde" en français', 2007)[30]

Once again, the 'postcolonial' challenge to Frenchness is not built on communitarianist separatism; rather, it is a form of liberation for the majority French population also. French universalism will live on but in a new, revised transnational form.

Does this mean, then, that the *littérature-monde* manifesto shares the vision of the other postcolonial manifestos that we have examined? In broad terms, I think it does, but there are also major dividing lines. A significant difference between Le Bris and Rouaud's manifesto and the three others lies in the former's singularly vague attention to historical, political, social and even literary questions: the sense of a pressing and immediate threat present in the other manifestos examined here (marginalization, repressive legislation, etc.) is replaced by a general threat of Parisian domination; there is no analysis of the literary system, no engagement with the hostile political landscape in France. This is no doubt in part due to the highly lyrical and romanticized nature of the *littérature-monde* manifesto, which seeks almost to soar above the petty concerns of the everyday world in its flight towards a dynamic, travelling, world-literature in French. Indeed, unlike the other manifestos, *littérature-monde* presents a world that has already changed; they now just need the Parisian-centred literary scene to follow suit. However, the text struggles to cover with one blanket the different members of its loose coalition: its depiction of the Paris-dominated literary scene is very much viewed from within Le Bris's permanently oppositional, post-'68 position; and, as I have argued elsewhere (Murphy, 2010; see also Toledo, 2008), the insistence on an aesthetic of the 'real', as imagined within the framework of French literary politics, simply does not reflect the aesthetic choices of many of the 'Francophone' signatories. Situating *littérature-monde* within the context of other postcolonial manifestos more rooted in historical concerns, and unconcerned with the incandescent powers of literature, is thus a necessary corrective to the premature celebration of the post-political world of literary globalization: as Charles Forsdick, citing the work of Amitiva Kumar, states

---

[30] 'With the center placed on an equal plane with other centers, we are witnessing the birth of a new constellation, in which language freed from every other power hereafter but the powers of poetry and the imaginary, will have no other frontiers but those of the spirit.' ('Toward a "World-Literature" in French', 2009: 56).

elsewhere in this volume, a grounded, 'World Bank Literature' would place the cosmopolitan text of World Literature in dialogue with counter-canonical texts such as pamphlets, memoirs and economic reports, in order to produce a more complex vision of post-imperial global relations.

A final factor that clearly distinguishes the manifestos I have examined is their site of publication. The two 'Appels' announced themselves to the world in relatively marginalized forums: on-line for 'L'Appel des indigènes'; small circulation journal for 'Appel pour une République'; 'Qui fait la France?' was more high profile with publication in fairly high circulation magazines and with a renowned Parisian publisher, Stock. However, the *littérature-monde* manifesto and the associated collection of essays were published in by far the most prestigious sites of high French culture, and, perhaps paradoxically, this might most profitably be viewed as an attempt by what were the 'margins' to occupy a space within the centre: for, despite the outsiderism cultivated by Le Bris in particular, the fact remains that the manifesto was published in *Le Monde* and the edited collection was published by the major French publisher, Gallimard (not quite in its top-of-the range 'Collection blanche' but not relegated to its highly controversial 'Continents noirs' series for 'black writers'). Le Bris, Rouaud and their fellow signatories are, of course, correct that something is happening in the Paris-centred world of publishing in French: spaces have now opened up for a wide body of 'Francophone' authors in ways that would have seemed unimaginable a decade ago but does this mean that the world of publishing in French has really been revolutionized? I would suggest that the manifesto might best be interpreted as an appeal by those who have (almost) 'made it' culturally to dismantle the framework that prevents others from joining them. This process of claiming a place in the centre is always fraught with danger and can lead to accusations of 'selling out'; and the fact that the manifesto stresses mobility is, in many ways, unfortunate for it seems to sanction a certain type of cosmopolitan writer/writing at the expense of 'local' writing whether from the former colonies (in particular, those writers published outside of France) or from France itself (as was mentioned above, the *banlieue* writers who constitute the Collectif Qui fait la France? are a glaring absence from the *littérature-monde* project). Equally, the media-savvy way in which the *littérature-monde* project was able to announce and sustain its existence has led some to view it purely as a media creation. While I sympathize with such critiques, I believe that they also run the risk of overlooking the very real significance of the way in which the project has managed to popularize debates and ideas that are usually relegated to academic journals.

Finally, then, what of Angenot's critique of the pamphleteer? As we have seen, all four manifestos share a vision of a new, de-centred France, a Republic made anew: but does this, in Angenot's terms, leave them trapped within the terms of reference of the discourse that they seek to challenge? Perhaps it does to an extent but, then, manifestos are never the absolute break with the past that they proclaim themselves to be. It is a legitimate response to identify and even critique the ongoing belief in the universal values of the Republic but does this not neglect the 'political' strategies being deployed, the necessary compromise and engagement with 'actually existing' systems and beliefs?

Conclusion:
Criticism and the Partisanship of the Manifesto

What, then, of the critic's relationship to the postcolonial manifesto? Critics have been absolutely right to signal the issues glossed over in the manifesto's rush to see a new world order: from the (unacknowledged) irony of French literary prizes being viewed as symbols of a challenge to the centre, to the ambiguity of two white French authors adopting a stance that posits the emergence of a *littérature-monde* as a way of 'saving' French literature from itself (see Kleppinger 2010: 79–80).[31] Dominic Thomas articulates the disquiet felt by many academics at the attempt to 'banish' the term 'Francophone' in a utopian gesture that seeks to 'perform' the change it desires to see: 'the issue has never been exclusively about "incorporating" Francophone authors to the curriculum but rather more importantly about rethinking the ways in which cultural inquiries are conducted' (Thomas, 2010: 50). Do the successful Francophone authors of the *littérature-monde* project simply constitute the trees that hide the forest of a literary world still dominated by Paris? Like many other critics, I would argue that they do, but I would also like to suggest that focusing on these failings in this way may be seen to 'miss the point' of the manifesto. As I have argued at length in this chapter, the manifesto calls on us to take sides in the name of bringing about, or at least creating the possibility of, change. This may lead to simplifications or errors but in placing the critical focus on these 'flaws' are we in effect neglecting the primary impulse behind these texts, namely motivating/inspiring the reader to embrace change? As Timothy Brennan has remarked in relation to a rather different context, namely the anti-colonial writings of Amilcar Cabral, the independence leader of Guinea-Bissau:

---

[31] For a more scathing critique of Le Bris and Rouaud, dismissed as 'quelques Européens tropiques' [a handful of tropical Europeans], see de Toledo (2008: 108–09).

[T]he dialectic of colonizer and colonized was simply not supposed to represent either a sociological explanation or a nuanced cultural model [for Cabral]. It was itself a focus – that is, a careful exclusion. He was not lumping difference together, nor was he unaware of multiple communities with their disparate interests. He did not emphasize the disparate because it would not then, in that project, have led to more than the impossibility of doing. (Brennan, 1997: 3)

I would suggest that Le Bris, Rouaud and their fellow signatories similarly situate themselves within a landscape of friends and enemies where it is necessary to take sides in order to effect change. The binary oppositions and truncated histories to be found in their manifesto (as in other postcolonial manifestos) are critically 'suspect' but, in their view, strategically necessary. We must beware the pitfalls of inclusive taxonomic gestures that in fact signal the ongoing marginalization of certain peoples or groups; but to argue that the victory of several non-French authors in the autumn prize season in 2006 signals a revolution in 'French letters' is in fact both deeply naive and, for a significant number of readers, inspirational. Scholars must thus recognize the value of postcolonial manifestos that seek to challenge the legacy of Empire in ways that may seem intellectually problematic but which may in fact help to produce change, however imperfect that change may be.

Works Cited

Angenot, Marc. 1982. *La Parole pamphlétaire: contribution à la typologie des discours modernes*. Paris: Payot.

'L'Appel des indigènes de la République'. 2005. Les Indigènes de la République. <www.indigenes-republique.fr>. Consulted on 8 April 2010.

'Appel pour une République multiculturelle et postraciale'. 2010. Initial signatories: Lilian Thuram, François Durpaire, Rokhaya Diallo, Marc Cheb Sun, Pascal Blanchard. *Respect Mag: urbain, social et métissé* 24 (January–March): Supplement.

Bongie, Chris. 2008. *Friends and Enemies: The Scribal Politics of Post/Colonial Studies*. Liverpool: Liverpool University Press.

Brennan, Timothy. 1997. *At Home in the World: Cosmopolitanism Now*. Cambridge, MA: Harvard University Press.

Burger, Marcel. 2002. *Les Manifestes: paroles de combat - De Marx à Breton*. Paris: Delachaux et Niestlé.

Caws, Mary Ann. (ed.) 2001. *Manifesto: A Century of Isms*. Lincoln and London: University of Nebraska Press.

Célestin, Roger, William J. Cloonan, Eliane DalMolin, and Alec G. Hargreaves (eds). 2010. *Contemporary French and Francophone Studies: Sites* 14.1 [Special issue: William J. Cloonan and Alec G. Hargreaves (eds), '*Littérature-Monde*: New Wave or New Hype?']

Collectif Qui fait la France?. 2007. *Chroniques d'une société annoncée*. Paris: Stock.

Diouf, Abdou. 2007. 'La francophonie, une réalité oubliée'. *Le Monde* 20 March.

Duneton, Claude, and Jean-Pierre Pagliano. 1978. *Anti-manuel de français*. Paris: Seuil.

'Ecrivains du monde: Round Table Discussions Featuring Azouz Begag, Michel Le Bris, Alain Mabanckou, Anna Moï, Jean Rouaud, and Abdourahman Waberi'. 2010. *Contemporary French and Francophone Studies: Sites* 14.1: 93–112 [Special issue: William J. Cloonan and Alec G. Hargreaves (eds), '*Littérature-Monde*: New Wave or New Hype?']

Forsdick, Charles, and Andrew Stafford (eds). 2005. *The Modern Essay in French: Movement, Instability, Performance*. Oxford: Peter Lang.

Forsdick, Charles, and David Murphy (eds). 2007. 'France in a Postcolonial Europe: History, Memory, Identity'. Special issue of *Francophone Postcolonial Studies* 5.2 (Autumn/Winter).

—. 2009. 'Situating Francophone Postcolonial Thought'. In Charles Forsdick and David Murphy (eds), *Postcolonial Thought in the French-Speaking World*. Liverpool: Liverpool University Press: 1–27.

'Identité nationale et passé colonial: pour un véritable débat'. 2009. Rue 89. <http://www.rue89.com/2009/12/18/identite-nationale-et-passe-colonial-pour-un-veritable-debat-130562>. Consulted on 6 May 2010.

Kleppinger, Kathryn. 2010. 'What's Wrong with the Littérature-Monde Manifesto?'. *Contemporary French and Francophone Studies: Sites* 14.1: 77–84. [Special issue: William J. Cloonan and Alec G. Hargreaves (eds), '*Littérature-Monde*: New Wave or New Hype?']

Le Bris, Michel, and Jean Rouaud (eds). 2007. *Pour une littérature-monde*. Paris: Gallimard.

'Liberté pour l'histoire: une pétition pour l'abrogation des articles de loi contraignant la recherche et l'enseignement de cette discipline'. 2005. *Libération* 13 December.

Lyon, Janet. 1999. *Manifestoes: Provocations of the Modern*. Ithaca, NY and London: Cornell University Press.

Murphy, David. 2010. 'Literature after Empire: A Comparative Reading of Two Literary Manifestos'. *Contemporary French and Francophone Studies: Sites* 14.1: 67–75. [Special issue: William J. Cloonan and Alec G. Hargreaves (eds), '*Littérature-Monde*: New Wave or New Hype?']

Najjar, Alexandre. 2007. 'Un intellectuel libanais s'élève contre le manifeste "Pour une littérature-monde en français": Expliquer l'eau par l'eau'. *Le Monde* 30 March.

'La pétition des historiens: 1001 signatures et après … '. 2005. *Le Monde* 25 March.

'Pour une "littérature-monde" en français'. 2007. *Le Monde* 16 March.

Puchner, Martin. 2006. *Poetry of the Revolution: Marx, Manifestos and the Avant-garde*. Princeton, NJ: Princeton University Press.

'Qui fait la France?' 2007. Qui fait la France? 17 September. <http://www.quifait-lafrance.com/content/view/45/59/>. Consulted on 26 May 2010.

Sarkozy, Nicolas. 2007. 'Pour une francophonie vivante et populaire'. *Le Figaro* 22 March.

Somigli, Luca. 2003. *Legitimizing the Artist: Manifesto Writing and European Modernism 1885–1915*. Toronto: University of Toronto Press.

Thomas, Dominic. 2010. Decolonizing France: From National Literatures to World Literatures'. *Contemporary French and Francophone Studies: Sites* 14.1: 47–55. [Special issue: William J. Cloonan and Alec G. Hargreaves (eds), '*Littérature-Monde*: New Wave or New Hype?']

Toledo, Camille de. 2008. *Visiter le Flurkistan, ou les illusions de la littérature-monde*. Paris: Presses Universitaires de France.

'Toward a "World-Literature" in French'. 2009. Trans. by Daniel Simon. *World Literature Today* (March–April): 54–56.

Postcolonialism, Politics
and the 'Becoming-Transnational'
of French Studies

'On the Abolition
of the French Department'?
Exploring the Disciplinary Contexts
of *Littérature-monde*

Charles Forsdick

Framing the Manifesto:
Between the National and the Transnational

In an interview published twenty years ago in *Le Débat*, Pascal Quignard called for 'une déprogammation de la littérature' (1989: 88), a deprogramming of contemporary French literature that would both avoid prescription and challenge orthodoxy. Quignard continued: 'Nous avons besoin de cesser de rationaliser, de cesser d'ordonner ceci, de cesser d'interdire cela ...'.[1] Critics of late twentieth- and early twenty-first-century French literature, most prominently Dominique Viart (2005), have demonstrated that contemporary writing in France no longer presents itself as programmatic, preferring instead to engage with the immediacy of the present or with the everyday, or, alternatively, to tease out traces of the past through various processes of excavation. Such tendencies may be seen as a reflection of the wider uncertainty regarding the future, evident in – although, of course, not restricted to – turn-of-the-century France. They may also relate to the increasing dislocation of literature from an explicitly national identity or cultural project. It is arguable that the relative absence, since the late 1970s, of the literary manifesto, a form that had hitherto provided key landmarks in the literary field, is a further clear indication of the reluctance

---

[1] 'We need to stop rationalizing, to stop ordering this, to stop forbidding that ... '. Unless otherwise indicated, all translations from French into English are by the author of this chapter.

of writers to align themselves with the confidently Modernist tendencies of forward-facing, collective movements.

Emerging in the nineteenth century, where it often took the alternative form of letters, prefaces or more general critical interventions, the manifesto was increasingly privileged in the context of Modernism as the preferred vehicle of self-performance by avant-garde literary groups. Its proliferation as a type of ideological or aesthetic intervention in the early twentieth century has been tracked meticulously by Mary Ann Caws, whose invaluable study *Manifesto: A Century of Isms* provides an extensive and remarkably rich anthology of the genre. Acknowledging the concentration of manifestos in the first three decades of the last century, Caws points to a possible explanation for its steady decline: 'High on its own presence, the manifesto is Modernist rather than ironically Postmodernist. It takes itself and its own spoof seriously' (2001: p. xxi). Militant manifestos persist, of course, in the post-modern, postcolonial present, but literary projects tend on the whole to elaborate, define and present themselves in new and different ways. The 2007 publication of the manifesto 'Pour une "littérature-monde" en français' was, therefore, a familiar event in wider literary-historical terms, and yet an unexpected and even unusual one in a context where such formalized collective utterances (especially petitions and 'appels') were – as David Murphy suggests in his contribution to this volume – increasingly the preserve of historians and activists engaging in vociferous memory wars around the colonial past and the postcolonial present. As the contributors to this volume reveal, such an event merits study, not only on the grounds of its intrinsic significance, but also because of the wider repercussions – literary, cultural, political, intellectual and academic – of the programmatic project with which the manifesto is associated.

The immediate debates triggered by the manifesto (Dutton, 2008) were rapidly eclipsed in France itself, not least by related but more openly political controversies regarding national identity and the institutions (such as ministries and museums) whereby such identity is manufactured, sustained and regulated. A critical essay on the concept of *littérature-monde* appeared the following year (Toledo, 2008), much to the irritation of Michel Le Bris, who devotes several pages of his recent autobiography to denouncing the inadequacies of the text (2009: 354–56). More generally, attention to the concept within France remains largely restricted to activities surrounding the annual Etonnants Voyageurs festival in Saint-Malo. Since the publication of the manifesto, there have been plans to launch a related journal, entitled *Gulliver* (like that associated with the earlier 'Pour une littérature voyageuse' movement emerging from Saint-Malo), but it is striking that the principal impact of the manifesto appears to have been outside France itself, and even beyond the parameters of the French-speaking world. According to a self-fulfilling logic, this external attention is perceived by authors central to the manifesto, such as Le Bris and Jean Rouaud, to be evidence of the continued centripetalism of the Parisian literary establishment, and of the consequently persistent hierarchies of 'French' and 'Francophone' literatures. There is no denying – as even Nicolas Sarkozy acknowledged in a *Figaro* article written in response to the manifesto (2007) – that, with several notable exceptions, the academic interest in French-language literatures produced (if not published) outside France (and also even produced in France by authors of, or perceived to be of, non-French origin) is indeed most apparent in the non-French-speaking world. The implications of this external, almost 'ethnographic' interest in *littérature-monde* – often drawing on associated debates on 'world literature' or *Weltliteratur*, and more critical than the manifesto's signatories perhaps imagined – are twofold: on the one hand, elaborating on a critique articulated by Jean-Pierre Cavaillé in another early article on the text (2007), such attention has highlighted and interrogated the latent Gallocentrism of the assumptions by which the notion is underpinned; on the other (and by extension), external responses have suggested that the manifesto possesses blind spots relating to cognate concepts in other language traditions, and fails to register the oxymoronic contradictions of a phenomenon that claims a global reach but persists with a monolingual definition of 'en français' (see Forsdick, 2010).

This explicit commitment to a poetics of writing the world must thus be seen to have an immediate, contemporary context, political and socio-cultural, associated not only with a particular critique of the abstraction of a specifically French literature from the world it purports to represent, but also with a residual perpetuation of the distinction between the 'French' and the 'Francophone'. Yet it would be a mistake to reduce the manifesto to a storm in a Parisian teacup, for, perhaps not surprisingly, given the attention the document has attracted outside France, the concept of *littérature-monde en français* has had a genuinely wider impact, not least on the field of French studies where it echoes important debates regarding national frames and shifting objects of study. The aim of this chapter is to explore the place and role of *littérature-monde* in the interrogation and redefinition of disciplinary boundaries as French studies continues to pass through a period of 'renewal crisis'. Such debates relate not only to the forms of connection that link together the geographically disparate elements of the Francosphere, but also to the associations between politics and poetics that those negotiating these connections, especially in the cross-disciplinary field of Francophone postcolonial studies, are invariably obliged to address.

World Literature
and the Globalization of French Studies

The shifts in French studies – and the 'becoming-transnational' of the area (to borrow the term coined by Françoise Lionnet (2003: 784)), a process of which this volume constitutes an active exploration – reflect wider transformations in the Humanities evident in Edward Said's introduction to a special 2001 issue of *PMLA* devoted to 'Globalizing Literary Studies'. 'An increasing number of us', Said notes, 'feel that there is something basically unworkable or at least drastically changed about the traditional frameworks in which we study literature' (2001: 64). In illustration of his concern, Said cites the work of Arjun Appadurai – specifically *Modernity at Large* (1996) – to describe a radically reshaped literary and cultural landscape, in which 'diasporic communities replace settled ones, new mythologies and fantasies energize as well as deaden the mind, and consumption on a new scale animates markets all across the globe' (Said, 2001: 65). Such an analysis is one that most scholars active in the field of Francophone postcolonial studies would share, and a realization along these lines is often central to their commitment to the project that such an apparently sub-disciplinary appellation may be seen to betoken.

The destabilization of national frameworks, the impact of commercial factors, and the increasing mobility, even instability of the cultural (and principally literary) object on which Said's analyses rest are not, of course, new phenomena. The originality of Said's observation – focused in no small measure, unsurprisingly perhaps for one of the twentieth century's leading comparatists, on the erosion of national boundaries in considerations of cultural production – is nevertheless to be attenuated. Some 180 years before the publication of the *littérature-monde* manifesto to which the current chapter in part reacts – i.e., in January 1827, Goethe had written along similar lines, about such frameworks, to the young Johann Peter Eckermann: 'National literature is now a rather unmeaning term; the epoch of world literature [*Weltliteratur* was his recently coined term] is at hand, and everyone must strive to hasten its approach' (cited in Damrosch, 2003: 1). Goethe remained restricted and essentially Eurocentric in his vision of a 'kind of grand cosmopolitan gathering' (Prendergast, 2001: 100) that would permit 'mutually fruitful dialogue among discrete national literatures' (Pizer, 2007: 6), but he nevertheless gestured towards a broader literary world to which the provincial writer, eschewing mediation through the national, might turn. Two decades later, in what for many commentators is the first 'modern' manifesto, Marx and Engels adopted the notion of *Weltliteratur* and harnessed it to world revolutionary aspirations: 'National one-sidedness and narrow-mindedness become more and more impossible, and from the numerous national and local literatures there arises a world literature' (cited in Damrosch, 2003: 4). Although the context has changed rapidly and radically, the issues that underpin the quotations from these key European intellectuals from the first half of the nineteenth century resonate in contemporary debates.

These twenty-first-century debates are themselves increasingly international, centred on the work of scholars such as Pascale Casanova, David Damrosch, Franco Moretti and Christopher Prendergast, concerning the intersections and complex iterations of five cognate fields associated with the current state of French studies at its current stage of evolution : post-national studies; transnational studies; postcolonialism; comparative literature; and, of course, World Literature. Between, on the one hand, a totalizing 'World Literature' – or *littérature mondiale* – with its overtones of a dangerously capacious glory hole in which eclectic global literary production may be stuffed and, on the other, *littérature-monde*, there are, of course, important terminological and conceptual distinctions on which this chapter endeavours to touch. Nevertheless, with the publication of the *littérature-monde* manifesto in March 2007, we have a clear example of discussions hitherto restricted to academia, or at best to the pages of *World Literature Today* or the *New Left Review*, spilling out into the public sphere and popularizing key debates about the pitfalls, challenges and opportunities associated with the globalization of literature – and linked in particular to the notion that globalized, globalizing conceptions of literature might no longer remain notional or aspirational, but are moving instead towards a stage of realization.

The implications of, and reactions to, the destabilization of what Said dubs 'traditional frameworks' nevertheless continue to attract hostility both within and outside the academy, as the Pancho cartoon discussed by Thomas Spear in his contribution to this volume reveals. Accompanying Colombe Schneck's 1994 article in *Le Monde* on 'le français piégé par le multiculturalisme américain' [French ambushed by American multiculturalism], the image encapsulates an anti-American incredulity concerning the audacity of those studying French outside France: these are scholars and students who, to summarize the accompanying article, (i) dare to study texts (by authors such as Ken Bugul and Aminata Sow Fall) that are 'pratiquement introuvables en France' [practically unfindable in France], (ii) 'ghettoize' authors according to their ethnicity, gender or sexuality ('refusant la portée universelle d'un texte' [refusing the universal reach of a text]) and (iii) further question the identitarian unity of French universalism by suggesting, for instance – in the context of 'politiquement correct' censorship – that the 'Déclaration universelle' of 1789 might be 'un texte écrit par des hommes pour des hommes ...' [a text written by men for men ...]. It is with these questions of disciplinary ownership and interdisciplinary mix, of identitarian unity and of hybridized diversity, and of the associated issues relating to the national and the post-national that this chapter engages. It is structured into three main and interlinking sections: (i) reflecting on the way in which recent shifts in French studies have necessitated a search for new scholarly paradigms, (ii) suggesting that the emergence of new models has triggered an urgent and radical rethinking of inherited practices and assumptions (a process read in this context, following Ngũgĩ, as a form of 'abolition') and (iii) exploring the ways in which a critical reading of the *littérature-monde* manifesto might in fact permit us to outline the beginnings of a constructive response to these current disciplinary and institutional debates.

Becoming Post-national:
The Search for New Paradigms

The rapid evolution of French studies over the past decade has been characterized by two key shifts, both of which continue trends apparent in the field since the cracking of its coherence from the 1970s onwards. On the one hand, the geographical parameters of the object of enquiry has been expanded to encompass a wider Francosphere; on the other, the primarily literary object of study, with which a nascent French studies (drawing on the national French paradigm of *lettres modernes*) traditionally and initially engaged, has been progressively replaced by a more diverse range of subjects produced by an equally diverse range of agents. To take a parallel example of the field of French historical studies, the methodological and pedagogical implications of the transnational manoeuvres that may be seen as implicit in the *littérature-monde* manifesto are addressed by Alice Conklin in her complementary explorations of the ways in which we might teach 'French history as colonial history and colonial history as French history' (2000), a suggestion further illustrated by the work of a range of scholars – including Yves Benot, Laurent Dubois and John Garrigus – who have all followed C. L. R. James's example in reading the shortcomings of the French Revolution in the light of its Haitian counterpart (and not, as is customary, vice versa). Such approaches, in their various ways, negotiate the pitfalls identified by historian Gregory Mann, who warns against 'the new colonial history [that] risks ending where it began, in a national history of a different nation – one that takes the imperial archive into account but does not go beyond it – rather than in a post-national history that might better help historians understand the world in which they and others live' (2005: para. 42).

At the same time, such renewed approaches are expressed quite consciously in a context of growing disciplinary uncertainty for Modern Languages in general: what for the past twenty years has been known euphemistically as 'renewal crisis' has recently been transformed into more urgent reviews of actual 'viability'. A recent series of reports produced for UK Higher Education, most notably by the British Academy and the Higher Education Funding Council for England (HEFCE), have identified the paradoxical situation we now find ourselves in: as Higher Education and research practices gesture increasingly towards internationalization, Anglophone monolingualism (manifest in particular in a national 'language skills deficit') seems more apparent than ever. The British Academy recommendations – recognition that a whole generation 'risks being "lost to languages"'; introduction of language requirements for university entrance; increased language proficiency amongst all students, especially research students; challenging the increasing insularity of Humanities and Social Science Research ('Language Matters') – are laudable, and it is likely that few would challenge them. They remain limited, however, presenting languages as primarily functional and associated with issues of proficiency, and do not necessarily speak to the more complex disciplinary debates that concern Modern Linguists directly. In the final section of the chapter, I am going to suggest that the *littérature-monde* manifesto – as unsatisfactory as it might be – continues to challenge us to ask more searching questions about French studies as the field becomes post-national, transnational, postcolonial. These are questions that have been implicit in the work of those engaged in Francophone postcolonial studies (and it might be suggested of French studies more generally) for a number of years now. First, they are associated with the development of research practices that permit us to negotiate a path between ethics and aesthetics, politics and poetics, without privileging one to the detriment of the other. Secondly, as I have suggested already, they challenge us to rethink our objects of study in spatial terms, in relation to a wider and fundamentally uneven or unstable French-speaking space (or series of overlapping, interlocking French-speaking spaces, the contact zones existing between which or at the limits of which are themselves crucial subjects for study); and, finally, they signal the need to return to – or possibly even assert for the first time – a sense of the disciplinariness of French studies, which may provide a clear foundation for the interdisciplinary dialogues in which we are invariably and inevitably engaged, but that will at the same time ensure that the enabling diversity by which our field has been characterized for several decades now does not tip into a disabling, disintegrating fragmentation. In this optic, I share Peter Cryle's sense of a doggedly optimistic perplexity relating to the coherence of French studies as a field:

Perhaps this is what characterizes us best, what makes it possible, indeed, to say 'us' without presumptuousness: we know that what we do does not converge or cohere according to the principles of a classical epistemology, but we are determined that our work should hang together in some way. In fact, we know that it already does, and we teach our students accordingly. It's just that it's sometimes a bit hard to explain. (Cryle, 1997: 154)

A quotation from Milan Kundera's recent collection of essays *Le Rideau*, his intervention in debates around world literature, provides a helpful way in to these questions of disciplinary identity. I cite from the English translation, but am mindful that Kundera's adoption of French as his language of expression associates him closely with the post-national *littérature-monde* project:

And what about the professors of foreign literatures? Is it not their very natural mission to study works in the context of world literature? Not a chance. In order to demonstrate their competence as experts, they make a great point of identifying with the small (national) context of the literatures they teach. They adopt its opinions, its tastes, its prejudices. Not a chance – it is in foreign universities that a work of art is most intractably mired in its home province. (Kundera, 2007: 37)

Kundera's analysis is to be recognized in certain persistent forms of French studies, but I would suggest that his observation is now largely outmoded, and reflects a time when the paradigms and practices of our field were principally derivative, based exclusively on national models and on close observation of *lettres modernes*, much in the same way that German studies remained for a long time indebted to *Germanistik*. I do not believe that I am the only scholar in French studies to bristle and baulk at the suggestion, articulated surprisingly frequently in France, that relative proficiency in the French language and an interest in things French are ineluctable markers of Francophilia. Ross Chambers claims that: 'it is one of the disciplinary assumptions of French that the test of legitimacy and achievement for a French scholar is the ability to "pass for French" (and not, by the way, for any other native speaker of French) [...] Francophilia, in other words, is not a by-product of our teaching, but one of the things we teach, like Frenchness itself' (1996: 141–42). The progressive shift from the 'French' to the more openly 'Francophone' makes any such nationally based aspiration increasingly difficult to defend – and even redundant. The response to Kundera's assumption of blinding Francophilia is not, of course, an equally negative Francophobia, but a claim that those of us who study France, French, Frenchness, Francophonia and the wider Francosphere *from outside* must acknowledge the potential privilege of ethnographic distance and develop what Herman Lebovics has identified as 'tough love for France' (2006). A form of participant observation may remain essential to our work, and is certainly central to undergraduate programmes with which it is associated, but this is not the same as cultural insiderism, and is certainly not the mimicry that, in Kundera's terms, risks 'intractably mir[ing]' our object of study 'in its home province'. To the contrary, enacting the manifesto's aim of uncoupling the object of study from a national frame represents a potential liberation from the strictures of those earlier paradigms to which Kundera refers.

On the Abolition of the French Department?

In relation to such debates, a key question is: to what extent does the post-national French studies to which I have been alluding – and which it might be argued is embodied in the idea of a *littérature-monde en français* – imply, in the terms of my title, the 'Abolition of the French Department' as we know it? 'Abolition' does not refer directly to the structural changes to which many teachers and researchers have been subject as unitary French departments have been absorbed into Schools of Modern Languages or even larger structures; nor does it allude to the alarming, literal abolition associated with actual departmental closures. The title of this chapter relates instead to a seminal if rarely cited document in the early institutional history of postcolonial studies, Ngũgĩ's 1968 text, 'On the Abolition of the English Department', reproduced in his 1972 collection of essays *Homecoming*. The text, a blueprint responding to papers submitted to the Arts Faculty Board at the University of Nairobi, had prophetic implications for the academic discipline of English literary studies not just in sub-Saharan Africa but also elsewhere, including of course in Britain itself.

The importance of texts such as Ngũgĩ's is becoming increasingly apparent as postcolonial studies and its linguistically defined subfields reach a maturity and relative stability as areas of enquiry. Such shifts are reflected in two recent developments: first, an increasing interest in the institutional history of postcolonialism, evident in recent essays by key figures such as Graham Huggan (2002) and David Scott (2005); and, secondly, the organization of conferences and seminars marking the anniversaries of foundational texts in the area, such as Said's *Orientalism* (published in 1978) and Ashcroft, Griffiths and Tiffin's *The Empire Writes Back* (whose twenty years were marked in 2009). There is, I would suggest, a distinction between institutional history and intellectual genealogy, and one of the most striking elements inherent in asserting the Francophone dimensions of postcolonial criticism has been the emergence of alternative birth narratives, reliant on 'travelling' theory and more specifically on the now well-rehearsed narrative of the transatlantic displacement of an unwieldy body of French-language writing on anti-colonialism and post-structuralism and their re-emergence in the North American academy. The telling of alternative disciplinary histories allows us to diversify our sense of foundational texts, drawing on studies such as Ngũgĩ's 'On the Abolition' and John Docker's conference paper from 1977, 'The Neocolonial Assumption in the University Teaching of English' (1978).[2]

Ngũgĩ's text concerns the teaching of African writing in English in sub-Saharan Africa, suggesting that a decolonization of the English department will entail consideration of 'the place of modern languages, especially French', and 'the place of African languages, especially Swahili', in the curriculum. Denouncing 'the current, rather apologetic attempt to smuggle African writing into an English syllabus' (1995 [1972]: 439), he outlines a range of proposals to expand the syllabus by acknowledging multilingualism, the place of the oral tradition, the need to work on contemporary literature and to adopt what he calls a 'multi-disciplinary outlook' (440). Ngũgĩ's argument relates to the emergence of a postcolonial curriculum in the wake of independence, and challenges what John Docker dubs – in the second paper alluded to above – the 'ruling anglocentric assumption in the university teaching of English' (1978: 26), with its implication that the study of 'post-colonial literature' (Docker uses the phrase already, with the epithet still hyphenated) depends on the application of 'values & standards learnt from studying English literature' (1978: 27). Docker's conclusion is a stirring one:

> The challenge of post-colonial literature is that by exposing and attacking anglocentric assumptions directly it can replace 'English literature' with 'world literature in English'. [...] It is the challenge of those interested in post-colonial literature not simply to offer empirical studies of particular authors, but to see it as questioning our received methods of literary criticism and of university teaching of English. (Docker, 1978: 30–31).

Ngũgĩ's conclusion, occupying similar territory to Docker's, is of interest to those seeking to address associated questions, already outlined above, concerning research in and teaching of *French*. Postcolonial writing and culture are not, Ngũgĩ writes, 'an appendix or a satellite of other countries and literatures' (1995 [1972]: 441), which is another way of stating that the

---

[2] Although they have attracted relatively little critical attention, they are nevertheless to be found together in the Routledge *Postcolonial Studies Reader* (Ashcroft, Griffiths and Tiffin, 1995: 438–46).

'becoming-postcolonial' and 'becoming post-national' of a field is not a matter of bolting on subsidiary material or of appointing a 'Francophone hire' (Gould, 2003: 26) who is asked to teach everything from the Indian Ocean to Quebec. Instead, the process implies a radical rethinking of the epistemological and geographical boundaries of the field in which we operate, a rethinking that might usefully be seen as an essential reinvigoration rather than evidence of a spiralling crisis: perhaps abolition of those 'traditional frameworks' (to cite Said) with which our field has long been familiar. In a controversial *Times Higher* article from September 2003, the Latin Americanist Jon Beasley-Murray explained along these lines why he thought the languages crisis could in fact be helpful:

> Globalization induces the definitive crisis of modern languages. As national borders fade, so does the notion of national languages. [...] The crisis, its causes and contexts should become the very substance of modern languages. We should amplify and propagate the crisis, exposing the complacency of disciplines (English and history, again) that carry on as usual. Modern languages, more affected than most by globalisation and the practical and political challenges it raises, are also best placed to study these processes. (Beasley-Murray, 2003)

Underpinning the soapbox polemicism is a desire to move beyond threats of split or fears of crisis through a privileging of the transnational and intercultural connections by which a field such as French studies is increasingly defined.

In the midst of such change and uncertainty – seen by some as a proliferation of French Studies (in the plural), situated somewhere between enriching diversity and fatal fragmentation – one is struck by a residual quest for much-needed coherence or focus at a time of apparent crisis and instability. Such a quest is particularly evident in Sandy Petrey's robust defences of the literary dimensions of French Studies, narrowing this object whilst – in deceptively commonsensical terms – suggesting the only practical approach to it:

> To try to cover everything is to condemn ourselves to watered-down, dumbed-down versions of history, political science, art, economics, sociology, and the many other areas pertinent to things French. [...] We've learnt how to deal with words, and chances are very good that we will do more things that deserve doing if we address words than if we address immigration statistics, changing styles on Maghreb Dance floors, or the status attached to owning a pit bull in French housing projects. [...] We can be serious about pit bulls and dance fashions in any language we choose,

we can be serious about Bâ and Baudelaire, Colette and Montaigne, only
if we know French. (Petrey, 1998: 12, 17)

Petrey's interventions in recent debates (see also Petrey, 1995; 2003)
concerning disciplinary identity deserve attention, not least because he is
one of the few to articulate in print a conservative position in which France
is privileged to the detriment of other Francophone spaces, and literature
to the detriment of other forms of cultural production. A number of the
assumptions underpinning such an intervention – the existence or otherwise
of a collective 'we', the fetishization of literature, the foregrounding of a
Francophile cultural insider-ism – are questionable, but what strikes me most
is the desire to force coherence on a field that has in fact long refused it.

   In contrast to these ideas, and pursuing the logic of Ngũgĩ's rhetoric of
'abolition' and Beasley-Murray's call to capitalize on perceived crisis, there
seems to be an equally urgent need to interrogate the 'French' of 'French
studies', a disciplinary term that reflects – as Christophe Campos explains
in a contribution to a volume on *French in the 90s* – the 'unusual, but
not quite unique' designation of a subject area 'by an adjective instead of
a noun', or, perhaps more accurately, by an adjective used as a denotative
noun – i.e., a part of speech whose field of reference is notoriously arbitrary
or unpredictable (1992: 33–34). Whether the 'French' relates to language,
culture, geography, literature, history, politics, sociology or any other field
of enquiry, the term has traditionally been understood hexagonally, mapped
onto metropolitan France (and, when convenient, onto representatives of
contiguous Francophone spaces – e.g., Rousseau, Michaux, Simenon, Bouvier
– who are deemed to have transcended the nationality or regional identity to
which the location of their birth might quite easily have condemned them).
The steady transformation of France throughout the twentieth century
– subject to a range of forces such as two World Wars, decolonization,
urbanization, the emergence of the European Community – means that
this centre (to the extent that it ever was a free-standing, autonomous
centre) cannot hold. Richard Klein, reflecting in 1998 on the advent of the
Euro, stated that 'French studies may be nothing other than the study of
the disappearance of French' (1998: 6), an observation supported by Nelly
Furman who (adopting the perspective of Benedict Anderson) sees the field
as one of a number of 'traditional disciplines in the humanities and the
social sciences established a century ago in the age of nationhood and print
culture [that] seem of little interest to entering college students who flock to
new curricula and new majors' (1998: 69). Despite what Thomas Spear dubs
France's reluctance to 'se faire métisser par sa "propre" francophonie' [be
hybridized by its own *francophonie*] (2002: 12), these national shifts (and the

emergence of new transnational connections by which they are caused) make necessary – on an immediate level – an inevitable recognition of changes to what remains the 'symbolic and real capital' (Furman, 1998: 70) of most French studies programmes – i.e., the French language itself, used by up to 300 million people outside France as some means of communication, in many cases as a second language or lingua franca. As Robert Chaudenson has outlined in a series of publications, despite the confident rhetoric and linguistic chauvinism of *Francophonie*, it is other geostrategic considerations – such as the fragmentation of the Eastern bloc and the shift of the balance of influence in sub-Saharan Africa towards South Africa – that will determine the future of French as a world language: '[T]he future of French in the world will be determined in Africa [...] It follows that the fate of French in Europe itself will be determined not in that space but precisely outside that space' (2003: 297).

It is undeniable that these shifts, away from the 'certaine idée de la France' that dominated French studies for much of the twentieth century, entail 'a possible threat to the genuine intellectual convictions as well as the hard-earned, existing "cultural capital" of many members of French departments' (LaCapra, 2000: 170). Lawrence Kritzman asks two questions that may be seen to underpin the deliberations central to this chapter: 'Can French Studies survive the death of the traditional idea of the nation, and the teleology of its progress? Does France's own identity crisis – the loss of its exceptional status, the progressive erosion of its role as an imperial messianic nation, its integration into the European community – endanger our own discipline of French studies?' (1995: 19; see also 2003). Kritzman is one of a number of US commentators who have countered Sandy Petrey's pessimism by seeing the current situation as one of urgent opportunity: the rapid transformation of French studies coincides with a growing monolingualism in the English-speaking world, which reveals itself, at its extremes, in increased xenophobia; at the same time, with languages at best perceived in functional terms, the manifestations of multiculturalism are explored monolingually, resulting, in Michael Cronin's words, from 'the desire to maintain the benefits of connect-edness without the pain of connection' (2003: 49).

Some – and again, Sandy Petrey seems to epitomize this response – have reacted by reasserting a sense of tradition, characterized by a largely imaginary coherence, a disciplinary autonomy and even passivity in the face of other disciplines (with which sustained dialogue is perceived as potentially harmful), an unabashed elitism, and a sustained focus on 'Frenchness' or France itself; yet a further challenge almost immediately made itself apparent in the relatively rapid emergence of what was known, initially at least, as 'Francophone studies'. As Naomi Schor made clear, any 'postcolonial turn' in French Studies should be seen as part of the ongoing process, alluded to above, of transformation, epistemological and otherwise, continuing and further developing in many ways the impact of feminism in the 1970s and Cultural Studies in the 1980s: 'Francophone literatures did not arrive alone and did not arrive first. The dismantling of the Enlightenment universal handed down, and nowhere more so than in and by France, was well underway by the time Francophone literatures emerged. Indeed their emergence may be viewed less as a cause than an effect' (2003: 164–65). The 'postcolonial turn' nevertheless produced the most manifest challenge to the assumptions underpinning French Studies by prizing open the field's Eurocentric identity and positing a more complex, 'globalized' Francophone space as a legitimate object of enquiry.

Disciplinary labels have not yet evolved to reflect this significant change: an etymological understanding of 'Francophone' continues to be undermined by neo-colonial understandings of centre and periphery; a postcolonial understanding often tends 'to perceive the francophone as a monolithic bloc and to obscure the multiple, at times mutually contestatory, differences and differentiations with it' (LaCapra, 2000: 224); and 'French' itself has not yet perhaps acquired the post-national status that would permit its wider application. Nevertheless, the ambiguous conjunction of 'French' and 'Francophone' reflects what Dominick LaCapra goes on to see as one of the principal challenges of the 'postcolonial turn' – i.e., 'a turning of both the Francophone and the metropolitan towards one another in order to elicit their tangled relations, their often lost opportunities, and their possibilities for the future' (225). Such an integrative approach avoids the risks of extremes suggested by, on the one hand, Sandy Petrey's designation of Francophone Studies as a form of 'Francophobic inquiry' (2003: 135), and, on the other, Mireille Rosello's provocative suggestion that 'Hexagonal literature is a branch of Francophone Studies' (2003: 131). In an article on the 'World Literature and Cultural Studies Program' at Santa Cruz, Kristin Ross spells out the potential of 'present[ing] both dominant and emergent cultures as dynamically related' anticipating in many ways the notion of *littérature-monde*: 'Cultural "classics" would not be excluded from our program; rather they would be recontextualized and approached in such a way as not to presume their monumental status' (1993: 667). I would argue that the future of French Studies may lie in negotiating a course between the two extremes that seem at times to characterize the contemporary field: on the one hand, 'those who wish to confirm the dissolution of any fetishized notion of Frenchness, insisting on the multiplicity of *Francophonies* and the fragmenting effects of globalization on anything that claims to be a specifically French identity'; and, on the other, 'those who promote French studies precisely as the defence of an irreducible specificity of all things French, which is threatened by changes in the university and the world' (Culler and Klein, 1998: 3).

Contested Sites:
At the Intersection of French Studies and *Littérature-monde*

In conclusion, I suggest that the tensions explored above are not so much resolved as embodied in the complexities of the 2007 *littérature-monde* manifesto, the implications of which appear to be at least double. On the one hand, the manifesto triggers questions concerned with what we might call this 'becoming-postnational' (and by implication, perhaps, 'becoming-transnational') of French literature and culture discussed above, a process reliant in part on the decolonization of the epithet 'French' and on the now familiar observation of the neo-colonial implications of any exclusive understanding of 'Francophone'. On the other hand, the manifesto articulates an associated critique of the poetics of metropolitan culture and literature, highlighting its potential short-sightedness, solipsism and, in a global context, provincialism. (The manifesto might thus be seen in part at least as an element of what Chakrabarty calls the 'provincialization of Europe' (2000).) The relationship of these two aspects challenges the reader with a key, and I would suggest unresolved, tension that underpins the manifesto, a tension that exists beyond the oppositions presented within the manifesto itself, between the national and the global, between cultural introversion and extroversion, between sickness and health, between sessility and mobility. For, in addition to these polemical, polarizing binaries there is an unresolved tension between the political (i.e., the search for a globalized, postcolonial literary field of creation and production) and the poetic (i.e., the search for a specific form in which the cultures of the contemporary world might find their expression).

Littérature-monde, like a hyphenated 'world-literature', is not the accumulated literary production of the (in this case, French-speaking) world, but indicates rather a world system in which literature is produced and allowed to circulate. The term *littérature-monde*, reminiscent of – to take one prominent example – Braudel's *économie-monde* of the sixteenth-century Mediterranean, encourages engagement with world-systems theory and reflection on the usefulness of, and persistence or otherwise of, the nation state (Beecroft, 2008). This is the key issue on which contemporary debates concerning globalized understandings of literature focus, and what the manifesto perhaps lacks, despite references to the need to free language 'de son pacte avec la nation' [from its exclusive pact with the nation], is any serious engagement with, or indication of, what we might call a postcolonial sociology of literature and culture, by which I understand the production of an inevitably challenging awareness of the literary and cultural systems and forms of circulation and exchange through which the relationship between former centre and former periphery is not only adjusted but also, crucially, often permitted to persist. This tendency is perhaps most apparent in the manifesto's opening reference to prize culture, and in particular the award of five of the seven major French literary prizes in Autumn 2006 to 'des écrivains d'outre-France' [foreign born writers] ('Pour une "littérature-monde" en français'; 'Toward a "World-Literature" in French', 2009: 54). Graham Huggan, in *The Postcolonial Exotic* (2001), suggests, however, that literary prizes – in particular the Booker, but by extension the Goncourt – may actually *contain* cultural critique by commodifying difference. The exotic is domesticated via a prize-system that itself may be seen to channel and even suppress creativity by perpetuating the inequalities within the French-language publishing industry and by reinforcing its centripetal structures. And literary prizes are only part of an axial division of labour in the literary field, according to which – in Alexander Beecroft's terms – '[p]eripheral production is only of value once recognized by the centre' (2008: 89).

We are moving here in this analysis from 'world literature' to what Amitiva Kumar (2001) has provocatively dubbed 'World Bank Literature'. Implicit in this term is a suggestion that the postcolonial globalization of literature 'must include a countercanonical formation that mixes together novels with pamphlets, short stories with journalism, memoirs with economic reports' (224) – must, in short, be accompanied by the acknowledgement of a literature that reasserts what Said called the 'worldiness' of the text, according to the complex understanding of that term. A postcolonial engagement with the notion of *littérature-monde* reveals convergences and divergences. It underlines the potential contribution of post-national engagements with literary texts to our understanding of postcolonial cultural production, but at the same time signals the persistent risks of what Spivak dubbed 'worlding' – i.e., the way in which colonized space may be brought into the 'world', made to exist as part of a world essentially constructed according to the assumptions of Eurocentrism. There is no denying that the *littérature-monde* debate is to be welcomed, albeit cautiously, not least for its popularization of what are long-standing calls – well-established in certain strands of postcolonial criticism – for sustained critical scrutiny of *Francophonie*: calls for recognition, elaboration and consolidation of an expanded French-speaking space in which literary production is no longer freighted via residually asymmetrical structures of power. Such debates relate directly to the questioning of disciplinary shape, frameworks, methods and assumptions alluded to earlier in this chapter. The manifesto boldly presents itself as a response to, perhaps even an encapsulation of, a 'moment historique'; if, on the contrary, it is to avoid reduction to the status of footnote in early twenty-first-century literary history, the contestatory movement it purports to represent must ask searching questions about the *littérature-monde* for which it aims to act as vehicle.

The complex institutional history, methodological complexity and intellectual maturity of French Studies mean that the field is now well placed – in the light of enabling, but ultimately problematic, catalysts such as *littérature-monde en français* – to encourage close reflection on, and even perhaps an engagement with, the supercomplexity characterizing contemporary societies that such a conception of the Francosphere implies. This notion of such supercomplexity should be seen as both a specific challenge to – and opportunity for – the Humanities. It is possible, therefore, that French studies – led by subfields such as the Francophone postcolonial – will continue to emerge 'not as an enclosed area or a strictly bounded discipline but as a contested site on which important issues – literary, cultural, historical and other, focused on the French and the Francophone (but not restricted to them) – may be explored' (LaCapra, 2000: 226).

Works Cited

Appadurai, Arjun. 1996. *Modernity at Large: Cultural Dimensions of Globalization*. Minneapolis and London: University of Minnesota Press.

Ashcroft, Bill, Gareth Griffiths, and Helen Tiffin (eds). 1995. *The Postcolonial Studies Reader*. London: Routledge.

Beasley-Murray, Jon. 2003. 'Why I ... think the languages crisis is helpful'. *Times Higher Education* 26 September: 18.

Beecroft, Alexander. 2008. 'World Literature Without a Hyphen'. *New Left Review* 54: 87–100.

Campos, Christophe. 1992. 'The Scope and Methodology of French'. In Jennifer Birkett and Michael Kelly (eds), *French in the 90s: A Transbinary Conference July 1991*. Birmingham: Birmingham Modern Languages Publications: 33–38.

Cavaillé, Jean-Pierre. 2007. 'Francophones, l'écriture est polyglotte'. *Libération* 30 March.

Caws, Mary Ann. (ed.) 2001. *Manifesto: A Century of Isms*. Lincoln and London: University of Nebraska Press.

Chakrabarty, Dipesh. 2000. *Provincializing Europe: Postcolonial Thought and Historical Difference*. Princeton, NJ: Princeton University Press.

Chambers, Ross. 1996. 'Cultural Studies as a Challenge to French Studies'. *Australian Journal of French Studies* 33.2: 137–56.

Chaudenson, Robert. 2003. 'Geolinguistics, Geopolitics, Geostrategy: The Case of French'. In Jacques Maurais and Michael A, Morris (eds), *Languages in a Globalizing World*. Cambridge: Cambridge University Press: 291–97.

Conklin, Alice L. 2000. 'Boundaries Unbound: Teaching French History as Colonial History and Colonial History as French History'. *French Historical Studies* 23.2: 215–38.

Cronin, Michael. 2003. *Translation and Globalization*. London: Routledge.

Cryle, Peter. 1997. 'Is There a Research Paradigm in Australian French Studies?'. In Philippe Lane and John West-Sooby (eds), *Traditions and Mutations in French Studies: The Australian Scene*. Brisbane: Boombana Publications: 143–54.

Culler, Jonathan, and Richard Klein. 1998. 'Preface'. *Diacritics* 28.2: 2–3. [Special issue: 'Doing French Studies'.]

Damrosch, David. 2003. *What is World Literature?* Princeton, NJ and Oxford: Princeton University Press.

Docker, John. 1978. 'The Neocolonial Assumption in the University Teaching of English'. In Chris Tiffin (ed.), *South Pacific Images*. St. Lucia, Queensland: SPACLALS [South Pacific Association for Commonwealth Literature and Language Studies]: 26–31. [Reproduced in Bill Ashcroft, Gareth Griffiths and Helen Tiffin (eds), *The Postcolonial Studies Reader*. London: Routledge: 443–46.]

Dutton, Jacqueline. 2008. '*Littérature-monde* or Francophonie? From the Manifesto to the Great Debate'. *Essays in French Literature and Culture* 45: 43–68.

Forsdick, Charles. 2010. 'From "littérature voyageuse" to "littérature-monde": The Manifesto in Context'. *Contemporary French and Francophone Studies* 14.1: 9–17.

Furman, Nelly. 1998. 'French Studies: Back to the Future'. *Profession*: 68–80.

Gould, Karen L. 2003. 'Nationalism, Feminism, Cultural Pluralism: American Interest in Quebec Literature and Culture'. *Yale French Studies* 103: 24–32.

Huggan, Graham. 2001. *The Postcolonial Exotic: Marketing the Margins*. London and New York: Routledge.

—. 2002. 'Postcolonial Studies and the Anxiety of Interdisciplinarity'. *Postcolonial Studies* 5.3: 245–75.

Klein, Richard. 1998. 'The Object of French Studies – *Gebrauchkunst*'. *Diacritics* 28.3: 5–11.

Kritzman, Lawrence D. 1995. 'Identity Crises: France, Culture and the Idea of the Nation'. *SubStance* 76–77: 5–20.

—. 2003. 'A Certain Idea of French: Cultural Studies, Literature and Theory'. *Yale French Studies* 103: 146–60.

Kumar, Amitiva. 2001. 'World Bank Literature 101'. In Henry A. Giroux (ed.),

Beyond the Corporate University: Culture and Pedagogy in the New Millennium. New York: Rowman & Littlefield: 213–26.

Kundera, Milan. 2007. *The Curtain: An Essay in Seven Parts.* Trans. by Linda Asher. London: Faber and Faber. [First published as *Le Rideau.* Paris: Gallimard (2005).]

LaCapra, Dominick. 2000. 'Reconfiguring French Studies'. *History and Reading: Toqueville, Foucault, French Studies.* Toronto: University of Toronto Press: 169–226.

'Language Matters: A Position Paper'. 2009. London: British Academy. <http://www.britac.ac.uk/policy/language-matters.cfm>. Consulted on 1 February 2010.

Le Bris, Michel. 2009. *Nous ne sommes pas d'ici: autobiographie.* Paris: Grasset.

Lebovics, Herman. 2006. 'Tough Love for France'. In Laura Lee Downs and Stéphane Gerson (eds), *Why France?* Ithaca, NY: Cornell University Press: 47–60.

Lionnet, Françoise. 2003. 'Introduction'. *Modern Language Notes* 118.4: 783–86. [Special issue: 'Francophone Studies: New Landscapes', edited by Françoise Lionnet and Dominic Thomas.]

Mann, Gregory. 2005. 'Locating Colonial Histories: Between France and West Africa'. *American Historical Review* 110.2: <http://www.historycooperative.org/journals/ahr/110.2/mann.html>. Consulted on 9 October 2010.

Ngũgĩ Wa Thiong'o. 1995. 'On the Abolition of the English Department'. In Bill Ashcroft, Gareth Griffiths and Helen Tiffin (eds), *The Postcolonial Studies Reader.* London: Routledge: 438–42. [First published in *Homecoming: Essays on African and Caribbean Literature, Culture and Politics.* New York: Lawrence Hill and Co. (1972).]

Petrey, Sandy. 1995. 'French Studies/Cultural Studies: Reciprocal Invigoration or Mutual Destruction'. *French Review* 68.3: 381–92.

—. 1998. 'When Did Literature Stop Being Cultural?'. *Diacritics* 28.3: 12–22.

—. 2003. 'Language Charged with Meaning'. *Yale French Studies* 103: 133–45.

Pizer, John. 2007. 'Towards a Productive Interdisciplinary Relationship: Between Comparative Literature and World Literature'. *Comparatist* 31: 6–28.

'Pour une "littérature-monde" en français'. 2007. *Le Monde* 16 March.

Prendergast, Christopher. 2001. 'Negotiating World Literature', *New Left Review* 8: 100–21.

Quignard, Pascal. 1989. 'La déprogammation de la littérature'. *Le Débat* 54: 77–88.

Rosello, Mireille. 2003. 'Unhoming Francophone Studies: A House in the Middle of the Current'. *Yale French Studies* 103: 123–32.

Ross, Kristin. 1993. 'The World Literature and Cultural Studies Program'. *Critical Inquiry* 19: 666–76.

Said, Edward W. 2001. 'Globalizing Literary Study'. *PMLA* 116.1: 64–68.

Sarkozy, Nicolas. 2007. 'Pour une francophonie vivante et populaire'. *Le Figaro* 22 March.

Schneck, Colombe. 1994. 'Le français piégé par le multiculturalisme américain'. *Le Monde* 17 February.

Schor, Naomi. 2003. 'Feminism and Francophone Literature: From One Revolution to Another'. *Yale French Studies* 103: 164–65.

Scott, David. 2005. 'The Social Construction of Postcolonial Studies'. In Ania Loomba, Suvir Kaul, Matti Bunzi, Antoinette Burton and Jed Esty (eds), *Postcolonial Studies and Beyond*. Durham, NC and London: Duke University Press: 385–400.

Spear, Thomas (ed.). 2002. *La Culture française vue d'ici et d'ailleurs*. Paris: Karthala.

Toledo, Camille de. 2008. *Visiter le Flurkistan, ou les illusions de la littérature monde*. Paris: Presses Universitaires de France.

'Toward a "World-Literature" in French'. 2009. Trans. by Daniel Simon. *World Literature Today* (March–April): 54–56.

Viart, Domnique. 2005. 'Programmes and Projects in the Contemporary Literary Field'. In Johnnie Gratton and Michael Sheringham (eds), *The Art of the Project: Projects and Experiments in Modern French Culture*. Oxford: Berghahn: 172–87.

Francophonie:
Trash or Recycle?

Lydie Moudileno

The May 2007 issue of *PMLA* devoted its editor's column to the question, 'The End of Postcolonial Theory?' The year before, a roundtable discussion at the University of Michigan had apparently sparked such lively debate and controversy that *PMLA* wanted to address the validity of postcolonial theory today in a more public fashion. As the editors put it, the time had come to 'investigate [...] the potential exhaustion of postcolonialism as a paradigm' (Yaeger, 2007: 633). To question its validity and to talk about its 'potential exhaustion' amounts to announcing, if not its death, at least that something is wrong with postcolonialism and postcolonial studies today.

Indeed, the field has come under criticism in the last few decades for a number of reasons. The most frequently stated is postcolonialism's failure to account for the state of the global world, be it new imperialisms brought about by the events of 9/11, increasingly complex geopolitical configurations, or twenty-first-century identities and conditions. Another, perhaps more dismissive, reason is that postcolonial studies has become an 'exceptionally self-reflexive field' (Yaeger, 2007: 643), concerned less with the state of the world than with the state of the discipline itself and the position of its interpreters. To be brief, the world has changed, and postcolonial theory/ studies may no longer provide the necessary tools to interpret it. Rather than the actual arguments of the debate, what interests me here is the performative act of announcing – or hinting at – the 'end' of the discipline. Simon Gikandi reminds us in the same *PMLA* issue:

> Lately, there has been a lot of talk about the end of postcolonial theory [...].
> For me the presumed end or death of postcolonial theory, like all narratives

of ending, triggers an ambivalent response. It seems to designate, on the one hand, an arrival into the institution of interpretation, and, on the other hand, an evacuation from the same edifice [...]. Stories of ending – the end of history, the end of philosophy, the end of art – have functioned, at least in the Western tradition, as authorized moments of closure and sublation. And that is not a bad thing [...]. Our challenge here is to figure out what this talk about the end of postcolonial theory means. Is the end of postcolonial theory a mere stopping, a symptom of its decline and impotence? Or is it the completion of a theoretical project whose work has become ensconced as an authorized version of literary and cultural analysis? If postcolonial theory has ended, what exactly ended, and what was its task? (Yaeger, 2007: 635)

Taking my cue from Gikandi, I would like to reflect on a similar pronouncement in a different context, the end of *Francophonie*. As my facetious title suggests, *Francophonie* and Francophone studies can be said to be at a point where their currency as a concept and a discipline needs to be re-examined. Should we keep *Francophonie* as an operative category or should we seriously think about 'trashing it' (keeping in mind both senses of 'trashing': to get rid of it but also to speak badly about it)? As I will show, recent events in academia and *belles-lettres* have brought about a re-examination of *Francophonie* not unlike the one affecting postcolonial studies. The two contexts – the American and the French and Francophone academies – are obviously different, historically, culturally and institutionally. But it is not a coincidence that the two spheres almost simultaneously arrived at a crucial moment of reappraisal of the relevance of their discipline, against the background of the new century's political, cultural and literary shifts.

I speak of simultaneity because in 2007, the year that the American institution, via its 'official' organ, raised the question of 'the end of postcolonial theory', a manifesto appeared in *Le Monde* declaring in no uncertain terms 'the end of *Francophonie*'. Signed by forty-four writers, among them future Nobel prize-winner J.-M. G. Le Clézio as well as Tahar Ben Jelloun, Eric Orsena, Nancy Houston, Édouard Glissant, Maryse Condé and other major literary figures, the manifesto, under the title 'Pour une "littérature-monde" en français', announced not only 'the end of *Francophonie*', but also the birth of 'world literature in French'. Taking as a starting point the fact that five of the seven main French literary prizes the previous autumn (2006) had been awarded to foreign-born writers, the manifesto stated:

Plus tard, on dira peut-être que ce fut un moment historique [...]. [Une] révolution copernicienne. Copernicienne, parce qu'elle révèle ce que le milieu littéraire savait déjà, sans l'admettre: le centre, ce point depuis lequel était supposée rayonner une littérature franco-française n'est plus le centre. [...] [L]e centre, nous disent les prix d'automne, est désormais partout, aux quatre coins du monde. Fin de la francophonie. Et naissance d'une littérature-monde en français.[1] ('Pour une "littérature-monde" en français', 2007)

Positing that 'en toute rigueur l'idée de "francophonie" se donne [...] comme le dernier avatar du colonialisme' [in a strict sense the 'francophone' concept presents itself as the last avatar of colonialism] (2007; 2009: 56), they argued: 'Ce qu'entérinent ces prix d'automne est le constat inverse: que le pacte colonial se trouve brisé, que la langue délivrée devient l'affaire de tous, et que, si l'on s'y tient fermement, c'en sera fini des temps du mépris et de la suffisance. Fin de la "francophonie", et naissance d'une littérature-monde en français [...]' ('Pour une "littérature-monde" en français', 2007).[2]

Reaction to the manifesto was tremendous. Within days, in the same section of *Le Monde*, Abdou Diouf, president of the Organisation Internationale de la Francophonie, responded with a detailed defence of his institution (Diouf, 2007), as did a number of individual writers (see Najjar, 2007). As one can imagine, the internet has been even more effervescent. Roundtables and public debates proliferated, and by 2009 the *littérature-monde* manifesto had been the subject of two books, two special issues of journals, several international conferences (Copenhagen, Tallahassee, Algiers, Djibouti), with many more planned around the world in the subsequent years.

I would like to examine some of the circumstances that led to the manifesto's formidable success and its increasingly evident status as a literary event. In *Qu'est-ce qu'un événement littéraire au XIXe siècle?*, Corinne Saminadayar-Perrin insists that in order to explain a literary event one must take into account the multiplicity of factors that allowed it to happen. Thinking about the event, she notes, not only places it in a specific literary

---

[1] 'In due course, it will perhaps be said that this was a historic moment [...]. A Copernican revolution. Copernican because it reveals what the literary milieu already knew without admitting it: the center, from which supposedly radiated a Franco-French literature, is no longer the center. [...] [T]he centre, these fall prizes tell us, is henceforth everywhere, at the four corners of the world. The result? The end of "francophone" literature – and the birth of a world literature in French.' ('Toward a "World-Literature" in French', 2009: 54.)

[2] 'What these fall prizes confirm is the inverse notion: that the colonial pact is broken, that language thus liberated has become everyone's concern, and that, if one firmly subscribes to it, the era of contempt and adequacy has ended. The end, then, of "francophone" literature, and the birth of a world-literature in French [...]' ('Toward a "World-Literature" in French', 2009: 56.)

history, but also forces us to think about the status of writing itself, and the condition of writers at a particular time and place (2008: 10). In short, to understand the scope of the manifesto as an event one must look at the conditions of possibility of its success. If a literary event is a *mise-en-scène* of the value of literature at a given moment in history, what exactly is at stake with this particular event? What elements have contributed to its visibility and magnitude? Beyond its performative enunciation, does the event allow for real epistemological change? To put it more bluntly, to what extent, and how successfully, does it 'trash' the old *Francophonie*? To begin to answer these questions, I will first chart the contemporary spheres that this idea of a 'world literature in French' challenges. Then I will look in more detail at the rhetoric of the manifesto as it proposes a paradigmatic shift from *Francophonie* to 'world literature in French'.

In order to better contextualize these issues, it is useful to examine three distinct but sometimes overlapping 'scenes' as they appear in 2009: the French literary scene and discourse on the state of French letters; the Francophone scene; and the international and postcolonial scene.

A Timely Event

As far as the first scene – the French, hexagonal sphere – is concerned, the last few decades have apparently been marked by a dual movement. On the one hand, we can observe a proliferation of new writers, mostly novelists, like Beigbeder, Houellebecq, Amelie Nothomb, or those of 'la nouvelle école de Minuit' and the 'nouveau nouveau roman'. On the other hand, we hear constantly of an alleged crisis of French literature. Richard Millet speaks of 'désenchantement de la littérature' [disenchantment of literature]; Tzvetan Todorov speaks of 'littérature en péril' [literature in jeopardy]; Pierre Jourde decries a 'littérature sans estomac' [literature without guts]; Jean-Philippe Domecq asks 'Qui a peur de la littérature?' [Who's afraid of literature?]; Jean-Pierre Otte announces 'La Littérature prend le maquis' [Literature goes AWOL]; and Jean Bessière likewise asks, 'Qu'est-il arrivé aux écrivains français?' [What happened to French writers?]. According to all these observers, the sad truth is that French literature is just not what it used to be. Even if we bear in mind that declinology is a French national pastime, the accumulating works deploring the state of *belles-lettres* nonetheless signal the need to assess the state of contemporary literature. There is, it would appear, an urgent need to diagnose the literary body's worrisome symptoms. While these essays all deserve full analysis, briefly stated, they indicate that the symptoms of this decline would be narcissism, solipsism, lack of referentiality, obscenity, imposture and stupidity. Contemporary French writers and their work are defined through a series of binary oppositions, good/bad, of course, but also best seller/masterpiece, authentic/fake, original/cliché and so forth.

In an article entitled 'Pourquoi ils se haïssent. De Houellebecq à Benamou: onze duels littéraires' ['Why They Hate Each Other. From Houellebecq to Benamou: Eleven Literary Duels'] the magazine *Le Nouvel Observateur*, in what it calls 'A Chronicle of Parisian Literary Hatreds', depicts the Parisian literary scene in these words: 'Ils se traitent de fachos, de plagiaires, de moins que rien, d'antisémites, de va-t-en guerre, de nuls, d'obsédés sexuels. Petite chronique parisienne des détestations littéraires'.[3] Note that the accusations go in all directions. Contrary to the situation in previous 'crises', today it is difficult to identify a particular movement or group responsible for the alleged decline. In other words, everybody is under attack. Or, rather, not quite everybody. Writers of African, colonial or postcolonial origin, for instance, are never mentioned – neither criticized nor praised, but simply absent from the polemics. This absence is striking, indeed, in the work of critics who do not hesitate to identify 'bad' writers by name, to establish taxonomies according to aesthetic criteria, and to question a given writer's right to be included in great French literature. Is it that authors of colonial origin are all, without exception, above average and above criticism? Or is the Francophone (postcolonial) ignored by critics for other reasons, such as fear of suspicion of racism? Certainly, people such as Renaud Camus and Houellebecq do not let political correctness keep them from anti-Semitic and xenophobic statements. Could it be, then, because Francophone postcolonial literature is in essence outside the debate? The writings of an author of African or Caribbean origin who publishes at Le Seuil, Gallimard or Albin Michel cannot be blamed for the decline of French literature because a priori it is not *part* of French literature. It is against the background of this limited, exclusionary conception of French literature, as I will show below, that the manifesto constitutes an event.

The second, obvious context that I would like to examine briefly is the Francophone scene. While the 1990s confirmed the tremendous diversity of French-speaking literary productions, mostly in terms of genres, origin of authors and editorial venues, the expansion of the field has also increasingly revealed profound structural inequalities. The most obvious and perhaps most problematic is the widening gap between North and South, those who reside and work in Western countries and cities, and those who reside

---

3 'They call each other fascists, plagiarists, zeros, anti-Semites, crusaders, worthless, sexual perverts.' Unless otherwise indicated, all translations from French into English are by the author of this chapter.

and work in the African continent, the Caribbean *départements*, Haiti, the Indian Ocean or the Pacific Rim. One of the major developments in Francophone studies in the last few years has been the steady consolidation of a Francophone canon. If we agree with Roland Barthes that a 'canon is what is taught', there is no denying the existence of such a canon. However, typical of the process of canon-formation, new forms of marginalization have emerged within the discipline. While some award-wining writers have reached canonical status, others, of course, have not made their way into our syllabuses, for a number of reasons. Minor genres like poetry or more popular productions, for instance, remain outside the Francophone canon as we practise it. This kind of criticism has also been levelled at postcolonial studies in the Anglophone context. I bring it up in connection with the manifesto because one of the objectives of the text is precisely to open up the category of French writing to 'the world', to its diverse voices and by extension diverse modes of self-representation. It is also, as I will demonstrate later, one of its potential pitfalls.

Concerning the third scene, the international postcolonial sphere, one can say that the twenty-first century is marked in France by a remarkable effervescence around the issue of 'postcolonial studies'. Jim Cohen remarks that France has taken a noticeable 'postcolonial turn' in the first years of the century. Converging factors in the humanities in general, like the first translations of Homi Bhabha, Stuart Hall and Paul Gilroy and the collective work of historians such as Nicolas Bancel, Sandrine Lemaire and Pascal Blanchard's groundbreaking *La Fracture coloniale*, in addition to events like the commemoration of the abolition of slavery, have increasingly set the stage for the appearance of 'postcolonial studies in the Francophone context'. In literary criticism more specifically, the 1999 publication of Jean-Marc Moura's *Littératures francophones et théorie postcoloniale* with the prestigious Presses Universitaires de France was a significant paradigm shift. But as far as literature is concerned, Moura's scholarship remains an exception in France. By contrast, a good number of Francophone studies scholars working in the Anglo-Saxon world have forcefully called for both a reassessment of Francophone studies and advocated for a 'translation' of postcolonial literary criticism at the turn of the century, starting with Alec Hargreaves and Mark McKinney in their 1997 *Post-Colonial Cultures in France*, followed with the almost simultaneous publication, in the first years of the twenty-first century, of Forsdick and Murphy's 2003 *Francophone Postcolonial Studies: A Critical Introduction* and Kamal Salhi's 2003 *Francophone Post-colonial Cultures: Critical Essays* from the United Kingdom, and, from the USA, Anne Donadey and H. Adlai Murdoch's 2005 volume *Postcolonial Theory and Francophone Literary Studies*. However, as

Moura, one of the first advocates and practitioners of postcolonial literary criticism in France, remarks, the move is not as natural as it sounds. According to Hargreaves and Moura:

> 'Francophone' and 'Postcolonial' studies have often been seen as rival if not antagonistic academic fields. Where work in the second has been led by Anglophone scholars for whom the politics of culture have been of primordial importance, the first has generally been preferred by scholars in France who have seen in postcolonialism an overly simplified and unduly politicized 'Anglo-Saxon' approach to the cultures of formerly colonized people. (Hargreaves and Moura, 2007: 307)

Although the overall French institutional attitude has traditionally been suspicion and disdain for 'postcolonial studies', one can definitely see a move away from *Francophonie* toward 'postcolonial Francophone' studies in the last few years. In France, 2006 alone saw an amazing number of special issues devoted not just to postcolonial studies, but also to an interrogation of the relevance to the French context of postcolonialism as a discipline. Journal special issues with titles such as 'Postcolonialisme et immigration' (*Contretemps*); 'Faut-il être postcolonial?' (*Labyrinthe*); 'Pour comprendre la pensée postcoloniale' (*Esprit*); 'Qui a peur du postcolonial?' (*Mouvements*); 'Qui a peur des Post Colonial Studies en France?' (*Multitudes*) all point to this 'postcolonial turn'.[4] Acknowledging this increased interest in French and Francophone studies, critics Azzedine Haddour and Margaret A. Majumdar recall the move from Commonwealth literature to postcolonial studies in the early 1980s: 'Just as this new field of critical inquiry subsumed literary criticism and Commonwealth literature, so is it possible to identify parallels in the attempts of francophone postcolonial studies to subsume francophone literature. Indeed, for some, this interest in French postcolonialism signals the end of the discourse of francophonie' (Haddour and Majumdar, 2007: 11). We might thus be at a moment of paradigmatic and disciplinary shift when 'French postcolonialism' or 'French postcolonial studies' renders *Francophonie* obsolete. Postcolonial studies would ultimately achieve disavowal of *Francophonie* in favour of the broader interdisciplinary, transnational, less Francocentred approach to historical and cultural productions.

In this context the concept of *littérature-monde*/'world literature' constitutes a welcome addition to the conversation. First, and most importantly, it re-centres the debate around artistic–literary issues, and re-conceptualizes the heterogeneous and transnational body of texts coming out of the

---

4 On this 'French postcolonial turn', see Cohen, 2007; Haddour and Majumdar, 2007; Hargreaves and Moura, 2007; and Smouts, 2007.

French-speaking world (including France). At this most opportune moment, when French literature is supposedly 'declining' and *Francophonie* increasingly superseded by postcolonial studies, the idea of a 'world literature in French' is attractive because it provides a concept that does not seem to be borrowed from the Anglo-Saxon world. This is also the first time since the 1970s that a literary concept has caught the French imagination to such an extent. By comparison, the little Parisian battles I described above sound petty. Neither a movement nor a programmatic call, the manifesto has caught on, I believe, because it is able to discard *Francophonie* while proposing a concept that can account for the increasingly diverse and fragmented production of the contemporary scene.

The signatories to the manifesto announce what they call 'good news': 'Le monde revient' [The world is back]. The statement means, among other things, that those who had been excluded from the French sphere are inviting themselves to the debate on the state of French literature. Published in the pages of *Le Monde*, the manifesto also performs a media and institutional coup: French literature now has to deal with the *monde*, i.e., the rest of the world. With this move, literature written in French by writers of all origins takes its place not just *in* French literature, but as its vital core and cultural horizon. This being said, is the concept a valid substitute for *Francophonie*?

Limits and Paradoxes

Again, beyond its immediate attraction, to what extent can the concept of *littérature-monde* indeed replace that of *Francophonie*? To go back to my alternative – trash or recycle – does the idea of a '"littérature-monde" en français' allow scholars as well as writers to get rid of, to 'trash', *Francophonie* altogether? What would be the implications? Does it really make *Francophonie* obsolete, or is it merely a catchy neologism that veils and then recycles the same cultural practices?

To introduce some of the potential criticism to *littérature-monde*, I would like to mention yet another event. In July 2007, cultural life in Guadeloupe, in the French West Indies, was shaken: Maryse Condé, a world-renowned novelist originally from Guadeloupe, considered 'la grande dame des Antilles' and one of the canonical figures of Francophone studies, announced on the local radio station that she had decided to 'leave Guadeloupe and the Caribbean forever'. Seventy-one-year-old Condé first invoked personal, family and health reasons to justify her decision to settle in Paris and New York. As the interview progressed, however, she mentioned a more philosophical reason: she claimed that though the Caribbean island of Guadeloupe had been an essential source of inspiration, the people of Guadeloupe had not given her anything other than the occasional school visit or book signing at the local cultural centre.

Condé is alleged to have concluded by saying: 'The people did not give me anything. But I don't blame them. A people which has nothing cannot give anything'.[5] While many Guadeloupians reiterated their pride and admiration for Maryse Condé on her final move, many others found her statements shocking, condescending and humiliating for Guadeloupians. Some, like public commentator and famous blogger Pierre Papaya, violently criticized Condé's move in terms of abandonment, if not disavowal of 'the people' in favour of the wider 'world':

> Maryse Condé quitte donc son pays natal, définitivement ... Elle s'en va donc vers le tout-monde. Un tout-monde qui exclut nos peuples. Un tout-monde partagé entre New-York et Paris [...]. Elle va chérir ces capitales reconnaissantes qui pourtant ont apporté tant de désolation dans le monde: l'extermination de peuples, la traite, le code noir, les camps d'exter-mination ... Deux capitales qui agissent avec mépris et arrogance vis à vis des autres peuples. Deux capitales qui œuvrent pour maintenir les peuples de Palestine, d'Irak, d'Haïti, d'Afghanistan et d'ailleurs sous occupation![6] (Papaya, 2007)

This perceived disavowal of – or defection from – the local in favour of a new and implicitly more glamorous postcolonial subjectivity reflects, I believe, some of the potential pitfalls of *littérature-monde* as a modality. Condé's signing of the manifesto, which doubles the symbolic departure from the

---

5   Condé made a public appearance on Radio France Outremer on 13 July 2007, discussing the reasons behind her decision to sell her house in Montebello, Guadeloupe, and leave Guadeloupe 'forever'. Unfortunately I have not been able to find a video or transcript of the interview. Part of her interview is cited by J. S. Sahai: 'Le pays m'a beaucoup donné et m'a permis d'écrire mes livres. Mais les gens ne m'ont pas donné grand-chose, dit-elle pour glisser vers le tout-monde et s'offrir une aventure autrement actuelle. Et de conclure, réaliste et sans reproche, qu'elle ne saurait reprocher à son pays de ne pas lui avoir donné ce qu'il ... n'a pas' (Sahai, 2007).

6   'Maryse Condé is thus leaving her native land forever ... She is going towards the *tout-monde*. A *tout-monde* that excludes our people. A *tout-monde* shared between New York and Paris [...]. She is leaving to cherish those grateful metropolises that have brought so much desolation in the world: extermination, the slave trade, the *Code noir*, the extermination camps ... Two capital cities that act with disdain and arrogance towards other peoples. Two capital cities that work to maintain the peoples of Palestine, Iraq, Haiti, Afghanistan and elsewhere under permanent occupation!'

native land, confirms the gap between a global, privileged and highly visible group – the *tout-monde* – and what it necessarily leaves behind, the local.

This is in fact my first and primary critique of the rhetoric surrounding *littérature-monde*. On the one hand, it claims that the eruption of foreign-born writers has achieved a radical destabilization of the field, a 'Copernican revolution' ('Toward a "World-Literature" in French', 2009: 54). On the other hand, this conception of the 'world' entails a problematic valorization of mobility which, I think, further excludes other 'worldly' identities and positions.

The manifesto has its origin in the Etonnants Voyageurs project, organized for the first time by Michel Le Bris in 1989. Now in its third decade, Etonnants Voyageurs is a festival originally designed to bring together artists engaged one way or another with travel writing in different cities (such as Saint-Malo, Bamako and Port-au-Prince). It may seem unfair to blame a manifesto that is the offspring of Etonnants Voyageurs for valorizing mobility. However, its publication represents a significant shift from festival and cultural events to an actual literary movement, if not a theory of world representation. In this context the valorization of travel and mobility becomes problematic. If indeed mobility becomes a privileged mode of access to the 'real' world – as opposed to, say, rootedness – where does this rhetoric leave writers who do not travel? If cosmopolitanism is the condition of this 'Copernican revolution', what is the status of sedentariness? As Camille de Toledo, one of the harsher critics of the *littérature-monde* manifesto, points out, 'le combat pour créer un espace postcolonial – passe par une polarisation esthétique très caricaturale: autrement dit, d'un côté, les écrivains de chambre, de l'autre, les voyageurs' (2008: 17).[7]

The case of Condé shows, and the rhetoric of mobility confirms, a state of affairs that was already characteristic of Anglo-Saxon postcolonial studies. Defining postcoloniality in the 1990s, Anthony Appiah famously talked about a 'comprador intelligentsia' to account for those whose careers are born of and depend on passages between the West and the rest of the world:

> Postcoloniality is the condition of what we might ungenerously call a comprador intelligentsia of a relatively small, Western-style, Western trained, group of writers and thinkers who mediate the trade in cultural commodities of world capitalism at the periphery. In the west they are

---

7 'the struggle to create a postcolonial space – involves an aesthetic polarization which is very caricatural: with on the one hand, stay-at-home writers [écrivains de chambre], and on the other, travellers'.

known through the Africa they offer; their compatriots know them through an Africa they have invented for the world, for each other, and for Africa. (Appiah, 1991: 348)

The concept of *littérature-monde en français* clearly stands at the intersection of *Francophonie*, postcolonialism and cosmopolitanism. Writers such as Condé would thus practise a transnational cosmopolitanism rather similar to the one advocated by, for example, Homi Bhabha, but in which the French language would remain the fundamental creative anchor. To account for this cosmopolitan figure I propose the term 'Francosmopolitan': one whose personal and professional itineraries and migrations have him/her evolve in the centrifugal, nomadic, ever-changing and endlessly hybridized modes of transnational circulation, but whose miles accumulate on Air France (rather than, say, British Airways), and whose privileged linguistic affiliation and creative home remain (in) French. The 'Francosmopolitan', like *littérature-monde en français*, operates within a subtle – if not artificial – negotiation of the centrifugal appeal of the 'world' and the more materialistic, centripetal *pied-à-terre* of France and the French metropole.

We would now have, on the one hand, the 'French-French' writer, anchored in national borders, and, on the other, the Francosmopolitan. An exclusion becomes clear: how do we account for the writer who is neither French nor cosmopolitan, that is, the former 'Francophone writer'? Is s/he, together with *Francophonie*, also declared 'dead'? How do we account for those who, while not residents of the hexagon, live and work in New Caledonia, Burkina Faso, Madagascar or Algiers, and do not travel? Are not the so-called 'peripheries' such as the Guadeloupe Maryse Condé is leaving behind sometimes called *ultrapéripheries* – i.e., spaces marginalized as soon as opening to the 'world' is conceived only in terms of mobility, nomadism, multiple citizenship and dual residence? This, I believe, is one of the main reasons why *littérature-monde* cannot fully function as a substitute for the language-based *Francophonie*, however flawed, outdated and unsatisfactory the latter might be. In its effort to 'provincialize' France, the valorization of mobility has the paradoxical potential of transforming an opening-up gesture into an exclusionary one, by which the explosion of the Parisian centre ultimately consolidates the marginal status of the cultural spheres already at the margins of the *monde*.

A close reading of the manifesto would reveal other problematic rhetorical traits as well, among them, the over-reliance on the old opposition between a Western deliquescent world and a vital, revitalizing creative energy originating from an exotic elsewhere. My second criticism touches on this polarization: the contrast between a tired and depleted France and a dynamic 'world'. A few relevant passages demonstrate this easily. The call is one that involves 'se frotter au monde pour en capter le souffle, les énergies vitales [...] [c]e désir nouveau de retrouver les voies du monde, ce retour aux puissances incandescences de la littérature'.[8] Finally, the sentence: 'Et les regards se tournaient de nouveau vers les littératures "francophones", particulièrement caribéennes, comme si, loin des modèles français sclérosés, s'affirmait là-bas, héritière de Saint-John Perse et de Césaire, une effervescence romanesque et poétique dont le secret, ailleurs, semblait avoir été perdu' leaves no doubt about the manifesto's problematic reliance on a rhetoric of exoticism and vitalism.[9]

As William Cloonan convincingly demonstrates in his 2008 essay 'Littérature-monde and the Novel in 2007', this polarization does not hold under rigorous scrunity: hexagonal literature lacks neither vitality nor originality and recycling the opposition between an old and tired France and an incandescent world is simply a misrepresentation of the present state of contemporary literature. Or, at least, if it ever did, it is certainly not the case in 2007. This misrepresentation aside, it may be more problematic that the manifesto's overvaluation of 'vitalism' sends us back to familiar and longstanding rhetoric positing the 'primitive' as a source of inspiration for the West. Repetition of words such as 'incandescent', 'secret', 'elsewhere', 'breath' echoes Jean-Paul Sartre in his famous 'Black Orpheus', with which, more than sixty years ago, he introduced the *Anthologie de la nouvelle poésie nègre et malgache.* Indeed, the encounter with an elsewhere in which is preserved the natural essence of the human is perhaps the grounding topos of discourses on the 'exotic'. Thus, Sartre saw in the poets of *Négritude* the 'Black Africans' who 'au contraire, sont encore dans la grande période de fécondité mythique' [unlike us are still the grand era of mythical fecundity] (Sartre, 1948). Closer to our own time, the director of Gallimard's 'Continents noirs' collection introduced his 1998 collection by stating in the prefatory text included in each volume: '*Nous parions, ici, sur les Africains d'Afrique et d'ailleurs, de langue française et de toute langue écrite, parlée et sans doute pas écrite encore, nous parions sur l'écriture des continents noirs pour dégeler l'esprit romanesque et la langue française du nouveau siècle. Nous parions sur les fétiches en papier qui prennent le relais de fétiches en bois*' (Schiffano,

[8] 'rub up against the world in order to capture its essence and vital energies [...] this renewed desire to rejoin the world's routes, this return to literature's powers of incandescence' ('Toward a "World Literature" in French', 2007: 54).

[9] 'And "francophone" literatures were receiving renewed attention, particularly in the Caribbean, as if, far away from vitiated French models, a novelistic and poetic effervescence – inherited from Saint-John Perse and Aimé Césaire – was being affirmed there' ('Toward a "World Literature" in French', 2007: 55).

2000).[10] If this statement recycles the vitalistic trope of the exotic other, the manifesto equally participates in the doubled register of agony and vitality. The African text, in other words, would allow a European modernity in ruins to return to the sources of the 'world' in all its authenticity. As such, the *littérature-monde* manifesto is an opportunity for: (i) authors of European (non-colonial) origin to situate themselves on the side of the diverse and thus the vitality of Francophone letters and not the moribund Occident; and (ii) authors of colonial origin to approach the Western universal, since the presence of non-Africans, non-Caribbeans, and so on brings with it a kind of guarantee of the essential worth of their vitality. In other words, they are not reduced to the diverse, though they may participate in it. In the group of signatories, one side helps sidestep accusations of narcissism, ethnocentrism and so on, while the other helps escape the dangers of representativity. Each thereby serves as an alibi for the other. Together, they offer the French literary scene an intellectual community in which personal origin is made to appear insignificant while it is simultaneously the very foundation of the diversity the group explicitly and programmatically projects. What is different is that the group of manifesto signatories, in alphabetical order, presents itself like a heterogeneous assembly, in which the apprentice–master relationship (or the white author's preface as in the era of Leiris and Sartre) has disappeared. What persists, however, and remains perhaps even more problematic, is that, beyond the levelling gesture, the historical relationship between Europe and its Elsewhere(s) is preserved, with all the hierarchical implications that historically produced binary carries with it.

One should not forget, at this point, the fundamental distinction between *Francophonie* as a geopolitical institution represented by the Organisation Internationale de la Francophonie (OIF) and *Francophonie*, or, to be exact, Francophone studies as an academic discipline. The first corresponds to a specific *projet* – organizing French-speaking nations around the world – the origins and developments of which can be duly dated, and which bears on an ideological conception of transnational and French relations to France that some might consider neo-colonial. The second, born in great part in US and French academic departments, is a scholarly category, akin to periodic or area studies.

As I mentioned at the beginning, among the many reactions elicited

---

[10] 'We are gambling here on the Africans of Africa and elsewhere, writing in French or any other written language, or spoken and perhaps not even yet written, we are gambling on the writing of the Black Continents to thaw the literary spirit and the French tongue of the new century, We are gambling on the paper fetishes who are taking over for the wooden ones'.

by the publication of the manifesto was a statement by Abdou Diouf, president of the OIF. Ironically or deliberately, the text was published just four days before the official 'Journée mondiale de la Francophonie', 20 March. As thousands around the world were busy organizing festivities for the world day of *Francophonie*, Diouf published a 'droit de réponse' [right of response] in *Le Monde* (2007). Calling the signatories 'fossoyeurs de la francophonie' [gravediggers of *Francophonie*], he stated: 'Vous contribuez, dans ce manifeste, avec toute l'autorité que votre talent confère à votre parole, à entretenir le plus grave des contresens sur la francophonie, en confondant francocentrisme et francophonie, en confondant exception culturelle et diversité culturelle'.[11] Here again a distinction needs to be made between discarding or embracing *Francophonie* and discarding or embracing Francophone studies, the discipline that explores the work of French-speaking authors around the world, perhaps more aptly called 'Francophone postcolonial studies'. To be sure, the lines are sometimes blurred, especially when considering pragmatic issues such as editorial practices, distribution and availability. However, Francophone studies as practised in the American academia is not intellectually or ideologically dependent on the OIF. 'We' scholars of Francophone studies are not paid by, or intellectually or politically aligned with, Abdou Diouf's institution. Reminding ourselves of this distinction allows us to agree with the manifesto's call for a long overdue gesture of destabilizing France and Paris as the hegemonic centres of cultural productions in French, and thus, at least for now, continue using the term, of course with quotation marks. While it would be naive to think that the two do not overlap or have never overlapped, this distinction nevertheless remains useful as we think strategically about our practice as scholars and literary critics.

As an affirmation of the significant contributions made by non-French-born artists, the *ras-le-bol* expressed in the manifesto is absolutely understandable. Talking about the discipline requires more nuance. Francophone studies has allowed us to expose students to a variety of texts and artists from the French-speaking world. Although it has undoubtedly found its place in our departments and curricula, its legitimacy remains fragile. Some of our colleagues would be only too happy to see 'the end of Francophone studies' as the inevitable fate of a fad not in any way competitive with the good old canon. Can we, then, afford to trash the particular *Francophonie* we have

---

[11] 'You contribute in this manifesto, with all the authority that your talent gives your speech, to maintain the gravest of contradictions concerning *Francophonie*, by confusing *Francocentrism* with *Francophonie*, by confusing cultural exceptionalism with cultural diversity'.

fought hard to impose? What would be the implications of a radical disavowal of *Francophonie* as a field of scholarly investigation? Is *Francophonie* meant to be, as Sartre prophesied about Negritude, just the negative moment of a dialectical progression toward something more universal, *littérature-monde*? I tend to think that the battle for the legitimacy of Francophone studies in the Anglo-Saxon and French worlds is not over. As a practitioner of *Francophonie* and someone who is very aware of the past, present and future battles in the field, as well as of its inevitable paradoxes, I, for one, do not think we can afford to trash it just yet.

Works Cited

Appiah, Kwame Anthony. 1991. 'Is the "Post" in "Postcolonial" the "Post" in "Postmodern"?'. *Critical Inquiry* 17: 336–57.

Bessière, Jean. 2006. *Qu'est-il arrivé aux écrivains francais? D'Alain Robbe-Grillet à Jonathan Littell*. Loverval: Éditions Labor: Espaces de Libertés.

Cloonan, William J. 2007. 'Littérature-monde and the Novel in 2007'. *French Review* 82.1: 33–50.

Cohen, Jim. 2007. 'La bibliothèque coloniale en pleine expansion'. *Mouvements* 51: 166–70.

Contretemps. 2006. Special issue: 'Postcolonialisme et immigration'. 16.

Diouf, Abdou. 2007. 'La francophonie, une réalité oubliée'. *Le Monde* 20 March.

Domecq, Jean-Philippe. 2002. *Qui a peur de la littérature?* Paris: Les Mille et une nuits.

Donadey, Anne, and H. Adlai Murdoch (eds). 2005. *Postcolonial Theory and Francophone Literary Studies*. Gainesville: University of Florida Press.

Esprit. 2006. 'Pour comprendre la pensée postcoloniale'. 12.

Forsdick, Charles, and David Murphy (eds). 2003. *Francophone Postcolonial Studies: A Critical Introduction*. London: Arnold.

Haddour, Azzedine, and Margaret A. Majumdar. 2007. 'Whither Francophone Studies? Launching the Debate: Editorial Introduction'. *International Journal of Francophone Studies* 10.1–2: 7–16.

Hargreaves, Alec G., and Mark McKinney (eds). 1997. *Post-Colonial Cultures in France*. London: Routledge.

Hargreaves, Alec G., and Jean-Marc Moura. 2007. 'Extending the Boundaries of Francophone Postcolonial Studies: Editorial Introduction'. *International Journal of Francophone Studies* 10.3: 307–11.

Jourde, Pierre. 2003. *La Littérature sans estomac*. Paris: Pocket Agora.

Labyrinthe. 2006. Dossier: 'Faut-il être postcolonial?'. 24.

Le Bris, Michel, and Jean Rouaud (eds). 2007. *Pour une littérature-monde*. Paris: Gallimard.

Millet, Richard. 2007. *Désenchantement de la littérature*. Paris: Gallimard.

Moura, Jean-Marc. 1999. *Littératures francophones et théorie postcoloniale*. Paris: Presses Universitaires de France.

Mouvements. 2007. 'Qui a peur du postcolonial? Dénis et controverses'. 51.

Multitudes. 2004. 'Qui a peur des Post Colonial Studies en France?'. 19, Winter.

Najjar, Alexandre. 2007. 'Un intellectuel libanais s'élève contre le manifeste "Pour une littérature-monde en français": Expliquer l'eau par l'eau'. *Le Monde* 30 March.

Le Nouvel Observateur. 2009. 'Pourquoi ils se haïssent. De Houellebecq à Benamou: onze duels littéraires'. 2 January. <http://bibliobs.nouvelobs.com/20090122/10161/pourquoi-ils-se-haissent-2>. Consulted on 25 January 2009.

Otte, Jean-Pierre. 2005. *La Littérature prend le maquis*. Paris: Sens et Tonka.

Papaya, Pierre. 2007. 'MARYSE CONDÉ S'EN VA, WOULO BA SA KI DÉSIDÉ RÉTÉ!'. Le bloc-note de Pierre Papaya. 21 July. <http://www.montraykreyol.org/spip.php?article483>. Consulted on 20 February 2009.

'Pour une "littérature-monde" en français'. 2007. *Le Monde* 16 March.

Sahai, J. S. 2007. 'MARYSE CONDÉ: COGNÉE D'UN DÉTOUR, Ô PAYS NATAL!'. Montray Kréyol. 17 July. <http://www.montraykreyol.org/spip.php?article472>. Consulted on 25 February 2009.

Salhi, Kamal (ed.). 2003. *Francophone Post-colonial Cultures: Critical Essays*. Lanham, MD: Lexington Books.

Saminadayar-Perrin, Corinne (ed.). 2008. *Qu'est-ce qu'un événement littéraire au XIXᵉ siècle?* Saint-Étienne: Presses Universitaires de Saint-Étienne.

Sartre, Jean-Paul. 1948. 'Orphée noir'. In Léopold Sédar Senghor (ed.), *Anthologie de la nouvelle poésie nègre et malgache de langue française*. Paris: Presses Universitaires de France: pp. ix–xliv.

Schiffano, Jean-Noël. 2000. 'Postface'. Éditions Gallimard, collection 'Continents noirs'.

Smouts, Marie-Claude (ed.). 2007. *La Situation postcoloniale: Les postcolonial studies dans le débat français*. Paris: Les Presses de Sciences Po.

Todorov, Tzvetan. 2006. *La Littérature en péril*. Paris: Flammarion.

Toledo, Camille de. 2008. *Visiter le Flurkistan, ou les illusions perdues de la littérature-monde*. Paris: Presses Universitaires de France.

'Toward a "World-Literature" in French'. 2009. Trans. by Daniel Simon. *World Literature Today* (March–April): 54–56.

Yaeger, Patricia. 2007. 'Editor's Column: The End of Postcolonial Theory? A Roundtable with Sunil Agnani, Fernando Coronil, Gaurav Desai, Mamadou Diouf, Simon Gikandi, Susie Tharu, and Jennifer Wenzel'. *PMLA* 122: 633–51.

(Not) Razing the Walls:
Glissant, Trouillot and
the Post-Politics of World 'Literature'

Chris Bongie

Despite a great deal of cultural materialist work over the past several decades devoted to the insight that literature is, in Alan Sinfield's words, 'an institutional arrangement we have made to dignify some writing (at the expense of other)' (2004: 31), Francophone postcolonial studies, as I have argued on more than one occasion, remains invested in an idealist conception of the literary text as '"rising above" its conditions of production and reception' (Sinfield, 2004: 31). One might venture that there is no greater proof of this belated investment than the excessive amount of scholarly ink that has been spilled – and that, as this volume testifies, continues to be spilled – over the manifesto 'Pour une "littérature-monde" en français' since its publication by Michel Le Bris, Jean Rouaud *et consortes* in March 2007. What, we might well ask, is at stake in their (our) continuing investment in the salvific virtues of 'literature' – a word that might, at first glance, seem the least problematic component of a seductive buzz phrase like 'world literature (in French)'?[1] That is the question I want to address here, not by lingering over the actual manifesto and interrogating its purported deconstruction of the French/Francophone binary (authentic act of literary decolonization or yet another instance of Franco-phony rhetoric? ... readers will have little difficulty identifying where I stand on that score), but by

---

[1] As Christopher Prendergast remarked in the Introduction to his edited volume *Debating World Literature*, 'even in the field of literary studies, it is really only the first term in the expression "world literature" that has elicited serious interest' (2004, p. ix).

focusing on two Caribbean-born writers who contributed to the eponymous follow-up collection of essays published later that year by Gallimard (*Pour une littérature-monde*). In zeroing in on Édouard Glissant and, especially, the Haitian novelist Lyonel Trouillot, both co-signatories of the original manifesto, I aim to draw out the 'post-political' dimension of the manifesto's commitment to a 'retour aux puissances d'incandescence de la littérature' [return to the incandescent powers of literature] and of its insistence that this *retour* is part and parcel of the equally felicitous 'effondrement des grandes idéologies' [collapse of grand-scale ideologies] symbolized by the fall of the Berlin Wall ('Pour une "littérature-monde" en français', 2007).[2]

If post-politics is defined as 'a politics which claims to leave behind old ideological struggles and instead focus on expert management and administration' (Žižek, 2008c: 40), then a writer like Trouillot ably fits this bill in his dual capacity as purveyor of a (self-styled) non-ideological literary product and outspoken critic of the supposed Prophet-turned-Dictator Jean-Bertrand Aristide, about whom, he has authoritatively claimed, everything was anticipated by François Duvalier (Trouillot, 2004b; 'tout Aristide est dans François Duvalier'). From the post-political perspective of a Trouillot – who over the past decade has taken every possible opportunity to trumpet his status as someone who does 'not belong to any political party' and does 'not defend any particular political ideology', but who 'share[s] in the demands of the civil society for the respect of democratic norms' (Trouillot, 2004c) – inscribing one's name at the bottom of a literary manifesto alongside those of forty-three other 'great' writers would appear to be of a piece with signing on the dotted line as a member of the anti-Aristide *Collectif Non* in the months preceding the ouster of Haiti's democratically elected President in 2004, participating in 'pitifully blunt instruments of Haiti's tiny ruling class' such as the 'US-funded' Group of 184 (Hallward, 2007b: 102, 72), and then generously contributing his 'expert' services to the regime that was installed after the Franco-American-Canadian coup.

Trouillot's work for the Haitian Ministry of Culture (as *directeur de cabinet auprès de la Secrétaire d'État à la Culture*) in the months following upon the fall of Aristide – his willingness, in Peter Hallward's words, 'to participate in an interim administration that lacked the merest pretence of any democratic or constitutional legitimacy' (2009: 185) – helps clarify what is at stake in Trouillot's self-flattering insistence upon his lack of any formal adhesion to political parties and particular political ideologies. It is precisely this purported 'lack' that *defines* the post-political subject, both

---

[2] Unless otherwise indicated, all translations from French into English are by the author of this chapter.

in terms of legitimizing his managerial expertise *and* in terms of securing his identity as a creative writer, at a purifying distance from the sordid play of partisan politics. In an age when a rejection of any such politics seems like substantive proof that one is an 'enlightened and responsible person' of the sort who can, alone, expertly manage and administer a 'failed state' like Haiti,[3] the partisans of 'literature', authors and critics alike, assume a new authority that helps divert attention away from both the *'untrammeled* triumph of neo-liberal imperialism in Haiti' (Hallward, 2007b: 182) and, more broadly, 'the global tendency of new dams and walls that have been popping out everywhere since 11 September 2001, confronting us with the inner truth of "globalisation", the underlying lines of division which sustain it' (Žižek, 2008a). That *littérature-monde* does not simply divert attention away from, but may actually help perpetuate, the very lines of division that its 'incandescent powers' supposedly abolish is the guiding hypothesis of what follows.

The brunt of my comments will be concentrated on Trouillot here, but before turning the critical spotlight on him it will be helpful to make two preliminary moves, both of which draw attention to a central component of my argument, namely the binary thinking that is at the heart of the manifesto's efforts to re-attach 'literature' to the world. First, I will supply a few pertinent details regarding the original manifesto's fetishistic represen- tation of 'literature' under threat, which is more fully developed in Le Bris and Rouaud's contributions to their subsequent edited collection of essays. Second, I will briefly examine Glissant's contribution to that collection, which perhaps best exemplifies its post-political ethos: an interview entitled 'Solitaire et solidaire', where the author of *Poétique de la Relation* rehashes any number of the hyperbolic claims for the virtues of his chosen profession that have been a stock in trade of his work over the last two decades.

It is important to remember that the manifesto, along with the follow- up chapters that Rouaud and Le Bris contributed to their edited collection, is haunted by the potential dissolution of *French* literature and, indeed, of *literature itself.* A narrative of decline frames the entire project, not just of national and cultural decline (see Porra, 2008: 48), but one which is grounded in the belief that creative writers in the closing decades of the twentieth century were being treated as, and turned into, little more than nameless functionaries. This narrative is summed up in a passage from the book's

---

[3] Trouillot's anti-Aristide agenda is completely at one with Alex Dupuy's neo- paternalist and anti-populist insistence that, when it comes to Haitian politics, 'between the leader and the masses there must exist a structured organization controlled by enlightened and responsible people' (2007: 95).

opening chapter, 'Mort d'une certaine idée' (7–22), where Rouaud laments that the novelist, who had been a surveyor of space, an inventor of the imaginary, a discoverer of hidden worlds, had been reduced to a lowly managerial role (19; 'était ramené à un rôle de syndic'). For Rouaud, the 'syndicated' nature of the late-twentieth-century literary scene in France can be traced, most obviously, to the French language's sterilizing connection to the French nation: only the breaking of that language's pact with the nation, its ongoing liberation from the grasp of the *source-mère* and its embracing of, and by, the world can reverse this decline and jump-start 'une autre aventure poétique' [another poetic adventure] (21). However, more importantly for our purposes, that lamentable state of affairs can also be attributed to the subservient role to which 'literature' had been reduced by the (post/structuralist) critics who falsely claimed authority over it, those who Le Bris dismissively refers to in his chapter (23–53) as 'la foule des petits hommes gris, déconstructeurs, intertextualistes, structuralistes' (43).[4] This *foule* of pedantic formalists were both the purveyors and the advocates of *mauvaise littérature* (29), the badness of which stems from its failure to meet 'l'épreuve de l'autre, de l'ailleurs, du monde, qui, seule, peut empêcher la littérature de se scléroser en "littérature"' (29).[5] For Le Bris, (great) writers have for decades been suffering under the parochial sway of dictatorial critics who contaminated the literary field with their 'deadly discourse': these critics (writers themselves, to be sure, but doomed never to produce anything of value because of their perverse allegiance to the nefarious 'Sign-king') have exhibited the 'arrogance' of 'dwarves' in their attempts at channelling the unmasterable mastery of (great) writing and thereby 'assassinating literature' in the service of their delusive theories (26; 'Comment supporter ces nains plus longtemps, leurs discours mortifères, leur arrogance? C'était la littérature qu'ils assassinaient chaque jour … ').

This *doubling* of author-giants and critic-dwarves, exemplary of the binary thinking that dominates the manifesto, proves inseparable from an equally blunt opposition between good and bad universalisms. If Le Bris can so confidently contest the authority of the little grey men, that *foule ennemie*, it is because the 'littérature mondiale' of which he sings the praises is one and the same as 'la littérature *universelle*' (39; my italics). The very concept of (world) literature in French proves inseparable from claims of its universality – a *true* universality that is to be contrasted with any and all false mirror images such as that offered by *Francophonie*, which depends on an erroneous

---

  [4] 'the crowd of little grey men, deconstructors, intertextualists, structuralists'.
  [5] 'the challenge of the other, of the elsewhere, of the world, which alone can prevent literature from ossifying into "literature"'.

vision of France as 'dépositaire de l'universel' [repository of the universal] (45). Not surprisingly, for the editors of *Pour une littérature-monde*, the dwarfish critics against whom they rail work in the service of that same false universal, as Le Bris makes clear when, recalling the abject literary scene in France in the early 1990s, he labels the haughty schoolmaster's assistants (*pions*) who held sway back then as 'fonctionnaires autoproclamés de l'universel' [self-proclaimed civil servants of the universal] (25). It is this unholy state of affairs that (world) 'literature' is called upon to redress, and that redemptive mission, as we have seen, cannot be articulated without the positing of a starkly antagonistic relation (or, as it were, the building of an identitarian wall) between two types of writers, good and bad, and two types of universals, true and false.

It is this same Manichean opposition that pervades the work of late Glissant, whose euphoric detailing of the diverse incitements of the *Tout-monde* emphatically draws attention to itself as both the theoretical explanation and practical manifestation of worldly complexity, but ultimately boils down to nothing more (or less) than the repeated staging of a straightforward opposition between those capable – as he and Patrick Chamoiseau put it in *Quand les murs tombent* (published in English as *Raze the Walls*) – of being opened up 'par un imaginaire libéré, par une poétique clairvoyante du Tout-Monde' (2008: 14–15),[6] and those unenlightened souls whose imaginaries remain closed to 'mystery' and 'beauty', and whose lives are lived in the shadow of identitarian walls that 'ne protège[nt] plus, n'ouvre[nt] à rien sinon à l'involution des régressions, à l'asphyxie insidieuse de l'esprit, à la perte de soi' (11).[7] This is not the place to examine the contradictory logic that generates late Glissant's universalizing anti-universalism and his fulsome embrace of the *Tout-monde*.[8] What is important to register here is simply the insistence in Glissant's late work, including the interview in *Pour une littérature-monde* (77–86), upon the same binary vision that one finds in Le Bris and Rouaud, as when he distinguishes between mere *littéralité* and its more properly literary double, between 'poètes militants qui écrivent des poèmes comme on écrit des tracts ... des gens qui, littéralement, copient le monde' (84),[9] and true 'artists', who are the *only* people capable of seeing what's happening deep

---

[6] 'by a liberated imaginary, by a clairvoyant poetics of the *Tout-Monde*'.

[7] 'no longer protect, and open onto nothing except the involution of regressions, the insidious asphyxia of the spirit, of the loss of self'.

[8] For an extended analysis of late Glissant along these lines, see Bongie, 2008: 322–70.

[9] 'militant poets who write poems as if they were tracts ... people who, literally, copy the world'.

down, the *only* ones capable of making deep connections between poetry and politics.¹⁰ Such time-honoured appeals to 'the surface/depths model' have been a stock in trade for several centuries now when it comes to efforts at distinguishing 'literature' from the disreputable forms of textual production that so resemble it,¹¹ but they take on a renewed force in the here-and-now of the post-political moment: when Glissant privileges the clairvoyance of the poet and identifies it with a 'deeper' form of the political, to be distinguished from 'une activité politique au sens littéral du terme' [political activity in the literal sense of the term] (84), he is making a fundamentally post-political move, in which political action at the 'literal' level can always be written off as superficial or false (mere 'ideology'). True politics is elsewhere, and it is an elsewhere best accessed by those who have earned the name of 'poets': those who have left behind 'old ideological struggles' and are uniquely equipped to show the rest of the world the right way forward. To be sure, this managerial cadre is made up of poets not just in the literal sense, but of all those who have 'une conception du vrai rapport entre poétique et politique' [a conception of the true relation between poetics and politics] (84), and yet, predictably, the only examples provided in the interview are taken from among Glissant's fellow authors, such as Saint-John Perse (80), or Lezama Lima, whose 'absolutely subversive' novel *Paradiso* is, Glissant assures us, 'ce qui est arrivé de mieux à la révolution cubaine' [the best thing to come out of the Cuban Revolution] (86).

It is this same hyperbolic investment in literature that one finds in Trouillot's contribution to *Pour une littérature-monde*, which self-consciously gestures toward Glissant's archipelagic poetics of relation in its title, 'Langues, voyages et archipels'. For Glissant, 'becoming-archipelago' (*archipélisation*) is not a symptom of fracturing and weakness but, rather, something that allows for the spurning of ready-made ideas (Glissant and Chamoiseau, 2009: 38), and it is this anti-conventional vision of a fragmented but ever-approximating

---

¹⁰ 'Or, ce qu'il y a de fondamental dans l'art, c'est le moment où on abandonne le littéral, la thèse, etc., et où on essaie de voir ce qui se passe *au fond*, ce que le poète est le *seul* à voir' [The fundamental aspect of art is that moment when the literal, the argument, etc. get left behind, and one tries to see what's happening *deep down*, which is something the poet *alone* sees]; 'le poète possède une clairvoyance car il est le *seul* à relier *en profondeur* poésie et politique' [the poet has a clairvoyance that comes from being the *only one* who makes *deep* connections between poetry and politics] (84; my italics).
¹¹ 'In our culture, this model is a powerful means through which one side of an opposition can be credited with the authority of profundity, and the other dismissed as superficial' (Sinfield, 2004: 168).

reality that Trouillot sees world literature (in French) as promoting. An international readership open to this 'multiple', non-hierarchical reality will be able, he writes at the conclusion of his essay, to migrate from one French-language text to another, 'tisser les liens qui font les archipels, avoir le monde à portée de lecture, en ses différences, en ses utopies, comprendre, connaître, rêver, inventer' (Trouillot, 2007: 204).[12] To widen a reader's horizons and make possible this relational thinking is the urgent task – an urgency, he specifies, *d'ordre politique* – that can be accomplished by an *écriture-monde en français*, which will enrich French-language readers with a sense both of local concerns and of 'ce qui, dans l'écriture, dépasse la condition immédiate, rapproche' [what, in writing, transcends immediate conditions, draws together] (203).

As is clear from the previous quotation, Trouillot's privileged term is *écriture*, which functions as a sort of universal that binds together the diverse parts of the literary archipelago through its ability to go beyond 'immediate conditions'. Again, a version of the binary opposition – that essential move in the rhetoric through which the ideological investments in, and of, 'literature' are legitimized – is predictably central to his account: here, it does not take the form of the straightforward good/bad oppositions of Rouaud and Le Bris, but of a seemingly less polemical distinction between this all-embracing *écriture* and the (national, regional, etc.) specificities of what he calls *littérature*. Trouillot's essay begins by establishing the difference between the two: the former (which includes oral production) is a timeless product of 'the human' ('l'écriture relève de l'humain, comme un mal de l'espèce'), whereas the latter is ever-changing and belongs only to the particular societies in which it is produced (Trouillot, 2007: 197). *Écriture*, in the singular, is a humanly necessary activity that comes from within ('une activité nécessaire à la personne, de l'intérieur de la personne') and that has no *langue fétiche*, whereas literatures, in the plural, do (197). Haitian writers were for a long time guilty of fetishizing the French language, and hence their literature fell well short of *écriture*, being nothing more than a 'schizophrenic' pursuit of a French model that had falsely assumed the mantle of universality (197). In order for Haitian literature to be infused with the incandescent powers of *écriture*, it was necessary to 'porter quelques bons coups à la notion d'universel' [give the idea of universals a good pummelling] (198). Mercifully, those 'quelques bons coups' have had the desired effect: the French language today is neither wrong nor right; it is henceforth a language like any other

---

12 'create the links through which archipelagos are formed, keep the world within reach of reading, in its differences, in its utopias, understand, know, dream, invent'.

(200), no more and no less capable of performing the 'subversive' task of *écriture*, which involves transcribing and interpellating 'multiple realities', and promoting a 'plurality of genres and forms' (202). Thus runs Trouillot's familiar, indeed supremely banal, historical scenario: the (anti-)universal power of *écriture* wins out against the unhealthy, indeed pathological ('schizophrenic', 'fetishistic') preoccupations of what belongs merely to 'society'; what comes from the 'inside' supplants external forces that threaten, in their conventionality, a form of 'dictatorship'.[13] From within the confines of the ideology of literature, such binary distinctions are only 'natural', and it is precisely within the shadow of these ideological partitions that any sympathetic engagement with the tenets of *Pour une littérature-monde* must take place: to embrace the transnational possibilities of *littérature-monde* is inevitably to invest in something like what Trouillot calls *écriture*, a quasi-universalizing force that underlies the seeming insistence on diversity and pluralism, and that functions as a privileged means, in Trouillot's words, '[d]'appréhender l'humain' [of apprehending the human] (202). It is a good investment, at least for the literary critic.

Trouillot's binary oppositions are hardly contentious in the way that Le Bris and Rouaud's are: in *their* interventions, friends and enemies are clearly identified. By contrast, as with Glissant's beatific vision of a relational *Tout-monde*, the emphasis in Trouillot's archipelagic meditations is on the positive or on the hierarchical imbalances of the past, when particular languages were fetishized and false conceptions of the universal reigned. And yet, as the coded reference to 'dictatorial' conventions attests, we are really not all that far away in this irenic effusion from the anti-Aristide publicist who served as an expert advisor to the post-coup government. The literary author's partisan double does give a brief glimpse of himself in the article's one explicit allusion to the current state of his native Haiti, where he speaks in general but positive terms of 'un intellectuel haïtien fatigué d'une société sans sphère commune de citoyenneté parce que les relations de dépendance (économique, culturelle) liant une élite corrompue au pouvoir du centre ont empêché un peuple de naître à lui-même' (200).[14] This one specific comment

---

[13] 'Peut-on parler d'une littérature-monde en français si elle est soumise à la dictature d'un genre, d'un marché, d'un contenu?' [Can one speak of a world literature in French if it is subject to the dictatorship of a genre, a market, a subject matter?] (202).

[14] 'a Haitian intellectual tired of a society that lacks any common sphere of citizenship because the relations of (economic, cultural) dependency binding a corrupt elite to the power-centre have prevented a people from coming into its own'.

intrudes upon the post-political calm of the chapter, disrupting its elegant prose and high-sounding arguments, supplying a visible reminder (not that any is needed) of its 'immediate conditions' of production.

In making this clear-cut distinction between the exasperated Haitian intellectual on the margins (a figure through whom Trouillot coyly points to himself) and a corrupt elite in cahoots with the *pouvoir du centre*, Trouillot conveniently denies any and all relation of himself to the scapegoated double. This gesture of disavowal – this refusal to take into account what I have dubbed 'scribal politics': that is to say the *relation to and with power* in which 'literature' as a cultural institution has been entangled since its inception – is common to literary studies as a whole, but it is one to which postcolonial literary studies, Francophone or otherwise, has been especially committed (it being a field where the materialist critique associated with cultural studies has, strangely, made few inroads; see Bongie, 2008: 280–321). Our field is committed to fêting cultural producers for their creativity and genius, rather than attending to the ways in which they pursue 'immediate' agendas – agendas that in the case of a 'conservative G184 intellectual' like Trouillot may well be, and always have been, in contradiction with the pursuit of 'principles of freedom, equality, solidarity, justice' (Hallward, 2007b: 182, p. xxxiv). We are trained to lionize Haitian writers and film-makers such as Lyonel Trouillot or Raoul Peck,[15] to represent them as 'speaking up for those who are essentially speechless in their own society, those who rage at their suffering, those whose violence has coursed through Haiti's history like the lifeblood of the body politic, those who are, in a way, still trapped in the anger that is their very birthright' (Coverdale, 2003: p. xxiii). Self-styled opponents

---

15 In Peck's glowing preface to journalist Michael Deibert's stridently anti-Lavalas *Notes from the Last Testament* (2005: pp. xv–xix), he identifies Aristide with neo-Duvalierism and promotes the eminently falsifiable idea that in late 2003 and early 2004 'a vast popular opposition to [Aristide's] rule finally took to the streets he has been monopolizing through years of terror' (p. xviii). Like Trouillot, Peck repeatedly identifies the 'democratic' opposition with one of the more appealing, and empty, catch-phrases of our contemporary moment, 'civil society', which is, in Peck's words, constituted by 'a wide range of valid and critical opinions that are neither submissive to any local or foreign powers, nor aligned with the wealthy, the former military, the Lavalas extremists or the infrastructure of corruption' (p. xix). 'Civil society' becomes a collective equivalent to the individual 'artist–intellectual', both free of any taint whatsoever. As George Yúdice has suggested, the increasingly popular legitimation narrative of 'civil society' perhaps ought to be looked upon not 'as the Habermasian space of free debate and opinion shaping, but as a handmaiden to neoliberal policies that reduce and privatize the social and the cultural' (2003: 7).

of 'dictators and prophets' they might well be, but in the case of these particular anti-Aristide members of the Haitian elite that in no way precludes their also being, in Peter Hallward's terms, 'conservative intellectuals' whose seemingly benign appeals to 'civil society' tacitly promote the interests of the neo-liberalizing/colonizing nation states that overthrew Aristide as well as those of the unelectable politicians and industrialists in Haiti who supported the coup and with whom the 'Haitian intellectual', à la Trouillot, is so closely – if uneasily, to be sure – aligned.

From the perspective of the author and of the literary critics who trade in that author, tracing Trouillot's essay back to these 'immediate conditions' must, of course, seem like a naively deterministic move, of the sort that every materialist approach to 'literature' is accused of making by those who, overtly or covertly, subscribe to an 'idealist aesthetics' intent on 'discern[ing] an essential quality of literariness in admired texts' (Sinfield, 2004: 32). Hallward's critique of 'francophiliac intellectuals and artists' such as Laënnec Hurbon and Raoul Peck (2007b: 114), who have authoritatively denounced 'the Aristidean apparatus of repression' and deprecated those (mostly black) US politicians who spoke out against the 2004 coup as at best dupes and at worst people who have benefited from the 'dividends' ('gifts, payments, jobs, and lucrative arrangements') that are a 'long accepted practice in politics' (Peck, 2005: p. xvi), is not one that they are likely to take sitting down, as can be seen, for instance, from Trouillot's recent, vitriolic response in the pages of *Small Axe* to Hallward's sympathetic account of the Lavalas movement in *Damming the Flood: Haiti, Aristide, and the Politics of Containment*. In that article, the 'non-partisan' front of the pluralizing writer of 'world literature (in French)' falls away, revealing a wildly partisan individual ready to engage in self-flattering arguments that depend upon the starkest of binary oppositions: between, on the one hand, the Duvalier-emulating Aristide and the wicked or misguided people like Hallward who lend their support to the 'Empire's slave' (2009: 130), and on the other, 'the majority of Haitians' who, regardless of class divisions, were all supposedly 'agreed on one thing' in their opposition to Aristide, namely 'the political expression of social conflicts within the context of formal democracy' (131).

While the polemical dynamics of Trouillot's attack on the 'intellectual' Hallward, and of Hallward's equally polemical response to that attack, are supremely relevant to the argument about the post-politics of 'literature' that I am developing here,[16] my goal in the remainder of this chapter will be to

---

[16] A more extended version of this article concludes with a detailed account of the Trouillot–Hallward debate, part of which can be found in the inaugural issue of the *Bulletin of Francophone Postcolonial Studies*.

provide a more fleshed-out account of the idealist framework within which 'great' writers like Trouillot are 'naturally' read – and within which, I am claiming more broadly, the otherwise nugatory project of a 'world literature (in French)' alone makes sense. I will do so by providing a specific example of the unconsidered deference that characterizes the field's approach to cultural producers such as Trouillot, outlining the way that a recent article in *Small Axe* devoted to the latter's 2004 novella *Bicentenaire* seeks authority for its chosen subject (and legitimizes its own investment in that subject) by completely occluding the politics *in* and *of* that novella and insisting upon its 'universal' status as 'literature' – a universality and literariness that are said to be evidenced by the (literary and cultural) 'complexity' of the author's vision.

The article in question is entitled 'Interdependence and Intertextuality in Lyonel Trouillot's *Bicentenaire*' (Munro, 2008), and as its title suggests it is intent on showing: (i) that Trouillot's novel 'invokes tropes and situations that recall, often indirectly, previous literary works' (49) and (ii) that these tropes and references support the novel's thematic emphasis on 'the underlying interdependence between different social classes' (46). The critic in question, Martin Munro, had already dealt briefly with Trouillot's novella and its 'twisting, confusing, and contradictory morality' (2007: 98) in a book-length account of post-Second World War Haitian literature – an account that, perhaps revealingly, plays its contemporary political cards very close to the vest, with but two, extremely in passing, references to Aristide.[17] In that earlier intervention, the critic's main point had been to draw allegorical connections between the two brothers in the novella, Lucien and Little Joe, and the two leaders of the Haitian Revolution, Toussaint Louverture and Jean-Jacques Dessalines. The poor university student Lucien, who takes to the streets in a march on the National Palace in Port-au-Prince, and is shot dead at the end of the novel, is doubled by his drug-addled, gun-toting Dessalines-like brother, whose gang is paid to support the police in their crackdown on the demonstrators. While retaining an interest in that allegory, as part of a more

---

[17] These two references certainly do anticipate the implicitly anti-Aristide agenda of the subsequent article: for instance, we hear tell, in a discussion of 'the autocratic rule that has shaped the nation', of 'the messianic rulers that have returned to power there, from Dessalines to Aristide in an unbroken cycle' (Munro, 2007: 22). Further along in the book, we are informed that 'the successive waves of emigration, the rise of Duvalierism, and the subsequent failures of Jean-Bertrand Aristide and his party, Fanmi Lavalas' are the most obvious factors that have disrupted and rendered untenable 'the belief in a fully representable and recoverable Haitian people' (259).

ambitious exploration of the workings of intertextuality in *Bicentenaire*, the article places its main emphasis on detailing, and valorizing, the ways in which Trouillot maturely asserts the 'fundamental interdependence' of all the characters. In line with an archipelagic poetics of relation, Trouillot's stressing of 'the underlying interdependence between different social classes and between individual Haitians', our critic insists, 'makes a strong statement on the impossibility of living discrete, insulated existences' (2008: 52).

What soon becomes clear to anyone with a modicum of knowledge of the text, and of contemporary Haitian history, is that Munro is able to ground his approving emphasis on archipelagic 'interdependence' in the novel only through an extremely distorted presentation/occlusion of its historical framework. Here is all that one learns of this framework from the article in question: 'Although all of the events in the novel take place on one morning in December 2003, in many ways Trouillot's work encapsulates two hundred years of Haitian history, and in particular the cycles of hatred and revenge that seem to have no time, and to be ever-present' (45). What we have here is an obvious diversion away from what the novel is actually representing, namely the student protests that month against Aristide's government, part of a wave of anti-government protests that took place in the months leading up to the coup, and which were in turn repeatedly 'dwarfed' by pro-government rallies.[18] One does not have to hold to Peter Hallward's account of these events – one does not have to argue that if 'the student protests were intended to expose a government intent on the suppression of dissent, what they actually indicated was a tolerance verging on complacency', and to point to the 'remarkably low' levels of violence under the circumstances (2007b: 198) – in order to see through the move our literary critic is here making, one that echoes his earlier claim that the characters are to be read 'as timeless manifestations of an unending, recurring history' (Munro, 2007: 101). A mere polemicist, the author of a *roman à thèse*, might write about something as historically precise as the student protests, but a novelist worthy of his salt, and of academic study, does much more (indeed, cannot even be said to be doing what he's most obviously doing): rather, he 'encapsulates' two hundred years of history, meditates upon time-less 'cycles' of hatred and revenge, is attuned to the 'ever-present'. And, of course, the literary critic is

---

[18] 'Pro-government rallies continued to dwarf anti-government protest – no G184 or FEUH [Federation of Students at the University of Haiti] rally came close to attracting the tens of thousands of people who turned out in support of Aristide on 26 December, let alone the estimated 100,000 or so people present at what was probably the largest rally of Aristide's entire presidency, on 7 February 2004' (Hallward, 2007b: 199).

doing no more here than replicating the author's own diversionary tactics, for Trouillot makes the same de-historicizing moves in his novel, where he plays down the local significance of the demonstrations, while not being quite as adept as the literary critic at removing all traces of the partisan stakes generating his particular choice of subject matter. Trouillot, after all, cannot resist providing us with a little more context than the literary critic: be it in the coy preface where he chastens certain readers who might wish to 'établir un lien entre ce récit et les événements politiques qui marquèrent le bicentenaire de l'indépendance de la république d'Haïti' (2004a: 9),[19] an erroneous reading because, as he grandiloquently puts it, 'tout ici ne renvoie qu'à l'incommunicable, au silence que cachent le bruit et la fureur' (9);[20] or in various passages in the novel, all ignored by our literary critic, in which an anti-Aristide agenda is insinuated, as when we are told that Lucien has a premonition that he will be 'massacred', because he knows from his brother 'que la police a reçu l'ordre de donner la charge et que les bandes de voyous appelées en soutien ont déjà touché une avance sur salaire' (34; see also 84, where the same convenient passive voice construction is used).[21]

The literary critic's transubstantiation of a specific historical event into a manifestation of the 'ever-present' is not the matter for a simple corrective footnote, however, because the entire thematic interpretation of the novel, in its effusive emphasis on 'interdependence', hinges upon valorizing the very event that is also being occluded: for our critic, the march in which Lucien participates is the primary symbol of this much valued 'interdependence'. We are told that this march 'breaks down the social barriers' that formerly separated the marchers, 'leaving behind the deeper truth of their essential interconnectedness' (48), without ever being told why the march is happening, and who is paying thuggish crack-heads to break it up, superficial details that one must assume bear no relation to 'deeper' and 'essential' truths. In buying into this symbol of interconnectedness, which sounds so pleasant in the abstract, our literary critic avoids any confrontation with the obvious real-world translations of that consensual emphasis, to which Trouillot himself gave crystal-clear articulation in the pages of the *New York Times* (2004c), only days before the coup: 'For the first time, I am seeing Haitians of all origins united in a common goal. With the exception of Carnival, demonstrations

---

[19] 'to establish a link between this story and the political events that marked the bicentenary of the independence of the republic of Haiti'.

[20] 'everything here refers only to the incommunicable, to the silence hidden by the sound and the fury'.

[21] 'that the police have received the order to attack and that the bands of hoodlums enlisted in support have already been paid off in advance'.

against Mr Aristide have been the only public events joining all ethnicities and all social groups. This constitutes enormous progress in light of the discrimination that has tarnished our past'. The march in *Bicentenaire* against nefarious if nebulous 'policing' forces provides a literary mirror of this carnivalesque real-life joining together of 'all' ethnicities and social groups in the common struggle against the dictatorial rule of Aristide. It's a good symbol, at least for members of the Haitian elite and their publicists, who are understandably invested in the idea of a broad-based coalition as the only legitimate form of democratic expression, even if it is made up of a small number of people and its opponents are legion (and even if the very idea of this coalition depends upon *naturalizing* divisions between 'social groups' in order to narrate their coming together, and resorting to characterological compromise-formations in order to create a central protagonist who can assume the burden of being both 'poor' and 'literate').[22]

In his critical reading of Alex Dupuy's *The Prophet and Power*, Peter Hallward has ably demonstrated the way that this 'consensual' rhetoric works: commenting on Dupuy's disapproval of Aristide's 'failure' to rely more on the Haitian bourgeoisie in his first years in office, his 'failure' to form 'a broad coalition government that included representatives' from among his 'opponents in the National Assembly' (Dupuy, 2007: 119), Hallward points out that sceptics may wonder 'whether his repeated preference for a "broad-based" as opposed to a "mass-based" government is altogether compatible with his apparent enthusiasm for democracy', and that it is hard to grasp 'how a decision to pursue policies emphatically endorsed by the great majority of the population and authorised by several repeated and overwhelming election victories is best interpreted as a rejection of "consensus"' (2007a). It is hardly surprising that this 'consensual' position, which is at the very heart of the post-political *dépassement* of 'old ideological struggles', should be the structuring device (through symbolic and narratological means) at the heart of a novel written by someone who sees himself as giving voice to the 'true' wishes of the Haitian people; what is more surprising, perhaps, given many decades of materialist critique devoted to understanding the ideological

---

[22] Whereas Trouillot's representation of the thuggish Little Joe straightforwardly relies upon disparaging representations of Aristide's *chimères*, in order to create an affective investment in Lucien as the focalizer through whom the anti-Aristide march is experienced by the reader, when it comes to Lucien Trouillot resorts to the compromise-formation of the 'poor student' in order to match material impoverishment with bourgeois insight, conflating the elite intellectual and the abject 'part-of-no-part' as a way of both representing and avoiding the realities of social exclusion in contemporary Haiti.

underpinnings of the literary text, is that the Francophone postcolonial critic should forego any and all investigation of what might be at stake in his chosen author's seemingly benign insistence on the virtues of 'interdependence'.

In lieu of such contextualizing work we are instead treated to a string of grand claims that symptomatically reveal the ideological assumptions (and self-identifications) at work in the production of Trouillot's novella and its critical reception within the field of postcolonial literary studies. If 'interdependence' is a virtue, and the author who promotes it is thus virtuous, that is because both can be characterized as 'complex', a favourite word in our critic's vocabulary. Trouillot's novel, we are told, 'is pushing toward a more *complex* understanding of personal and collective identity and destiny in Haiti, and how it thereby offers a potential way out of the repetitive, circular history that revenge engenders' (Munro, 2008: 43; my italics). This 'complex' understanding requires the rejection of all 'us versus them' distinctions (except, of course, the distinction between those who have arrived at a 'complex understanding' of the need for broad-based consensus and those who have not), and the consequent rejection of anyone 'simple' enough to lend credence to binary oppositions between, say, 'the great mass of the Haitian people on one side, and a small elite who remain identified with today's colonizers on the other' (Aristide, 2008: p. xix). Whatever their merits, earlier Haitian novels, we are informed, remained shaped by 'dualistic models of revenge and hatred' (Munro, 2008: 43), whereas Trouillot 'sets up a *complex*, multi-dimensional system of interdependent grudges, actions, and characters' (43; my italics). Timothy Brennan has ably exposed 'the general assumption that the lucubrations of complexity are inherently more accurate than binary confrontation in determining their object' (1997: 85); more to the point in relation to Le Bris and Rouaud's claims about 'world literature (in French)' is that it is a very short step from complexity of vision to *universality* of vision, and the re-assertion of seemingly outdated claims about the salvific powers of 'literature' that are gaining a new resonance in 'our "post-political" epoch of the culturalization of the political' (Žižek, 2008b: 349). Trouillot, our critic feels compelled to declare, is not only 'one of the most incisive and uncompromising of all contemporary Caribbean writers', but he has, as fellow novelist Madison Smartt Bell maintains, 'a true "claim to universal greatness"' (Munro, 2008: 52).

This truth-claim might be grounded in some 'universal' insight, but our critic is also obscurely aware that such claims cannot be staked by just anyone: he thus goes on to clarify that Trouillot's insights are due to the fact that he 'is at once deeply immersed in the conflicts and traumas of contemporary Haitian existence, while also sufficiently distanced from that reality to be able to evaluate it and offer tentative solutions to longstanding social issues' (52) – solutions that must be portrayed as free of the taint of ideology.[23] The description of the 'complex' subject-position of the 'universally great' author, his capacity for simultaneous immersion and distance, is as vague and evasive as the critic's account of the novella's historical context, but it can be readily translated into more sociologically revealing terms. What is being described here, after all, if not one of those 'enlightened and responsible people' whom Alex Dupuy insists must remain in control of a 'structured organization' capable of mediating between the leader and the Haitian masses (see n. 3)? What is being described here, in other words, if not the very figure of the *scribe*, the cultural producer who represents, for better and worse, the interests of the leader (or the interests of some other partisan force intent upon displacing that leader)? That which is disavowed by Trouillot and the critic intent on consecrating him is the scribal component of the former's work: within their framework of understanding, there can be no consideration of the extent to which cultural production is entangled in, dare I say it, a complex relation with power, rather than simply at a purifying distance from it.[24] Trouillot, of course, is someone who has, of late,[25] left enough traces of his partisan activity *at* the side, rather than *to* the side, of men of state such as Monsieur Gérard Latortue that it has not been hard,

---

[23] 'In Trouillot's novel, ideas, morality, and meaning are never clear, and there is no absolute truth, only a swirling, conflicting series of half-truths, lies, and broken ideologies' (51). What the literary critic insists upon here, in rigorously post-political fashion, is the essentially broken nature of 'ideologies'; this insistence becomes the *absolute* truth capable of grounding a relativizing poetics, and (post-)politics, of 'interdependence'.

[24] For an extensive account of 'the disavowed relation between "mercenary scribes" and their uncanny doubles – the intellectual, the man of letters, and so on', see Bongie, 2008.

[25] From a chronological perspective, it might well be argued that Trouillot's work this decade marks a partial break with earlier practice, where he was better able to maintain the fiction of writerly autonomy. In an article from 2004, commenting on his work from the 1990s, one critic approvingly notes that Trouillot 'claims the right to personal choices and non-involvement in politics' and that 'again and again, he indirectly advocates the writer's right to stay clear of political involvement' (N'Zengou-Tayo, 2004: 339, 340). This apparent de-linkage of politics and literature can, the critic argues, be seen as positive: 'in a country in which literature has sometimes been the ladder to political position, Trouillot's work could be considered a promising new trend in spite of its dark tone' (339). Trouillot's work (both literary and political) over the course of this decade, it might be ventured, openly breaks with that promise and reveals the 'idealist' assumptions upon which it is based.

for heuristic purposes, to demonstrate through a reading of one exemplary article devoted to the 'universal greatness' of this *directeur de cabinet* what might be far harder to draw to the surface in a vast array of other fawning literary-critical interventions devoted to Francophone postcolonial writers that are dependent upon the same acts of disavowal.

The point here is not, of course, to question whether Trouillot should or should not be listed among those 'enjoying unprecedented international exposure in what is surely a golden age of Haitian writing' (Munro, 2007: 206), and to deny him his rightful place alongside the likes of Laferrière, Victor, Dalembert, Des Rosiers, Péan, Frankétienne or Evelyne Trouillot. Such is the evaluative work that is proper to literary critics, and that makes perfectly good sense within the discursive limits of their field of study. Nor, for that matter, does an awareness of the scribal dimension of 'literature' foreclose upon the possibility that there might remain some 'utopian' dimension that escapes, or perhaps even emerges from, an emphasis on the ideological conditioning and institutional status of all such texts. The 'political turn' of postcolonial studies over the course of the past decade,[26] and its consequent scepticism towards the sort of 'idealist' arguments we have been examining here, is inevitably being matched by an 'aesthetic turn', which insists upon the radical potential of the literary project. This insistence can take, for instance, the form of a Frankfurt School-ish insistence that the literary project, in its 'excessive' relation 'to the factual record', and notwithstanding its potential for 'political evasion, even ideological capitulation', 'is also the freedom essential to creating possibilities that evade the conditions of the given world' (Bahri, 2003: 80); or it can take the form of Deleuzian expostulations that 'writing is expressive of a desire that is irreducible to the dimension of representation, and that exceeds the categories of a macropolitics' (Vallury, 2008: 183). It is, there can be no doubt, the disciplinary work of the literary critic both to engage in qualitative evaluations, and to seek for such redemptive excesses.

But when the literary critic feels entitled to engage in positive effusions about the role of 'interdependence' in a work like *Bicentenaire*, and to ground his thematic analysis in an astute analysis of the ways in which a formal technique such as free indirect discourse supports this theme,[27] without ever once pausing to consider the ideological implications of this thematic emphasis or the formal techniques through which that emphasis

---

[26] On this 'political turn', see Bongie, 2008, especially 3–4 and 15–24.

[27] The use of free indirect discourse 'permits the narrator to enter into each character's subjective experience and to further bind them, their experiences, and their destinies together' (Munro, 2008: 49).

is pursued, then one must indeed question the disciplinary limits within which, alone, the speculative fiction of literary value can be thought to hold true. Our exemplary literary critic's unwillingness to move beyond Trouillot's own flattering self-presentation as a 'non-partisan' author, a man possessed of a self-evident 'respect of democratic norms', is not idiosyncratic but exemplary of a generalized tendency in (Francophone) postcolonial studies to avoid any full reckoning with the scribal dimension of 'literature', its institutional status and the strategies of legitimization through which it perpetuates itself. And, of course, to return to our point of departure, it is this very act of avoidance that generates the production, and in large part reception, of a collection of essays like *Pour une littérature-monde*, with its hyper-valorization of 'authentic' writers and consequent scapegoating of 'dwarfish' functionary-critics, who serve as the symptomatic figuration of that to which these consecrated writers cannot confess. Their 'partisan' doubles are made to carry the burden of scribal identity, confirming by way of antithesis the pleasingly 'non-partisan' images that these writers have of themselves (the free-floating adventurer in Le Bris and Rouaud, the clairvoyant young poet in Glissant, the archipelagic intellectual in Trouillot, etc.). It is this supposedly autonomous status, a *singular* openness to multiple realities rather than a *specific* relation to a certain reality,[28] which allows these writers to (claim) access to the 'universality' of literature and which, in a paradoxical turn, endows them with the 'heteronomous power' (in Bourdieu's phrase) to comment authoritatively on the inadequacies of 'mere' politicians and scribes, as if a clown's ability at juggling somehow qualified him to construct a bridge, or at least to go about stating what was a well-built or poorly-built bridge.

The simile is, of course, a poorly chosen one. 'Great' writers are not clowns, although it may occasionally behove the literary critic to portray their verbal juggling as such, in order to establish an essential distinction between them and the humourless crowd of 'little grey functionaries' who 'in our allegedly "post-ideological" era' (Žižek, 2008b: 296) have come to be seen as at best otiose and at worst dangerous in their commitment to the sort of engineering projects without which real bridges cannot be built. Such distinctions notwithstanding, my suggestion in this chapter, scandalous and disloyal as it must surely appear to many of those who work alongside me in the bounteous field of (world) 'literature' (in any language), is that a 'universally great' writer like Trouillot cannot be simply and conveniently detached from such projects, or from the administrative (as opposed to

---

[28] On the opposition between the singular and the specific, see Hallward, 2001, *passim*.

purely poetic) imaginary that generates them. There is indeed a good deal of real-world construction work going on in an 'incandescent' novella like *Bicentenaire*, as there is in the exuberant puffery of a post-political manifesto like 'Pour une "littérature-monde" en français', only it does not always involve the sort of work one might 'naturally' expect from those who authored them, given their vocal insistence upon the necessity of razing walls and busting dams, and the unremitting emphasis on their own expertise in managing such matters. It may well be the case, as their admiring publicists maintain, that the adventurous practitioners of world 'literature' have a privileged role to play when it comes to offering 'tentative solutions' to the challenge of gaining a 'deeper' understanding of how best to navigate our way through the global(izing) archipelago; what I have argued here, by way of querying (our investment in) this particular sort of understanding, is that the assuming of this role, and its privileges, depends as much on a proven ability to construct new dams and walls as it does on a loudly proclaimed willingness to tear down old ones.

Works Cited

Aristide, Jean-Bertrand. 2008. 'Introduction'. In Nick Nesbitt (ed.), *Toussaint L'Ouverture: The Haitian Revolution*. London: Verso: pp. vii–xxxiii.

Bahri, Deepika. 2003. *Native Intelligence: Aesthetics, Politics, and Postcolonial Literature*. Minneapolis: University of Minnesota Press.

Bongie, Chris. 2008. *Friends and Enemies: The Scribal Politics of Post/Colonial Literature*. Liverpool: Liverpool University Press.

Brennan, Timothy. 1997. *At Home in the World: Cosmopolitanism Now*. Cambridge, MA: Harvard University Press.

Coverdale, Linda. 2003. 'Translator's Introduction'. In Lyonel Trouillot, *Street of Lost Footsteps*. Trans. by L. Coverdale. Lincoln: University of Nebraska Press: pp. xi–xxiii.

Dupuy, Alex. 2007. *The Prophet and Power: Jean-Bertrand Aristide, the International Community and Haiti*. New York: Rowman & Littlefield.

Glissant, Édouard. 2007. '"Solitaire et solidaire": Entretien avec Édouard Glissant'. In Michel Le Bris and Jean Rouaud (eds), *Pour une littérature-monde*. Paris: Gallimard: 77–86.

Glissant, Édouard, and Patrick Chamoiseau. 2008. *Quand les murs tombent: l'identité nationale hors-la-loi?* Paris: Galaade Éditions.

—. 2009. *L'Intraitable beauté du monde: Adresse à Barack Obama*. Paris: Galaade Éditions.

Hallward, Peter. 2001. *Absolutely Postcolonial: Writing Between the Singular and the Specific*. Manchester: Manchester University Press.

—. 2007a. 'Aristide and the Violence of Democracy'. ZNet. 9 September. <http:// www.zmag.org/znet/viewArticle/14525>. Consulted on 1 June 2010.

—. 2007b. *Damming the Flood: Haiti, Aristide, and the Politics of Containment.* London: Verso.

—. 2009. 'Lyonel Trouillot, or The Fictions of Formal Democracy'. *Small Axe* 13.3 (30): 174–85.

Le Bris, Michel. 2007. 'Pour une littérature-monde en français'. In Michel Le Bris and Jean Rouaud (eds), *Pour une littérature-monde.* Paris: Gallimard: 23–53.

Le Bris, Michel, and Jean Rouaud (eds). 2007. *Pour une littérature-monde.* Paris: Gallimard.

Munro, Martin. 2007. *Exile and Post-1946 Haitian Literature: Alexis, Depestre, Ollivier, Laferrière, Danticat.* Liverpool: Liverpool University Press.

—. 2008. 'Interdependence and Intertextuality in Lyonel Trouillot's *Bicentenaire*'. *Small Axe* 12.3 (27): 42–52.

N'Zengou-Tayo, Marie-José. 2004. 'The End of the Committed Intellectual: The Case of Lyonel Trouillot'. In Marie-Agnès Sourieau and Kathleen M. Balutansky (eds), *Écrire en pays assiégé – Haïti – Writing Under Siege.* Amsterdam: Rodopi: 323–43.

Peck, Raoul. 2005. 'Introduction'. In Michael Deibert, *Notes from the Last Testament: The Struggle for Haiti.* New York: Seven Stories Press: pp. xv–xix.

Porra, Véronique. 2008. '"Pour une littérature-monde en français": Les limites d'un discours utopique'. *Intercâmbio* (2nd Ser.) 1: 33–54.

'Pour une "littérature-monde" en français'. 2007. *Le Monde* 16 March.

Prendergast, Christopher. 2004. 'Introduction'. In Christopher Prendergast (ed.), *Debating World Literature.* London: Verso: pp. vii–xiii.

Rouaud, Jean. 2007. 'Mort d'une certaine idée'. In Michel Le Bris and Jean Rouaud (eds), *Pour une littérature-monde.* Paris: Gallimard: 7–22.

Sinfield, Alan. 2004. *Literature, Politics and Culture in Postwar Britain.* 3rd Edn. London: Continuum.

Trouillot, Lyonel. 2004a. *Bicentenaire.* Arles: Actes Sud.

—. 2004b. 'Ce sont bien les Haïtiens qui ont renversé Aristide'. *L'Humanité* 9 March. <http://www.humanite.fr/2004-03-09_International_-Lyonel-Trouillot-Ce-sont-bien-les-Haitiens-qui-ont>. Consulted on 1 June 2010.

—. 2004c. 'In Haiti, All the Bridges Are Burned'. *New York Times* 26 February. <http://www.nytimes.com/2004/02/26/opinion/in-haiti-all-the-bridges-are-burned.html>. Consulted on 1 June 2010.

—. 2007. 'Langues, voyages et archipels'. In Michel Le Bris and Jean Rouaud (eds), *Pour une littérature-monde.* Paris: Gallimard: 197–204.

—. 2009. 'Hallward, or The Hidden Face of Racism'. Trans. by Nadève Ménard. *Small Axe* 13.3 (30): 128–36.

Vallury, Rajeshwari S. 2008. *'Surfacing' the Politics of Desire: Literature, Feminism, and Myth*. Toronto: University of Toronto Press.

Yúdice, George. 2003. *The Expediency of Culture: Uses of Culture in the Global Era*. Durham, NC: Duke University Press.

Žižek, Slavoj. 2008a. 'Democracy versus the People'. *New Statesman*. 14 August. <http://www.newstatesman.com/books/2008/08/haiti-aristide-lavalas>. Consulted on 1 June 2010.

—. 2008b. *In Defense of Lost Causes*. London: Verso.

—. 2008c. *Violence*. New York: Picador.

The 'Marie NDiaye Affair' or the Coming of a Postcolonial *Evoluée*

Dominic Thomas

Conrad portrays a void; Hamidou Kane celebrates a human presence and a heroic if doomed struggle. The difference between the two stories is very clear. You might say *that* difference was the very reason the African writer came into being. His story had been told for him, and he had found the telling quite unsatisfactory.

Chinua Achebe, *The Education of
a British-Protected Child* (2009), 117–18.

The awarding of the Prix Goncourt to Marie NDiaye in November 2009 may at first sight appear to have brought further confirmation of the 'Copernican revolution' which, according to signatories of the manifesto 'Pour une "littérature-monde" en français', has been sweeping through the world of literatures of French expression, casting aside hierarchical distinctions inherited from the colonial era. Yet scarcely had the announcement of NDiaye's triumph been made when it unleashed a furore that showed her to be trapped in a web of identity politics which, in the optic of the manifesto, had supposedly been consigned to the trash can of history. Though the word was not publicly used, NDiaye was, I will argue, treated as a latter-day *évoluée*.

While deferring unconditional membership to that privileged club that was Frenchness, the French colonial authorities coined the category of *évolués* in order to designate certain colonized subjects who, through exposure to colonial educational and assimilationist mechanisms, had internalized French cultural and social norms. The racial advocacy organization founded in 2005 known as *Les Indigènes de la République* has emphasized the transcolonial and transhistorical connections inherent in such mechanisms of hierarchization in terms of their representation of 'descendants of slaves and deported Africans, daughters and sons of the colonized and of immigrants' (Mouvement des Indigènes de la République). The treatment meted out to NDiaye highlights the complex positions the writer has negotiated in the process of 'belonging' in France as a person of African descent, in a nation state whose Republican ideals and values are supposed to render ethnicity indistinguishable. In practice, NDiaye's racial differentiation explains the disquieting statements formulated by an elected member of the French National Assembly (Éric Raoult) in response to comments she had made concerning the impact on ethnic minorities and immigrants of President Nicolas Sarkozy's policies. In Raoult's view, these statements put into question her allegiance to France. Raoult's claims betrayed deep-seated expectations concerning the standards to which immigrants – treated in effect as postcolonial incarnations of *évolués* – should adhere. Wider social tensions on these issues have been heightened since November 2009 when the French government launched a national debate on what it means to be French, a debate implicitly structured around outdated notions of a pristine, white Europe-bound French history (Grand débat sur l'identité nationale). At the same time, NDiaye herself has been outspoken concerning the limits of her 'Africanness' and her conceptualizations and paradigms of Africa in her own writings raise many important questions. This complex web of issues makes it particularly challenging to situate NDiaye clearly in relation to existing theorizations of a *littérature-monde* in French.

The connection between *littérature-monde* and major literary prizes in France has been foundational to the process of thinking about the parameters of such a literary model. In response to the award of three important prizes in one season to 'non-natives', Jonathan Littell (Goncourt), Alain Mabanckou (Renaudot) and Nancy Huston (Femina), the initial manifesto 'Pour une "littérature-monde" en français' [Toward a 'World-Literature' in French] published 16 March 2007 in *Le Monde* proclaimed: 'le centre, nous disent les prix d'automne, est désormais partout, aux quatre coins du monde'.[1] Francophone precursors had, of course, included Tahar Ben Jelloun, Patrick Chamoiseau, Andreï Makine, Amin Maalouf and Ahmadou Kourouma, and new authors have added their names to an ever-expanding list of twenty-first-century prize recipients – Atiq Rahimi (Goncourt, 2008) and Tierno Monénembo (Renaudot, 2008), a list further

---

[1] 'the centre, these autumn prizes tell us, is henceforth everywhere, at the four corners of the world' ('Toward a "World-Literature" in French', 2009: 54).

augmented by the award of the Prix Goncourt to Marie NDiaye and the Prix Médicis to Dany Laferrière in 2009. Naturally, not all of these writers were signatories of the original manifesto. Certainly, since the award of the Goncourt prize in 1921 to René Maran (a Black French Guyanese author) for his novel *Batouala: véritable roman nègre*, the question of diversity – both gendered and racial – has been inseparable from the para-discourse that has accompanied prize-giving. Competition between publishing houses is fierce, and it might be worth reminding ourselves at this juncture that since the Goncourt was established in 1903 and the Renaudot in 1926, the overwhelming majority of awards have gone to male authors published for the most part by the three most prestigious publishing houses (Gallimard, Grasset and Seuil) or by commercial branches of these (L'Olivier, Denöel, Mercure de France, etc.).

Given the considerable media and scholarly attention devoted in recent years to these questions and to the national and international impact of the debate on 'littérature-monde', the award of the Prix Goncourt in 2009 to a mixed-race woman published by the Éditions Gallimard thus becomes all the more interesting particularly when one considers the range of responses this announcement has triggered. After all, as one of the Goncourt jury members, Tahar Ben Jelloun, claimed after the announcement was made at the Drouant restaurant, 'C'est bien de rappeler que la France a des écrivains aussi qui ne sont pas tout blancs. Finalement, Marie NDiaye est une française dont l'identité est métisse, d'un père sénégalais et d'une mère bourgogne'.[2] However, such statements warrant further analysis. Why, one may well ask, is this 'bien' [good]? How does Marie NDiaye's own understanding of her racial identity connect with such a statement? And, how do such statements correlate with Republican imperatives concerning racial invisibility or for that matter with broader questions pertaining to racial constructs in France today? And finally, to what extent can NDiaye's work – to rejoin Maran's title – be considered a 'véritable roman nègre' [authentic Negro novel]? Lydie Moudileno provides a compelling analysis of these complex factors, revealing how NDiaye:

> has controlled the conditions of her visibility. She has done so, I would suggest, through a systematic strategy involving two positions. The first

---

[2] 'It is good to remind people that France has writers that are not lily white. In the end, Marie NDiaye is a mixed-race French woman with a Senegalese father and mother from Burgundy'. This and subsequent quotations, unless otherwise indicated, were translated from French into English by the author of this chapter.

involves playing down, or distancing herself from her 'African' origins. When she first published, though her family name gave away a connection to Senegal, her physical body – therefore, her 'race' – remained an enigma because she would not give interviews. As is typical of Minuit [her previous publisher], no pictures appeared on its famous blank white cover. (Moudileno, forthcoming)

Of course, NDiaye's case is all the more interesting precisely because of her background and the comments she has made pertaining to Francophone literature in a more general manner.

Marie NDiaye is not the first Black woman on the French literary scene. In 2006, with reference to Calixthe Beyala (a Cameroonian writer who resides in France), Nicki Hitchcott had written that 'Only Marie NDiaye has experienced anything close to comparable commercial success with her novels published by the prestigious Éditions de Minuit [...]. However, born in France of a French mother and a Senegalese father, NDiaye has never been represented (or represented herself) as a Black African writer; indeed, she is keen to reject any suggestion that she is "francophone" rather than "French"' (2006b: 30). In response to a questionnaire prepared by Beverley Ormerod and Jean-Marie Volet in their book *Romancières africaines d'expression française: le sud du Sahara*, NDiaye emphasizes how 'n'ayant jamais vécu en Afrique, et pratiquement pas connu mon père (je suis métisse), je ne puis être considéré comme une romancière francophone, c'est-à-dire une étrangère de langue française' (Ormerod and Volet, 2004: 111).[3] However, as Hitchcott rightly suggests, 'NDiaye poses an important question about what constitutes an African woman writer, especially as her fiction is not recognizable as that of an African author since it has neither an African context nor African characters' (2000: 24). As African literature has become increasingly globalized, diasporic and transnational, many of these questions have gained in complexity. African authors and/or writers of African descent are now located on every continent, thereby complicating the question of defining that which constitutes an African work of literature: does the author, for example, have to be the bearer of a passport from an African country, reside on the African continent, write in 'African' languages or for that matter situate the narrative in Africa? As I have argued elsewhere:

What is particularly striking [...] in texts produced by francophone sub-Saharan African authors who have chosen to situate their narratives in

---

[3] 'never having lived in Africa, and having scarcely known my father (I am of mixed race), I cannot be considered to a be a francophone novelist, that is a French-speaking foreigner' (cited in Hitchcott 2000: 24).

both Africa and France [...] is the variety of ways in which transnational
communities are organized outside the homeland, how cultural practices
are maintained, challenged and transformed as they are subjected to
multiple influences [...]. At what point, then, does Beyala stop being
a Cameroonian novelist and become an Afro-Parisian one? Is she, for
example, Afro-Parisian when she writes about immigration in France [...]
and Cameroonian when the focus is Africa [...]? (Thomas, 2001: 167)

Likewise, other African and/or Franco-African authors such as Fatou Diome
(2003; 2006; 2008) have authored works that address the challenges that
come with having to negotiate multiple identities as both they *and* their
protagonists circulate between Africa and France *and* Africa in France.
Beyala's perception of the French literary establishment becomes all the more
interesting when one considers recent developments. As Hitchcott has shown,
'Throughout these various tactical shifts, the one constant has been Beyala's
emphasis on her "otherness." [...] Her adopted position of victim extends to
her disingenuous explanation of her failure to win the Prix Goncourt: "I'm
not going to kid myself: to give the prize to a Black African woman, even
me, that would be a bit much for the Goncourt"' (2006a: 105). To a certain
extent, Beyala's complaint has now become redundant, because a 'Black
African woman' – whether NDiaye accepts this categorization or not may
well be secondary since the range of responses to her recognition have only
further confirmed her 'Africanness' – has now won the Goncourt (Senegalese
novelist Aminata Sow Fall's *L'appel des arènes* had been short-listed in 1982).
But for NDiaye the question has always posed itself differently than for Beyala
and Diome: at what point, one may ask, does NDiaye stop being a French
novelist and *become* an African one? Such a reversal to the conditions of
analysis accrue currency given that the Goncourt has been awarded to what
is unambiguously her most 'African' book – in terms of geography, choice
of protagonists, engagement with global migration patterns, human rights
issues, and so on. Perhaps then what the *World Republic of Letters* evoked by
Pascale Casanova (2005) has deemed the most authentic, the most 'véritable'
[authentic] of African works, produced by a writer who exceeds the norms
of Frenchness and who as such, though the self-proclaimed 'least' African
of 'Black' writers in France, is nevertheless simultaneously equipped with
the unquestioned authority of a *native* informer when she writes *about*
Africa, and in particular when she writes in the way she does about the
continent. Such an argument would find support in the conclusion Nelly
Kaprièlian reaches: 'Qui de mieux placé que Marie Ndiaye[4] pour traiter de la

---

[4] It should be noted that the author's preferred spelling of her name, NDiaye, is

monstruosité d'un temps où "l'étranger" est aussi maltraité' (2009b: 10).[5] As such, NDiaye is invested with an ethnographic authority which, as we shall see, rather than destabilizing and displacing prevalent constructs, paradoxically reproduces, performs, the kind of comfortable and reductive representations of Africa that fulfil the expectations of readers whose projections cannot then be decoupled from popular views of Africans and African migrants that influence insensitive policy-making initiatives. These observations require further analysis and we will return to them later. But the important point to retain at this juncture is that while NDiaye is 'indigenous' to France – she was born *on* French soil – the manner in which she is treated by certain elements in French society is analogous to the treatment of *indigènes* in French colonies, namely those individuals who were not considered *évolués* and therefore deemed unworthy of rights.

In the past, NDiaye has invoked her lack of familiarity with the African continent as a way of pointing to the inappropriateness of the label and category 'Francophone' to describe her. In *Trois femmes puissantes*, Africa becomes an 'imagined' topographic space, mediated through a broad range of constructs, territorial associations and references (NDiaye, 2009). According to Kaprièlian, the novel stands 'comme un antidote au roman classique, linéaire, qui incarnerait une normalité bourgeoise, une littérature cent pour cent française' (2009a: 29).[6] Somehow, the framework adopted by NDiaye can no longer be accommodated by traditional categories ascribed to the French novel; it is now marked by its otherness, its difference, its non-Frenchness. Kaprièlian stops just short of adding it to the library of *littérature-monde* in French, of calling it 'Francophone'. In one of the first mainstream appraisals and assessments of NDiaye's new novel, Kaprièlian asked the author: 'Vos personnages sont africains. Votre père est sénégalais. Vous revendiquez-vous d'une culture africaine?' (Kaprièlian, 2009a: 31).[7] NDiaye replied:

> Je m'en revendiquerais, m'en sentirais proche, si j'avais effectivement eu une culture double. [...] La seule chose qui change quand on a une origine africaine, c'est qu'on est noir, c'est visible. [...] J'ai été élevée dans un univers 100% français. Dans ma vie, l'origine africaine n'a pas vraiment de sens

---

sometimes incorrectly rendered as Ndiaye, as in the title and text of the interview by Kaprièlian.

[5] 'There is no one better positioned to deal with this monstrous era in which "outsiders" are treated so poorly'.

[6] 'as an antidote to the traditional linear novel that embodies bourgeois norms, a one hundred percent French literature'

[7] 'Your characters are African. Your father is Senegalese. Do you proclaim an African identity?'

– sinon qu'on le sait à cause de mon nom et de la couleur de ma peau.[8]
(Kaprièlian, 2009a: 31)

This 'only thing' though cannot be played down since this racialized identity informs the status of citizens in the postcolonial French Republic (even those who have participated in every aspect of French life), and serves as a constant reminder of a marginal status in a context in which there exists little ambiguity concerning the parameters of Frenchness (Tshimanga, Gondola and Bloom 2009).

Kaprièlian takes NDiaye's responses at face value and does not go on to challenge her further on this, pointing to the fact that she refuses to 'justifier son geste littéraire par cet élément biographique. Comme elle ne fait pas de son roman une allégorie des rapports entre la France et l'Afrique' (2009a: 29);[9] yet she goes on to argue how 'Marie Ndiaye raconte des vies déchirées entre l'Afrique et la France. Une interrogation sur la condition humaine [...] si peu représentés dans la littérature française' (Kaprièlian, 2009a: 29–30).[10] But the fact nevertheless remains that these subjects – which she claims are 'so rarely represented in French literature' – do pertain to contemporary relations between France and Africa, providing the structure and theme of the third section of the novel (pp. 247–317) which, while fictionalizing perilous Mediterranean crossings, remain *fictions* anchored in decipherable evidentiary modes that have captured the author's attention: 'j'étais très intéressée et bouleversée par les histoires de réfugiés qui arrivent à Malte ou en Sicile ou ailleurs' (Kaprièlian, 2009a: 30).[11] Could, one may wonder, NDiaye's growing consciousness of racial hierarchies in France have allowed for identification with and greater sensitivity to circumstances in Africa?

---

[8] 'I would claim such an identity and feel proximity to it if I actually had a dual culture. [...] The only thing that is different when one's origins are African is that one is Black, this difference is visible. [...] But I was raised in an environment that was one hundred percent French. And so in my life, African origins don't mean very much – except for that fact that I can't hide it because of my surname and the colour of my skin'.

[9] 'justify her literary work through this biographical element. Much in the same way that her novel is not to be interpreted as an allegory for relations between France and Africa'.

[10] 'Marie NDiaye recounts stories of lives torn between Africa and France. There is an interrogation on the human condition today [...] so rarely represented in French literature'.

[11] 'I was very interested and shaken by accounts of refugees arriving on the shoreline in Malta or in Sicily or elsewhere'.

Possible answers are perhaps to be found in an interview with Lucie Clair (2009b: 26–29), 'La discrète empathie', published in October 2009. The notion of 'empathy' emerges as a key indicator here as to NDiaye's relationality to the plight of Africa and Africans, and a review of *Trois femmes puissantes* written by Clair confirms this connection. Clair writes: 'C'est aussi le lieu où [...] se posent les questions de l'esclavage moderne, des mariages forcés' (2009c: 25).[12] But this 'empathy' to which Clair alludes for a 'site' of concern happens to be a *real* geographic zone, namely sub-Saharan Africa; the context is precise, identifiable, it becomes a documentary in nature. We know that such violence exists, has been recognized as such, and that these are sites (among numerous others) of patriarchal oppression. They are thus not products of the imagination but rather concrete realities, albeit realities that also inform the collective European imagination when it comes to Africa and that have often been recuperated at the service of a paternalistic France, the kind of France that invests in debates on a twenty-first-century 'national identity'. As Gérard Noiriel has demonstrated, 'Le but est toujours de définir l'identité nationale en dénonçant son contraire, dans la logique classique du "eux" et "nous" [...] procédant par allusions, en laissant le soin aux commentateurs et aux électeurs de compléter le raisonnement' (2007: 95–96).[13] In a discussion of works produced by second-generation Maghrebi women authors, Alec G. Hargreaves (2006: 45) identifies a disturbing pattern, whereby 'There is also a danger that narratives denouncing the subjection of minority women to sexual and other forms of abuse may play into the hands of those who argue that today's postcolonial minorities are as inherently barbarous as were yesterday's colonized "natives"'. An assessment therefore remains to be made as to the extent to which NDiaye's novel inscribes itself or not within this tradition.

The evidence is certainly there when it comes to ascribing to the work a sense of political commitment, a dimension NDiaye has not ignored: 'si ces gens fuient la misère, elle a une raison, elle est liée à des politiques, à des gouvernants' (Kaprèlian, 2009a: 29).[14] These comments pertain to the third section of the novel where the focus is provided by the sociological

---

[12] 'This is also the site [...] where the problem of contemporary slavery and forced marriages is to be found'.

[13] 'The objective is always to achieve a definition of national identity by denouncing its opposite, through a classical logic that juxtaposes the "them" with the "us" [...] through allusions, this leaves it up to commentators and electoral supporters to fill in the gaps'.

[14] 'there is a reason why these characters flee hardship; it is the result of policies, of inadequate governance'.

circumstances of migration from the African continent into the European Union. In this instance, the reader observes these conditions through the eyes of the central protagonist Khady (a pain that is now also hers), and contemplates the spectacle of human suffering, 'Elle jeta un coup d'œil au groupe indistinct de paquets et d'êtres' [She glanced at an undifferentiated mass of packages and beings] (NDiaye, 2009: 276), gathered here with shared hopes and expectations for what lies beyond, in anticipation 'qu'il arriverait un jour en Europe' [that there might one day come a day in Europe] (NDiaye, 2009: 286). It has become common knowledge that globalization has exacerbated economic dissymmetries, and NDiaye's characterization of the political climate in France since President Sarkozy's election in 2007 is apt: 'Je trouve cette France monstrueuse' [I find this France monstrous] (Kaprèlian, 2009a: 32). But NDiaye also shares in the responsibility of exercising caution when it comes to representing socio-cultural dynamics in Africa itself, because the overwhelming image one gets from her novel is one of violence and despair.

Rejoining the epigraph in which Chinua Achebe distinguishes between the works of Joseph Conrad and Cheikh Hamidou Kane, whereby the former presents Africa as a void, this void re-emerges in NDiaye's novel; for while she acknowledges the complexity of gender relations, she nevertheless reintroduces a Conradian void that is now filled with an overwhelming range of negative representations and stereotypes. Thus, as argued earlier, the risk is that her novel serves to reassure a French audience with received notions as to what constitutes Africa *and* Africans – thereby perpetuating the kinds of negative constructs that have served to justify those very repressive measures adopted by the newly created Ministry of Immigration, National Identity, Integration and Co-Development and which she herself has denounced. Ultimately, her novel can be potentially 'reconstructed as a sensational rhetorics that appeals to an official French audience whose prejudices can only be further confirmed by the authenticity of a narrative delivered by an African "native" informer' (Thomas, 2007: 140). Furthermore, when NDiaye claims that her work provides a space for beings 'so rarely represented in French literature', she reveals the degree to which she is blinded by her own ignorance of the vast corpus of works that has already addressed these postcolonial concerns in recent years, including works by J. R. Essomba (1996), Alain Mabanckou (1998), Mahi Binebine (1999), Fatou Diome (2003), Laurent Gaudé (2006), Abdourahman A. Waberi, (2006) and Antoine Matha (2009): writers that have been warning people for years that what awaits them beyond the perilous crossing is of course a 'monstrous' France (Thomas, 2009).

These entangled transcolonial and transnational histories are of course intrinsic to NDiaye's novel, and she has not herself been immune from racist critiques. Her comments concerning Sarkozy's France first appeared in print in the August 2009 interview she granted the magazine *Les inrockuptibles* with Nelly Kaprièlian – therefore several months before receiving the Goncourt prize and not in an attempt to exploit the platform and visibility accorded to recipients of such prestigious awards. However, upon being awarded the prize – an award which coincidently was given on the very same day that Minister Éric Besson launched the Great National Identity Debate – Éric Raoult (UMP [Union for a Popular Movement] Mayor of Raincy and elected Deputy for the Department of Seine-Saint-Denis) got wind of NDiaye's remarks and immediately wrote a letter sent to Frédéric Mitterrand, the Minister of Culture and Communication:

> Monsieur Éric Raoult attire l'attention de M. le ministre de la culture et de la communication sur le devoir de réserve, dû aux lauréats du Prix Goncourt. [...] [L]e message délivré par les lauréats se doit de respecter la cohésion nationale et l'image de notre pays. Les prises de position de Marie Ndiaye [...] sont inacceptables. [...] Une personnalité qui défend les couleurs littéraires de la France se doit de faire preuve d'un certain respect à l'égard de nos institutions.[15] (Polloni and Siankowski, 2009)

Perhaps it is unnecessary to linger on the disturbing implications of patriotic fervour and the principle of moderation if it weren't for the fact that these comments were also accompanied by additional statements by Raoult: 'Nous lui avons accordé le prix Goncourt parce qu'elle a du talent. [...] Maintenant qu'elle a le Goncourt, elle peut penser comme elle veut, mais, en l'occurrence, il faut qu'elle soit un peu l'ambassadrice de notre culture [...] La France lui a donné le Prix Goncourt' (Raoult, 2009).[16] The context of the national identity debate is of course all-important, since it has (wilfully?) stirred up racial tensions, and, as Kaprièlian (2009b: 10) has argued, 'Ce n'est pas un hasard si c'est à l'écrivain d'un tel livre, un écrivain d'origine sénégalaise de surcroît, que s'en prend un élu UMP en

---

15 'Mr. Éric Raoult would like to draw the attention of the Minister of Culture and Communication to the principle of moderation expected of Goncourt Prize winners. [...] [W]inners of this prize must uphold national cohesion and the image of our country. Marie NDiaye's statements [...] are unacceptable. [...] A personality who carries the French literary flag must show a certain respect for our institutions'.

16 'We awarded her the Goncourt Prize because she has talent. [...] Now that she has received this prize, she can think as she likes, but as it happens she now has to be a kind of ambassador for our culture [...] France has given her the Goncourt Prize'.

plein débat sur l'identité nationale'.[17] Effectively, Raoult sets in motion a mechanism in which outdated expectations and hierarchies associated with an assimilated colonial *évolué* category are here reorganized and rationalized only to then be subsequently mapped onto the postcolonial subject as contemporary recipient of French generosity. We are reminded here of NDiaye's inability to escape her perpetual status at the periphery, dependent on admission according to the imperatives of the dominant racial class, and sanctioned here for not having learned the 'assimilation' lesson. Exemplars of integration exist and have been rewarded, such as Gaston Kelman (2003), whose book *Je suis noir et je n'aime pas le manioc* [I'm Black and I don't care for manioc] is effectively a defence and illustration of the possibility of successful insertion into a colour-blind Republic that can be called upon to invalidate the assertions and claims of visible minorities. Kelman's public statements on race have afforded him the appointment as adviser to Besson at the Ministry of Immigration, National Identity, Integration and Co-Development.

In the public debate that ensued, both NDiaye and Raoult called upon the Minister of Culture and Communication to weigh in. When Mitterrand finally intervened on 12 November he was non-committal and merely defended the principle of free speech. The background to the question of belonging in French society can only be fully understood by considering some of the objectives of the national identity debate as well as other recent incidents that have underscored the lingering presence of racial constructs in French society. In his appointment letter of 31 March 2009, Besson is reminded that 'La promotion de notre identité nationale doit être placée au cœur de votre action' [The promotion of our national identity should find itself at the heart of your action] ('Lettre de mission', 2009: 6), a prerequisite to achieving 'appartenance' [belonging]. This question of belonging has emerged as a central tenet in contemporary French politics. Sarkozy as a presidential candidate had become fond of repeating 'La France, tu l'aimes ou tu la quittes' [France, love her or leave her], thereby insisting upon the necessity embracing the collective 'we'. During a session devoted to the national identity debate in the French National Assembly on 8 December 2009, Minister Besson presented the main issues and then responded to questions from other deputies. Among his most controversial claims was the suggestion that there existed a 'hiérarchie entre les appartenances' [hierarchy between forms of belonging] (Assemblée Nationale, 2009) that could be employed

---

[17] 'It is no coincidence that an elected UMP official should have attacked the author – moreover one of Senegalese origin – of such a book at the height of the debate on national identity'.

to distinguish between different forms of societal belonging. Naturally, the subtext here has everything to do with what it means *to be* French (Besson, 2009a). Thus, when Raoult (cited earlier) calls upon NDiaye to 'uphold national cohesion' and to 'carry the French literary flag', he is merely echoing Besson's calls for patriotism (Besson, 2009b).

Not surprisingly, there is a fascinating precedent to this polemic. Senegalese-born Rama Yade, the former Secretary of State for Human Rights and now Secretary of State for Sports, has developed a reputation in the French media as an outspoken member of Sarkozy's administration. She has been described as 'insoumise' [rebellious, insubordinate], criticized for not being a 'team player' and for refusing to tow the Party line ('Fillon', 2009). In *Comment je suis devenu français* [How I became French], a book edited by Jacqueline Rémy (2007), Rama Yade evokes her surprise at being informed of the need to respect Republican values in the official letter of notification she received informing her that her petition for French citizenship had been successful. When Yade added that she had received the news at a time in her life when she had not yet come to terms with her biculturalism and 'national allegiance' (she was twenty-one at the time), two UMP deputies (Jacques Myard and Christian Vanneste) denounced this 'double allégeance' [divided allegiance] ('Fillon', 2009). To observers in Britain and the United States, to cite just two examples, such a reaction to the perceived incompatibility of national origin with citizenship of a different state may seem striking, yet in France the very individuals concerned by these responses have often been the first to reject the positive qualities of such diverse backgrounds (Soudan, 2009).

The parallels between Marie NDiaye's and Rama Yade's exposure to the French authorities are compelling, sharpening the need further to evaluate the question of race consciousness in France today. In the case of NDiaye, there was already an interesting way of approaching this, given that she had written the preface to her brother Pap Ndiaye's 2007 book *La condition noire: Essai sur une minorité ethnique française*.[18] The intersection of their respective intellectual trajectories – the one as a writer of fiction and the other as a social scientist – around the question of 'race' and 'Africa' is interesting. The short story, 'Les sœurs' (NDiaye, 2007: 9–15), that serves as a preface to the essay on ethnic minorities in France, addresses the complexity of multiracial identities, divided allegiances and the self-definition of identity balanced against the perceptions and expectations of others. Marie NDiaye has stated that her growing consciousness of being Black in France came as a result of discussions with her brother and from reading his work: 'Je ne m'étais jamais

---

[18] Marie NDiaye and her brother Pap Ndiaye have elected to spell their surnames differently, in his case with a lower case 'd' following the capitalized 'N'.

posée cette question avant de le lire et qu'il m'en parle' (Kaprèlian, 2009a: 32).[19] In other words, a 'discovery' that must have been relatively recent given that Pap Ndiaye's own research had focused almost exclusively on the United States and the Black American experience until after the 2005 uprisings in France and the creation of the Conseil représentatif des associations noires (CRAN) [Representative Council for Black Associations], in which he has been active. This new way of conceptualizing and interpreting a complicated African-French history as a colonial and postcolonial experience – affording a mixed-race novelist a newfound 'empathy' with African women and a social scientist a shift in fieldwork orientation from ethnic minorities in the United States to those in contemporary France – has surely infused the narrative of *Trois femmes puissantes.* To this end, the arguments formulated by Pap Ndiaye in his *La condition noire* become relevant because of the insights they can offer us. A symbiotic link can therefore be established between the preface to a work of social science and the findings of social science in turn refracted into a work of fiction.

For Pap Ndiaye, new forms of identification and solidarity originate in the shared experience of discrimination (Ndiaye, 2007: 21–24). When one relocates visibility within French Republican structures as the primary factor in the experience of discrimination – that is, of social exclusion – then one can only conclude that 'La différence entre les Français noirs et les autres Français dont les parents sont venus d'ailleurs est que l'identité française se trouve constamment suspectée dans le cas des premiers' (Ndiaye, 2007: 42).[20] Hence President Sarkozy's electoral campaign mantra ('France, love her or leave her') and the Ministry of Immigration and National Identity's activities, under cover of which the real objectives of the national identity debate are to foster and reinforce social hierarchies, perceptions that some 'French' people are *more* French than others, or that others are 'communau-taires' [factionalist]. These constructs have roots that can be traced back to the colonial era because 'The idea of race – understood as the hierarchical difference between groups – concerns Republican citizenship. Some are more citizens than others: the creation of a *colonial citizenship* in 1946 that was different to the citizenship applied in the metropole, was the most striking example of this' (Bancel, Blanchard and Vergès, 2003: 122–23).

For the writer Faïza Guène, who grew up in a French *banlieue* [housing

---

19   'I never asked myself the question until I read his work and he talked to me about it'.

20   'The difference between Black French people and other French people whose parents came from elsewhere is that the French identity of the former will always be treated suspiciously'.

project], this has given rise to a form of oppositional politics: 'I realized something important, which is that not many people from my background, with my social and cultural origins, are represented in the media or have a voice. I got this opportunity, and now I realize I don't have the right to pass it up. It's rare for someone to speak out, especially in a field that's not normally reserved for us. "La littérature française" – I've got no right to touch it!' (Guène, 2006). When interviewing NDiaye, Kaprèlian raised an important question: 'En Angleterre ou aux Etats-Unis, beaucoup d'écrivains sont issus d'origines ethniques différentes comme Zadie Smith, Monica Ali, Hari Kunzru, etc. En France, nous n'avons pas ce type d'écrivains. Comment l'expliquez-vous?' (2009a: 33).[21] In response, NDiaye remarked:

> En général, les écrivains sont des gens qui ont fait des études, savent manier la langue et peut-être que ça n'est pas encore le cas pour nos minorités, qui se sentent peut-être exclues d'un certain savoir [...] il semblerait que les écrivains français viennent tous d'une bourgeoisie éclairée, cultivée, qui est un milieu assez restreint.[22] (Kaprèlian, 2009a: 33)

Raoult's comments reveal deep-seated assumptions and prejudice against certain categories of French people, they are reprehensible and to be denounced as such. Yet, as much as NDiaye's work has endeavoured to feature those 'victims' of African social relations, those 'so rarely represented in French literature', one has to wonder whether her experiences before and after the Goncourt have altered her way of conceiving internal (domestic) cultural and political dynamics and to recognize that 'French writers DO NOT ALL come out of an enlightened bourgeoisie' (my capitalized alterations) but rather from diverse ethnic backgrounds and *banlieues* neighbourhoods, often those very spaces in French society in which the 'monstrous' France she has evoked is most tangible. As Moudileno has argued:

> When NDiaye issues an almost legal disclaimer of any affiliation with 'African novelists', she is not only resisting an identity. What she also refuses is the socio-literary label – 'romancière africaine' (African novelist) – which would ultimately exclude her from the French hexagonal corpus

---

[21] 'In England and in the United States, there are many writers from different ethnic backgrounds, such as Zadie Smith, Monica Ali, Hari Kunzru, etc. In France, we don't have the same kind of writers. How do you account for this?'

[22] 'For the most part, writers are people who have pursued advanced studies, who know how to handle language, and that might not be the case yet for our minorities who feel left out of a certain kind of knowledge [...] most French writers seem to come out of an enlightened bourgeoisie, they are educated, and this is a fairly restricted milieu'.

she has worked so hard to conquer. Having resisted that label earlier in her career, she has, in a way, refused the temptation of celebrity. It is now from a position of freedom that years later, the postcolonial origin can find its way back into her private and professional identity. (Moudileno, forthcoming)

In fact, for a long time, NDiaye claims, she was 'classée parmi les auteurs francophones à la Fnac, à cause de son nom' [shelved in the Francophone section in the Fnac, because of her name] (Clair, 2009a: 22). Having now vacated a space on the 'Francophone' shelves, and rejoined the 'literary we', it remains crucial for the author to remain attentive to and aware of the existence of those others who have been left behind. Their names are Azouz Begag, Farida Belghoul, Mehdi Charef, Fatou Diome, Rachid Djaïdani, Gaston-Paul Effa, Faïza Guène, Ferrudja Kessas, Alain Mabanckou, Léonora Miano, Soraya Nini, Mohamed Razane, Thomté Ryam and Abdourahman A. Waberi... A similar critique can be made of the *littérature-monde* movement which, in its own concern with having 'the center placed on an equal plane with other centers' ('Toward a "World-Literature" in French', 2009: 56), also neglected to include any *Beur* or *banlieue* authors in their manifesto (Thomas, 2010).

The fact that Marie NDiaye currently resides in Berlin may seem all the more paradoxical given that the twentieth anniversary of the dismantling of the Berlin Wall has only just been celebrated. At this historic moment, people have been calling for the dismantling of another symbolic wall (the Ministry of Immigration and National Identity), one that is being erected brick by brick through fear-mongering and ignorance in Germany's neighbour to the west. As one reflects on the cultural, economic, political and social challenges that have come to define existing forms of global communication, contact and exchange, one can only hope that it will be possible to move beyond the kind of divisive discourse epitomized by political figures such as Besson, Raoult and Sarkozy (among a long list of others, of course) when the homeostasis that is in place is displaced and those mechanisms deployed at the service of the imposition of hierarchies of belonging are rendered obsolete by newly configured models of empathy.

Works Cited

Achebe, Chinua. 2009. *The Education of a British-Protected Child*. New York: Alfred A. Knopf.

Assemblée nationale. 2009. <http://www.assemblee-nationale.fr/13/cri/2009-2010/20100079.asp>. Consulted on 3 January 2010.

Bancel, Nicolas, Pascal Blanchard and Françoise Vergès. 2003. *La République coloniale: Essai sur une utopie.* Paris: Albin Michel.

Besson, Éric. 2009a. 'Faire connaître et partager l'identité nationale'. Grand débat sur l'identité nationale. 31 October. <http://www.debatidentitenationale.fr/propositions-d-eric-besson/faire-connaitre-et-partager-l.html>. Consulted on 3 January 2010.

—. 2009b. 'Valoriser l'identité nationale'. Grand débat sur l'identité nationale. 31 October. <http://www.debatidentitenationale.fr/propositions-d-eric-besson/valoriser-l-identite-nationale.html>. Consulted on 3 January 2010.

Binebine, Mahi. 1999. *Cannibales: Traversée dans l'enfer de Gibraltar.* Paris: Fayard.

Casanova, Pascale. 2005. *The World Republic of Letters.* Trans. by M. B. DeBevoise. Cambridge, MA: Harvard University Press.

Clair, Lucie. 2009a. 'Écrire, quoi d'autre?'. *Le Matricule des anges: Le mensuel de la littérature contemporaine* 107 (October): 20–24.

—. 2009b. 'Interview with Marie NDiaye. 'La discrète empathie'. *Le Matricule des anges: Le mensuel de la littérature contemporaine* 107 (October): 26–29.

—. 2009c. 'Tenir tête'. *Le Matricule des anges: Le mensuel de la littérature contemporaine* 107 (October): 25.

Diome, Fatou. 2003. *Le ventre de l'Atlantique.* Paris: Éditions Anne Carrière.

—. 2006. *Kétala.* Paris: Flammarion.

—. 2008. *Inasouvies, nos vies.* Paris: Flammarion.

Essomba, J. R. 1996. *Le paradis du Nord.* Paris: Présence Africaine.

Fall, Aminata Sow. 1982. *L'appel des arènes.* Dakar: Les Nouvelles Éditions Africaines.

'Fillon se paye Rama Yade et Guiano'. 2009. *Le Post.* 3 November. <http://www.lepost.fr/article/2009/11/25/1808877_rama-yade-et-ses-racines-senegalaises-2-deputes-ump-attaquent.html>. Consulted on 3 January 2010.

Gaudé, Laurent. 2006. *Eldorado.* Arles: Actes Sud.

Grand débat sur l'identité nationale. <www.debatidentitenationale.fr>. Consulted on 3 January 2010.

Guène, Faïza. 2006. Interview with Sarah Adams. 'Voice of the People'. *Guardian* 10 May. <http://www.guardian.co.uk/society/2006/may/10/books.socialexclusion>. Consulted on 3 January 2010.

Hargreaves, Alec G. 2006. 'Testimony, Co-Authorship, and Dispossession among Women of Maghrebi Origin in France'. *Research in African Literatures* 37.1: 42–54.

Hitchcott, Nicki. 2000. *Women Writers in Francophone Africa.* Oxford: Berg.

—. 2006a. 'Calixthe Beyala: Prizes, Plagiarism, and "Authenticity"'. *Research in African Literatures* 37.1: 100–09.

—. 2006b. *Calixthe Beyala: Performances of Migration*. Liverpool: Liverpool University Press.

Kaprièlian, Nelly. 2009a. Dossier littéraire. 'Marie Ndiaye: aux prises avec le monde'. *Les inrockuptibles* 716 (18–24 August): 28–33.

—. 2009b. Interview with Marie Ndiaye. 'Écris et tais-toi'. *Les inrockuptibles* 729 (18–24 November): 8–11.

Kelman, Gaston. 2003. *Je suis noir et je n'aime pas le manioc*. Paris: Max Milo Éditions.

Le Bris, Michel, and Jean Rouaud (eds). 2007. *Pour une littérature-monde*. Paris: Gallimard.

'Lettre de mission' from President Nicolas Sarkozy to Éric Besson. 2009. Ministère de l'immigration, l'intégration, de l'identité nationale et du développement solidaire. 31 March. <http://www.immigration.gouv.fr/spip.php?page=dossiers_them_org&numrubrique=341>. Consulted on 3 January 2010.

Mabanckou, Alain. 1998. *Bleu, Blanc, Rouge*. Paris: Présence Africaine.

Matha, Antoine. 2009. *Épitaphe*. Paris: Gallimard.

Moudileno, Lydie. forthcoming. 'Fame, Celebrity, and the Conditions of Visibility of the Postcolonial Writer'. *Yale French Studies*.

Mouvement des indigènes de la république. 2005. <http://indigenes-republique.org>. Consulted on 3 January 2010.

NDiaye, Marie. 2007. 'Les sœurs'. In Pap Ndiaye, *La condition noire: Essai sur une minorité ethnique française*. Paris: Éditions Calmann-Lévy: 9–15.

—. 2009. *Trois femmes puissantes*. Paris: Gallimard.

Ndiaye, Pap. 2007. *La condition noire: Essai sur une minorité ethnique française*. Paris: Éditions Calmann-Lévy.

Noiriel, Gérard. 2007. *A quoi sert "l'identité nationale"*. Marseille: Agone.

Ormerod, Beverley, and Jean-Marie Volet. 2004. *Romancières africaines d'expression française: le sud du Sahara*. Paris: L'Harmattan.

Polloni, Camille, and Pierre Siankowski. 2009. 'Eric Raoult s'attaque à Marie Ndiaye et invente un "devoir de réserve" pour les prix Goncourt'. Les Inrockuptibles. 10 November. <http://www.lesinrocks.com/actualite/actu-article/article/eric-raoult-sattaque-a-marie-ndiaye-et-invente-un-devoir-de-reserve-pour-les-prix-goncourt/>. Consulted on 3 January 2010.

'Pour une "littérature-monde" en français'. 2007. *Le Monde* 16 March.

Raoult, Éric. 2009. 'Eric Raoult rappelle Marie NDiaye à son "devoir de réserve" pour le Goncourt'. YouTube. <http://www.youtube.com/watch?v= IN_Yh4AHB5I>. Consulted on 3 January 2010.

Rémy, Jacqueline (ed.). 2007. *Comment je suis devenu français*. Paris: Seuil.

Soudan, François. 2009. 'Rama Yade: "Sarkozy, les Africains et moi"'. *Jeune Afrique* 25 (25 February). <http://www.jeuneafrique.com/Article/ARTJAJA2511p022-029-bis.xml0/france-interview-rama-yade-secretaire-d-

etatrama-yade-sarkozy-les-africains-et-moi.html>. Consulted on 3 January 2010.

Thomas, Dominic. 2001. 'Daniel Biyaoula: Exile, Immigration, and Transnational Cultural Productions'. In Susan Ireland and Patrice J. Proulx (eds), *Immigrant Narratives in Contemporary France*. Westport, CT: Greenwood Press: 165–76.

—. 2007. *Black France: Colonialism, Immigration, and Transnationalism*. Bloomington: Indiana University Press.

—. 2009. 'Sarkozy's Law: The Institutionalization of Xenophobia in the New Europe'. *Radical Philosophy* 153: 7–12.

—. 2010. 'Decolonizing France: from National Literatures to World Literatures'. *SITES: Contemporary French and Francophone Cultures* 14.1: 47–55. [Special issue: William J. Cloonan and Alec G. Hargreaves (eds), '*Littérature-Monde*: New Wave or New Hype?']

'Toward a "World-Literature" in French'. 2009. Trans. by Daniel Simon. *World Literature Today* (March–April): 54–56.

Tshimanga, Charles, Didier Gondola and Peter J. Bloom (eds). 2009. *Frenchness and the African Diaspora: Identity and Uprising in Contemporary France*. Bloomington: Indiana University Press.

Waberi, Abdourahman A. 2006. *Aux États-Unis d'Afrique*. Paris: Éditions JC Lattès.

(R)Evolutions

Thomas C. Spear

There is no need for a *littérature-monde*. The hot topic among the literary and publishing circles of Saint-Germain-des-Prés does, nevertheless, provide an opportunity for specialists in Francophone writing and cultures to exchange views on the evolution of our fields of research in a global context, and to do so from an academic standpoint.

Littérature-monde? No revolution here, at least not when seen from the North-American side of the Atlantic. This is a literary and publishing phenomenon which chiefly concerns Paris. It is not the group of young writers in Port-au-Prince associated with the publication *La Ruche* who brought down a government in 1946. Neither is it the 'total revolution' proposed by the Refus Global [total refusal] manifesto in 1948 which was intended to cut off all ties with social conventions, including the church, in Quebec. And it is not the young authors and creators of the journal *Souffles* in Rabat whose foray into international solidarity led to long prison sentences from 1972 onwards. In those manifestos where politics is involved, and where artistic movements extend to the plastic arts, singers, film-makers or simple 'philosophers', the debates are weightier, more urgent.

Much ado about nothing or, to quote Louis-Ferdinand Céline, these debates about Parisian publishing serve only to: 'troufignoliser l'adjectif... goncourtiser... merde! enculagailler la moumouche, frénétiser l'Insignifiance, babiller ténu dans la pompe, plastroniser, cocoriquer dans les micros...' (1937: 11).[1] Everything about Céline sets him apart from the authors of the manifesto, except for his defence of the French language:

---

[1] 'poncificate adjectives up the arse ... academize ... crap! nitshitpick, franticize

164

Il n'y a qu'une seule langue, Colonel, en ce monde paracafouilleux! une
seule langue valable! respectable! la langue impériale de ce monde: la nôtre!
... charabias, les autres, vous m'entendez? ... dialectes bien trop tard venus!
... mal sapés, mal léchés, arlequinades! Rauques ou miaulants à-peu-près
pour rastaquouères! Zozoteries pour clowns![2] (Céline, 1955: 87)

The manifesto of the forty-four writers is 'Toward a "World-Literature" *in
French*', not to be confused with a *French* literature.

It is good that the manifesto should proclaim 'la fin de la francophonie'
[the end of *Francophonie*] in its institutional form ('Pour une "literature-
monde" en français'; 'Toward a "World-Literature" in French', 2009: 54). But
in literature we have reached the end of the first decade of the twenty-first
century. Hello? Don't the French publishing houses, even those in Paris,
publish Francophone writers from all around the world? For example, Albin
Michel may not be located near Gallimard on the rue Sébastien-Bottin, but
it is nearly a century since one of their 'non-hexagonal' authors, René Maran,
won the Prix Goncourt (1921), and authors such as Calixthe Beyala and Émile
Ollivier have been among their published authors for quite some time. Is this
not a *littérature-monde*? Canadian writers such as Ying Chen, Nancy Huston
and Michel Tremblay can be found at Actes Sud, as the result of a partnership
with the Leméac publishing house in Montreal. The paperback series at
Actes Sud (Babel) includes classic writers such as Amadou Hampâté Bâ and
contemporaries such as Vénus Khoury-Ghata and Lyonel Trouillot. And the
list of authors published by Pierre Astier at Le Serpent à Plumes (1988–2004)
has allowed readers to get to know an attractively packaged *littérature-monde*
that includes authors from all geographical backgrounds.

Galligrasseuil

Rather than a revolution, the manifesto for a *littérature-monde* represents (or,
at least, is intended to represent) a minor change of perspective on the part
of the establishment as it is embodied by the newspaper *Le Monde* and the
'Galligrasseuil' publishers (Gallimard, Grasset and Seuil).

---

the Insignificant, pen a fine whine, swagger, crow into the microphones ...'. All
translations of citations from French into English are by the translator of this
chapter.

[2] 'There is only one language, Colonel, in this parashambolic world! one
language that is valid! respectable! the imperial language of this world: our own!
... gibberish, the others, do you hear me? ... far-too-tardy dialects! ... poorly
rigged out, lacking polish, buffoonery! Raucous or caterwauling approximations
for flashy foreigners! Lispings for clowns!'

At Gallimard, René Depestre and Patrick Chamoiseau are among the few 'negroes' in the *Collection blanche* [White Series] (Édouard Glissant joined this famous series during the 1990s). Gallimard created the *Continents noirs* [Dark Continents] series in 2000, confining African authors to a publishing ghetto of books which are, moreover, aesthetically impoverished (as exemplified by the collection's typeface and cover designs). Éloïse Brezault reminds us that 'on a reproché à Continents noirs d'enfermer les auteurs dans une couleur de peau qu'ils ne voulaient pas forcément revendiquer[,] et la collection "Naïve francophones" [dirigé par Pierre Astier] a conduit le critique Pierre Assouline à parler de *"ghettoïsation d'une catégorie de langue française"'* (2008: 352).[3] Some of the *Continents noirs* writers have left to go to other publishers; others have remained in the ghetto. Of those who have left the series, Ananda Devi – whose island (and by extension herself) was at first exotically 'dark' – is the only writer that Gallimard has managed to keep by transferring her to the *Collection blanche*. *Ève de ses décombres* [Eve from her rubble] appeared in 2006: not a revolution, but an evolution in *littérature-monde* at Gallimard.

Grasset has published Xavier Orville, Raphaël Confiant (at the beginning of his career in French) and, recently, Dany Laferrière. Gaston-Paul Effa also began his career in Grasset's series before being drawn for a short period into the *Continents noirs* collection. Although it does not practise geographical or ethnic exclusion in the form of a separate series for such authors, Grasset nevertheless remains a traditional Franco-French publisher.

Of the three Galligrasseuil publishers, Seuil differentiates the least between the geographical origins of the authors on its lists. Here, we can find the work of Anne Hébert from 1958 onwards and that of Jacques Godbout since 1962; the paperback list includes similar authors from Quebec, the Maghreb, Africa, and a few from the Caribbean. Seuil published the second edition of Ahmadou Kourouma's *Les Soleils des indépendances* [The Suns of Independence] in 1970 (we often forget the reasons for a first edition in Montreal in 1968), as well as the works of some of the signatories of the manifesto for a *littérature-monde*, including Tahar Ben Jelloun and Alain Mabanckou.

Littérature-monde is thus not new. If the presence of writers from so-called Francophone backgrounds is now more visible (for example, during the

---

[3] 'the *Continents noirs* series has been criticized for locking up its authors in a skin colour which they did not necessarily wish to claim[,] and the *'Naïve francophones'* collection [edited by Pierre Astier for the Naïve record label] led the critic Pierre Assouline to speak of *"ghettoization of a French language group"'*.

literary prize season of autumn 2006), this is simply an indication that the 'major' publishing houses are putting more energy into promoting them. We no longer live in an era when only publishers such as L'Harmattan, Hatier, Karthala and Présence Africaine published French-language writers who were not French. Nevertheless, authors on the lists of the smaller publishers rarely appear among the literary prize-winners and fewer columns are devoted to them in the general literary press. There are certainly some exceptions to this rule which promote writers from further afield – for example, *La Quinzaine Littéraire*, directed for the past forty years by Maurice Nadeau and, for the past twenty years, the Etonnants Voyageurs festival organized by Michel Le Bris. Nonetheless, books published in Montreal or Brussels never appear on the shortlists for French literary prizes; we should not expect a 'World Goncourt Prize' for a novel published in Dakar or Port-au-Prince to be forthcoming any time soon. Reference to 'Galligrasseuil' exaggerates the importance of these three publishing houses; what should be understood by this term is the exclusion, in the French literary institution, of all books in the French language that are published by small publishers, provincial publishers and, especially, publishers outside France. If we think there is anything new in the manifesto for a *littérature-monde*, we should re-read Jacques Godbout's text 'La Question préalable' [the preliminary question]:

> Une transformation profonde de l'attitude des Français vis-à-vis de la francophonie doit accompagner l'affirmation d'une littérature-monde en français. Paris doit modifier son appareil éditorial et critique. Il ne s'agit pas de créer une mode 'francophone', il s'agit de changer la 'culture' de l'institution littéraire en France. Est-ce réalisable? On peut comprendre notre scepticisme, c'est un débat qui, pour nous, date de plus de quarante ans.[4] (Godbout, 2007: 107)

Dates without (R)Evolution

The distribution and circulation of books in French should be of concern to the authors of the manifesto, all of whom are published in Paris (with two (Swiss) exceptions). As for a 'revolution' – or rather 'evolution' – in

---

[4] 'A profound transformation in the attitude of the French towards *Francophonie* has to accompany the declaration of a *littérature-monde* in French. Paris must change its editorial and critical machine. This is not a question of creating a 'Francophone' fashion; it is a question of changing the 'culture' of the literary institution in France. Can this be achieved? Our scepticism is understandable, since this debate has, for us, been going on for over forty years'.

littérature-monde in French, I shall mention a few dates which suggest, rather, that there is no shift in French literary habits. The passing of Bill 101 in Quebec in 1977 (the Charter of the French language) should mark the beginning of the chronological sequence, but the linguistic independence of Quebec is of little concern to French publishers. Nowadays, France is more resistant to the revolution of electronic publishing than is North America (and the Anglophone world), but the e-book will certainly change the look of tomorrow's *littérature-monde*. In the meantime, three dates from the current generation can provide an insight into the evolution of the Francophone cultural space in France.

The first date is 1994, when we can test the Parisian pulse and sense how quickly its heart beats for *littérature-monde* through an article by Colombe Schneck, 'Le français piégé par le multiculturalisme américain' [The French language trapped by American multiculturalism], which appeared in *Le Monde* (17 February 1994). From her Parisian viewpoint, Schneck found the passion for Francophone studies in the United States strange. The Pancho drawing which accompanied the article showed three multi-ethnic students outside an American 'French Dept' door. In it, a tall black student was protesting 'Mais j'aurais aimé étudier Balzac, moi!' [But *I* would have liked to study Balzac] while a short white student replied 'Oui, mais il n'était pas transsexuel, lui … ' [Yes, but *he* wasn't transsexual]. Schneck, like Pancho, laughed at these odd Americans, obsessed by the 'politically correct', stuffing their students with non-European authors when, in fact, students would have preferred to read the writers of the City of Light. In France, nobody understood that a passion for Mongo Beti or Marie Chauvet was as valid as one for a Gustave Flaubert or a Marcel Proust. Many Francophone writers (including French ones) teach in the United States (and Canada): Maryse Condé, Assia Djebar, Emmanuel Dongala, Édouard Glissant, Alain Mabanckou, V. Y. Mudimbe, Abdelhak Serhane, to mention but a few, as the broad horizons of North American campuses are not at issue here. Abdourahman Waberi reminds us, moreover, of the number of Francophone writers with teaching posts west of the Atlantic (2007: 70). For what reasons? Political correctness? The financial lure of the Ivy League universities? Or the power of such a vast continent, compared with France itself? We can certainly say that the many examinations and entrance tests required to obtain a university post in France – including a doctorate, the *agrégation* (sometimes), successful defence of the *qualification* and *habilitation* exams, and contacts (always) – are not an encouragement for creative writers. In all senses, the doors of 'French Depts' in France are not particularly open to writers. To avoid embarking on a list of acquaintances who are qualified (but without 'Gaulish' ancestry) and frustrated by the current French university system, I need only remind you of the example of Mongo Beti's career (he was a high-school teacher in Rouen) to show the position of creative writers as university professors in France, compared with Francophone writers in the United States.

Second date: in 2002, Karthala published the collection of essays I edited, *La Culture française vue d'ici et d'ailleurs* [French culture seen from here and elsewhere]. This volume was well received despite the fact that Karthala is certainly not Gallimard and no manifesto was published in *Le Monde des Livres* to accompany the book! Nevertheless, the testimonies from the thirteen Francophone writers with dual or multiple nationalities on the love–hate they feel towards France (its culture and its language) raised the problems which are expressed in *Pour une littérature-monde*. A number of them, educated under the colonial system, experienced great disappointment on discovering that the supposed icons of the 'universal' values promoted by France as the 'cradle of human rights' had nothing to do with them.

In an article on the 'crisis' of French universalism, Naomi Schor reminds us of those excluded by such universalism: at the time of the French Revolution, it was women and slaves. Today, through a strategy of assimilation, various minority groups are excluded from a place in the French Republic:

> One thing is certain: the pressure to assimilate in France is such that identity politics cannot thrive there; there is a logical and insuperable incompatibility between promoting assimilation and encouraging identitarian micro-communities based on gender, race, and sexual orientation, what we in the United States have taken to lumping under the term multiculturalism. Viewed from the French perspective, *multiculturalism* is nothing short of a cultural disaster, threatening the polity with fragmentation, and the nation with dissolution. (Schor, 2001: 52–53)

When I was invited to appear on Bernard Pivot's television programme *'Double je'* [Double I, Double game] in May 2004, I found it hard to believe that this literary star of French television did not know the Présence Africaine bookshop which I had chosen as a location for the interview. This example – the non-recognition of a publishing company founded in Paris over fifty years ago – demonstrates the (non-)position to which the establishment in France relegates literature *in French* published outside certain major Parisian publishing houses. Why does a song cross geographical boundaries more easily than a book? Disc jockeys on Parisian radio stations are certainly more open to a Francophone world music than Parisian editors and journalists are to *littérature-monde*; we should play the latter the refrain from Sally Nyolo's 1998 hit: 'multiculti, multiculti, multiculti chantons | ô ô ô ô ô ô ô'.

Third date: 2006 was named the 'year of *Francophonie*' in France. Serving as the theme for the spring book fair in Paris, the *FrancoFFFonies* (Francophone

Festival in France) lasted for almost the whole year. It was Mexico's turn to be the special guest country for the 2009 Paris book fair. With its 110 million inhabitants and a large literary output, Mexico deserved this degree of attention. But when we look at the population of certain countries (or the number of speakers of the relevant languages) which have been guests of honour at this book fair, we have to ask why only Quebec (with a population of 9 million) should have been accorded this position at the fair, in 1999, a position never offered to an independent Francophone country such as Algeria (34 million inhabitants), Cameroon (18 million), Senegal (13 million) or Congo-Kinshasa (67 million). To hold a book fair which honoured the *Francofffonies* was a way to deal with all these countries in one go, and to avoid giving too great a place to literature from ex-French (or Belgian) colonies. Of the forty writers invited from five continents in 2006, not one represented France. Europe was represented by the Belgian and Swiss Francophone communities. But there was no Corsican or Breton writer, nor any writer from the Paris region, because such writers are *French*, not Francophone. In France in 2006 the term '*Francofffonies*' always referred to *others*. The drawing by Tomi Ungerer on the front page of *Le Monde des Livres* for the week of the Paris book fair, on 17 March 2006, provides a perfect illustration of the exotic and inevitably foreign character of *Francofffonie* in France (see my article, 'Lectures francophones ex-centrées' [Ex-centric Francophone readings], 2006): a characteristic detail is the (black) woman in the illustration smacking her lips over an ice cream in the red, white and blue colours of the French Republic.

Far from the Capital

This is why I am pleased to work in my North American context. Bernard Pivot was not the only Frenchman who seemed surprised to hear me say that Paris is not the centre of the universe for all Francophones. This is why it is a pleasure to return to Jacques Godbout's contribution to the collection *Pour une littérature-monde*. In an ironic manner, Godbout encourages us to attempt 'une fois de plus de déniaiser la province parisienne!' [once again to de-stupidify Parisian provinciality!] (2007: 110), reminding us that 'Par ignorance ou par arrogance, la France est restée accrochée à son espace littéraire national, et ses maisons d'édition à leurs réseaux hexagonaux. L'institution littéraire française n'a pas eu vraiment envie, à ce jour, de participer à une littérature-monde' (2007: 104–05).[5] Pascale Casanova, too, in *La République*

---

[5] 'Through ignorance or through arrogance, France has remained attached to its national literary space, as its publishers have to their networks within

mondiale des lettres [The World Republic of Letters] emphasizes that 'Paris ne s'est jamais intéressé aux écrivains issus de ses territoires coloniaux' [Paris has never been interested in writers from its colonial territories] and suggests that when such writers do receive the occasional rare award in France, this occurs for 'considérations néo-coloniales évidentes' [obvious neo-colonial reasons] (1999: 174). The irony, in Casanova's view, lies in the fact that all writers – who confront assimilation or differentiation imposed by national norms (1999: 246) and who seek autonomy and universality on the world stage (1999: 125) – are obliged to draw on the literary 'capital' (in the sense of both capital city and material resources) which operates as a 'banque centrale' [central bank] where authors from the periphery gain their literary 'credit' (1999: 180–81). Paris is thus not so very different from other literary capitals since '[l]es académiques (souvent académiciens) du monde entier forment la plus grande cohorte de tous les retardataires de la littérature' (1999: 145)![6] Casanova's study emphasizes the influence of literary capitals such as Paris, and the advantages and disadvantages of their 'credit'. Her adjective 'démuni' [deprived] to describe writers who do not belong to the centre is appropriate to the writers of *littérature-monde*:

> La mise au jour des contraintes qui pèsent sur tous les écrivains démunis n'a naturellement rien d'une mise à l'index ou à l'écart: il s'agit au contraire de montrer que leurs œuvres sont plus improbables encore que les autres, qu'elles parviennent presque miraculeusement à émerger et à se faire reconnaître en subvertissant, par l'invention de solutions littéraires inédites, les lois littéraires établies par les centres.[7] (Casanova, 1999 : 254)

It is not necessarily through a miracle that the works of these authors who are 'deprived' by the centre should reappear in the North American curriculum. While, in signing the manifesto for a *littérature-monde*, the writers concerned may have been seeking in some way to subvert the laws of

---

France itself. The French literary establishment has not really wanted, so far, to participate in a *littérature-monde'*.

⁶ 'academics (and sometimes academicians) across the world form the largest cohort of literary reactionaries'.

⁷ 'The exposure of the constraints which burden all deprived writers is of course in no sense an act of proscription or exclusion; it instead serves to demonstrate that their works are even more unlikely than the others, that it is almost a miracle that they should manage to appear and gain recognition while subverting, through the invention of fresh literary solutions, the literary laws established by the centres'.

the Parisian centre, it is no less true that outside 'the' Francophone capital, we have other centres (and other Haitian *lwa* [laws/gods]) which determine our perspectives and our literary 'laws' alike.

The official structures of what is known as *Francophonie* – including the Organisation Internationale de la Francophonie [International *Francophonie* Organization] (the OIF) and the Agence Universitaire de la Francophonie [University Agency for *Francophonie*] (the AUF) – are certainly evolving, but the divide between the 'Northern' and 'Southern' member countries can still be felt in areas such as book distribution and circulation networks (bookshops, associations, translations, publishing houses and universities). The digital evolution allows access, for the fortunate, to an increasing number of press agencies, websites, discussion groups and Francophone databases. The Internet also offers a beneficial form of decentralization compared with the traditional centre – in publishing and education – represented by France itself. Nevertheless, the continued focus on Paris as the centre of book publishing and French-language book circulation remains, for now, quite a destructive force for Francophone authors publishing outside the French capital. In his study *Éditer dans l'espace francophone* [Publishing in the Francophone World] (2005), Luc Pinhas examines the forces of power in all areas where French-language books are published. His overview of publishing history reminds us of the roles of Holland and Switzerland in the eighteenth century. In his survey, Pinhas brings out the importance of French-language publishing in other countries as well, such as Algeria, Lebanon and Quebec. In Quebec, for example, more books per inhabitant are published each year than in France (and more than double the figure per inhabitant in the United States), and, unlike in France (but as in the United States), the university presses occupy an important position in Quebec's publishing landscape (2005: 52, 54). According to Pinhas, 'l'édition française est sans doute aujourd'hui l'une des plus concentrées au monde' (2005: 48);[8] a few large publishing groups (including the two leading publishers in France: Hachette, which is part of the Lagardère group, and Éditis, which has belonged since 2008 to the Spanish group Planeta) control most of the French publishing market. In reality, the city of Paris has occupied the entire Francophone publishing space since the end of its own occupation by the Nazis: 'l'après-guerre est marquée par le retour sur le devant de la scène des éditeurs français et la restauration du vieux réflexe parisien de centralisme outrancier' (2005: 37).[9] We could discuss the racism and colonialist attitudes of the Parisian

---

[8] 'French publishing today is probably one of the most concentrated publishing industries in the world'.

[9] 'the post-war period is characterized by the return of the French publishers

publishers, and the minimal space allowed to books published outside France in the French literary press. Pinhas prefers to write about the book itself as object, rather than about its contents: is it possible to find a book published in Africa or Canada, for example, on a shelf in a French bookshop? 'Or Paris et la France se montrent peu poreuse à l'influence des éditeurs étrangers qui publient en français et les instances de médiation, excepté à l'occasion de moments exceptionnels et extrêmement circonscrits, [...] les dédaignent ou au mieux les ignorent' (2005: 32).[10] This does not only apply to foreign publishers: provincial firms also suffer from limited distribution, and the large and ubiquitous publishers (Galligrasseuil) prevent the small publishing houses from achieving visibility in bookshops or in the press, and recognition in Paris.

Littérature-monde?

Littérature-monde? Not yet in Paris. The manifesto is evidence of yet another attempt to change the 'colour' of French publishing. It is in Paris that the signatories publish their work; it is in Paris that they want to see a greater visibility for the Francophone literary world and a more receptive attitude towards it. There is never any discussion of issues relating to the book trade, of African bookshops which survive by selling stationery or school supplies, or, for example, book prices in a country where the twenty euros it costs to buy a text published in Paris are the equivalent of half a month's salary. If there were a real *littérature-monde*, then the ladies of the up-market sixteenth *arrondissement* in Paris would have a wonderful time, I am sure, reading the most recent popular romance from Senegal or, for example, Kettly Mars's latest *roman-feuilleton* published in Haiti. But no, these books, like volumes of Tunisian or Mauritian poetry, Moroccan novels, and a fair proportion of the literature of Quebec – to give just a few examples – are not available in France. They are unaware in Paris of this world *littérature francophone* and there is no mention of it in the manifesto.

If a revolution in *littérature-monde* does exist in this slow evolution, it is to be found, rather, on the Internet. Whether you are in New York or Rio de Janeiro, if you cannot find a bookshop which sells Haitian authors published

---

to centre stage and the restoration of the old Parisian reflex of outrageous centralization'.

[10] Paris and France are rarely receptive to the influence of overseas French-language publishers and those in charge of cultural liaison, except in exceptional circumstances and for a very limited period, [...] either disdain them or, at most, pretend they don't exist'.

in Montreal, Paris and Port-au-Prince, on-line booksellers can provide what you need. With a few clicks of the mouse you can order all sorts of books, including rare out-of-print editions. We should deplore the fact that we are thereby contributing to the death of small independent booksellers, despite our awareness that some of the rare books bought at Chapitre.com or GibertJoseph.com have come from the shelves of such small bookshops. To help the latter, there has been a fixed book price law in France since 1981. Jack Lang, the French Minister of Culture of the time, would deserve praise for this were it not for the fact that his period of office also saw the end of boat cargo in the French postal system with reduced rates for shipping books. If you want to encourage the spread of a *littérature-monde* in the French language, any book policy needs to take account of the expenses and obstacles which hinder the free *circulation* of books, wherever boats and planes may take them.

The digital divide in the Francophone world remains a concern. One day, from the suburbs of Kinshasa to the hills of Jacmel, French speakers will find it easier to participate in an increasingly digital *littérature-monde*. For now, the gap between the Francophone countries of the north and so-called third-world countries is accentuated by economic, political and institutional factors. We contribute to this through our choice of reading and the way in which we 'rich' Francophones provide other French-speakers with access to 'our' heritage. And we need to make sure that 'their' Francophone heritage is digitized and made available to us, too. A real *littérature-monde* would be able to follow the example of J.-M. G. Le Clézio in promoting a literature which is not necessarily a written one. The stories narrated by Elvira, a storyteller from the forests of Panama, referred to by Le Clézio in his acceptance speech for the Nobel Prize for Literature in 2008, are as important to us as those published in a printed book by an African in Paris. The tattoos and songs of Polynesia contribute to the construction of a Polynesian literature, which also exists in book form and in French. At the Premier Congrès des écrivains de la Caraïbe [First Caribbean Writers' Congress] which took place in Guadeloupe in November 2008, the budget in euros paid for the receptions and the air tickets for many invited writers and celebrities (including myself, I have to admit), but I couldn't find any books published in Port-au-Prince in the bookshops of Pointe-à-Pitre. This demonstrates that the financial and intellectual priorities of official and cultural French bodies – the Ministère de la Culture [Ministry of Culture] and the Secrétaire d'État de la Francophonie [Secretary of State for *Francophonie*] as well as the literary press in print, on the radio and the television – still favour Parisian publishing.

We should broaden our geographical horizons if we want to talk about *littérature-monde* in the French language. We should talk about spoken, performed, oral literature. Researchers, like official bodies, contribute to the exclusion of some authors and the privileging of others. The written book – whether in print or digital form – is not yet available to all French speakers. Modes of book circulation and patterns of access vary, depending on nationality and income.

As Francophones, we share the weight of a cultural heritage with the French language and its literature, whether it takes the form of the linguistic freedom offered by Rabelais, the masterly and libertine construction of Laclos, the Proustian sentence or the fine vulgarity of Céline. We also share, through this language, the skills of poets such as Aimé Césaire, Andrée Chedid, Abdellatif Laâbi and Gaston Miron. This doesn't prevent our revolt at the underlying racist and anti-Semitic position of Céline, or our continuing envy of Proust or Gide, for their talents, certainly, but also for the fact that they never had to concern themselves with such a banal occupation as having to earn a living.

To distract myself from these Parisian 'niaiseries' [idiocies] (whether we like it or not, they are part of the bread and butter of teachers of French), I shall conclude by quoting an excerpt from one of Franketienne's recent volumes. At more than 800 pages, *Galaxie Chaos-Babel* is no lightweight read! The 'Nobel of Bel-Air' does not confine himself to the written language, far from it: the text is lavishly accompanied by his drawings, some of which are in colour. Franketienne exceeds the confines of the Parisian publishing world; his linguistic and visual innovations explode across the pages, along with collages of words cut out of newspapers. It is not just prose. And it is not only in French. The description of Franketienne could very well apply to the Parisian centre of *littérature-monde*. The signatories of the manifesto would like other centres of influence to be present on the Parisian landscape; in America, with a Francophone city in the north (Montreal) and an independent capital in the south (Port-au-Prince), the French City of Light is not our only beacon. Twenty years ago, in Louisiana, Édouard Glissant taught me to look with a critical eye on the concept of *Francophonie*. We should pay him homage for the '*-Monde*' [World], the *Tout-Monde*, which he introduced into our discussions. We can say that American practices (in the academic world, at least) are more 'politically correct', or quite simply more multidisciplinary than those we see in France. It is certain that we have a more triangulated, or archipelic, way of engaging with the self-obsession of the Parisian literary world, which could be described by borrowing a passage from Franketienne:

crocodiles alligators caïmans bagoulines marsinflins vangouloups bornugats cornigris mapotchos rhinocéros hippopotames et toute la

race des phaloupines voraces pataugeant barbotant magouillant dans les
marécages vaseux de la malouchonnerie locale régionale internationale
maffieuse omnipotente'.[11] (Frankétienne, 2006: 666)

Translated by Teresa Bridgeman.

Works Cited

Brezault, Éloïse. 2008. 'Qu'est-ce qu'un auteur francophone?'. In Catherine Coquio
(ed.), *Retours du colonial? Disculpation et réhabilitation de l'histoire coloniale.*
Nantes: L'Atalante: 347–57.

Casanova, Pascale. 1999. *La République mondiale des lettres.* Paris: Seuil.

Céline, Louis-Ferdinand. 1937. *Bagatelles pour un massacre.* Paris: Denoël.

—. 1955. *Entretiens avec le professeur Y.* Paris: Gallimard.

Devi, Ananda. 2006. *Eve de ses décombres.* Paris: Gallimard.

Frankétienne. 2006. *Galaxie Chaos-Babel.* Port-au-Prince: Spirale.

Godbout, Jacques. 2007. 'La Question préalable'. In Michel Le Bris and Jean
Rouaud (eds), *Pour une littérature-monde.* Paris: Gallimard: 103–11.

Kourouma, Ahmadou.1968. *Les Soleils des indépendances.* Montreal: Presses de
l'Université de Montréal.

—. 1970. *Les Soleils des indépendances.* Paris: Éditions du Seuil.

Le Clézio, Jean-Marie Gustave. 2008. Nobel Prize Banquet Speech. <http://
nobelprize.org/mediaplayer/index.php?id=1125>. Consulted on 9 June 2009.

Pinhas, Luc. 2005. *Éditer dans l'espace francophone.* Paris: Alliance des éditeurs
indépendants.

'Pour une "literature-monde" en français'. 2007. *Le Monde* 16 March.

Schneck, Colombe. 1994. 'Le français piégé par le multiculturalisme américain'.
Le Monde 17 February.

Schor, Naomi. 2001. 'The Crisis of French Universalism'. *Yale French Studies*
100: 43–64.

Spear, Thomas C. 2002. *La Culture française vue d'ici et d'ailleurs.* Paris:
Karthala.

—. 2003. 'Variations sur la langue de Molière; l'enseignement du français aux
États-Unis'. *Présence francophone* 60: 12–38.

—. 2006. 'Lectures francophones ex-centrées'. In *L'Écrivain dans l'espace
francophone.* Paris: Les Dossiers de la Société des Gens de Lettres: 95–97.

---

[11] 'crocodiles alligators caimans glibbers porposers winnowolves fishydogs
hornifuddles mapotchos rhinoceros hippopotamus and the whole race of
voracious phallupines floundering wading fiddling in the muddy marshes of
local regional international all-powerful mafioso malpracticery'.

<http://www.sgdl.org/la-documentation/les-dossiers/271>. Consulted on 9 June 2009.

'Toward a "World-Literature" in French'. 2009. Trans. by Daniel Simon. *World Literature Today* (March–April): 54–56.

Waberi, Abdourahman. 2007. 'Écrivains en position d'entraver'. In Michel Le Bris and Jean Rouaud (eds), *Pour une littérature-monde*. Paris: Gallimard: 67–75.

Littérature-monde
and Old/New Humanism

Jane Hiddleston

The *littérature-monde* movement, as it is elucidated in the 2007 volume *Pour une littérature-monde*, has at its heart the ambition to uncouple literature from the nation. Frustrated with the neo-colonial undertones of *Francophonie*, with the term's perpetuation of an imperialist conception of the benefits of French culture and language for the 'natives' of its supposedly inferior colonies and ex-colonies, Rouaud and Le Bris propose *littérature-monde* as a more liberating, all-encompassing term for the literature of diverse cultures throughout the world. The last vestige of French colonialism, *Francophonie* is described by Le Bris as 'un espace sur lequel la France mère des arts, dépositaire de l'universel, dispenserait ses lumières' (Le Bris, 2007: 45),[1] and *littérature-monde* will sound the death knell of this essentially nationalist and ultimately reductive conception of literary production in French. Moreover, at the same time *littérature-monde* offers a challenge not only to the strict association of literature with the nation, but also to an excessive self-consciousness or 'textualism' detected in literature in French in the wake of post-structuralism and the *nouveau roman*. *Littérature-monde* refuses what is seen as an inward-looking preoccupation with language in order to embrace lived realities. If this two-pronged critique of *Francophonie* is carried out in the name of a celebration of plurality and diversity, however, it is striking that this plurality is couched in terms

---

[1] 'a space upon which France, the mother of the arts and trustee of the universal, would bestow her enlightenment'. Unless otherwise indicated, all translations from French into English are by the author of this chapter.

of a new humanism. On the one hand, Rouaud and Le Bris affirm that their movement addresses a universal humanity, rather than simply the citizens of the French nation and its colonies or ex-colonies, and they conceive literature as a site for the exploration of human beings above and beyond their national affiliations. *Littérature-monde* celebrates the enriching intermingling of human cultures, the vast, chaotic network of interactions that affects and defines all human life. On the other hand, Rouaud and Le Bris equally champion a commitment to humanity as opposed to pure textuality, and recommend an exploration of 'l'humaine condition' [the human condition] (Le Bris, 2007: 26, 41) in contradistinction to what they perceive as French literature's recent and arid focus on literature itself.

References to humanity and to the human condition are abundant throughout the collection of essays that makes up *Pour une littérature-monde*. Two initial references to 'l'humaine condition' are cited above, and both Rouaud and Le Bris repeatedly emphasize the capacity of *littérature-monde* to embrace the human in ways that they believe French literature has tended to foreclose. In addition to denouncing the introspective formalism of the *nouveau roman*, for example, Le Bris also condemns in particular the structuralist desire to subordinate humanity to 'l'Empire du Signe' [the Empire of the Sign], and argues that, since signs are also translatable, 'prétendre soumettre l'espace humain à l'Empire du Signe revenait donc à vouloir des hommes traduisibles eux aussi les uns dans les autres, eux aussi interchangeables' (Le Bris, 2007: 46).[2] This excessive emphasis on signs, then, obscures according to Le Bris the infinite diversity of humanity. Furthermore, many of the authors of the essays in the body of the volume affirm the importance for literature to probe and celebrate human experience in all its manifold forms. Abdourahman Waberi, for example, asks what is a poem if not an attempt to 'caresser des yeux et du cœur le visage humain toujours si semblable et si différent?' (Waberi, 2007: 72).[3] Grégoire Polet underlines the universal shared experience of humanity in his affirmation that 'la Terre est ronde, quoi qu'en disent les esprits chagrins et scolastiques. L'humanité est une!' (Polet, 2007: 125).[4] Lyonel Trouillot differentiates 'écriture' [writing]

---

[2] 'the claim to submit the human race to the Empire of the Sign amounted to wanting men to be translatable one to the other, as interchangeable as signs themselves'.

[3] 'caress with one's eyes and one's heart the human face which is always so similar and always so different'.

[4] 'the Earth is round, whatever despondent and scholarly minds say about it. Humanity is unified!'

from 'littérature' [literature] by arguing that, while the latter belongs to society, the former precisely 'relève de l'humain' [comes under the aegis of the human] (Trouillot, 2007: 197). Literature is grounded in history, and yet 'l'écriture', or more specifically Trouillot's conception of 'écriture-monde', would have at its heart 'l'exploration des thèmes, des formes qui posent à la vie humaine la question de son sens' (Trouillot, 2007: 202–03).[5] And for Gary Victor, literature is 'un lieu où l'humain peut constamment se recréer et se redécouvrir' [a site where the human can constantly recreate and rediscover itself] (Victor, 2007: 315). This humanism recognizes humanity's simultaneous universality and diversity, and anchors literature in human life rather than in the abstract realm of language.

The humanism of the *littérature-monde* movement is conceived to celebrate human diversity, and yet it is intriguing that some of its supporters uphold a notion of universality that echoes the very humanism that fuelled the colonial mission. It is perhaps ironic that Le Bris precisely notes that the movement grew out of a dissatisfaction with the state of French literature, 'devenue sourde et aveugle, me semblait-il, à la course du monde, à force de se croire la seule, l'unique, l'ultime référence, à jamais admirable, modèle livré à l'humanité' (Le Bris, 2007: 25);[6] and yet Le Bris too conceives his movement as a model for all humanity. In many ways, the humanism of the *littérature-monde* movement indeed seems not unrelated to that of the Republic seeking to embrace and assimilate cultural differences into an overarching framework, governed by liberty, equality and fraternity. Many of the writers cited above may set out to advocate the exploration of human diversity through literature, but the idea of 'l'humaine condition' continues to imply a degree of sameness that could quickly become reductive. Indeed, a 'condition' suggests a recognized set of experiences inevitably shared by all. Moreover, if they seek to reinvent humanism and to create a more dynamic understanding of the human than that which fuelled the *mission civilisatrice*, this is also a gesture clearly inherited from much earlier anti-colonial thinkers such as Césaire and Fanon, and, indeed, the humanism of the present collection lacks the sophistication and nuance of these earlier versions. I want to argue, then, that despite the laudable aims of the collection, its call for a form of writing that is 'multiple, diverse, colorée, multipolaire et non pas uniforme comme le craignaient les esprits chagrins'

---

[5] 'the exploration of themes, of forms which pose fundamental questions about human life itself'.

[6] 'which has become deaf and blind, it seems to me, to the world's development, because it conceives itself the single, unique, the ultimate reference, a forever admirable model bestowed to humanity'.

(Le Bris, 2007: 41),[7] its humanism at times seems less innovative than its proponents claim. Moreover, this humanism fails to take into account the sophisticated input not only of previous anti-colonials such as Césaire and Fanon, but also the humanism found in the very post-structuralism vilified by Rouaud and Le Bris. Finally, I shall conclude by suggesting that, most recently, Edward Said offers a theory not only of humanist writing but also, crucially, of humanist reading, from which the movement may have much to learn.

One of the first difficulties of the humanism of the *littérature-monde* movement is, perhaps, this notion of the universal 'human condition' and its potential complicity with the assimilatory forms of Eurocentric humanism that the writers of the *littérature-monde* movement set out to reject. Indeed, at times the celebration of the human condition implies that the metropolitan authors Rouaud and Le Bris perceive a clear and perceptible relation between their own experiences and those of the indigenous peoples in France's colonies and ex-colonies. It is possible that, in their eagerness to liberate literature from 'son pacte avec la nation' [its pact with the nation] (Rouaud, 2007: 21), Rouaud and Le Bris undermine the specific differences between national and cultural histories. As David Murphy (2010) points out, Le Bris's essay also seems hasty in its announcement of the 'fin aussi d'une conception impérialiste de la langue' [end also of an imperialist conception of language] (Le Bris, 2007: 45), and there is the risk that, so eager are they to abolish the legacy of colonialism, Le Bris and Rouaud finish by eradicating and denying tensions that indubitably still exist. *Littérature-monde* is conceived to put an end to the imperialist overtones of *Francophonie*, but in rejecting the term *Francophonie* it may at the same time fail to account for the specific postcolonial anxieties that affect authors from the DOM-ROM (départements d'outre-mer/régions d'outre-mer) and the ex-colonies writing in French. Many such writers still write consciously in the wake of colonialism and their writing is still plagued by their country's colonial past or present. The universality of the humanism of the *littérature-monde* movement for this reason risks positing a sameness that would occlude diverse experiences of colonialism and that would flatten out tensions that persist in disturbing ways in the writing of a plethora of authors from countries that suffered or still suffer from particular forms of political, economic and cultural oppression. Le Bris and Rouaud may set out to insist on human diversity as well as sameness, but their refusal to explore the ongoing effects of colonialism, together with their retention of

---

[7] 'multiple, diverse, colourful, multipolar and not uniform as was feared by doom-mongers'.

a notion of a shared 'condition', means that their humanism, like that of the past, again risks obscuring certain kinds of difference.

In addition, a form of humanism reminiscent of that of the *littérature-monde* movement is detectable in the work of a number of former anti-colonial thinkers, and is articulated with considerably more nuance. First, in addition to asserting the specificity of black identity, Aimé Césaire affirms the black man's humanity as a statement of resistance to the dehumanizing drive of colonial exploitation. If colonialism is 'thingification', then anti-colonialism requires the restoration of the black man's humanity, and that humanity, as for the proponents of the *littérature-monde* movement, must be recognized as infinitely diverse (Césaire, 1972: 21). In particular, it is significant that in Césaire's *Cahier d'un retour au pays natal*, humanism exists not in contradiction with the affirmation of a specific identity, but in dialogue with the poet's very celebration of Negritude. While the advocates of the *littérature-monde* movement tend to champion a broad humanism which, though claiming to embrace diversity, in reality makes little mention of the specific experiences of colonized peoples, and which is overtly opposed to national identity, Césaire's humanism precisely grows out of his attempt to redefine both black specificity and Martinican identity. Having decried the diseased state of Martinique in the first section, for example, Césaire explores in the middle section of the poem the heritage and experience of the black self that was denied by colonialism and slavery, and black subjectivity is portrayed both as historically specific and as open, relational and dynamic as a result of its interaction with the rest of the world. Negritude is a specific claiming of black identity but it affirms not a state of being but an action or process, 'it reaches deep down into the red flesh of the soil | it reaches deep into the blazing flesh of the sky' (Césaire, 1995: 115). Moreover, the closing pages of the *Cahier* serve to elucidate the relationality of both black identity and humanity. Black experience may be historically specific, but black subjectivity is created out of its contacts with the world and with humanity as a whole, and, even more, it is the celebration of these contacts that serves as a force of resistance against the constraints of colonialism. The poet beseeches: 'bind me with your vast arms to the luminous clay | bind my black vibration to the very navel of the world | bind me, bind me, bitter brotherhood' (Césaire, 1995: 135). The poetic self is integrated into the very stuff of the earth, and his black identity is connected with the core of the world as if by an umbilical cord. Black subjectivity is also global, linked to the history of humanity as well as to the natural world. At the same time, moreover, this affirmation does not serve as a final apotheosis or endpoint. The closing assertion, 'I now want to fish the night's malevalent tongue in its immobile verrition', evokes at once stasis and movement, movement in stasis, but not completion (Césaire, 1995: 135).[8] The interpenetration of Negritude and humanism is not a culmination but sets both concepts in motion; both continually evolve as a result of their contact with the other and with the world.

So Césaire keeps a productive tension between black specificity and universal humanism in his *Cahier*, and though his definitions of humanity as relational and diverse anticipate some of the proposals of the *littérature-monde* movement, he offers a more nuanced vision of how the specific plays into the universal. Similarly, Frantz Fanon's humanism in *Peau noire, masques blancs* and *Les Damnés de la terre* foreshadows both the dynamism and the materiality of the humanism of Rouaud and Le Bris, and yet it is more clearly worked out of the emancipation of specific colonized peoples. Gary Victor's assertion, quoted above, that literature might be 'un lieu où l'humain peut constamment se recréer et se redécouvrir' [a site where the human can constantly recreate and rediscover itself] (Victor, 2007: 315) contains powerful echoes of Fanonian thinking, and yet Fanon's texts tie this process of reinvention much more explicitly to a historical moment of liberation from colonialism and such references to historical specificity are frequently what the *littérature-monde* essays by Le Bris and Rouaud lack. In the conclusion to *Peau noire, masques blancs*, for example, Fanon argues that if the black man is to be recognized for his humanity, this requires precisely the celebration of difference. For Gary Victor, and equally for Rouaud and Le Bris, humanity is championed because it is dynamic, and each individual capable of endless self-invention. The term *homme* is a sort of empty signifier; it is deployed as a call for a recognition of the freedom of all, and as an affirmation of the power and the needs of every human body. This celebration both of diversity and of concrete materiality and lived experience, then, seems very close to the mission of the *littérature-monde* movement, and both polemics also share a suspicion towards theoretical abstraction. But although Fanon's conclusion refuses a humanism based on the past, on the weight of history – 'I am not a prisoner of history. I should not seek there for the meaning of my destiny' (Fanon, 1967: 229) – he clearly conceives the process of human reinvention as one that emerges from specific instances of oppression. Fanon also calls for the liberation of all men and for the celebration of human diversity, but this occurs at the same time as the oppressed black man is compelled to assert: 'my cry grew more violent: I am a Negro, I am a Negro, I am a Negro' (Fanon,

---

[8] A. James Arnold comments on the link between Césaire's 'immobile verrition' and Breton's 'explosante fixe'. Reminiscent also of Rimbaud, the image conveys the idea of holding onto a moment of pure energy and dynamism (see Arnold, 1981: 167).

1967: 138). Like that of Césaire, Fanon's humanism grows directly out of his embrace of Negritude and the specific lived experience of the colonized black man. His work conceptualizes in this way the tension between the universal and the particular in more nuanced ways than the proponents of *littérature-monde*, who propose a more overtly Glissantian system of relationality that risks glossing over specific instances of oppression.

Equally, in *Les Damnés de la terre*, Fanon's humanism seems closely related to his celebration of national culture. While Rouaud and Le Bris argue that the concept of *littérature-monde* should liberate literature from its pact with the nation, Fanon's text shows how literature and culture can precisely retain a dynamic relationship both with nationalism and with humanism. National culture for Fanon is not necessarily reductive and limiting, but can function as the means of expression for a dynamically emerging people. His example is that of Algerian national culture at the time of the independence movement, and he argues that literature and art emerge spontaneously from the combat. Evidently, the example of Algerian nationalism is very different from the protection of the French nation vilified by the proponents of *littérature-monde*, and, indeed, Fanon's predictions of national unity turned out to be disastrously utopian. Yet it is nevertheless significant that Fanon offers a vision of literature and national identity that is much more dynamic than that presupposed by Rouaud and Le Bris. National culture for Fanon should not fall into reproducing stereotypes but emerges from the creative activity of the people. Fanon takes as an example a poem by Keita Fodeba, Minister of the Interior in the Republic of Guinea, in which the poet narrates the hero Naman's participation in the Second World War and subsequent murder when protesting against the white leaders in Dakar. He praises the poem's clarity and frankness, 'it is a precise, forward-looking exposition' (Fanon, 1967: 186), and applauds the way in which it communicates to the people the injustice of the colonial system and the necessity of resistance. Above all, Fanon argues that it is the poem's rootedness in action, in the reality of the combat that gives it its revolutionary force. It is also acted out both on the page and in the body, and maintains the immediacy of Fanon's concept of lived experience explored and upheld in *Peau noire, masques blancs*. The intellectual or poet does not inhabit merely the realm of abstract contemplation but involves both body and mind in his expression of resistance: 'to ensure that hope and give it form, he must take part in action and throw himself body and soul into the national struggle' (Fanon, 1967: 187). This physicality, this immersion of intellectual and poetic work into the everyday realities of the conflict lends to Fanon's vision of national culture a unique dynamism. National culture is necessarily always being recreated and refuses both abstraction and stereotype. Fanon's conception of national culture as the product of a collaborative present could perhaps also be used, then, to reimagine the link between literature and *Francophonie* as a similarly dynamic and spontaneous process of dialogue.

Moreover, this national culture is a part of Fanon's humanism, as it is celebrated in the text's conclusion. Once again, humanism does not replace national identity but emerges from it, as Fanon's conception of the human closely echoes the subjective agency crucial to the national culture essay. The most important feature of Fanon's conception of humanism is precisely its novelty. Fanon's humanism will not imitate European culture, and, indeed, he enjoins the Algerian people to imagine a universality that Europe struggled to achieve: 'let us try to create the whole man, whom Europe has been incapable of bringing to triumphant birth' (Fanon, 1967: 252). Like the national culture that he also upholds, then, humanism for Fanon is not weighed down by a specific heritage determined by the past, but he instead repeats numerous times that decolonization will lead to the invention of new men. Fanon's closing demand reinforces the novelty that the rest of the text has been seeking, and yet this novelty is more important than any determined identity: 'we must turn over a new leaf, we must work out new concepts, and try to set afoot a new nation' (Fanon, 1967: 255). In addition, as well as providing a link with Fanon's conception of national culture, Fanon's new humanism retains an openness that the concept of the 'humaine condition' found in the *littérature-monde* essays can seem to lack. While Rouaud and Le Bris claim to celebrate the multiplicity of humanity, they also fail properly to interrogate specifically how the term 'human' signifies. For Fanon, however, the human is a crucial but a much more fraught concept; it is both maintained and emptied out; it is a residual category without content, and signifies only a fundamental ethical need for recognition. And, even more, while Le Bris and Rouaud imply an embrace of lived reality as opposed to textualism, it is Fanon who inscribes the corporeal at the heart of postcolonial humanism. If, according to Fanon, colonialism causes a tension in the colonized's muscles, then liberation will bring the redirection and release of that muscular energy: 'let us decide not to imitate Europe; let us combine our muscles and our brains in a new direction' (Fanon, 1967: 252). This call for physical reassertion is not according to Fanon a simplistic return to Nature, but rather a reclaiming of corporeal dignity: 'it is simply a very concrete question of not dragging men towards mutilation, of not imposing on the brain rhythms which very quickly obliterate it and wreck it' (Fanon, 1967: 253–54). Fanon's vision of humanist freedom is conceived as the liberation of the human body, as freedom of movement and as a seizing of energy. Fanon's humanism is nothing other than the reintegration of mind and body, the renewed energizing of the body in defiance of colonial oppression, and his writing conceives this corporeal energizing in more precise and more pressing terms than the rather more woolly phraseology of Le Bris and Rouaud.

Another difficulty with the humanism of Rouaud and Le Bris's essays is that this championing of something akin to Fanon's lived experience is expressed as a highly irate rejection of a certain reflection on language found in the work of *nouveaux romanciers* such as Claude Simon and Alain Robbe-Grillet. Even more, in Le Bris's essay the distaste for self-consciousness in literature expands to become a rejection of what he terms 'la Théorie du Signe' [the Theory of the Sign], as he suggests that structuralism was itself just a 'prise du pouvoir' [seizing of power] (Le Bris, 2007: 26) that occluded real people. Yet although it is no doubt true that both structuralism and the *nouveau roman* set as the object of their investigations the mechanics of signification, the highly generalized criticisms thrown out in Rouaud and Le Bris's essays suggest too stark an opposition between textualism or linguistics and humanism. Le Bris actually cites Tzvetan Todorov as an example of a thinker who has shifted away from structuralism to an awareness of the danger posed to literature by excessive self-consciousness, but fails to see that there might be a continuum between the two phases of Todorov's work.[9] Indeed, Todorov's exploration of literary form and function in texts such as *La Notion de littérature* of 1987 is bound up specifically with reflection on how texts impact on real readers, and his *Nous et les autres* [On human diversity] of 1989 is precisely an investigation of how human others are figured and conceived in texts. Furthermore, thinkers such as Roland Barthes and Jacques Derrida combine equally strikingly an early reflection on structuralist linguistics with later contemplation of the affect that lies at the heart of human experience. Such apparently diverse subjects of investigation are at the same time not related to distinct and separate areas of thought, but clearly emerge one from the other. Barthes's study of Japanese cultural signs in *The Empire of Signs*, for example, is at once a highly technical semiotic reflection and the result of a direct encounter with human difference. Most explicitly, the work of Jacques Derrida has become more and more explicitly concerned with the relation between processes of signification and forms of human experience that resist that signification – that compel us to narrate but that at the same time defy narration. 'Circumfession', a sort of circum-locutionary contemplation of the philosopher's Jewishness, his circumcision and the death of his mother, and *The Work of Mourning*, his collection of funerary orations, are deeply concerned both with language and 'text', and at the same time with irreducible human affect. For Lou F. Caton, in his texts on cosmopolitanism, mourning and the secret, Derrida is constantly engaging

---

[9] Le Bris cites Todorov's *La Littérature en péril* (2006).

with humanism even as he explores the ways in which language signifies, and these questions are inextricably linked: 'the human has a discursive definition, of course, and notoriously shows how language continually fails in its adequacy to that textuality. But there is always excess; there is always more than language can handle. The disruption of writing, then, may tear at the human but does not destroy her' (Caton, 2004: 800).[10] It seems, then, that Le Bris calls for attention to the human in contradistinction to textuality, while many of the major theorists of textuality precisely offer a more subtle integration between (post)structuralism, linguistics and humanism.

Finally, it is perhaps the humanism of Edward Said that appears at face value to be closest to that of the proponents of *littérature-monde*, and yet once again I shall argue that Said offers a further perspective on the relation between literature and humanism that is problematically lacking in the essays of Le Bris and Rouaud. First, it is perhaps significant that, as far back as 1983, Said invented the notion of 'worldliness' as a way of thinking about how texts are intricately bound up with specific places and experiences. In *The World, The Text and The Critic*, Said asserts that literary works are necessarily embedded in the cultural communities in which they are born, and that even the most abstract and abstruse work is tied to a human context. Said's argument is that 'texts are worldly, to some degree they are events, and, even when they appear to deny it, they are nevertheless part of the social world, human life, and of course the historical moments in which they are located and interpreted' (Said, 1983: 4). The problem with recent American literary criticism for Said is that it has tended to forget this worldliness, and has become preoccupied with merely conforming to the demands of the market and strengthening its institutional status. Said's denunciation of contemporary criticism here may be distinct from Rouaud and Le Bris's vilification of the self-consciousness of French literature, and yet it is clear that their mistrust of abstraction and embrace of the human through literature finds its roots in Said's work published at least twenty years previously. Said also laments the 'philosophy of pure textuality' associated for him with the ascendancy of Reaganism and a turn to the political right, and his call for attention to human experience, history and politics anticipates the assumed challenge to conservatism in Le Bris and Rouaud's critique of the imperialism of *Francophonie* (Said, 1983: 4).

It is in *Humanism and Democratic Criticism* (2004), however, that Said's humanism reaches its fullest expression, and again this is accompanied by a concept of 'worldliness' very close to that of the *littérature-monde* movement.

---

10 This is from Lou F. Caton's review essay on *A Taste for the Secret* (Derrida and Ferraris, 2001). See also Derrida 2001a and 2001b.

As in *The World, The Text and The Critic*, Said conceives his humanism as a critique of what he perceives as structuralist antihumanism, and he states somewhat dismissively:

> despite the (in my opinion) shallow but influential ideas of a certain facile type of radical antifoundationalism, with its insistence that real events are at most linguistic effects, and its close relative, the end of history thesis, these are so contradicted by the historical impact of human agency and labor as to make a detailed refutation of them here unnecessary. (Said, 2004: 10)

Once again, his embrace of the human resonates with Rouaud and Le Bris's suspicion of an excessive attention to linguistic effects in French literature. In addition, however, Said now also calls for a rethinking of national identity, and 'worldliness' is more explicitly bound up with a celebration of cultural plurality and interaction. Furthermore, humanism is concerned with listening to the voices of marginalized peoples, those excluded from mainstream national discourses, the testimonies of 'barely surviving groups, the places of exclusion and invisibility', located outside the metropolitan centre (Said, 2004: 81). Still like Rouaud and Le Bris, Said is recommending a way of conceiving literary production outside of imperialist structures as well as across national frontiers.

Yet one of the most pressing demands of Said's *Humanism and Democratic Criticism* is its call not for a humanist form of writing but for humanist reading. While the essays of *Pour une littérature-monde* argue that literature should broadly be *conceived* as originating in its relations with the world, for Said this actually means that we should *read* in a different way. His humanism, then, is not merely a banal celebration of literature's ability to reflect on life, but a specific ethics of reading that recommends a thorough attention to how texts change our understanding of the world. Rouaud and Le Bris may repeatedly affirm the diversity associated with *littérature-monde*, what Le Bris describes as 'le télescopage, dans le creuset des mégapoles modernes, de cultures multiples, et l'enfantement d'un monde nouveau' (Le Bris, 2007: 41).[11] But for Said, it is not enough repeatedly to affirm the existence of literary multiplicity; we need also to learn how to read properly, to attend to difference without appropriating it and reducing it to the familiar. Numerous times throughout *Humanism and Democratic Criticism*, Said stresses how humanism is precisely a process of careful reading, such as when he cites Richard Poirier (1987) on active reading and concludes that 'only acts of

---

[11] 'the telescoping, in the melting pot of modern agglomerations, of multiple cultures, and the birth of a new world'.

reading done more and more carefully, as Poirier suggests, more and more attentively, more and more widely, more and more receptively and resistantly (if I may coin a word) can provide humanism with an adequate exercise of its essential worth' (Said, 2004: 60–61). This attentive reading means first understanding the text as a specific object, then tracing its relations with history, culture and society, and conceiving these as a vast and complex network. It is also this form of diligent reading that allows the humanist to look beyond national categories, to attend to voices that are outside norms and institutions, and that gives his practice an ethical openness to the complexity of cultural difference. And, even more, Said explores how this commitment to careful reading precisely originates not in Europe, not in colonial cultures, but in Islam itself. The interpretation of the Koran, or *ijtihad*, is conceived as such an infinite and challenging process, that the reader must expend considerable and ongoing effort, as well as paying due attention to the community of readers that precedes her.

In this way, Said sketches a more compelling ethics than that of the *littérature-monde* movement, and he does so at the same time by means of a more rigorous reference to a non-European culture. His references to humanism and worldliness work not simply as a means of staving off excessive textualism, but serve precisely to recommend a degree of rigour and effort when approaching literary texts. While, like Rouaud and Le Bris, Said retains something of a stereotypical view of 'structuralist antihumanism', he is nevertheless much more specific in his discussion of how to read texts in such a way as to decipher the manner in which their language might alter our understanding of the worlds of which they speak. The difference between the approaches of Said and the founders of *littérature-monde*, then, is that Said's announces an ethics of scholarship and admits precisely to the anxiety and difficulty of humanist reading. For Said, 'the intellectual's provisional home is the domain of an exigent, resistant, intransigent art into which, alas, one can neither retreat nor search for solutions. But only in that precarious exilic realm can one first truly grasp the difficulty of what cannot be grasped and then go forth and try anyway' (Said, 2004: 144). For Rouaud and Le Bris, however, the humanity of *littérature-monde* is much more a cause for celebration, and diversity is perceived as stimulating but not necessarily opaque or difficult to grasp. Their essays are also much less geared towards intellectual engagement than towards marketing. The jubilant call for worldliness is an attempt to sell a new movement in the wake of *Francophonie* but the level of intellectual engagement with processes of reading and interpretation is relatively low. The collection may be aimed at writers, booksellers and the public at large as much as at intellectuals, but it is nevertheless undeniable that the humanism embedded within it is more seductive than it is rigorous. It also lacks the dynamic tensions of Césaire and Fanon's humanism between the specific and the universal, and adds little to the various concepts of the human found in the existing anti-colonial thinkers. Ultimately, while vilifying abstraction, Rouaud and Le Bris's vision remains a relatively abstract and superficial reworking of previous forms of postcolonial humanism, and fails, moreover, to elucidate the vital ethics at that humanism's core. It champions human diversity, but lacks a notion of the work of reading and attending to that diversity, which in turn would serve to give humanism both rigour and substance.

Works Cited

Arnold, A. James. 1981. *Modernism and Negritude: The Poetry and Poetics of Aimé Césaire*. Cambridge, MA: Harvard University Press.

Barthes, Roland. 1980. *L'Empire des signes*. Paris: Flammarion.

—. 1983. *The Empire of Signs*. Trans. by Richard Howard. London: Cape.

Caton, Lou F. 2004. 'The Impossible Humanism for Today's Cosmopolitan: Jacques Derrida's Recent Books on Mourning, Forgiveness, and Secrets'. *Critical Sociology* 30.3: 799–815.

Césaire, Aimé. 1972. *Discourse on Colonialism*. Trans. by Joan Pinkham. London: Monthly Review Press.

—. 1995. *Cahier d'un retour au pays natal*. Newcastle upon Tyne: Bloodaxe. [First published in 1939.]

Derrida, Jacques. 1993. 'Circumfession'. In Geoffrey Bennington and Jacques Derrida, *Jacques Derrida*. Trans. by Geoffrey Bennington. Chicago: University of Chicago Press.

—. 2001a. *On Cosmopolitanism and Forgiveness*. Trans. by Mark Dooley and Michael Hughes. London and New York: Routledge. [First published as *Cosmopolites de tous les pays, encore un effort*. Paris: Galilée (1997).]

—. 2001b. *The Work of Mourning*. Ed. by Pascale-Anne Brault and Michael Naas. Chicago: University of Chicago Press.

Derrida, Jacques, and Maurizio Ferraris. 2001. *A Taste for the Secret*. Trans. by Giacomo Donis. Ed. by Giacomo Donis and David Webb. Malden, MA: Blackwell.

Fanon, Frantz. 1952. *Peau noire, masques blancs*. Paris: Seuil.

—. 1967. *Black Skin, White Masks*. Trans. by Charles Lam Markmann. London: Pluto Press.

—. 1991. *Les Damnés de la terre*. Paris: Gallimard. [First published in 1961.]

Le Bris, Michel. 2007. 'Pour une littérature-monde en français'. In Michel Le Bris and Jean Rouaud (eds), *Pour une littérature-monde*. Paris: Gallimard: 23–53.

Le Bris, Michel, and Jean Rouaud (eds). 2007. *Pour une littérature-monde*. Paris: Gallimard.

Murphy, David. 2010. 'Literature after Empire: A Comparative Reading of Two Literary Manifestos'. *Contemporary French and Francophone Studies* 14.1: 67–75. [Special issue: William J. Cloonan and Alec G. Hargreaves (eds), '*Littérature-Monde*: New Wave or New Hype?']

Poirier, Richard. 1987. *The Renewal of Literature: Emersonian Reflections*. New York: Random House.

Polet, Grégoire. 2007. 'L'Atlas du monde'. In Michel Le Bris and Jean Rouaud (eds), *Pour une littérature-monde*. Paris: Gallimard: 125–34.

Rouaud, Jean. 2007. 'Mort d'une certaine idée'. In Michel Le Bris and Jean Rouaud (eds), *Pour une littérature-monde*. Paris: Gallimard: 7–22.

Said, Edward. 1983. *The World, the Text, and the Critic*. London and Boston: Faber and Faber.

—. 2004. *Humanism and Democratic Criticism*. London: Palgrave.

Todorov, Tzvetan. 1987. *La Notion de littérature, et autres essais*. Paris: Seuil.

—. 1989. *Nous et les autres: La réflexion française sur la diversité humaine*. Paris: Seuil.

—. 1993. *On Human Diversity: Nationalism, Racism, and Exoticism in French Thought*. Trans. by Catherine Porter. Cambridge, MA: Harvard University Press.

—. 2006. *La littérature en péril*. Paris: Flammarion.

Trouillot, Lyonel. 2007. 'Langues, voyages et archipels'. In Michel Le Bris and Jean Rouaud (eds), *Pour une littérature-monde*. Paris: Gallimard: 197–204.

Victor, Gary. 2007. 'Littérature-monde ou liberté d'être'. In Michel Le Bris and Jean Rouaud (eds), *Pour une littérature-monde*. Paris: Gallimard: 315–20.

Waberi, Abdourahman A. 2007. 'Ecrivains en position d'entraver'. In Michel Le Bris and Jean Rouaud (eds), *Pour une littérature-monde*. Paris: Gallimard: 67–75.

Mapping *Littérature-monde*

Littérature-monde,
or Redefining Exotic Literature?

Jean-Xavier Ridon

The argument developed within this chapter is framed within a paradox that is central to the notions of *littérature-monde* and Francophone literature. Each of these literatures challenges, and frequently denounces, exoticism as a concept directly inherited from the colonial past whilst simultaneously pursuing a search for new forms capable of representing the world's diversity. For both *littérature-monde* and Francophone literature, exoticism is the appropriation of the other expressed through a hegemonic discourse that more often than not returns us to the West. Whether it functions as the source of dreams or of fantasies of the other, exoticism is one of the driving forces of all forms of Orientalism.

Criticism of exoticism thus forms part of the worthwhile project of deconstructing the Western subject insofar as the latter must now recognize and reveal the ideologies that subject brings to bear on his or her perception of the other. However, the aim of this disclosure is not so much to silence the Western subject as to seek out the places where the voice of the other can be found and heard and also to reveal the location of exoticism's formulation. In this way, the very idea of *Francophonie* can be said to have arisen from the desire to recognize the position of non-hexagonal French literary voices and the contribution of their cultural, geographic and linguistic differences. As a site of recognition, Francophone literature made audible the voice of writers who hitherto had been deprived of a space within which to disseminate such difference. For this reason, it would be inaccurate to reduce the notion of *Francophonie* to an act of subjugation to a centre that imposes its own identity. For to do so would be to ignore the participation of those very marginal voices that contributed to its construction. There is, nonetheless, consensus amongst each of the contributing writers to *Pour une littérature monde* that the very definition of Francophone literature, as well as the institutions of *Francophonie*, are built upon a dynamic of opposition between centre and periphery. The concept of *Francophonie* recreates a border aimed at distinguishing literatures that share the same language. With its reproduction of a hierarchy in which France is the instance of power determining criteria of literary inclusion and exclusion, this notion is clearly not so far removed from a certain form of neo-colonialism.[1] In this way, the sign of recognition of the other's difference instigates forms of representation allowing the Western subject to apply his/her power. Thus, by conforming to a description imposed from outside, Francophone literature unconsciously defines a representation of the other that may be perceived as a new form of exoticism. Francophone literature is exotic if it is limited and defined from a centre that qualifies it as the other of a norm.

But in what way does the concept of *littérature-monde* allow us to escape this paradox? And can exoticism be avoided if, as Alain Mabanckou remarks, most so-called Francophone authors do not exist and are not recognized until they sign with a French, invariably Parisian, editor.[2] For these authors, literary success is confirmed with the unqualified adoption by the French literary establishment: in other words, 'l'auteur de l'espace francophone ne commencerait à exister que lorsque la place parisienne tout entière lui aurait discerné un passeport' (Mabanckou, 2007: 58).[3] After all, in his opening pages, Michel Le Bris reproduces this paradox when he notes that the event revealing there has been a 'Copernican' revolution is the fact that: 'pour la

---

[1] In his contribution to the Manifesto, 'La Question préalable', Jacques Godbout describes this situation clearly: 'Les Français ont plutôt perpétué l'approche coloniale en acceptant de nommer "francophonie" leur relation nouvelle avec les nations libérées. Le nouvel espace serait "francophone", la France magnanime faisait don de sa langue aux peuples du monde, mais Paris restait le banquier de la littérature' [The French perpetuated the colonial approach in agreeing to name their new relationship with liberated nations *Francophonie*. This new space would be 'Francophone', a magnanimous France made a gift of its language to the people of the world, but Paris remained the banker of literature] (Godbout, 2007: 104). Unless otherwise indicated, all translations from French into English are by the author of this chapter.

[2] In the Francophone world, only Morocco and Quebec have developed a publishing industry that ensures they have significant amount of independence in relation to France.

[3] 'the Francophone author does not exist until the entire Parisian establishment has granted him/her official entry'.

première fois dans la vie littéraire française, cinq des sept principaux prix littéraires de l'automne ont été décernés à quatre des auteurs que l'on dit d'ordinaire, avec un rien de condescendance, "francophones'" (Le Bris, 2007: 23).[4] Here, change is said to have come from recognizing the power of these peripheral voices whereas one might have in fact thought that the refusal by four Francophone authors to accept these prizes would have constituted a more effective challenge of what they represented and, more importantly, would have underlined these authors' independence with regard to the Parisian literary establishment. Furthermore, how is the reproduction of an exotic representative type to be avoided when the very concept of *littérature-monde* is linked, by Le Bris and others, to travel literature? For, despite claims to the contrary, the driving force of this particular genre is the dream and discovery of an elsewhere. Indeed, how can a literature anxious to 'speak of' the world avoid reproducing an exotic discourse? Above and beyond the vague nature of the expression, what precisely does 'express the world' mean? If it means rubbing up against diversity and the world's differences and thereby providing us with a vision of the multiple cultures that surround us, then this literature is inseparable from exoticism whether this be Western or defined by another location. Indeed, this means it is situated in the interstice between discovery and the unknown that is the very motor of the exotic imagination. The remainder of this essay thus looks more closely at the links between exoticism and travel writing, as this genre is defined in the different publications and activities of the Etonnants Voyageurs festival as well as in the most recent manifesto. Do the authors redefine this term? If so, do they completely succeed in escaping an ideology of elsewhere that can be traced directly to colonial discourse?

The Genealogy of Travel

The idea of exoticism that the authors rightly contest is one which returns us to the clichés and stereotypes of the other criticized by Victor Segalen in his *Essai sur l'exotisme* (1978). Rather than expressing an interest in the world's cultural diversity, this type of exoticism uses the other as a pretext for representing an image of the same. The other is neutralized/sterilized in a form of appropriation that renders it palatable for a Western readership. If a narrative should aim to find a truth about the world, then exoticism places us at the centre of a fabulation/simulation, that of a dream of elsewhere which

---

[4] 'for the first time in French literary history, five of the seven major literary prizes of the Autumn have been awarded to four authors who would normally be described, with a hint of condescension, as "Francophone"'.

is only used to escape, momentarily, the realities that surround us. From the outset, Le Bris establishes a distinction between the literature he champions and another type of writing that, precisely, contents itself with exploiting local particularities: 'Le meilleur moyen de ne rien comprendre, me semblait-il, était de réduire cette effervescence à un "genre", une catégorie exotique, sinon une variante des littératures "régionales" ou "ethniques" – un peu de pittoresque en somme, quelques épices pour réveiller un temps nos palais fatigués' (Le Bris, 2007: 34).[5] This is what Mabanckou's text is also echoing when he states: 'Certes, il ne s'agit pas de proposer une littérature de rêve, encore moins de décréter que la seule création qui vaille est celle qui s'éloigne de son propre univers, exalte un ailleurs lointain pour finir par s'autodétruire à force de ne pas avoir un point d'ancrage. Nous risquerions alors de réveiller les vieux démons de l'exotisme' (Mabanckou, 2007: 65).[6] Needless to say, if exoticism is the old devil to be avoided it is precisely because of the colonial ideology it conveys.

When one analyses the different editorial statements of the Saint-Malo Etonnants Voyageurs festivals it becomes clear that the exotic imaginary occupies a key place. The promotional literature for the first festival in 1990 begins with the following: 'La route de la soie, la piste de l'encens, les caravanes du sel dans le vent du désert – nous rêvons d'aventure, de saut dans l'inconnu, de la griserie de ce que serait la "première fois", et nous n'en finissons pas de mettre nos pas dans les pas de ceux qui nous ont précédés, aventuriers, nomades ou géographes' ('Archives 1990, Etonnants Voyageurs').[7] The 1995 festival devoted to the Orient is presented in the following terms: 'L'Empire des étonnants mystères, des richesses fabuleuses, des civilisations étranges et raffinées, si différentes de la nôtre – et tant de désirs, de nouvelles partances ... Mais l'Orient réel, aussi, et l'histoire d'un difficile face à face

---

[5] 'It seemed to me that the best way to understand nothing was to reduce this effervescence to a "genre", an exotic category, indeed a variant of "regional" or "ethnic" literature. In short, a little dose of the pittoresque or some spices to re-energize our weary palettes for a time'.

[6] 'Of course, this is not to propose a literature of fantasy, much less to decree that the only creative work worth anything is one that removes the reader from his/her world and exalts a distant elsewhere only to self-destruct because there is no stable point of reference. This would mean risking a return to the old devil that is exoticism'.

[7] 'From the silk route to the spice trail and the salt caravans in the desert wind, we dream of adventure, of a leap into the unknown, the intoxication of the "first time", and we never cease to follow in the steps of those adventurers, nomads and geographers who have gone before us'.

avec l'Occident' ('Archives 1995, L'Orient').[8] Here the exotic dimension of the Orient is acknowledged by juxtaposing it with a reality that does not always correspond to it. Nonetheless the two visions coexist. For the festival has built itself on the mythology of the great traveller or firebrand, in search of authentic spaces that would avoid the beaten track and the tourist hordes. Each of the writers (Alain Borer, Nicolas Bouvier and Kenneth White, to mention the best known) who has contributed to what might be termed an initial draft of the manifesto, the volume entitled *Pour une littérature voyageuse,* corresponds to this image of the firebrand. In her thesis on the *Littérature voyageuse* movement, Katy Hindson (2008) establishes that, for the French press, the town of Saint-Malo itself becomes the pretext for an exotic representation and comes to be seen as the antidote to Paris and its centrality. The fact that Saint-Malo is a port from where numerous ships sail also facilitates the association with an elsewhere and the dream of an exotic location that plunges us into the limits of the known:

> Saint-Malo, ses phares, ses remparts, ses bars. En ce weekend du 1er mai et pour sa sixième édition, 'Etonnants Voyageurs' fait escale sur les docks du vieux port. A quai, on s'embarque pour le plus beau des voyages, la lecture. A coups d'expos, de débats, de films, ce festival navigue aux confins de toutes les cultures … avec le capitaine Michel Le Bris à la barre.[9] (Laval, 1995: 68)

As Hindson notes, the Saint-Malo to which Le Bris refers is the town of Chateaubriand and pirates and not the French port that was amongst the most active in the slave trade (Hindson, 2008: 41). The decision to erase this aspect of the town's history forms part of the exoticization of the festival's location which in turn recalls the very literature it promotes by becoming a place of desires, of dreams or an elsewhere that prompt flights of imagination. At the same time, this allows for the creation of a new cultural centre that offers a counterpoint to Parisian dominance.

There is thus a tension at the very heart of *Pour une littérature monde*

---

[8] 'The empire of startling mysteries, fabulous riches, strange and refined civilizations, so different from our own, and so many desires and new departures … But also the real Orient and the history of a difficult confrontation with the West'.

[9] 'Saint-Malo with its lighthouses, its old city walls, its bars. On this May weekend the sixth "Etonnants Voyageurs" is docking at the old port. Once on the quays, we will leave for the most beautiful journey there is: reading. With exhibitions, debates and films, this festival will sail to the limits of all cultures, with the skipper Michel Le Bris at the helm'.

which is never quite resolved: how is an ideologically questionable form of exoticism to be avoided by a movement that has used the imagination to constitute itself? It is this that explains the reticence but also the desire to distinguish the festival from being simply connected with travel writing. In an interview with *Le Monde* journalist Alain Beuve-Méry in 2006, Michel Le Bris states: 'Je n'ai jamais dit que c'était un festival d'écrivains-voyageurs. Le mot s'est trouvé lancé comme ça, en référence à Baudelaire'.[10] According to Le Bris, it would be contradictory to believe that 'la littérature exotique' [exotic literature] is the festival's main source of inspiration when the key driving force is a literature that expresses the world as it is. Here Le Bris is acknowledging the reductive aspect of travel writing and noting the impossibility of uniting the differences of all the writers under one formal category. In fact, what the *littérature-monde* manifesto highlights is the genuine desire of the contributors to distance themselves from a literature of travel perceived as problematic and reductive and instead replace it with voices originating from elsewhere.

Multiple Voices and their Displacement

The exotic imaginary has thus ceded its place to voices from the periphery but these voices have in turn distanced the festival from its original link to travel. It is important to recognize here the success of a festival that was able to create a dynamic meeting place and more importantly provide the type of visibility required to discover various authors from all over the world. This is the most notable change that has taken place between the 1992 *Pour une littérature voyageuse* volume, edited by Le Bris and already acknowledging the need for a *littérature-monde*, and the most recent manifesto. Whereas *Pour une littérature voyageuse* offered a collection of relatively united voices, *Pour une littérature-monde* gives more space to the other, to this periphery that allows a redefinition of the centre's importance. Of the twenty-seven contributors to the most recent manifesto, only three are from hexagonal France and nine of the contributors are female.

At this point, it is important to distinguish each of the authors who contribute to the volume because their different location demands that the concept of exoticism be relativized. For the question of exoticism cannot be understood unless the location(s) of its enunciation and its destination(s) (who is being addressed?) are analysed. In most instances, given the dependent nature of publishing, it is a hexagonal French readership that is being

---

[10] 'I have never claimed it was a festival of travel writers. This term arrived from nowhere, in reference to Baudelaire'.

addressed (as we have already seen this readership represents an initial criterion for the success of the Francophone text). For this reason it is difficult for African writers, for example, to avoid being perceived exotically, even if they do not agree that this is the case. It is precisely this that Nimrod criticizes when he claims: 'Et que dire de l'écrivain africain? Tout se passe comme s'il devait produire une littérature exotique destinée aux Européens et à lui-même, ce qui revient à vouer à la nostalgie une Afrique qui a disparu depuis longtemps' (Nimrod, 2007: 223).[11] Exoticism is constructed on a dynamic of recognition: the reader must be able to recognize the author's place of origin, that is to say the cultural location from where s/he is speaking. This recognition reveals the distance separating the author and her/his reader and allows the latter to project on to the author the image s/he has of her/his difference. For an African author to conform, for example, to this expectation is to plunge her/himself into a form of 'Africanness', in other words to reproduce the stereotypical signs of Africa as it is imagined by the West. At the same time it means reproducing a certain form of authenticity. Indeed, this is akin to the syndrome of authenticity which Salman Rushdie speaks of in his article on the Commonwealth: '"authenticity" is the respectable child of old-fashioned exoticism. It demands that sources, forms, style, language and symbol all derive from a supposedly homogeneous and unbroken tradition' (Rushdie, 1992: 67). Asking an African author to be 'African in her/his text is akin to asking her/him to conform to the reader's exotic expectations and desires which presuppose a link between the identity of the author and her/his country. This resembles an identity prison constructed by the expectation Gary Victor highlights in his text '*Littérature-monde* ou liberté d'être' [*Littérature-monde*: the freedom of being]: 'Mais les auteurs dits francophones restent tributaires du regard d'un lieu qui n'est pas le leur, ce qui fausse largement la perspective dans le sens d'une littérature dite monde' (Victor, 2007: 318).[12] The perspective is skewed because it owes its allegiance to an exotic expectation that imposes a particular form. However, what contemporary Francophone literature shows us is that this link can no longer be fully established.

In fact, the location, in geographical terms, of the Francophone writer can no longer be identified in precise, unambiguous terms. The Francophone

---

[11] 'And what of the African writer? Everything proceeds as though s/he should produce exotic writing destined for Europeans and themselves, which is the same as condemning to nostalgia an Africa that has long since disappeared'.

[12] 'But the so-called Francophone authors are dependent on the gaze of a place which is not theirs, and this greatly falsifies the perspective of a so-called world literature'.

writers whose works have been recognized over the past two decades are voices in movement who blur geographical boundaries. For example, several Antillean writers have long since left their countries of origin and very frequently live and teach in the United States. From Édouard Glissant to Maryse Condé, we are in the presence of an itinerant voice. This development is also in evidence in the most recent manifesto with Mabanckou living in Los Angeles, Waberi in Berlin, Laferrière in Montreal, Ananda Devi in Switzerland and Nancy Huston in Paris. Exotic discourse is thus hijacked from the interior because the words of the author can no longer be associated with her/his place of origin and because we can no longer guess the point of reference chosen by the authors in their respective works. Maryse Condé can pen texts on Africa from a European location. It is no longer just language that is disconnected from the nation, the link connecting the writer's identity to her/his place of origin is also broken. As a result, defining what an exotic discourse might be becomes decidedly more problematic. The comparative element specific to this discourse is no longer self-evident because the location of the author's voice is no longer a stable one. The difference between here and there is blurred because one can no longer be defined by the other.

Thus it is not travel writing in itself that allows for the questioning of exotic discourse but the displacement of the authors who situate their voices in multiple locations. Is it still possible to speak of Devi as Mauritian or Mabanckou as Congolese? Here it becomes evident how the question of belonging implied by these descriptors of national identity no longer allows us to take account of the complex nature of these writers' situation. Of course they are still connected to their culture of origin, but they are also already elsewhere and reside in a distance that allows them at times to reinvent their place of origin from the new horizons they find themselves in. It is this else-where as a space of displacement rather than a dream of the other that allows for an understanding of what a *littérature-monde* rid of its exoticism might look like. Yet this displacement must not become an indeterminate form. It must be capable of reinventing places and these voices must find a stable point of reference from which to represent the specificity of their locations.

Métissage and Exoticism

These multiple locations return us to the concept of *métissage*, said to be a characteristic of *littérature-monde*. It is highlighted several times in the manifesto and in festival literature and I analyse it here in parallel with exoticism. Indeed, several of the volume's contributors return to the idea that we no longer live in a world where identities can be defined according to absolute terms or categorical opposites but can only be conceived according to variants of admixture and exchange which are best expressed by the figure of the *métis/métisse*. The geographical displacement of the authors echoes this *métissage* as it presupposes the author's distancing from her/his national identity whilst also suggesting an adaptation to new cultures, what we might term in other words a distant belonging. The Francophone writer can be seen as a hybrid figure existing between different languages and cultures. The editorial statement of the 1995 Etonnants Voyageurs festival argues: 'Et l'enjeu décisif de l'époque – entre les tentations d'un repli identitaire, les phantasmes intégristes de "pureté" – est la préfiguration d'une littérature du XXIᵉ siècle dans l'expérience d'un métissage, d'un dialogue des cultures' ('Archives 1995, L'Orient').[13] This affirmation is almost self-evident but raises, nonetheless, a number of problems.

It bears repeating that, for Segalen, *métissage* was an indication of the decline of exoticism seen as the confrontation with alterity as it implied the destruction of the essential difference between self and other that he was seeking. Such criticism of cultural mixing for this otherwise respectful commentator of other cultures suggests a conservative dimension that, at times, approaches a form of primitivism. Today, on the contrary, *métissage* offers a dialogue between cultures that are becoming more open to each other and forms part of an ultimately more tolerant humanity. But this also means, as indeed a more pessimistic Segalen foresaw it, a world where we no longer have the possibility of encountering alterity. Has the world become so Westernized that it offers only forms of difference, that is to say an alterity that is reduced and contained only within the tools of the same, or, in other words, reduced to this exoticism that has been rejected? This is the argument forwarded by Jean Baudrillard in the work he co-authored with Marc Guillaume, *Figures de l'altérité*: 'Et je dirai que l'on ne peut lutter efficacement contre cette rareté de l'autre qu'en construisant ce que j'appelle une "fiction mixte", c'est-à-dire quelque chose qui est construit à

---

[13] 'The decisive challenge of our time – given the temptation to retreat into identity and integrationist fantasies of purity – is the prefigurement of a twenty-first-century literature within the experience of *métissage* and dialogue between cultures'. The editorial for the 2002 festival, 'Aux nouvelles voix d'Afrique' [To new voices from Africa], proclaims: 'Littérature de l'exil, du métissage culturel, bousculant les idéologies identitaires, refusant de s'enfermer dans une quelconque africanité, affirmant au contraire sa vocation universelle [...]: une Afrique nouvelle est en train de prendre la parole' [Literature of exile, of cultural fusion, overthrowing the ideologies of identity, refusing to be bounded by some Africanness and affirming instead its universal vocation [...]: a New Africa is in the process of speaking up] ('Archives 2002, Nouvelles voix d'Afrique').

partir d'un réel qui ensuite est dopé d'une certaine quantité imaginaire, de fiction' (Baudrillard and Guillaume, 1994: 49).[14] Could *littérature-monde* be described as a 'mixed fiction', a means of reinvigorating through fiction the dispersed voices of 'Francophone' writers and injecting a little of the alterity they have lost? When Dany Laferrière reveals in his contribution to the collection of essays edited by Le Bris and Rouaud that 'je voyage en français' [I travel in French] and that he is 'en guerre contre l'uniformisation' [at war with the homogenization] of the world (Laferrière, 2007: 68), does it not suggest that this concept of *littérature-monde* has itself a homogenizing dimension that even if it contests a form of facile, stereotypical exoticism, also destroys the idea of diversity? It is this that Gary Victor clearly criticizes when he asks: 'Comment dépasser la mondialisation qui n'est dans les faits que la mainmise d'un centre sur le monde? Donc la marginalisation des authenticités, si ce n'est leur destruction' (Victor, 2007: 318).[15] This is precisely what the critics of *métissage* argue.

For such thinkers, the concept of *métissage* is used to denote all forms of blending and dialogue whilst simultaneously obfuscating the particular nature of places and history. In his contribution to the volume edited by Le Bris and Rouaud, Lyonel Trouillot underlines the problematic aspect of *métissage* from an ideological perspective: 'Le mot "métissage" peut couvrir ou masquer des réalités différentes. Son usage excessif peut relever du camouflage idéologique et du déni de ses origines: la conquête et le viol' (Trouillot, 2007: 200).[16] This echoes the criticism levelled by Roger Toumson in his 1998 volume *Mythologie du métissage* where he challenges Chamoiseau, Confiant and Bernabé's concept of creoleness, arguing: 'Le discours de la créolité est la forme dialectale inédite que revêt, dans le champ littéraire francophone, le vieux mythe colonial paternaliste du métissage' (Toumson, 1998: 20).[17] For Toumson, the term *métissage* is directly descended from colonial fantasy.

---

[14] 'And I would argue that the only way to struggle effectively against the rarity of the other is to construct what I term a "mixed fiction", that is to say something that is constructed from the real and then injected with a certain imaginary quantity or fiction'.

[15] 'How do we move beyond a globalization that in fact represents the control exerted by the centre over the world that represents the marginalization of authenticity, if not its destruction?'

[16] 'The term *métissage* can cover or mask very different realities. Its excessive use can be determined by ideological camouflage and denial of its origins: that is conquest and rape'.

[17] 'In the field of Francophone literature, the discourse of creolity is the new dialectal form assumed by the paternalistic colonial myth of *métissage*'.

Once again, it represents the imposition of a hegemonic discourse on the other and not a critique and questioning of this discourse. It is a subterfuge used by the centre to control and especially to obliterate problems such as racial tension which are far from being resolved in today's world. Of course, Toumson's perspective is informed by a Marxist position which means that, for him, it is dialectic dynamism that allows for the reconciliation of opposites whilst maintaining irreducible identities. Nonetheless, his question remains pertinent; that is to say whether the model of *métissage* is a concept produced by the very centre from which *littérature-monde* is attempting to uncouple itself.

It is on this issue that Jean-Marc Moura concludes his *L'Europe littéraire et l'ailleurs* when he speaks of 'World Fiction' in an argument that is also relevant to *littérature-monde*: 'Une question demeure pendante: la littérature postcoloniale est-elle réellement décolonisée ou bien est-elle en train de subir une reprise en main par l'Occident, la World Fiction ne devenant alors qu'une nouvelle ruse occidentale pour imposer ses valeurs sous couvert de métissage culturel?' (Moura, 1998: 195).[18] Indeed, by attempting to define its object, the persistently hazy *littérature-monde*, Le Bris's text reproduces the inclusion–exclusion dynamic that is common to any text aiming for federation. *Métissage* or peripheral location, like any new norm, will in turn produce their own facile models of exoticism that enclose *littérature-monde* within a stereotyped literary identity, in this case the slightly marginal literature mentioned above that is disconnected and permanently in motion. In *The Postcolonial Exotic*, Graham Huggan similarly analyses the way in which all marginal cultural forms are easily salvaged or commodified by the discourses of the centre that then uses them for its own purposes. As Huggan notes: 'And that dilemma might be posed as follows: is it possible to account for cultural difference without at the same time mystifying it? To locate and praise the other without also privileging the self? To promote the cultural margins without ministering to the needs of the mainstream?' (Huggan, 2001: 31). In this recuperative process, the margin loses its power to question and subvert and is incorporated into a norm which constitutes a lack of differentiation. In fact, it reproduces precisely what the exotic discourse it denounces produced in the past: that is to say a model of differences that is constructed on a dynamic of recognition. It is the danger uncovered by Salmon Rushdie in the notion of 'Commonwealth literature' when he highlights the invention

---

18 'One question remains unanswered: is postcolonial literature really decolonized or is it in the process of being taken over by the West, with World Fiction becoming another Western ploy that uses the notion of cultural *métissage* for imposing its values?'

of a new literary category in which essentially different authors are bracketed together. In other words, it is the invention of a category that reinvents an exotic model that paradoxically is driven by a failure to differentiate amongst other voices whilst above all highlighting their difference. Is this not precisely the danger of entropy against which Segalen asks for vigilance? After all, exoticism is also a form of control, a means to affix limits where none necessarily exists. The other potential problem is that *littérature-monde* might regroup the entirety of the world's diverse voices without any form of inclusion–exclusion, thereby producing a concept so unwieldy as to lose all particularity. In this way it would be impossible to define the particular features of any individual voice. After all, is there any novel which does not speak of the world?

Conclusion

In order to avoid the disappearance of different voices in an overly vague and eclectic collective, all authors need to reinvent their location, this foothold of which Mabanckou speaks and which constitutes one of the keys of Édouard Glissant's thought. This site could be identified as the taking control of geography and its histories which the writer's voice opens up to the rest of the world. In this way, it becomes difficult for most Francophone authors to avoid reproducing at some time in their work a discourse that will be perceived as exotic. Should *métissage* or hybridity be seen as the contemporary form of exoticism which can no longer present itself in terms of an absolute opposite but an exoticism that must be constantly redefined according to ever changing terms? No doubt this is why instead of pretending exoticism no longer exists, or that these authors are distancing themselves from it definitively, we need to acknowledge how they force us to question the terms of this exoticism, and the way in which they are constantly renegotiating their relationship with it. As I see it, there is also a lesson here for postcolonial readings that too often present the question of exoticism as resolved by the use of the concept of hybridity. For the question is far from being dealt with, a fact that the multiple voices of the Manifesto force us to recognize, these voices so diverse as to be impossible to unite under one concept.

Translated by Aedín Ní Loingsigh.

Works Cited

Albert, Christiane. 2008. '"La littérature-monde en français": une nouvelle catégorie littéraire?'. In Christiane Albert, Abel Kouvouama and Gisèle Prignitz (eds), *Le Statut de l'écrit*. Pau: Presses Universitaires de Pau: 161–70.

'Archives 1990, Etonnants Voyageurs'. Etonnants Voyageurs. <http://www. etonnants-voyageurs.com/spip.php?article20>. Consulted on 26 May 2009.

'Archives 1995, L'Orient'. Etonnants Voyageurs. <http://www.etonnants-voyageurs.com/spip.php?article25>. Consulted on 26 May 2009.

'Archives 2002, Nouvelles voix d'Afrique'. Etonnants Voyageurs. <http://www. etonnants-voyageurs.com/spip.php?article32>. Consulted on 26 May 2009.

Baudrillard, Jean, and Marc Guillaume. 1994. *Figures de l'altérité*. Paris: Descartes & Cie.

Beuve-Méry, Alain. 2006. 'À Saint-Malo, au rendez-vous de la "littérature-monde"'. *Le Monde* 20 June.

Etonnants Voyageurs. <www.etonnants-voyageurs.com>. Consulted on 2 June 2010.

Godbout, Jacques. 2007. 'La Question préalable'. In Michel Le Bris and Jean Rouaud (eds), *Pour une littérature-monde*. Paris: Gallimard: 103–11.

Hindson, Katy. 2008. '*Pour une littérature voyageuse*: Travel and Identity in Late Twentieth Century France'. Unpublished Ph.D. thesis: University of Liverpool.

Huggan, Graham. 2001. *The Postcolonial Exotic: Marketing the Margins*. London and New York: Routledge.

Laferrière, Dany. 2007. 'Je voyage en français'. In Michel Le Bris et Jean Rouaud (eds), *Pour une littérature-monde*. Paris: Gallimard: 87–101.

Laval, Martine. 1995. 'Quai des plumes'. *Télérama* 2365 (10 May): 68.

Le Bris, Michel (ed.). 1992. *Pour une littérature voyageuse*. Brussels: Éditions Complexe.

—. 2007. 'Pour une littérature-monde en français'. In Michel Le Bris et Jean Rouaud (eds), *Pour une littérature-monde*. Paris: Gallimard: 23–53.

Le Bris, Michel, and Jean Rouaud (eds). 2007. *Pour une littérature-monde*. Paris: Gallimard.

Mabanckou, Alain. 2007. 'Le chant de l'oiseau migrateur'. In Michel Le Bris and Jean Rouaud (eds), *Pour une littérature-monde*. Paris: Gallimard: 55–66.

Moura, Jean-Marc. 1998. *L'Europe littéraire et l'ailleurs*. Paris: Presses Universitaires de France.

Nimrod. 2007. '"La nouvelle chose française": Pour une littérature décolonisée'. In Michel Le Bris and Jean Rouaud (eds), *Pour une littérature-monde*. Paris: Gallimard: 217–35.

Rushdie, Salman. 1992. *Imaginary Homelands*. London: Granta.

Segalen, Victor. 1978. *Essai sur l'exotisme*. Montpellier: Fata Morgana.

Toumson, Roger. 1998. *Mythologie du métissage*. Paris: Presses Universitaires de France.

Trouillot, Lyonel. 2007. 'Langues, voyages et archipels'. In Michel Le Bris and Jean Rouaud (eds), *Pour une littérature-monde*. Paris: Gallimard: 197–204.

Victor, Gary. 2007. 'Littérature-monde ou liberté d'être'. In Michel Le Bris and Jean Rouaud (eds), *Pour une littérature-monde*. Paris: Gallimard: 315–20.

From *Littérature voyageuse* to *Littérature-monde* via Migrant Literatures: Towards an Ethics and Poetics of *Littérature-monde* through French-Australian Literature

Jacqueline Dutton

French-Australian literature – does this category of writing really exist? If so, how, when, where and ... why? These initial interrogations regarding the corpus for this study are unsurprising, given its unusual, even unexpected focus on a little known literary phenomenon that has, however, a longer history than one might expect – a history that is certainly too complex to outline in a prefatory note. As an indication of the significant corpus that does exist, however, French fictional writings on Australia pre-date European colonization and settlement of the Great South Land. They include Gabriel de Foigny's *La Terre Australe connue* (1676), Denis de Vairasse's *Histoire des Sévarambes* (1677), followed by Tyssot de Patot's *Voyages et avantures de Jacques Massé* (1710) and Rétif de la Bretonne's *La Découverte australe par un homme volant* (1784). The first published history of Australia, *Histoire de la colonisation pénale et des établissements de l'Angleterre en Australie* (1831) was written by a Frenchman, Ernest de Blosseville; the first play set in Australia, *Les Emigrés aux terres australes* (1792) was written by a Frenchman, Citizen Gamas; the first novel by a woman set in Australia, *Les Voleurs d'or* (1857) was written by a Frenchwoman, the Comtesse de Chabrillan.

The French have written about Australia from afar or from within the island-continent for centuries, and continue to do so in travel writing, novels and plays, but interestingly, to date, no French films have been set in or focus on Australia. The corpus selected for this case study includes three texts on Australia written by French authors that involve travelling tales or migratory experiences. David Fauquemberg's *Nullarbor* (2007), Catherine Rey's *Une femme en marche* (2007) and Josiane Behmoiras's *Dora B: A Memoir of My Mother* (2005)[1] are distinguished in terms of their mainly autobiographical content, and also by their overt attempts to engage with the intercultural challenges of travel writing or indeed to 'dire le monde' [describe the world] (in the words of the *littérature-monde* manifesto ('Pour une "littérature-monde" en français', 2007)), through migrant perspectives. By examining these texts, it may be possible to define through demonstration the ethics and poetics of *littérature-monde*, at least with regard to French-Australian literature, with potentially wider application for *littérature-monde* in general. French-Australian literature therefore does exist and it may be that the strange force of attraction that the antipodes exerts on the French imaginary serves as the catalyst to crystallize the transition from *littérature voyageuse* to *littérature-monde* via migrant literatures.

The publication of the 'Pour une "littérature-monde" en français' manifesto in *Le Monde* on 16 March 2007 launched a debate that extends well beyond the obvious binary of 'French' versus 'Francophone' literatures, and the corollary paradigm pitting centre against periphery that this 'Copernican' revolution attempts to dismantle. Although its original intentions appear to correspond to the three central tenets of the manifesto genre – self-sufficiency, newness and self-positioning (Caws, 2001) – this manifesto is inherently linked not only via its literary antecedents to Goethe's *Weltliteratur* and the rise of world literature in English as practised by Pico Iyer and Salman Rushdie, but also to French language phenomena such as Jean Bernabé, Patrick Chamoiseau and Raphaël Confiant's *Eloge de la créolité* (1989) and Édouard Glissant's *Tout-monde* (1993). The drive towards *littérature-monde* is thus anchored historically in international trends ranging from cosmopolitanism to postcolonialism, and inspired politically by movements including creolization and even globalization. The tentacular spread of the manifesto to draw together such a diversity of ideas builds up an ambitious agenda but also renders it somewhat bewildering. Definitions of the key terms of the debate remain elusive, which leave the manifesto open to criticism as an approximation rather than a structured argument against the constraints of the Parisian literary establishment. And references to the self-satisfied abstractions of French metropolitan literature appear isolated attacks and outdated angst harboured against an editorial edifice that no longer has the power that it once did.

However, despite the hazy terms and conditions of the manifesto, it is clear that it criticizes both the ethics and the poetics of the metropolitan French

---

[1] *Dora B* was republished by Bloomsbury in 2007 in the United Kingdom as *My Mother was a Bag Lady.*

literature that has dominated French language literatures for decades. By imposing its content and methods as prescriptive models, this 'littérature franco-française' is deemed to have exerted a hegemonic force and attempted to absorb and subvert any renegade forms: '[elle] contraignait les auteurs venus d'ailleurs à se dépouiller de leurs bagages avant de se fondre dans le creuset de la langue et de son histoire nationale'.[2] This questionable stance of metropolitan French literature is summed up in the final lines of the manifesto as 'impérialisme culturel' [cultural imperialism] against which the signatories and *littérature-monde* should rail. Such obviously debatable ethics are accompanied by a poetics condemned as 'un jeu de combinaisons sans fin', and 'sans autre objet qu'elle-même', displaying a reliance on '"sa propre critique dans le mouvement même de son énonciation"' rather than being inspired and open to the world all around.[3]

The pointed criticism of both the ethics and poetics of metropolitan French literature is extended and refined by many of the twenty-seven contributing authors in the collection of essays entitled *Pour une littérature-monde* that appeared in May 2007. Explicit references and more subtle allusions to the dubious hegemonic impositions and 'impérialisme culturel' of the Parisian literati underpin several contributions to the volume. Alain Mabanckou recognizes this 'phénomène de l'hégémonie parisienne, surtout en ce qui concerne les auteurs originaires de l'espace francophone' (Mabanckou, 2007: 57),[4] and cites this 'hiérarchisation' [hierarchical ordering] as the reason for the inferiority complex that makes these authors servile to the pressures of Paris: 'l'auteur de l'espace francophone ne commencerait à exister que lorsque la place parisienne tout entière lui aurait décerné un passeport' (Mabanckou, 2007: 58).[5] The problematic ethics of a literary marketplace dictated by globalization are the focus of Gary Victor's essay that condemns the economic and symbolic influences controlling 'la littérature dite francophone' [literature known as 'Francophone']: 'Tout passe ici par les grands circuits contrôlés

---

2 '[it] forced authors who came from elsewhere to rid themselves of their foreign trappings before melting in the crucible of the French language and its national history' ('Toward a "World-Literature" in French', 2009: 54).

3 'a game of endless combinations'; 'with no other object than itself'; '"its own critique in the very movement of its enunciation"' ('Toward a "World-Literature" in French', 2009: 54).

4 'phenomenon of Parisian hegemony, especially concerning authors from the Francophone space'. Unless otherwise indicated, all translations from French into English are by the author of this chapter.

5 'the author from the Francophone space could only begin to exist when the whole of Parisian society had issued him a passport'.

par des monopoles alors qu'aucun pays dit francophone n'est en mesure de se créer à la fois un marché et une force symbolique permettant à ses créations d'entrer en compétition à armes plus ou moins égales' (2007: 318).[6] Marginally less obvious critiques of France's imperialist strategies by Ananda Devi and Boualem Sansal make allegorical references to the ethical irresponsibility of the metropolitan French literary establishment through their tales of disowning progeny and refusing recognition. It is nevertheless evident that the 'parents' at fault are those that create and perpetuate the constraints imposed on literary publishing in French.

In their essays attacking the poetics of metropolitan French literature, Jean Rouaud and Michel Le Bris hone their argument to focus on particular proponents of the dominant literary regime that they wish to overturn, and in this way define the contours of the model they are seeking to obviate. For Rouaud, it is Claude Simon and Robbe-Grillet, the *nouveau roman* and the Oulipo, who exemplify the sacrifice of the novel to technique, of the novelist to technicians' advocate: 'Le romancier qui avait été un arpenteur d'espace, un inventeur d'imaginaire, un découvreur de mondes enfouis, était ramené à un rôle de syndic' (Rouaud, 2007: 19).[7] Le Bris adopts a potentially more dramatic strategy to define the enemies, referring to those former structuralists who have recognized the error of their (wicked?) ways and seen the light of the new poetics of *littérature-monde*. Tzvetan Todorov is the ideal convert after publishing *La Littérature en peril*, but Henri Meschonnic is somewhat recalcitrant. He takes off his linguist's hat to the poet, but has just published a collection of poems *De monde en monde* (2009), that could be interpreted as an ambiguous response to the *littérature-monde* manifesto – 'tous les mondes | sont en moi' [all worlds | are within me]. The overwhelming force to be overturned in Le Bris's essay is the 'Signe-Roi' [Sign-King], indicating his fundamental mistrust of Derrida, Barthes, *et al.* Jacques Godbout adds more names to the 'blacklist', stating that they could only be rehabilitated by becoming part of the Francophone stable: 'Avant de prétendre que l'institution littéraire française adhère à une véritable littérature-monde, Philippe Sollers, Philippe Labro et Bernard-Henri Lévy devraient se reconnaître comme "écrivains de langue française", c'est-à-

---

[6] 'Everything here passes through the great circuits controlled by monopolies so that no so-called Francophone country is up to creating at once a market and a symbolic force allowing its creations to enter into competition more or less adequately armed'.

[7] 'The novelist, who had been a surveyor of space, an inventor of the imaginary, a discoverer of hidden worlds, was reduced to an assigned representative of literature'.

dire comme "francophones"' (Godbout, 2007: 106).[8] And Patrick Raynal's evaluation of the poetics of metropolitan French literature dismisses both its narrative content and outmoded style: 'Non seulement leurs histoires étaient profondément ennuyeuses, mais leurs styles semblaient sortir d'un placard qui sentait plus la naphtaline que le vent du large' (Raynal, 2007: 136).[9]

Whether names are named or not, the lines around the enemy camp are clearly drawn, and the grounds on which the conflict is based are the faulty ethics and uninspiring poetics of its literary representatives. But *littérature-monde* is more than just a negatively defined concept. The manifesto and the collection of essays provide some details regarding the ethics and poetics of *littérature-monde* and include references to practitioners of *littérature-monde*, most of whom are also travel writers. In fact, the manifesto expresses its liberatory ethics through its ambition to promote *littérature-monde* that is 'ouverte sur le monde' [open to the world] and 'transnationale' in the same way that the 1992 manifesto *Pour une littérature voyageuse* states that 'toute littérature vivante se doit d'être peu ou prou voyageuse, aventureuse, ouverte sur le monde' (13).[10] Likewise, the manifesto's joyous announcement that 'le monde revient' [the world is returning] is an obvious reprise of the poetics valorized in Le Bris's exhortation to 'retrouver le monde' [rejoin the world] that also appears repeatedly in *Pour une littérature voyageuse*. The *littérature-monde* manifesto explicitly acknowledges the groundbreaking work accomplished by travel writing in preparing the way for world literature in French: 'Les récits de ces étonnants voyageurs, apparus au milieu des années soixante-dix, auront été les somptueux portails d'entrée du monde dans la fiction'.[11] Citing Bruce Chatwin's travels to Patagonia, Réjean Ducharme's *L'Hiver de force* and Nicolas Bouvier's *L'Usage du monde*, the manifesto praises travel writing as a means of literary renewal: 'se frotter au monde pour en capter le souffle, les énergies vitales'.[12] The collection of essays in

---

[8] 'Before claiming that the French literary institution adheres to a true world-literature, Philippe Sollers, Philippe Labro and Bernard Henri-Lévy would have to recognize themselves as "French language writers", as "francophones"'.

[9] 'Not only were their stories profoundly boring, but their styles seemed to come out of a cupboard that smelt of naphthalene rather than the sea breeze'.

[10] 'all living literature must be more or less travelling, adventurous, open to the world'.

[11] 'The tales of these astonishing voyageurs, who appeared in the mid-1970s, would turn out to be the world's sumptuous entryways into fiction' ('Toward a "World-Literature" in French', 2009: 55).

[12] 'rub up against the world in order to capture its essence and vital energies' ('Toward a "World-Literature" in French', 2009: 54).

Pour une littérature-monde develops the varied and at times contradictory points of view on *littérature-monde* presented by the contributing authors, to raise fundamental questions regarding the scope for *littérature-monde* in reconfiguring the imaginary of French language literatures. The writers' diverse perspectives result in a rich and complex panorama of possibilities for *littérature-monde*, in terms of its ethics and poetics, but consequently participate in a widening of the definitional field rather than clarifying its boundaries.

Although 'ouverture' is the ethical underpinning of this manifesto and 'dire le monde' determines its poetics, there is nevertheless a need for some kind of circumscribing ideals that are more clearly defined than those currently proposed. Otherwise, does it simply mean that any writer who does not subscribe to or follow the models of 'littérature franco-française' is writing *littérature-monde*? Or do they need to subscribe politically to *littérature-monde* in the manner of authors signing manifestos and writing for the cause? Indeed, by contributing to the manifesto and collection of essays, do those authors consider themselves to be writing *littérature-monde*? Apart from including those who overtly claim to be part of this movement, how can we define its parameters?

Littérature voyageuse may provide some answers to these questions, but also raise others. The links between *Pour une littérature-monde* and *Pour une littérature voyageuse* relating to their ethics, poetics and practitioners suggest that travelling literatures may be naturally predisposed to displaying the qualities sought in *littérature-monde*. However, while some travel writing may express the ethics of 'ouverture' and embrace poetics that 'dire le monde', other examples of the genre are awkwardly aligned with the metropolitan French literature that the manifesto disparages through their shared flaw of cultural imperialism. Travel writing has been widely criticized for its colonial underpinnings and dominating masculine discourse related to the imperial gaze (Pratt, 1992), and indeed some contributors to the *Pour une littérature voyageuse* publication acknowledge the genre's hierarchical legacy. The fact that the bibliography included in the *Pour une littérature voyageuse* publication lists well-known travel texts written mostly by young white European male travellers attests to this tendency.

The potential contradiction between the aims and ideals of *littérature-monde* and the practices inherent in at least some strands of *littérature voyageuse* appears to have passed unnoticed by Le Bris. According to his essay, the one binding factor that underpins most examples of *littérature-monde* is the trope of travel, including the classic travel account and the novel of displacement, the migrant narrative and the journey of (self) discovery. Whether it is the author who migrates or the narrator who travels, or indeed any permutations of these movements, mobility seems to be the grounding principle of *littérature-monde* for Le Bris. The possible misrepresentations that could arise from the temptation to elide *littérature voyageuse* and *littérature-monde* are numerous. A panoramic description of imperialist nostalgia for the exotic or an intricate examination of passages through proximity could both be considered as travelling texts that go beyond the insular contemplations that characterize the dominant strands of metropolitan French literature to embrace the wider world, and therefore equate to examples of *littérature-monde*, were this unmitigated approach to be adopted.

If we consider the manifesto's refusal of metropolitan French literature's nefarious 'impérialisme culturel', and the fact that such tendencies can also be identified in some examples of travel writing, then the evolution from *littérature voyageuse* to *littérature-monde* should be neither automatic nor inevitable. All travel writing cannot be considered part of the apparently anti-imperialist, anti-colonial, more democratic and egalitarian category of *littérature-monde*. But, on the other hand, we understand that *littérature-monde* should encode narratives that travel. How then can we distinguish the forms of *littérature voyageuse* that fulfil the criteria of *littérature-monde*?

This question echoes the probing interrogation that arises out of Charles Forsdick's examination of the relationship between the aims and intentions of *Pour une littérature voyageuse* and *Pour une littérature-monde*. He asks: 'Which *littérature*? Whose *monde*?' (Forsdick, 2010: 15). In response, this chapter proposes to add a caveat nuancing the defining features of the ethics and poetics of *littérature-monde* outlined above. The caveat that has already been suggested in the title is related to migrant literatures, and the hypothesis that the migrant experience may play a significant role in plotting the course that leads from *littérature voyageuse* to *littérature-monde* will now be further explored. Using this approach, it may be possible to add another layer to the definitional strata that are currently being constructed around the concept of *littérature-monde*, which will then be tested through the case study of some French-Australian texts.

The abundant scholarship on migrant literatures overlaps with studies of cosmopolitanism and postcolonial literatures to establish a field that goes well beyond the limited scope envisaged for this study (see Walkowitz, 2006). It cannot, for example, enter the debate on the relative merits of the epithets 'migrant', 'ethnic' or 'multicultural' to designate literatures that arise from transnational experiences (see Huggan, 2001; 2007: 115–17), nor examine migrant literatures as the production of elites whose 'weightlessness' may be interpreted as disengagement with the emerging literatures of post-colonial nations and a return to accordingly receptive neo-colonial centres (Boehmer, 2005: 229–33). Instead, the relationship between migrant literatures and travel writing is the present preoccupation, together with the frequent exclusion of the former from the latter category. Defining travel writing is almost as hazardous as attempting to define *littérature-monde*, as there are many different opinions on whether, for example, fictional works should be included under this rubric, or whether it should be limited to the traditional non-fictional first person autobiographical narrative recounting personal experiences of travel. There are also questions asked as to whether the itinerary should involve a return to the point of departure, implying a mode of reporting back to a national readership, or whether such notions are outdated vestiges of imperialist voyages of conquest and exploration. The numerous volumes of travel writing criticism and anthologies that do not include migrant literatures, are slowly being contested by texts such as Charles Forsdick's *Travel in Twentieth-Century French and Francophone Cultures* (2005), James Clifford's *Routes: Travel and Translation in the Late Twentieth Century* (1997) and Aedín Ní Loingsigh's *Postcolonial Eyes: Intercontinental Travel in Francophone Africa* (2009) that engage with migrant narratives of travel. The present study follows in this recent trend, embracing more-inclusive interpretations of travel writing,[13] but it is interesting that Jacques Lacarrière's contribution to *Pour une littérature voyageuse* contains an explicit rejection of various examples of migrants, travellers whose voyages are invalid: 'Eliminons d'emblée un certain nombre de voyages [...] le voyage civil forcé (l'exilé, le déplacé, le déporté)' (1992: 105).[14]

In contrast with this explicit refusal of the migrant as traveller, which is also implicit in the editorial notes, bibliography and many of the essays in *Pour une littérature voyageuse*, the *littérature-monde* manifesto demonstrates a much more supportive stance with regard to migrant literatures. Significantly, the manifesto clearly takes as its starting point the

---

[13] As Director of the Melbourne Festival of Travel Writing, my musings on the distinction between travel and migrant writing were further complicated when I began organizing the inaugural festival, which took place on 19–20 July 2008. In early discussions about the programme with participating authors, some dismissed migrant travel narratives as inappropriate for a travel writing festival. However, at least half of the thirty writers who participated in the festival were in fact migrants, whose texts trace either their voyage to Australia or, more acceptably for the travel writing genre it seems, their voyage of return to the country of origin. For more information on the migrant authors who participated in the Melbourne Festival of Travel Writing, see <www.mftw.com.au>. Please note that the festival has been renamed the Australian Festival of Travel Writing; see <www.aftw.com.au>.

[14] 'Let's eliminate straight away a certain number of travels [...] the civilian's forced voyage (exile, displacement, deportation).'

ground-breaking award in 2006 of five of France's seven major literary prizes to foreign-born writers of literature in French. Judging by this, it seems that migrant literatures were the determining factor, the necessary catalyst to effect the transition away from the colonial associations of travel writing towards the apparently postcolonial perspectives of *littérature-monde*. The manifesto praises the acuity and inventiveness of those migrants writers such as Kazuo Ishiguro and Salman Rushdie who, by expressing their plural cultures without being overcome by nostalgia, opened the door to a new world literature in English: 'c'était bien la première fois qu'une génération d'écrivains issus de l'émigration, au lieu de se couler dans sa culture d'adoption, entendait faire œuvre à partir du constat de son identité plurielle, dans le territoire ambigu et mouvant de ce frottement'.[15] It must also be recognized that most of the signatories of the manifesto, and contributors to the collection of essays on *littérature-monde* are migrant writers, many having undertaken multiple migrations and some of whom have spent lengthy periods living outside French-speaking cultures, such as Maryse Condé, Alain Mabanckou and Abdourahman Waberi.

This confluence of events and revision of perceptions regarding the importance of migrant literatures as both *littérature voyageuse* and *littérature-monde* suggest that migrant literatures may represent a validating stage in the process of reinterpreting *littérature voyageuse* as *littérature-monde*. It may therefore follow that migrant literatures constitute the key that allows some strands of travel writing entry into *littérature-monde*. This hypothesis will be tested through the case study of three French-Australian texts, in an attempt to demonstrate that migrant literatures may provide the means of transforming writing about travel into literature that takes in and takes on the world.

The French-Australian texts to be analysed include David Fauquemberg's *Nullarbor* (2007), which is a fairly traditional travelogue that traces the French author's journey across Australia, winning the inaugural prix Nicolas Bouvier in 2007 and voted best travel text by *Lire* magazine in 2008. *Une femme en marche* (2007) by Catherine Rey is labelled a novel but is a thinly disguised autobiography of the author's struggle for recognition as a writer in France before emigrating to Australia in 1997. And, finally, French-born Josiane Behmoiras's *Dora B: A Memoir of My Mother / My Mother was a Bag Lady* (2005) relates her troubled itinerary with her Turkish-Jewish

---

[15] 'For the first time, then, a generation of emigrant writers, instead of melting into their adopted culture, set out to create by drawing on the source of their plural identity, in the ambiguous and shifting territory in which they rubbed up against each other' ('Toward a "World-Literature" in French', 2009: 55).

mother from Paris to Montpellier, their deportation to Israel and subsequent separation when the author settles in Melbourne.

As the titles suggest, Fauquemberg's and Rey's texts were written in French, whereas Behmoiras's work appeared in English, and was subsequently translated into French and German. The latter work serves as a telling contrast to the other examples of migrant literature, representing a completely different point on the spectrum of *littérature-monde*, in part precisely because of the author's choice to write in English. All of the works are also relatively contemporaneous (2005–07). Using these texts as a representative corpus of contemporary French-Australian literature, it may be possible to show that through integrating migrant narratives into the genre of travel writing, travelling literatures can be reinvented and find their place in the wider sphere of *littérature-monde*.

The first example, David Fauquemberg's *Nullarbor*, bears an encouraging recommendation on its back cover, promising 'la découverte pour le lecteur d'une Australie loin des clichés faciles, âpre, cruelle, où les êtres semblent se perdre, au sens strict se défaire, dans l'immensité du paysage'.[16] There is also a comparison with the Coen brothers' film *Fargo*, but the one-page preface to the text reads more like a scene from a *Mad Max* movie, including as many clichés and stereotypes to set the scene in the Australian outback as can be put together in one page:

> Dehors, une voix hurlait mon nom. Arraché au sommeil, je n'ai pas compris tout de suite. Une moto passait en trombe sur l'autoroute, à quelques mètres. Et ce long cri, inhumain, qui semblait résonner encore dans les ténèbres du désert. Il m'évoquait, confus, de macabres cérémonies, pieds martelant le sol, claquements de bâtons, visages mats et obscures fardés de cendres grises, dénués de reflet à la lueur des flammes. Souffle court, je me suis redressé sous ma tente. Le moteur ronronnait au loin, là-bas vers l'est. Pourtant, je frissonnais. Ce cri ne pouvait être que celui d'un loup. Ou plutôt un dingo. J'étais en Australie, au milieu de la Nullarbor. Ce rêve mauvais ne me lâcherait plus. Les lances à bout de bras, le deuil et la colère – la mort rôdait à mes côtés. Monde sans prudence, où tout n'est que violence et ruine. Voilà comment j'ai tué l'homme.[17] (Fauquemberg, 2007: 9)

---

[16] 'the discovery for the reader of an Australia removed from reductive clichés, bitter and cruel, where individuals appear to get lost, in the strict sense of being undone, in the immensity of the landscape'.

[17] 'Outside, a voice yelled my name. Wrenched out of slumber, I didn't understand straight away. A motorbike whizzed past on the highway, a few metres away. And this long cry, inhuman, which seemed to resonate still in the shadows of the desert. In my confused state, it evoked for me macabre ceremonies, feet stamping

The main narrative then begins with a rejection of Melbourne, a city where the narrator has lived for two years, and considers to be 'cette Europe en exil' [this Europe in exile] (11), which is also a common stereotype in French travel writing on Australia. Refusal to acknowledge any value in urban centres or Australian multicultural communities, and often highly derogatory descriptions of such, are almost inevitably counterbalanced by an immediate acceptance and integration of the French traveller into the indigenous society, leading to his or her spiritual enlightenment (see Decoust, 1987; Gotlib, 1999). Fauquemberg is no different – he hitchhikes across the Nullarbor, the thousands of kilometres of desert that separate Melbourne in the East from Perth in the (Wild Wild) West, and, upon arriving, finds work with a bunch of violent, savage, hard-drinking, hard-swearing Australians and migrants on a fishing trawler to earn enough money to get to Broome, in the north-west of Australia. This is the most innovative and original section of the book, in its attempt to represent the brutality of humankind. These fishermen (and one fisherwoman) are 'machines à tuer' [killing machines] that terrorize each other as well as the better known 'machines à tuer' – the sharks inhabiting the Indian Ocean that are slaughtered for their fins. Reversing that cliché, Fauquemberg nevertheless takes up several others once the narrator leaves this environment and reaches Broome. The jaded and tortured individual, the 'Saleté de Français' [French filth] (45), or 'Putain d'Français' [Bloody Frenchman] (52, 58) gradually disappears as the indigenous world, the 'ailleurs fantastique' [fantastic otherworld] of the Bardi people opens up to him, and the pleasures of fishing and observing sacred sites and rituals render him human again, with a new name, 'Napoleon [*sic*]' (104). Just before the time comes for him to leave, he decides to go into a forbidden inlet even though he has been warned that it is inhabited by an old crocodile: 'Toi, *Napoleon*, sûr qu'il te louperait pas. Il verrait que t'es pas d'ici, que t'es perdu. [...] Il aime pas qu'on l'dérange. C'est chez lui, là-bas. Y'a aucune raison d'y aller' (162–63).[18] Of course, having entered the taboo place, he is doomed to be snapped up by the crocodile, but is

---

on the ground, blows of clubs, dark and unintelligible faces, painted with grey ashes, devoid of any glint in the glow of the flames. Hardly breathing, I got up in my tent. The motor was humming in the distance, far off towards the east. However, I was shivering. This cry could only be that of a wolf. Or rather a dingo. I was in Australia, in the middle of the Nullarbor. This bad dream wouldn't leave me alone. Spears at arm's length, mourning and anger – death hanging around me. A world without measure, where everything is violence and ruin. That is how I killed the man.'

18 'You, *Napoleon*, can be sure that he won't miss you. He'll see that you're not

rescued by the indigenous elder Augustus, who sacrifices himself to save the foolish Frenchman.

Despite the originality of the first section of the text, the rest of *Nullarbor* falls into a typical paradigm of French travel writing on Australia, and although it was acclaimed in France, it does not really go beyond previous examples of the genre. In fact, with the sacrificial death of the most respected and wise representative of the indigenous people to save the life of the French narrator, the text slips suspiciously easily into an imperialist discourse that perpetuates the superiority of the white traveller, elevating the 'noble savage' to hero status only when his recognition of his subservient status and expendable existence becomes evident through his voluntary sacrifice. The author's two-year period of residence in Australia does not result in a migrant narrative with efforts to negotiate a place within the new society. Although it could be seen to portray the features listed in the *littérature-monde* manifesto, with expressions of mobility and some attempts to 'dire le monde', Fauquemberg's text seems simply to repeat the primitivist tendencies that permeate so much European travel writing on Australia. The impression that this text leaves on the reader is more linked to imperialist ethics and traditionalist poetics of *littérature voyageuse* than to the 'ouverture' that should underpin *littérature-monde*.

Catherine Rey's autobiographical novel *Une femme en marche* is more promising as an example of *littérature-monde*. She refers to similar experiences as those expressed by contributors to the *Pour une littérature-monde* collection of essays, as a provincial writer trying to get her work published in Paris:

> Et comme je viens de Saint-Plouc sur Gironde, et pas de Paris, ça m'arrangera pas mes affaires. Paris, c'est chasse-gardée [...]. Des chapelles, des coteries. A Paris, il n'y a que ça. N'entre pas qui voudrait dans ces cercles. Si vous n'avez pas de bons parrains, le chemin sera rude. Que de barrières! Que de murs! Quel misérable poids pèsent l'effort et le talent face aux systèmes où les courtisans rodés à tous les coups bas font jongler leurs privilèges. Choisir d'écrire quand on vient de nulle part, c'est payer le prix de l'exclusion.[19] (Rey, 2007: 66–67)

---

from here, that you're lost [...] He doesn't like to be disturbed. It's his place, over there. There's no reason to go there.'

[19] 'And the fact that I'm from Hicksville and not Paris, won't help matters, either. Paris, that's a private hunting ground, no poachers [...]. Chapters, coteries. In Paris, that's all there is. And you don't get into such circles just by wanting to. If you don't have decent sponsors, the going will be tough. So many barriers! So many brick walls! Talent and effort don't weigh much in the face of set-ups

This literary journey involves travel to Australia, expressed in a migrant narrative that is actually a kind of narrative of return. Her paternal grandparents, who raised her in France, were among the few French migrants to Western Australia in the early years of the twentieth century. Hoping for a new life of prosperity and freedom, they worked hard, but returned to France when their son, Rey's embittered father, was still quite young. The stories of an Australian paradise lost infiltrated Rey's childhood, and the image of freedom from the constraints of French society, family, judgment and language is what drives her finally to leave France:

> Quand on s'exporte à l'autre bout du monde, il n'y a plus de jugement. Plus rien. Plus de Boileau ni de Voltaire. Adieu l'imparfait du subjonctif. Place au délire. Là-bas, c'est débraillé, libre, réjouissant, heureux. En Australie occidentale, le culturel, tout le monde s'en bat l'œil, il faut bien le dire, mais au moins les choses sont clairement dites. Paris est un lointain village. Le français, un dialecte. Le pouvoir de la relativité entre en action. Vous adoptez enfin le point de vue de Sirius, et vous l'adoptez au sens propre. Comme tous ceux qui ont quitté leur terre natale, j'ai pu m'accorder une liberté de pensée que je n'aurais jamais prise si je n'avais pas quitté mon pays. Le pays, c'est aussi lourd que le regard des siens. On ne peut pas faire un pas de travers sans qu'ils soient là à vous conseiller, à vous juger, à vous débiner. Ah! la patrie! quelle trappe![20] (Rey, 2007: 113)

The voyage to Australia is accompanied by a love story that ends in a nervous breakdown, and a slow reintegration into a new society forms the basis of her account of the world. *Une femme en marche* thus combines travel writing and migrant writing, its ethics and poetics are certainly in concert with those

---

where the courtiers who know the ropes make the most of their privileges – and use every trick in the book doing so. Choosing to write when you come from nowhere means paying the price of exclusion' (2008: 48–49).

[20] 'When you export yourself to the other side of the world, there is no more judgment. No more anything. No more Boileau or Voltaire. It's goodbye to the imperfect subjunctive. Make way for delirium. Down Under it's scruffy, free, exhilarating, gleeful. In Western Australia, no one gives two hoots about culture, I have to say, but at least things are said clearly. Paris is a distant village. French, a dialect. The power of relativity comes into play. You end up adopting the point of view of Sirius, and you adopt it in the proper sense. Like all who have left their native lands, I was able to think freely in a way I would never have allowed myself if I hadn't left my homeland. Your homeland weighs as heavily on you as the gaze of your family. You can't take a step off the beaten track without them being there to advise you, judge you, slag you off. Ah! Your Native Land! What a trap!' (2008: 84).

inherent in the *littérature-monde* manifesto, but is there enough of the 'monde' in this text? A voyage from one Western privileged society – France – to another – Australia – without any evocations of indigenous spirituality or spectacular nature might not be perceived as enough commitment to 'dire le monde'. This example suggests that the individualized migrant experience without the intercultural and observational revelations that *littérature voyageuse* implies might not pass the *littérature-monde* test for French-Australian literature.

Finally, Josiane Behmoiras's *Dora B: A Memoir of My Mother / My Mother was a Bag Lady* is a memoir of her peregrinations at her mother's side, to be continued alone towards Australia with her new love. A brief trip back to Israel with her daughter to visit her ailing mother, is repeated a week later for her mother's funeral. This zigzag itinerary that crosses cultures and continents seems to provide an exemplary model for *littérature-monde*. The text displays the intercultural encounters of travel writing, the negotiation of new spaces and cultures of migrant writing and adheres to the ethics of 'ouverture' and the poetics of 'dire le monde' that form the basic tenets of *littérature-monde*. But it is not written in the author's mother tongue of French – it is written in the author's third language, English, after having lived more than twenty years in Australia. It has been translated into French and German, and all of the translations retain dialogue and vocabulary in French and Hebrew. The world enters the memoir from the very first page with a phone conversation between mother in Israel and daughter in Australia that emphasizes the cultural, temporal and geographical distance between the two places:

> In Australia it's eight o'clock in the morning when the telephone rings. My daughter rushes to the phone, like children often do. As soon as she has answered the call she waves both arms, one holding a peanut-butter toast and the other holding the receiver, which she hands to me as if it were a hot brick. I immediately know it's my mother calling and I brace myself for the usual shriek, '*Allô, allô! C'est toi ma fille?*'. (Behmoiras, 2005: 1–2)

The closing paragraphs of the text describing the author's reflections and actions following her mother's burial in Israel are equally revealing of the travelling cycles and migratory flow of this literature that brings the world into its focus:

> The first light of day illuminates the waves and the long flight of steps that will take me down to the beach. It's six o'clock; the regular bathers are already arriving. I wonder if both the Calderon brothers will be there, as they used to be at this hour every day of the year, even on stormy winter days, always present to offer the few beach devotees shelter and a warm comforting drink on the kiosk veranda [...].

There it is. I catch my breath as I approach it. The place is animated with the regulars, their voices and movements indicating with the song of a wet man, the flap of a towel, their friendship and shared history. Nissim Calderon is carrying big breakfast plates for his customers. Of the two brothers he is the slim, introvert one. He hasn't changed much from the way I remember him when I was a child, except for his hair, which used to be sun-bleached blond and is now white.

'*Shalom*', I say to him.

'*Shalom u'beracha*', he answers.

'I haven't been here for a long time, I used to come with my mother when I was a child, some thirty-five years ago. She used to speak to you in Ladino. I live in Australia now.'

Nissim smiles at me. 'Yes, I remember,' he says.

He doesn't say much more; I am not sure if he really remembers. But the mere fact that I smell the sea as I eat breakfast in this place is a way of honouring Dora's life. (Behmoiras, 2005: 264)

Although Behmoiras's memoir is not written in French, its qualities should certainly validate its inclusion as *littérature-monde*, if not guarantee its admission to the category of French-Australian literature.

As one of the three examples in this case study of French-Australian literature, Josiane Behmoiras's *Dora B: A Memoir of My Mother / My Mother was a Bag Lady* stands out as a model for *littérature-monde*, despite its initial composition in English. Catherine Rey's *Une femme en marche* also appears to correspond to the ethics and poetics of this literary phenomenon, responding to the added caveat of migrant experiences related through the narrative, but perhaps focusing too closely on the individual (and inner) itinerary of the protagonist without opening out enough to the world. Conversely, David Fauquemberg's *Nullarbor* seems less likely to fulfil even the broadest criteria relating to the ethics and poetics of *littérature-monde*. As this study has demonstrated, the lack of 'ouverture' or a capacity to 'dire le monde' in Fauquemberg's text arises from the absence of adequately developed migrant experiences or authentic travelling tales in the writing. *Littérature-monde* needs to 'dire le monde', but it must also know what to say and what not to say. And the manifesto expressly advises its proponents to find this out by travelling: 'avec d'abord l'envie de goûter à la poussière des routes, au frisson du dehors, au regard croisé d'inconnus'.[21]

---

[21] 'With the desire, first of all, to savor the dust from the roads, the allure of the outdoors, the encounter of a stranger's glance' ('Toward a "World-Literature" in French', 2009: 55).

The absence of a nuanced understanding and respect of indigenous cultures deprives Fauquemberg's text of depth, relegating it to the realm of clichés and stereotypes rather than allowing it to 'dire le monde'. Devoid of the engagement with and negotiation of intercultural relations that migrant literatures demand, *Nullarbor* falls into a redundant poetics that may have been avoided had Fauquemberg chosen to write about his two-year experience in Melbourne, as opposed to his final foray into the 'outback'.

Whether or not this case study of French-Australian literature can be extrapolated for application to *littérature-monde* in general, it is clear that the ethics and poetics expressed in the manifesto and volume of essays entitled *Pour une littérature-monde* are relevant criteria in defining this literary field. But the role of migrant literatures in the transition from *littérature voyageuse* to *littérature-monde* is also significant as it constitutes the necessary catalyst to crystallize the expression of 'ouverture' and capacity to 'dire le monde'. Amongst the residue left after such a literary reaction are the remaining examples of travel writing that could not be converted into *littérature-monde* due to 'imperialist impurities', but at least some travel writing expressing the migrant experience passes this definitional experiment. Migrant literatures represent the key to determining a positive interpretation and more practical application of *littérature-monde*, leaving behind the definition through negation that has hindered its progress as a useful concept. This conclusion may seem to indicate that migrant literatures rather than *littérature voyageuse* represent the real roots of *littérature-monde*, but such an understanding of the argument would be illusory and easily refuted by the example of Catherine Rey's autobiographical novel. *Littérature-monde* must reach out to recount literature's way in the world, not just the individual or inner experiences related to migration. The final equation arising from this case study of French-Australian literature is therefore: *littérature voyageuse* + migrant literatures = *littérature-monde*.

Works Cited

Behmoiras, Josiane. 2005. *Dora B: A Memoir of My Mother*. Camberwell, VIC: Viking Penguin.

Bernabé, Jean, Patrick Chamoiseau and Raphaël Confiant. 1989. *Eloge de la créolité*. Paris: Gallimard.

Boehmer, Elleke. 2005. *Colonial and Postcolonial Literature: Migrant Metaphors*. 2nd Edn. Oxford: Oxford University Press.

Caws, Mary Ann. (ed.) 2001. *Manifesto: A Century of Isms*. Lincoln and London: University of Nebraska Press.

Clifford, James. 1997. *Routes: Travel and Translation in the Late Twentieth Century*. Cambridge, MA: Harvard University Press.

Decoust, Michèle. 1987. *L'Inversion des saisons*. Paris: Laffont.

Fauquemberg, David. 2007. *Nullarbor*. Paris: Hoëbeke.

Forsdick, Charles. 2005. *Travel in Twentieth-Century French and Francophone Cultures: The Persistence of Diversity*. Oxford: Oxford University Press.

—. 2010. 'From "literature voyageuse" to "littérature-monde": The Manifesto in Context'. *Contemporary French and Francophone Studies*, 14.1: 9–17.

Glissant, Édouard. 1993. *Tout-monde*. Paris: Gallimard.

—. 1997. *Traité du tout-monde. (Poétique IV)*. Paris: Gallimard.

Godbout, Jacques. 2007. 'La Question préalable'. In Michel Le Bris and Jean Rouaud (eds), *Pour une littérature-monde*. Paris: Gallimard: 103–11.

Gotlib, Patricia. 1999. *Australiades: Voyage d'une Parisienne aux antipodes*. Paris: L'Harmattan.

Huggan, Graham. 2001. *The Postcolonial Exotic: Marketing the Margins*. London and New York: Routledge.

—. 2007. *Australian Literature: Postcolonialism, Racism, Transnationalism*. Oxford: Oxford University Press.

Lacarrière, Jacques. 1992. 'Le Bernard-l'hermite ou le treizième voyage'. In Michel Le Bris (ed.), *Pour une littérature voyageuse*. Paris: Éditions Complexes: 105–08.

Le Bris, Michel (ed.). 1992. *Pour une littérature voyageuse*. Brussels: Éditions Complexe.

—. 2007. 'Pour une littérature-monde en français'. In Michel Le Bris et Jean Rouaud (eds), *Pour une littérature-monde*. Paris: Gallimard: 23–53.

Le Bris, Michel, and Jean Rouaud (eds). 2007. *Pour une littérature-monde*. Paris: Gallimard.

Mabanckou, Alain. 2006. 'La francophonie, oui, le ghetto: non!'. *Le Monde* 19 March.

—. 2007. 'Le chant de l'oiseau migrateur'. In Michel Le Bris and Jean Rouaud (eds), *Pour une littérature-monde*. Paris: Gallimard: 55–66.

Melbourne Festival of Travel Writing. 2008. <www.mftw.com.au>. Consulted on 4 June 2010.

Meschonnic, Henri. 2009. *De monde en monde*. Paris: Éditions Arfuyen.

Ní Loingsigh, Aedín. 2009. *Postcolonial Eyes: Intercontinental Travel in Francophone Africa*. Liverpool: Liverpool University Press.

'Pour une "littérature-monde" en français'. 2007. *Le Monde* 16 March.

Pratt, Mary-Louise. 1992. *Imperial Eyes: Studies in Travel Writing and Transculturation*. London and New York: Routledge.

Raynal, Patrick. 2007. 'L'Avenir du roman? Noir'. In Michel Le Bris and Jean Rouaud (eds), *Pour une littérature-monde*. Paris: Gallimard: 135–42.

Rey, Catherine. 2007. *Une femme en marche.* Paris: Phébus.

—. 2008. *Stepping Out.* Trans. by Julie Rose. Artarmon, NSW: Giramondo Publishing.

Rouaud, Jean. 2007. 'Mort d'une certaine idée'. In Michel Le Bris and Jean Rouaud (eds), *Pour une littérature-monde.* Paris: Gallimard: 7–22.

'Toward a "World-Literature" in French'. 2009. Trans. by Daniel Simon. *World Literature Today* (March–April): 54–56.

Victor, Gary. 2007. 'Littérature-monde ou liberté d'être'. In Michel Le Bris and Jean Rouaud (eds), *Pour une littérature-monde.* Paris: Gallimard: 315–20.

Walkowitz, Rebecca L. 2006. 'The Location of Literature: The Transnational Book and the Migrant Writer'. *Contemporary Literature* 47.4: 527–45.

Littérature-monde
and the Space of Translation,
or, Where is *Littérature-monde?*[1]

Jeanne Garane

The question concerning the 'location' of a 'littérature-monde en français' is not as easily answered as one might first think. One reason for this is that the seemingly obvious answer to the question is tautological and chiasmic: *littérature-monde* is 'in' the 'world', and the 'world' is 'in' it. Or, again, it is purportedly 'from' the world over. Indeed, Goethe's epiphany heralding the new era of *Weltliteratur* in 1827 came to him while reading a Chinese novel translated into German. As Antoine Berman explains it in *L'Epreuve de l'étranger*, 'en forçant à peine les choses, on pourrait dire que la langue allemande est devenue parfois pour Goethe *la langue-de-la-traduction*' (Berman, 1984: 93).[2] To pose the questions, 'What literature?', 'What world?', 'In what language?'[3] is also to pose the question of translation, for it is an activity that is as central to the project of *littérature-monde* as it is to *Weltliteratur*, world literature, and *littérature mondiale*, although it may not always be acknowledged as such. Indeed, it is not too far-fetched to say that *Weltliteratur* for Goethe was a kind of *littérature-monde* in German.

Despite this possibility, the relationship between *littérature-monde*,

---

[1] The title for this essay takes its cue from the book, *Où est la littérature mondiale?*, edited by Christophe Pradeau and Tiphaine Samoyault.

[2] 'it may be said without exaggerating that the German language, for Goethe, sometimes became *the-language-of-translation*' (Berman, 1992: 57).

[3] In his critical reading of Pascale Casanova's *World Republic of Letters*, Christopher Prendergast asks 'not only who is included in the "world", but also what counts as "literature"'(4).

littérature mondiale, and its German and English-language counterparts *Weltliteratur,* and world literature is made explicit neither in the manifesto, 'Pour une "littérature-monde" en français', nor in the two introductory essays by Jean Rouaud and Michel Le Bris, the editors of the collection of essays by some of the signatories of the manifesto published under the title, *Pour une littérature-monde.*[4] When asked to clarify further the term *littérature-monde,* Le Bris offered the following definition: *littérature-monde* is 'literature' of the 'world' and the hyphen is the space of the writer's creative agency.[5] Putting aside for the moment the fact that in that particular instance Le Bris defined neither *littérature* nor *monde,* I will first focus on the hyphen before moving on to examine the definitions of *littérature* and *monde,* in particular as they appear in Le Bris's essay, 'Pour une littérature-monde en français'.

As a spatio-temporal marker of 'in-betweenness' that can either divide or connect wor(l)ds (although in French the *trait-d'union* implies unification rather more than division), the hyphen figures an in-between space of translation, negotiation and agency, one where, as Bhabha puts it, the signs and symbols of any culture 'can be appropriated, translated, rehistoricized and read anew' (Bhabha, 1994: 37–39). Bhabha has also asserted that in this Third Space, 'the politics of polarity may be eluded', while other critics who privilege 'in-betweenness' are attentive to the possible violence of translation. For instance, Anuradha Dingwaney cautions that

> translation is one of the primary means by which texts written in one or another indigenous languages of the various countries arbitrarily grouped under the 'Third', or non-Western, World are made available in Western, metropolitan languages [...] translation is also the vehicle through which 'Third World' cultures (are made to) travel – transported or 'borne across' to and recuperated by audiences in the West. Thus, even texts written in [...] one of the metropolitan languages but originating in or about non-Western cultures can be considered under the rubric of translation. (Dingwaney, 1995: 4)

---

[4] It is interesting to note that the book title, *Pour une literature-monde,* drops the modifier, 'en français'.

[5] Le Bris responded to this question during the first international conference devoted to the topic held in February 2009, at the Winthrop-King Institute at Florida State University in Tallahassee. David Simon's English-language translation of the manifesto, published in *World Literature Today* uses the term 'world-literature' with a hyphen, presumably to differentiate it from the term 'world literature', just as the hyphen in *littérature-monde* appears to separate it from the term *littérature mondiale.*

While attention to the potential for violence is necessary, I contend that it is equally necessary to account for the agency of the writer, an agency that the term 'Francophone' has often denied by implying a secondary, derived or indeed 'amateur' relationship to French when it is used to categorize certain 'writers of French expression' as 'non-French'. Moreover, in maintaining a centre-periphery binary, the term 'Francophone' is informed by the same oppositions that divide the conventional view of translation between author and original text on the one hand, and translator and derived text on the other, where translation is cast as 'a weak and degraded version of authorship' (Simon, 1996: 39). Similarly, as Lawrence Venuti writes in *Rethinking Translation*, the contemporary translator is often viewed as 'a paradoxical hybrid, at once dilettante and artisan' (Venuti, 1992: 1), an amateur writer and scholar who works within a relationship of lack.

In his contribution to the collection of essays *Pour une littérature-monde*, entitled 'Ecrivains en position d'entraver', Abdourahman Waberi cites the description of Anna Moï that was posted on the official website of the *Centre national du livre* during the 2006 *Salon du livre*: 'Anna Moï a beau écrire en langue française, ses origines vietnamiennes font d'elle un écrivain francophone' (Waberi, 2007: 69).[6] This description of Moï is ironic, given that she had already enjoined against such ethnic epithets in her book *Espéranto, désespéranto*: 'Les écrivains francophones non français issus de la colonisation sont malgaches, maghrébins, vietnamiens avant d'être des écrivains, contrairement à Samuel Beckett ou Nancy Houston ... comme si la francophonie du ressortissant d'une ancienne colonie était une aliénation' (Moï, 2006: 54).[7] In his contribution to the collection *Pour une littérature-monde*, Raharimanana addresses this implicit notion of alienation with outrage. 'Un livre publié. On crie au génie: "Comment faites-vous pour écrire aussi bien en français? Traduisez-vous à partir de votre langue maternelle?"' (Raharimanana, 2007: 305).[8] As it is posed here, the question denies Raharimanana creative agency by implying that 'all' he has done is 'copy', or 'translate' (in the conventional understanding of the term), from

---

6 'Although Anna Moï writes in the French language, her Vietnamese origins make her a Francophone writer'. Unless otherwise indicated, all translations from French into English are by the author of this chapter.

7 'Non-French Francophone writers from former colonies are regarded as Malagasy, Maghrebi or Vietnamese, before being seen as writers, contrary to Samuel Beckett or Nancy Huston ... as if the *francophonie* of someone from a former colony amounted to a form of alienation'.

8 'A book is published. I'm declared a genius: "How is it that you write so well in French? Do you translate from your mother tongue?"'

some pre-existing cultural 'original'. It also denies a long history of French-language education in Madagascar, and it ignores the fact that French is one of the national languages of that country.

This is precisely why the forty-four signatories of the manifesto declare that the centre-periphery model of a literary universe with Paris at its centre and Francophone writers at its margins should be put to rest. In qualifying their writing as 'transnational' and 'open to the world' the forty-four collectively declare the death of *Francophonie*, for, they say, 'personne ne parle le francophone, ni n'écrit en francophone'.[9] In sum, they propose to liberate the French language from the French nation, and to sever the 'carnal link' between the two. It is in this sense that Anna Moï suggests that Francophone writing be understood as a kind of translation, but as a translation with no original. In *Espéranto, désespéranto* she writes, '[L]es langues ne sont qu'un instrument de traduction d'une langue indicible concoctée par l'auteur [...] Elles sont presque secondaires et certains auteurs [...] écrivent dans deux langues. Ils sont écrivains avant d'être francophone ou anglophone' (Moï, 2006: 16).[10] Similarly, in her contribution to the collective volume entitled 'Traduttore non è traditore', Nancy Huston explains that the writer writes 'pour agrandir le monde, pour en repousser les frontières [...] Ce faisant, l'écrivain traduit' (Huston, 2007: 153).[11]

The manifesto proclaiming a *littérature-monde* in French joins contemporary debates surrounding the nature of comparative literary studies, postcolonial studies, world literature and the role of translation as a crucial but sometimes under-analysed component of these fields. In his introduction to *Debating World Literature*, an anthology of critical essays devoted to the examination of 'world literature', Christopher Prendergast credits Pascale Casanova's *République mondiale des lettres*, published in 1999 and translated into English in 2005 under the title *The World Republic of Letters*, as the catalyst for the return of 'world literature' to the spotlight, given that Casanova herself uses Goethe's *Weltliteratur* as a starting point.[12] Despite this privileging of Goethe's vision, Prendergast rightly points out that in the

---

[9] 'nobody speaks *francophonie*, nobody writes in Francophone'.

[10] 'Languages are nothing more than an instrument of translation from an ineffable language concocted by the author [...] They are almost secondary and some authors [...] write in two languages. They are writers first and foremost before they are Anglophone or Francophone'.

[11] 'to enlarge the world, to push back its borders [...] In doing this, the writer translates'.

[12] See also David Damrosch's *What is World Literature*? In a different vein, one could also examine Édouard Glissant's use of the word *monde* in his *Tout-monde*

end Casanova manages to declare Paris as the centre of the literary universe even as she describes it (in Prendergast's words) as a

> de-nationalized locus of the Universal, home to the Classic, guardian of Taste, resolver of Quarrels, arbiter of the New, host to the Avant-Garde – in short all of the cultural appurtenances with which a geographical capital accumulates, hoards, and dispenses [...] literary capital [...]. (Prendergast, 2004: 9)

Given this 'French' precedent, one wonders to what extent this view of the literary 'world' with Paris at its centre may inadvertently inform certain aspects of *littérature-monde* as theorized by Jean Rouaud and Michel Le Bris. Because Rouaud and Le Bris's essays introduce, and in that sense partially define, the contours of *littérature-monde*, I use their texts as points of departure for my examination, with the understanding that the remaining chapters in the volume also propose a variety of valuable perspectives on the issue, all the more so in that a number of the chapters specifically address the question of translation.

For Jean Rouaud, in his introductory essay 'Mort d'une certaine idée', 'the world' lies both in a French language 'déliée de son pacte avec la nation, libérée de l'étreinte de la source-mère, devenue autonome [...] vue d'Afrique, d'Asie, ou des Caraïbes, de Chine ou d'Iran, d'Amérique du Nord ou du Vietnam, son interprétation du monde' (Rouaud, 2007: 21)[13] and in the return of a realist post-*nouveau roman* aesthetic of representation in the (French) novel (Rouaud, 2007: 17–18).

On the other hand, in 'Pour une littérature-monde en français', Le Bris's introductory essay, the term is more nebulous. Here, in another chiasmic formula, *littérature-monde* is at once a kind of travel writing, exemplified by writers like Bruce Chatwin and Nicolas Bouvier, and a writing that travels, a *littérature voyageuse*, that comes from elsewhere, *le monde*. At other points in Le Bris's essay, *littérature-monde* is a variety of *littérature mondiale*. Le Bris uses the latter term twice to refer to works by such writers as Joseph Conrad and Robert Louis Stephenson (Le Bris, 2007: 29) or more generally to works that had been read by the cohort of forty writers 'du monde entier' that Le Bris had included in his 1992 Etonnants Voyageurs literary festival.

---

and *Traité du Tout-monde*, an endeavour well beyond the scope of the present essay.

[13] 'disconnected from its pact with the nation, liberated from the embrace of a mother-origin, autonomous now [...] seen from Afria, Asia, or the Caribbean, from China or Iran, from North America or from Vietnam, in its interpretation of the world'.

Le Bris explains that 'tous ces jeunes écrivains se revendiquaient en effet du monde entier, avaient lu toute la littérature mondiale, et particulièrement les littératures européenne ou américaine' (Le Bris, 2007: 39)[14] – for example, Faulkner, Dostoevsky and Conrad – although Le Bris does not specify in what language(s) these works were read. In this schema, Western literature and the West are cast as the primary nourishment from which these young writers would somewhat cannibalistically partake.[15] According to Le Bris, 'dès lors que le monde absorbait l'Occident, il le digérait, le dissolvait, le transformait par un processus continu d'hybridisation multiples. Ce que nous montrait la production de ces jeunes auteurs était en quelque sorte la dissolution de l'Occident dans un vaste ensemble-monde polyphonique [...]' (Le Bris, 2007: 40).[16]

Given this passage, one might rightly ask to what extent the *monde* in Le Bris's configuration of *littérature-monde* replicates the *monde* in *Tiers-monde* and, likewise, to what extent the term *littérature-monde en français* simply refers to literature in French from outside of France. Moreover, one wonders, if that is the case, to what extent does the old definition of *Francophonie* with all of its attendant binary oppositions between centre (Paris) and periphery (not-France) remain operative in Le Bris's essay?

There is no denying that in the West the reception of 'Francophone' writers has been tempered by the question of ethnicity and 'national' origins. And, willy-nilly, ethnicity also seems to inform the composition of the *Pour une littérature-monde* collection of essays. For, despite the inclusion of Michel Le Bris, Patrick Raynal, Jean Rouaud and Fabienne Kanor, whose biographical notice specifies – in an ironic replication of the ethnic identification that Waberi and Moï critique – that she was born in Orléans but is of Martinican descent (Le Bris and Rouaud, 2007: 242), the remaining writers included in

---

[14] 'all of these young writers saw themselves as part of the world in its entirety, had read all of world literature, and particularly European and American literature'.

[15] Although Le Bris does not say so, the connections between a figurative cannibalism and translation is a *lieu commun*. See, for instance, the introduction to *Postcolonial Translation* by Bassnett and Trivedi, 'Of colonies, cannibals, and vernaculars', and in the same volume Else Ribeiro Pires Vieira's 'Liberating Calibans: Readings of *Antropofagia* and Haroldo da Campos' *Poetics of Transcreation*'.

[16] 'in absorbing the West, the world digested it, dissolved it, transformed it through a continual process of multiple hybridization. Which showed us that what these young authors were engaged in was in a sense the dissolution of the West in a vast polyphonic world-ensemble'.

the anthology are identified by citing their respective birthplaces outside of France, in the 'world'.

In this connection, however, it is interesting to note that the American Jonathan Littell, who received the 2006 *Grand Prix du roman de l'Académie française* and the *Prix Goncourt* for *Les Bienveillantes*, is not among the signatories of the manifesto, nor is he included in the collective volume, although Ananda Devi, Alain Mabanckou and Nancy Huston, all of whom also won literary prizes that year, are included. Could this be because Littell, an American who wrote a novel in French, is qualified neither as Francophone nor as a writer *d'expression française* by the literary and academic establishments in France or abroad? Would this put him in the same category as Beckett and Ionesco, writers who wrote in French but were never called Francophones? As Tahar Ben Jelloun remarks in 'La cave de ma mémoire, le toit de ma maison sont des mots français', it is rarely pointed out that Beckett and Ionesco 'n'écrivaient pas dans leur langue-mère ou bien qu'ils allaient d'une langue à l'autre sans que cela offusque ou fasse problème' (Ben Jelloun, 2007:118).[17] On the other hand, according to Ben Jelloun, 'Est considéré comme francophone l'écrivain métèque, celui qui vient d'ailleurs [...]. [...] Ceux qu'on désigne du doigt, ceux qui doivent se justifier, montrer leurs "papiers", ceux qu'on regarde avec suspicion [...]' (Ben Jelloun, 2007: 117–18).[18] Against this, say the forty-four, the French literary establishment now must acknowledge that the 'world' can no longer be excluded from literature written in French. Writers from the 'periphery' of France (most often former French colonies) must no longer feel obligated to 'se dépouiller de leurs bagages avant de se fonder dans le creuset de la langue et de l'histoire nationale' ('Pour une "littérature-monde" en français', 2007).[19] Instead, they say, it is because of the very fact of their cultural difference that the 'world' has returned to French letters. Given this acknowledgement of cultural, 'ethnic' difference, one might ask to what extent 'the world' that Le Bris describes in his essay replicates or rejects in some way 'the world' as it is seen in Pascale Casanova's *République mondiale des lettres*?

Included in Casanova's *World Republic of Letters* is a model of 'Third World' writing as derivative translation that coexists with essentialist conceptions of linguistic ownership as 'cultural property'. This view leads

---

[17] 'did not write in their mother tongue or that they went back and forth between one language and another without this causing any upset or problem'.

[18] 'The Francophone writer is a dirty foreigner, one who comes from elsewhere [...] They are the ones who are pointed at, who have to justify themselves, who have to show their "papers", who are looked upon with suspicion [...]'.

[19] 'rid themselves of their baggage before being absorbed into the melting pot of [France's] national language and history'.

Casanova to characterize the situation of bilingual or multi-lingual African writers as tragic, dispossessed and 'dominated'. Having declared Paris to be the centre of the literary universe, Casanova's literary model is informed by the same centre-periphery binary that not only informs conventional notions of translation, but also those of *Francophonie*. For example, in her chapter entitled, 'La Tragédie des "hommes traduits"' [The tragedy of translated men] the East African writers Abdourahman Waberi and Nuruddin Farah are deemed to be tragic, 'translated men'. Both speak Somali, but Waberi writes in French and Farah writes in English. Characterizing them as being from 'des espaces excentriques' [outlying spaces] (Casanova, 1999: 347, 254), presumably with respect to Europe, Casanova declares them (among others) to be 'par définition dépourvues de capital littéraire' [by definition lacking literary capital] (Casanova, 1999: 350, 256). Casanova judges Somalia and Djibouti (along with other parts of Africa) to be 'régions très démunies littérairement' [regions of extreme literary impoverishment] (Casanova, 1999: 354, 259), while the Somali language is deemed 'presque inexistante' [almost non-existent] (Casanova, 1999: 354, 260). Thus, she concludes, writers like Farah and Waberi are tragic (Casanova, 1999: 352) because they are 'écrivains traduits' [translated men] (354, 260). This excessively Eurocentric model leads Casanova completely to ignore the existence of a long tradition of oral literature in the Somali language, a tradition that continues to this day in public performances that are recorded and distributed throughout the Somali diaspora.[20] Moreover, in assuming a model of translation as a transfer from 'original' to diminished derivative, Casanova can only conclude that writers like Waberi and Farah are victims, 'condemned' to find a way out of their 'dénuement' and their 'dependency' (Casanova, 1999: 348) through the 'tragedy' of translation. While Waberi himself confirms that he writes in part to 'faire exister mon pays sur la planète littérature' [bring my country into existence on planet literature],[21] he also insists that it is time to untie 'le nœud gordien qui englobe tout à la fois la langue, "la race" et la nation françaises' [the Gordian knot that binds together French as a language, a 'race' and a nation] (Waberi, 2007: 72). Moreover, his offhanded definition of *franco-phonie* as 'l'espace d'imaginaire, de mots, de culture ouvert à quiconque sait aligner deux ou trois mots de français' (Garane, 2005: 139)[22] suggests that

---

[20] For a more in-depth critique of Casanova's book, see Christopher Prendergast's 'The World Republic of Letters'.

[21] See my interview, 'Comment faire exister son pays sur la planète littérature'.

[22] 'the space of the imaginary, of words, of culture open to whoever can align two or three words in French'.

his experience as a 'Francophone' writer may not be as 'tragic' as Casanova might think.

Indeed, it could be said that Waberi shares Jacques Derrida's understanding of language and translation as it is expressed in Derrida's *Monolinguisme de l'autre* [Monolingualism of the Other]. Defining what he calls 'the law of translation' and 'the law as translation' through a double postulation that reads, 'On ne parle jamais qu'une seule langue. [...] (Oui mais) – On ne parle jamais une seule langue' (Derrida, 1996: 25),[23] Derrida argues that all language is inhabited by alterity. Derrida does not deny the possibility of subservience and hegemony. However, he writes:

> [L]e maître ne possède pas en propre, *naturellement*, ce qu'il appelle pourtant sa langue [...] parce que la langue n'est pas son bien naturel, par cela même il peut historiquement, à travers le viol d'une usurpation culturelle [...] feindre de se l'approprier pour l'imposer comme la sienne'.[24]
> (Derrida, 1996: 12)

As if to counter this model of cultural usurpation, the signatories of the manifesto, and later Michel Le Bris in his introductory essay, cite Salman Rushdie's 'Imaginary Homelands'. Here, Rushdie uses translation as a metaphor not just for describing the richness of cultural pluralism, but also as a figure for the creative writer when he points to the importance of translation as a necessary component of cultural exchange and interaction. Given that the word 'translation' comes from the Latin for 'bearing across', writes Rushdie in *Imaginary Homelands*, 'having been borne across the world, we are translated men. It is normally supposed that something always gets lost in translation; I cling, obstinately, to the notion that something can also be gained' (Rushdie, 1991: 17). For the signatories of the manifesto, 'French' letters 'gain' entry into a 'world' beyond the borders of France (*outre-France*) even as that 'beyond' inserts the 'world' into 'French' letters. To the singularity of a national identity is thus ostensibly added a plethora of transnational identities. Here, the reference to Rushdie's metaphor constitutes a rejection of the marginalization of those 'translated men [and women]', formerly known as 'Francophones', in favour of a sort of postcolonial and postnational world literature in French.

---

23 'We only ever speak one language. [...] (yes, but) – We never speak only one language' (Derrida, 1998: 10).

24 '[T]he master does not possess exclusively, and naturally, what he calls his language [...] because language is not his natural possession, he can, thanks to that very fact, pretend historically, through the rape of cultural usurpation [...] to appropriate it in order to impose it as his own' (Derrida, 1998: 23).

And yet, what is surprising in the manifesto and especially in Le Bris's essay, is the absence of any mention of so-called 'Beur' literature as a possible precursor or component of *littérature-monde* in French. On the contrary, for Le Bris, the changes that were occurring in 1980s Great Britain represented 'la première fois qu'une génération d'écrivains issus de l'immigration [...] entendait faire œuvre à partir du constat de son identité plurielle' (Le Bris, 2007: 33).[25] Le Bris doesn't say a word about the book *Ecarts d'identité* by Azouz Begag and Abedellatif Chaouite, which saw that during the 1980s the question of the Beur vote and of French Islam within the framework of what was called 'l'immigration maghrébine en France' [Maghrebi immigration in France] had already changed what was at stake for the nation. According to Begag and Chaouite, 'Pour la première fois, l'enjeu reconnu et explicitement visé est la France même. Au-delà de celles des minorités ethniques, ce sont les frontières de l'ethnicité française qui jouent et qui bougent' (Begag and Chaouite, 1990: 7).[26] Moreover, while Le Bris mentions the riots 'qui avaient secoué les banlieues des grandes cités industrielles de Grande Bretagne' [that had shaken the suburbs of the big industrial cities of Great Britain] in the 1980s (Le Bris: 2007, 32), he makes no mention of the similar disturbances that took place during the same period in the French *banlieues* nor of the nationwide *Marche des Beurs* in 1983. The appearance in 1985 in Great Britain of the film *My Beautiful Laundrette*, with a screenplay by Hanif Kureishi, set in the South-Asian community of London, retains his attention, but not Mehdi Charef's *Le Thé au Harem d'Archimède*, released the same year in France, nor Azouz Begag's extremely successful novel *Le Gone du Chaâba*, published in 1986.[27] Charef's film was itself adapted from his novel *Le Thé au harem d'Archi Ahmed*, which had been published in 1983. Just as Le Bris says nothing about the appearance in France of 'Beur' literature in the 1980s, the same is the case regarding the development of so-called migrant literature in 1980s France, most often represented by the writings of the (Franco)-Cameroonian Calixthe Beyala. In fact, Beyala's novel *Les Honneurs perdues* won the *Grand Prix du roman de l'Académie française* in 1996, a full ten years before the 2006 literary prizes that triggered the manifesto. Lest we forget, as early as 1987 and 1992, Tahar Ben Jelloun and

---

[25] 'the first time that a generation of writers of immigrant descent set out to constitute a work of art from the observations surrounding its plural identity'.

[26] 'For the first time what is at stake and explicitly so is France itself. Beyond those of ethnic minorities, it is the borders of French ethnicity that are in play and that are changing'.

[27] Azouz Begag, who was present at the conference in Florida, pointed out that the shantytowns of Lyon where he grew up and where *Le Gone du Chaâba* is set were also *le monde*.

Patrick Chamoiseau had received the *Prix Goncourt* for *La Nuit sacrée* and *Texaco* respectively. Similarly, in 2000, Ahmadou Kourouma, who was living in Lyon and who is buried in that same city, won the *Prix Renaudot* and the *Prix Goncourt des lycéens* for *Allah n'est pas obligé*.[28]

In my view, to exclude the works of so-called 'Beur' or 'immigrant' writers from *littérature-monde* inadvertently reinforces the model of imperial geography implicit in the term 'Francophone'. In *Culture and Imperialism*, Edward Said had already begun to explore the links between 'world literature' and imperial cartography. As Said puts it,

> the salutary vision of a 'world literature' that acquired a redemptive status in the twentieth century coincides with what theorists of colonial geography also articulated [... where ...] empire and geographical space collaborate to produce a 'world-empire' commanded by Europe. (Said, 1993: 47–48)

Said emphasizes the 'coincidences and convergences' that connect 'world literature' to the imperial world map. And, although Said never mentions him, it is useful to recall here that Onésime Reclus, the inventor of the term *francophonie* in *France, Algérie, et Colonies* (1880), was of course a colonial geographer. Applying the word to 'l'ensemble des territoires où l'on parle français' [all territories in which French is spoken] (Deniau, 1983: 8) Reclus's concept also incorporated that of *la mission civilisatrice*, with France as 'la nation porte-flambeau qui doit servir le monde par son exemple' [the torch-bearing nation that must serve as an example to the world], where the French language would serve as the medium for 'le ferment mystique des idéaux proprement français' [the mystical ferment of truly French ideals] (Deniau, 1983: 9).

Happily, the hyphen that connects 'world' to 'empire' in Said's analysis is not the same hyphen that connects 'littérature' to 'monde' for Le Bris. For Said, the birth of 'world literature' implied the privilege 'of an observer located in the West who could actually survey the world's literary output with a kind of sovereign detachment' (48). For Le Bris, the purveyors of *le monde* are literary 'agents' who often come from elsewhere. They are Rushdie's 'translated' men (and women) who have something to gain and something to offer in translation. Indeed, the image of translation that Rushdie proposes in 'Imaginary Homelands' can lead to a resolution of the binary opposition that seems to oppose writers from inside the hexagon to those who have ostensibly come from outside its borders. By including so-called writers of

---

[28] And this is not to mention the Negritude movement or the Harlem Renaissance.

immigrant origin in an enlarged vision of *littérature-monde*, the ideology of centre and periphery can be further undone.

Works Cited

Bassnett, Susan, and Harish Trivedi. 1999. 'Introduction: Of Colonies, Cannibals, and Vernaculars'. In Susan Bassnett and Harish Trivedi (eds), *Post-colonial Translation: Theory and Practice*. London: Routledge: 1–18.

Begag, Azouz. 1996. *Le Gone du Chaâba*. Paris: Seuil.

Begag, Azouz, and Abdellatif Chaouite. 1990. *Ecarts d'identité*. Paris: Seuil.

Ben Jelloun, Tahar. 1987. *La Nuit sacrée*. Paris: Seuil.

—. 2007. 'La cave de ma mémoire, le toit de ma maison sont des mots français'. In Michel Le Bris and Jean Rouaud (eds), *Pour une littérature-monde*. Paris: Gallimard: 113–24.

Berman, Antoine. 1984. *L'Épreuve de l'étranger: Culture et traduction dans l'Allemagne romantique*. Paris: Gallimard.

—. 1992. *The Experience of the Foreign: Culture and Translation in Romantic Germany*. Trans. by Stefaan Heyvaert. Albany, NY: SUNY Press.

Beyala, Calixthe. 1996. *Les Honneurs perdues*. Paris: Albin Michel.

Bhabha, Homi. 1994. *The Location of Culture*. London: Routledge.

Casanova, Pascale. 1999. *La République mondiale des lettres*. Paris: Seuil.

—. 2005. *The World Republic of Letters*. Trans. by M. B. DeBevoise. Cambridge, MA: Harvard University Press.

Charef, Mehdi. 1983. *Le Thé au harem d'Archi Ahmed*. Paris: Mercure de France.

—. 1985. *Le Thé au harem d'Archimède*. (Feature Film).

Damrosch, David. 2003. *What is World Literature?* Princeton, NJ and Oxford: Princeton University Press.

Deniau, Xavier. 1983. *La Francophonie*. Paris: Presses Universitaires de France.

Derrida, Jacques. 1996. *Monolinguisme de l'autre, ou la prothèse d'origine*. Paris: Galilée.

—. 1998. *Monolingualism of the Other, or The Prosthesis of Origin*. Trans. by Patrick Mensah. Stanford, CA: Stanford University Press.

Dingwaney, Anuradha. 1995. 'Introduction: Translating "Third World" Cultures'. In Anuradha Dingwaney and Carol Maier (eds), *Between Languages and Cultures: Translation and Cross-Cultural Texts*. Pittsburgh, PA: University of Pittsburgh Press: 3–15.

Garane, Jeanne. 2005. 'Comment faire exister son pays sur la planète littérature. Entretien avec Abdourahman A. Waberi'. In Jeanne Garane (ed.), *Discursive*

Geographies: Writing Space and Place in French/Géographies Discursives: l'écriture de l'espace et du lieu en français. Amsterdam: Rodopi: 133–49.

Glissant, Édouard. 1993. *Tout-monde.* Paris: Gallimard.

—. 1997. *Traité du Tout-monde (Poétique IV).* Paris: Gallimard.

Huston, Nancy. 2007. 'Traduttore non è traditore'. In Michel Le Bris and Jean Rouaud (eds), *Pour une littérature-monde.* Paris: Gallimard: 151–60.

Kourouma, Ahmadou. 2000. *Allah n'est pas obligé.* Paris: Seuil.

Littell, Jonathan. 2006. *Les Bienveillantes.* Paris: Gallimard.

Le Bris, Michel. 2007. 'Pour une littérature-monde en français'. In Michel Le Bris and Jean Rouaud (eds), *Pour une littérature-monde.* Paris: Gallimard: 23–53.

Le Bris, Michel, and Jean Rouaud (eds). 2007. *Pour une littérature-monde.* Paris: Gallimard.

Moï, Anna. 2006. *Espéranto, désespéranto: La francophonie sans les Français.* Paris: Gallimard.

'Pour une "littérature-monde" en français'. 2007. *Le Monde* 16 March.

Pradeau, Christophe, and Tiphaine Samoyault (eds). 2005. *Où est la littérature mondiale?* Saint Denis: Presses Universitaires de Vincennes.

Prendergast, Christopher. 2004. 'The World Republic of Letters'. In Christopher Prendergast (ed.), *Debating World Literature.* London: Verso: 1–25.

Raharimanana. 2007. 'Le Creuset des possibles'. In Michel Le Bris and Jean Rouaud (eds), *Pour une littérature-monde.* Paris: Gallimard: 305–14.

Reclus, Onésime. 1880. *France, Algérie, et Colonies.* Paris: Hachette.

Rouaud, Jean. 2007 'Mort d'une certaine idée'. In Michel Le Bris and Jean Rouaud (eds), *Pour une littérature-monde.* Paris: Gallimard: 7–22.

Rushdie, Salman. 1991. *Imaginary Homelands.* London: Granta.

Said, Edward W. 1993. *Culture and Imperialism.* New York: Alfred A. Knopf.

Simon, Sherry. 1996. *Gender in Translation: Cultural Identity and the Politics of Transmission.* New York: Routledge.

Venuti, Lawrence. 1992. *Rethinking Translation: Discourse, Subjectivity, Ideology.* London: Routledge.

Vieira, Else Ribeiro Pires. 1999. 'Liberating Calibans: Readings of *Antropofagia* and Haroldo da Campos' *Poetics of Transcreation*'. In Susan Bassnett and Harish Trivedi (eds), *Post-colonial Translation: Theory and Practice.* London: Routledge: 95–113.

Waberi, Abourahman A. 2007. 'Ecrivains en position d'entraver'. In Michel Le Bris and Jean Rouaud (eds), *Pour une littérature-monde.* Paris: Gallimard: 67–75.

Littérature-monde
or *Littérature océanienne?*
Internationalism versus Regionalism
in Francophone Pacific Writing

Michelle Keown

In the 2007 manifesto 'Pour une "littérature-monde" en français', the notion of a 'world literature in French' is offered as an enabling alternative to the concept of *Francophonie*, widely criticized for its neo-colonial political associations and the way in which it is often used to 'emphasize ethnic or racial "difference" from a perceived [metropolitan] "French norm"' (Forsdick and Murphy, 2003: 7; see also Mabanckou, 2007). The signatories to the manifesto posit the 1970s rise of a 'world literature in English' as a key precedent for their project, citing writers such as Kazuo Ishiguro, Ben Okri, Hanif Kureishi, Michael Ondaatje and Salman Rushdie as part of a new generation of *métis* pioneers which, 'au lieu de se couler dans sa culture d'adoption, entendait faire œuvre à partir du constat de son identité plurielle', thereby taking 'possession des lettres anglaises' ('Pour une "littérature-monde" en français', 2007).[1] The year 2006, in which five of the seven major French literary prizes were awarded to 'foreign-born' writers, is taken as a similar watershed in French literary culture, heralding 'l'émergence d'une littérature-monde en langue française consciemment affirmée' ('Pour une "littérature-monde" en français', 2007).[2]

Though the signatories' invocation of the concept of 'world literature' is

---

[1] 'instead of melting into their adopted culture, set out to create by drawing on the source of their plural identity', thereby 'taking possession of English letters' (Toward a "World-Literature" in French', 2009: 55).

[2] 'the emergence of a consciously affirmed, transnational world-literature in the French language' (Toward a "World-Literature" in French', 2009: 56).

optimistic and celebratory, the reference to the literary precedent in English signals potential pitfalls in the valency and utility of the concept. The notion of a 'world literature in English' has, in its most idealistic sense, been invoked to promote global inclusivity and diversity (as, for example, in the American periodical *World Literature Today*), and in its broadest and most politically neutral sense it encompasses 'all literary works that circulate beyond their culture of origin' (Damrosch, 2003: 4). In other contexts, however, 'world literature' is often used, like the term 'world music', to denote literature that falls outside the British-American literary 'mainstream', circulated and received less as 'testimony to a wealth of cultural diversity' than as part of an exoticizing 'domestication' of the foreign (Damrosch, 2003: 17; Huggan, 2001). As Barbara Herrnstein Smith observes, literary cosmopolitanism can become another form of cultural imperialism, with the Western subject perceiving 'in every horizon of difference new peripheries of its own centrality, new pathologies through which its own normativity may be defined and must be asserted' (Herrnstein Smith, 1988: 54). Partly as a result of these associations, the notion of 'world literature in English' (like 'Commonwealth literature') has in many contexts been superseded by the near-ubiquitous designation 'postcolonial literature', which – though not without its own semantic limitations and contradictions – is often perceived as circumventing the Anglocentric associations of its predecessors.[3]

With these debates in mind, this chapter considers the relevance of the notion of a 'world literature in French' to the context of Indigenous Francophone Pacific literature,[4] which (I will argue) does not readily lend itself to incorporation within such a paradigm. This exceptionalism can be attributed to a number of factors, not least the fact that until very recently Indigenous Pacific literature in French has been published and circulated almost solely within its country of origin, remaining a marginalized area even within the burgeoning field of Francophone postcolonial studies,[5] and ignored almost completely within metropolitan France (Forsdick and

---

[3] The decision to change the title of the journal formerly known as *World Literature Written in English* to *Journal of Postcolonial Writing* in 2005 is a case in point.

[4] Though I have used the term 'postcolonial' in other published work, in this chapter I tend to use 'Indigenous' partly in order to reflect the ambiguous political status of the French Pacific territories (discussed below), and partly to distinguish Indigenous writers from white settler populations (who might in some contexts be classified as 'postcolonial').

[5] Notable exceptions include, *inter alia*, two special issues of the *International Journal of Francophone Studies* – 8.3 (2005) and 11.4 (2008), edited by Pascale

Murphy 2003: 12; De Souza 2009: 240; Mateata-Allain 2008: 19). Further, any sense of a *regional* collective of Francophone Pacific writers has been hampered partly by the very limited publishing resources and networks within and across France's Pacific 'territories'[6] (which include French Polynesia, Wallis and Futuna and New Caledonia) and by the dominance of Anglophone writing within regional models of Pacific or 'Oceanic' literature. The linguistic barrier between the Francophone and Anglophone Pacific has – to some degree – prevented Indigenous writers from the Francophone Pacific from taking part in the creative and political discursive networks from which writers of the Anglophone Pacific have benefited, and Francophone Pacific writing has often been overlooked in surveys of anti- or post-colonial Pacific writing.[7]

However, in keeping with recent developments in international postco-lonial studies – which have included increasing recognition of Francophone as well as Anglophone contributions to the field – the last decade has witnessed burgeoning dialogues and collaborations between Francophone and Anglophone Pacific writers, as well as the emergence of a number of English translations of Francophone Pacific texts. In discussing these translingual dialogues with particular reference to the work of Kanaky (Indigenous New Caledonian) writer Déwé Gorodé and Māʻohi (Tahitian) writer Chantal Spitz, this chapter will argue that these nascent regional affili-ations between Indigenous Francophone and Anglophone Pacific writers call into question the relevance (to the Pacific) of the argument for a transnational collective of Francophone writers.

In recognizing the importance of these regional 'Oceanic' affiliations, however, this chapter will also consider the pragmatics and problematics of translating Francophone Pacific literature for an Anglophone readership.

De Souza and H. Adlai Murdoch – which include essays on Francophone Pacific writing as well as translations of poetry by Māʻohi (Tahitian) poet Henri Hiro.

[6] I use the label 'territory' to reflect the fact that with the exception of Vanuatu (a former Anglo-French condominium which achieved independence in 1980), the 'French' Pacific is neither 'postcolonial' nor strictly 'colonial' in political status. Until relatively recently, French Polynesia, Wallis and Futuna and New Caledonia were designated French 'Territoires d'outre-mer', enjoying greater local autonomy than 'Départements d'outre-mer' such as French Guyana and Guadeloupe. As of 2003, however, French Polynesia and Wallis and Futuna became known as 'Collectivités d'outre-mer', while New Caledonia, following the Nouméa Accord of 1998, was uniquely designated 'Pays d'outre-mer' and granted even greater political decentralization (Brown 2004: p. xxxii).

[7] Exceptions include Nicole (1999; 2001); Keown (2007); and Mateata-Allain (2008).

Both Spitz and Gorodé engage with issues that are also prevalent in Indigenous Anglophone Pacific writing, but it is important to consider to what degree their work resists incorporation within Anglophone literary-cultural paradigms. In this context, it is also worth considering the degree to which their writing *does* resonate with the work of Francophone postcolonial writers elsewhere in the world. As I will demonstrate, although Francophone Pacific writers are a notable absence amongst the signatories to the 2007 manifesto,[8] and although Chantal Spitz in particular has expressed resistance to being incorporated within a global collective of Francophone writers, there are some identifiable thematic and stylistic connections that can be made between Spitz's and Gorodé's work, and the work of Francophone postcolonial writers beyond the Pacific.

Gorodé, Spitz
and Indigenous Francophone Pacific Writing

Gorodé's and Spitz's work has emerged, respectively, from the two main 'centres' of Indigenous Francophone Pacific writing: New Caledonia and French Polynesia.[9] In both areas, Eurocentric education policies have resulted in low literacy rates and severe under-representation of Indigenous peoples in many professions, including writing. Gorodé and Spitz belong to a small minority of Indigenous peoples of the Francophone Pacific to have received a university education in metropolitan France, and both have played an active role in fostering Indigenous creative writing within their respective societies. Gorodé was one of the first Kanak writers to enter a literary milieu dominated by Caldoche (white settler) authors: her début poetry collection, *Sous les cendres des conques* (1985), was followed by a number of other poetry and prose works, some of which are discussed further below. Much of Gorodé's work is inspired by her involvement in the Kanak-led independence movement, which gathered momentum in the 1970s and 1980s.[10] Gorodé was

---

[8] Vietnamese writer Anna Moï is the one signatory who could be defined as a 'Pacific' representative, but Vietnam is commonly categorized as belonging to the 'Asia-Pacific' or 'Pacific Rim', which are separate geopolitical entities from the 'Pacific Islands Region' in which the writers discussed in this essay are located (see Hau'ofa, 1998: 396–7).

[9] French Polynesia and New Caledonia have exponentially larger populations and concentrations of public resources than Wallis and Futuna, whose local economy is heavily dependent on remittances from expatriates located in New Caledonia (see Brown, 2004: p. ix).

[10] Kanak involvement in the movement was partly motivated by a perceived

one of the founders of the independence organizations Groupe 1878 (named after the year of a major anticolonial Kanak uprising) and PALIKA (Parti de Libération Kanak, formed in 1976), and was jailed twice in the 1970s for her involvement in anticolonial protest activity. Further political protests in the 1980s helped bring about the 1988 Matignon Accords, which restored relative peace by establishing a constitutional framework within which to debate the territory's future and to improve socio-economic conditions for Kanak peoples.[11] In the 1990s, such advances included better publishing opportunities for Kanak writers, with poets and playwrights such as Pierre Gope, Wanir Welepane, Billy Wapotro, Denis Pourawa and Paul Wamo publishing their first works during and beyond that decade.

Like Gorodé, Chantal Spitz is also an Indigenous literary pioneer, publishing the first Mā'ohi[12] novel (entitled *L'Île des rêves écrasés*) in 1991. The novel is stridently anticolonial, exploring the inimical effects of French imperialism across generations of Mā'ohi, with a particular focus on the devastating environmental and cultural impact of French nuclear testing (which took place across a thirty-year period from the mid-1960s). Spitz's counterdiscursive emphasis on Mā'ohi environmental conservationism and animism is redolent of the work of an earlier wave of Mā'ohi poets (including Hubert Brémond, Henri Hiro, Charles Manutahi, Turo Raapoto and Flora Devatine/Vaitiare) who emerged in the 1960s and 1970s, while a feminist strand in her novel resonates with the work of other female contemporaries such as Michou Chaze/Rai a Mai, Flora Devatine (again), Louise Peltzer, Titaua Peu and Célestine Hitiura Vaite. Vaite is an expatriate (now based in Australia) who has published a trilogy of novels in English – *Breadfruit*

---

need to protect Indigenous rights following an influx of new French settlers during the nickel 'boom' years of the late 1960s, when Melanesians became a minority ethnic group for the first time.

[11] Subsequently, the 1998 Nouméa Accord provided for devolution of state powers over the following fifteen years and a further referendum for independence is expected as early as 2013 (see Brown, 2004: pp. x–xii).

[12] French Polynesia comprises 118 islands and atolls grouped into five archipelagoes. The three largest of these archipelagoes include the Society Islands (encompassing Tahiti, Mo'orea, Huahine, Bora Bora, Ra'iatea, and Tahaa); the Austral Islands; and the Marquesas. The Gambier and Tuamotu archipelagos are smaller and less densely populated. This essay follows local convention in using the term Mā'ohi to refer only to the Indigenous people and languages of the Society Islands, and primarily Tahiti (where French Polynesia's capital Papeete, and most of Tahiti's main publishers, are located). I also follow conventional linguistic practice in using an inverted apostrophe to represent the glottal stop phoneme and a macron to represent the long 'a' vowel phoneme in 'Mā'ohi'.

(2000), *Frangipani* (2004) and *Tiare* (2006) – that has now been translated into French (published by Au vent des îles in Tahiti).

Vaite's success as a Mā'ohi author writing in English has coincided with a growing interest in Francophone Pacific writing in English translation, particularly within Pacific metropolitan centres such as Hawai'i, Australia and New Zealand. In 2006, for example, the University of Hawai'i Press published *Vārua Tupu*, an anthology of contemporary Mā'ohi writing in English translation.[13] In 2007, Chantal Spitz's *L'Île des rêves écrasés* was published in English translation (under the title *Island of Shattered Dreams*) by New Zealand publisher Huia. In 2001, Kanak writer Pierre Gope's play *Le Dernier Crépuscule* (which explores the impact of commercial nickel mining upon Kanak peoples) was published in English as *The Last Nightfall*,[14] while in 2004, two volumes of poetry and short fiction by Déwé Gorodé were published by Pandanus of Australia. Gorodé's poetry collection (entitled *Sharing as Custom Provides*) is a bilingual edition of previously published and new work, while the prose volume (*The Kanak Apple Season*) features English translations of work from Gorodé's two short story collections, *Utê Murunu* (1994) and *L'Agenda* (1996).

Regionalism and Translingualism in 'Oceanic' Literary Culture

The increasing availability of Indigenous Francophone Pacific writing in English translation is viewed by many Francophone writers as a crucial means by which to reunite Pacific Islanders divided by the experience of colonialism. Mā'ohi scholar Kareva Mateata-Allain links this growing regional consciousness with the theoretical writings of Tongan writer Epeli Hau'ofa, who, in the 1990s, published a series of influential essays advocating a regional 'Oceanic' identity based in the shared marine heritage of Pacific peoples (Mateata-Allain, 2008: 40). Pacific Islanders developed sophisticated maritime technologies that allowed them to navigate established trade routes throughout the Pacific long before Europeans arrived in the region, but many of these intercultural links were severed as the Pacific was divided into separate French, British and other colonial spheres of influence. Further schisms were created by French explorer Dumont d'Urville's 1832 division of the Pacific into three geocultural categories, based on his

---

[13] Featured writers include Devatine, Hiro, Peltzer, Peu, Rai a Mai, Vaite and other contemporaries such as Taaria Walker and Patrick Araia Amaru.

[14] This was a joint publication by Grain de Sable of Nouméa and the Institute of Pacific Studies in Suva, Fiji.

identification of two distinct 'races': the 'black' peoples of Melanesia and the 'copper-coloured' peoples of Polynesia and Micronesia (see Keown, 2007: 13). Hau'ofa's 'Oceanic' paradigm is designed to transcend these imposed divisions, uniting and protecting Pacific Islanders against the vicissitudes of global capitalism and climate change, as well as serving as a source of inspiration to contemporary Pacific artists and creative writers (see Hau'ofa, 1998). Hau'ofa's model has been enormously influential throughout the Indigenous Pacific, and Mateata-Allain draws upon his work to posit Māʻohi writing as a metaphorical *vaʻa* [voyaging canoe] that can reunite Anglophone and Francophone Pacific peoples through a process of 'intellectual cross-fertilization' (2008: 41). The word *vaʻa* has a clear pan-Polynesian valency, with cognates such as *waʻa* (in Hawaiʻian), *waka* (in New Zealand Māori) and *vaʻa* (in Samoan), signalling the importance for Mateata-Allain of a common ancestral language (proto-Polynesian), as well as the voyaging canoe itself, as a vehicle for interpelagic commun(icat)ion (see Lynch, 1998). Mateata-Allain's use of the term thus privileges the unifying potential of a pre-colonial Indigenous signifying system over colonial languages such as the globalized French celebrated in the 2007 manifesto. Significantly, images and metaphors of Oceanic voyaging abound in *Vārua Tupu* (the 2006 anthology mentioned above), and editors Frank Stewart, Kareva Mateata-Allain and Alexander Dale Mawyer anticipate that the volume 'will contribute to the work of reunifying the Polynesians' of the Francophone and Anglophone Pacific (p. xx).[15]

Chantal Spitz has also embraced the notion of a translingual fellowship of Indigenous Pacific writers as a means by which to combat the relative isolation of Francophone writers from the rest of Oceania. In an important series of essays published in *Littérama'ohi* – a Māʻohi literary journal established in 2002 by Spitz and other Māʻohi writers[16] – she rejects the notion of *Francophonie* in favour of fostering regional dialogues with fellow Pacific Islanders. In 'Identité Comment' (published in the first issue of *Littérama'ohi*), for example, she argues that by identifying themselves as 'implied French people', Māʻohi dissociate themselves 'from our [Oceanic] brothers while associating ourselves with ancient battles against a modernized perfidious Albion fighting francophony against anglophony' (Spitz, 2002a: 110; translation in Mateata-Allain, 2008: 46). Similarly, in her unpublished

---

[15] Also significantly, the title of the volume carries connotations of spiritual renewal.

[16] These include Patrick Amaru, Michou Chaze, Flora Devatine, Danièle-Taoahere Helma and Marie-Claude Teissier-Landgraf, as well as Jimmy Ly (of Hakka Chinese ancestry).

essay 'Écrire Colonisé', she argues Māʻohi must free themselves from the 'trap of francophony' in order to re-establish connections with other Pacific peoples and, more broadly, with other colonized people 'who resonate so much [...] deeper within me than some other human being speaking thinking French' (Spitz, 2003: 2; translation in Mateata-Allain, 2008: 49). It is significant that Spitz here prioritizes trans-Pacific connections but also identifies with an international community, not on the basis of a shared language (French) but rather the shared experience of colonization. Her most extended and vehement rejection of the notion of an international collective of Francophone writers appears in her essay 'Francophonie' (published in the second issue of *Littérama'ohi*), where she asserts: 'Francophony has nothing to do with me. [...] History produced me speaking-reading-writing in French but has not made me feeling-thinking French. I do not feel linked to other French speakers under the pretext of francophony. I do not feel linked to French thinkers under the pretext of a common language' (Spitz, 2002b: 122; translation in Mateata-Allain, 2008: 51). Such arguments clearly reject the notion of a global fraternity of Francophone writers upon which the 2007 manifesto is based, even though Spitz goes so far as to acknowledge a shared experience of colonial oppression amongst Francophone postcolonial peoples.

Spitz's arguments for fostering trans-Pacific and translingual literary connections were put into practice in the fifth issue of *Littérama'ohi* (entitled 'Rencontres Océaniennes'), which featured the work of a range of New Caledonian writers (of both European and Kanak descent), as well as translations into French of material by Anglophone Indigenous Pacific writers such as Russell Soaba (Papua New Guinea), Teresia Teaiwa,[17] Anita Heiss (Australia) and Sia Figiel (Samoa). The special issue is therefore doubly significant, establishing links between hitherto isolated literary communities both within the Francophone Pacific and within wider Oceania. As Spitz puts it in her introduction to the issue: 'After a gruellingly long night, the people of Oceania are once more taking a journey. Like it once was when we navigated to our destiny under the stars of the sky, we now trace our future through the sense of our words [...] shared and exchanged through transcribed and translated texts' (Spitz, 2004: 44; translation in Mateata-Allain, 2008: 49). Notable here, again, are the metaphors of trans-Oceanic voyaging discussed earlier in this chapter. Although by 2004 the work of Anglophone Indigenous Pacific writers such as Alan Duff and Albert Wendt had already been translated for a metropolitan French readership,

---

17 Raised in Fiji, Teaiwa is of I-Kiribati and African-American descent.

this was one of the first examples of a genuinely trans-Pacific translingual dialogue.[18]

Translingual and trans-Pacific creative exchanges have also taken place within New Caledonia in recent years, particularly since the 1998 Nouméa Accord, which – as noted above – included an official commitment to recognizing and promoting Kanak identity and culture. To this end, a biennial *Salon du livre* was inaugurated in 2003, located in the north-east coastal town of Poindimié in a specific attempt to foster literary culture beyond the wealthy, highly urbanized Southern province (in which New Caledonia's capital Nouméa, and most of the white settler population, are located). The 2003 *Salon du livre* brought writers from New Caledonia (including Gorodé) into contact with a range of Anglophone and Francophone Pacific writers (from Australia, Aotearoa/New Zealand, Fiji, Papua New Guinea, East Timor and Tahiti), and was so successful that a similar event took place in 2005 under the title *Salon international du livre océanien*. Significantly, the 2005 event included a series of round-table discussions addressing topics – such as attitudes toward the natural environment, language and translation, culture and creativity, and tradition and modernity – upon which both Anglophone and Francophone Indigenous participants found common ground (see Brown, 2006). Such affiliations suggest that the notion of a global collective of Francophone writers as advanced in the 2007 manifesto is less relevant to Kanak writers than it is to New Caledonia's white settlers and their descendants, many of whom *have* maintained close links with metropolitan French literary culture (see Brown, 2006).

In this context, it is significant that Gorodé, like Spitz, has established strong affiliations with Anglophone Pacific writers, particularly those of other Melanesian countries that share both the experience of colonialism, and particular sociocultural dynamics that (in Gorodé's view) have disadvantaged women. She has expressed a particular affinity with *ni-Vanuatu* writer Grace Mera Molisa, translating a selection of her (English-language) poetry into French for the 1997 volume *Pierre Noire*. Before achieving independence in 1980, Vanuatu (formerly the New Hebrides) was an Anglo-French condominium, but Gorodé's interest in Molisa appears based more in their common experience as politically active Melanesian women than any sense of a 'shared' history of French colonialism. Both women have been centrally involved in independence movements in their respective countries, also serving in government in order to improve educational, creative and other opportunities for their fellow indigenes. Both have played an active role in

---

[18] Since 2006, a wider range of Anglophone Pacific texts in French translation has been published by Au vent des îles of Tahiti (see www.auventdesiles.pf).

the Pacific anti-nuclear movement, and have also been leading proponents of feminist movements at both local and regional levels. In this context, it is unsurprising that the majority of the poems in *Pierre Noire* engage with socio-political issues (such as (neo-)colonialism, women's rights and Indigenous social dynamics) that are also prevalent in Gorodé's own work.

Gorodé includes a direct reference to the work of Molisa and other Anglophone Pacific writer-activists in her semi-autobiographical short story 'Dos Montes', which focuses on a group of Indigenous and women's rights activists gathered in Australia. The story includes an episode in which the narrator and a fellow feminist activist discuss 'collections of poetry by two Melanesian women, Grace Mera from Vanuatu and Julie Sipolo from the Solomons, as well as a book by the Fijian, Vanessa Griffen, dealing with the problems we as women have' (Gorodé, 2004a: 89). Significantly, Molisa, Sipolo and Griffen – like Gorodé – are all Indigenous Pacific feminist writer-activists, but the story also indexes Gorodé's interest in Pacific self-determination initiatives that operate beyond questions of gender, making references to the Kanak, West Papuan and East Timor independence movements (Gorodé, 2004a: 85).

Unlike Spitz, however, Gorodé has also conveyed a sense of belonging to a wider global community of nations colonized by France. For example, her story 'Benjie, My Brother', which features a group of young Kanak men who become involved in the independence movement in the 1980s, includes references to anticolonial uprisings in French colonies beyond the Pacific. The narrator of the story meets a fellow Kanak who is an avid reader of Maspero publications such as Frantz Fanon's *The Wretched of the Earth* and Amilcar Cabral's *Unity and Struggle*, as well as *Afrique-Asie* (a France-based periodical that has supported independence movements in French and other colonial territories). Further, during military service in France, the narrator gains a detailed knowledge of anticolonial struggles in Algeria after befriending an Arab Algerian fellow serviceman, and at the end of the story he quotes a verse from the Koran alongside three anticolonial poems by Senegalese poet Malik Fall, thereby situating the Kanak nationalist movement within the context of an international struggle against French colonialism. The story, which clearly draws upon Gorodé's experiences as a university student in France during the 1970s, does in some ways conform to the 2007 signatories' model of 'une littérature-monde en langue française consciemment affirmée' ('Pour une "littérature-monde" en français', 2007),[19] but it is also very firmly grounded within its unique national context, confronting controversial contemporary

---

[19] 'a consciously affirmed, transnational world-literature in the French language' ('Toward a "World-Literature" in French', 2009: 56).

social issues affecting young Kanak men (such as the spread of AIDS through drug use and sexual activity). Though aware of anticolonial struggles in other parts of the Francophone world, Gorodé has channelled her energies into fostering local and regional independence movements, and her writing, like Spitz's, is attuned more to a trans-Pacific literary milieu than a transnational collective of Francophone writers.

The Pragmatics and Problematics of Translation

As I have demonstrated, writers such as Gorodé and Spitz have actively fostered translingual dialogues between Indigenous Francophone and Anglophone Pacific writers, but while much of this dialogue has focused on political matters – the need to unite Pacific peoples divided by colonialism; the desire to consolidate regional anticolonial, anti-nuclear and feminist movements – it is also important to consider some of the aesthetic and pragmatic issues at stake during the translation process. One of the risks associated with the translation of Francophone Pacific literature for an Anglophone readership – even if it is a regional Pacific audience with political and cultural affiliations to the source culture – is that some of the unique stylistic properties of the source text may be lost to this new audience. In the case of Spitz's writing in particular – which uses a radically non-standard variety of French – this could obscure one of the most important counter-discursive aspects of the source text, diluting its impact as a 'postcolonial' work that may indeed have a place in a transnational comparative study of Francophone literature. The translators of Spitz's *L'Île des rêves écrasés* (*Island of Shattered Dreams*) and Gorodé's *Sharing as Custom Provides* – upon which I will focus in the final part of this chapter – have addressed these potential problems in various ways.

Jean Anderson, translator of Spitz's novel, is an advocate of 'resistant translation', a practice that resembles Lawrence Venuti's concept of 'foreignization' in that it seeks to 'respect and reproduce', as far as possible, unique stylistic and other elements of the source culture without making significant allowances for a foreign reader (Anderson, 2009). To this end, her translation contains very little contextual or framing matter: a brief glossary of Mā'ohi terms (which appear mainly as isolated words and phrases in the source text) is added at the end of the book and a short translator's note is included in the prefatory matter. Here, Anderson outlines some of the aesthetic properties of the source text that are central to its counterdiscursive aims, revealing that Spitz 'radically disrupt[s] many of the parameters of accepted literary French', making heavy use of repetition, capitalization to 'stress cultural importance', and frequent code-switching between prose and lyric poetry, as well as between French and Māʻohi. These stylistic features are preserved in the translation, serving to emphasize the importance of orality over writing in Māʻohi culture, which – like many other Pacific cultures – had no orthography prior to the arrival of European explorers and missionaries. In the source text, Spitz decentralizes the authority of European discourse by beginning her narrative with an untranslated Māʻohi creation myth, which is then followed by a version of the biblical creation story in French. This discursive dialectic continues throughout the text through strategic code-switching from French into Māʻohi. Though the source text contains no glossary and little in the way of contextual translation, Anderson includes a short glossary in her translation, but is able to preserve the estranging effect of the code-switching into Māʻohi within the main body of the narrative,[20] while also deciding against offering a translation of the eighty-six-line Māʻohi creation poem that opens the story.

Anderson indicates, however, that she was unable to find a viable way in which to signal an important distinction that Spitz makes throughout the text between *parole* (which refers not just to the spoken word but specifically to Māʻohi oral culture) and *mot* (associated not just with writing but also French culture). However, her translator's note successfully alerts the reader to this distinction, which is traceable through the repetition of 'word' in contexts clearly associated with the oral tradition. Near the beginning of the narrative, for example, the Māʻohi patriarch Maevarua is told that his son Tematua has volunteered to fight for France during the First World War, and (as is the case with instances of heightened emotion elsewhere in the text) he expresses himself here through a passage of lyric poetry that reminds Tematua of his ancestral connections with the land and the rhythms of the natural world. The section of poetry is prefaced with an account of Maevarua's search for the right 'words', and it is clear from the context that these are the *paroles* associated with the Māʻohi oral tradition:

---

[20] On page 19, for example, Anderson is able to preserve an important distinction between 'traitorous' Māʻohi (Māʻohi hoʻo ʻaiʻa) and 'patriots' (Māʻohi here ʻaiʻa) by using Spitz's original Māʻohi terms, also retaining Spitz's strategy of opposing Māʻohi and French military terminology as a means by which to signal a cultural as well as linguistic standoff. Thus, Spitz's original sentence 'Nous avons alors commencé à nous entre-tuer: canons contre ômore, fusils contre toi, acier contre àito' is translated as 'And thus we began to kill one another: cannon against 'ōmore, rifle against to'i, steel against 'aito' (Spitz 1991: 26; Spitz 2007: 19). In the glossary, 'ōmore is translated as 'spear', to'i as 'axe' and 'aito as 'ironwood tree'. (Neither edition uses inverted apostrophes for glottal stops as I do elsewhere in this essay; see n. 12.)

And then, because since the beginning of time his people have always expressed themselves through the Word, Maevarua searches deep in his soul to find words to offer his son, his flesh and blood. Words, the music of love that he will be able to hear in his memory when he misses his Land too much. Words chosen amongst the multitudes of words in their language to make this world live in him, this world he is preparing to leave to go to distant parts. (Spitz, 2007: 29)

Notable in this passage, as in the source text, is the structural repetition used in Mā'ohi and other Polynesian oral traditions both for rhetorical emphasis and as an *aide-mémoire*. Where this section of the translation is clearly associated with the vitality of the Mā'ohi oral tradition, the association between writing and the formal restrictions of French literary culture is contrastingly evoked in a later passage in which letters arrive informing Mā'ohi parents of the deaths of their sons in the war: 'Twelve letters take the place of twelve children, letters full of leaden words that only the minister can make out, written in that incomprehensible language' (33). Here, again, it is clear from the context that 'leaden words' corresponds with a reference to *mots* (specifically, 'des mots inertes') in Spitz's original text (1991: 44).

Given Anderson's commitment to preserving Spitz's emphasis on the vitality of the Mā'ohi oral tradition, and the fact that this tradition is closely associated with the passages of poetry in the novel, it is perhaps surprising that in his review of the translation Paul Sharrad finds the sections of free verse 'banal and melodramatic', arguing that Anderson could have provided 'some greater sense of the original structuring of rhythm and sounds' in the source text (Sharrad, 2009: 191–92). A comparison of source text and translation reveals that Anderson has in fact faithfully reproduced the syntactic and semantic patterns of the original,[21] but Sharrad's response is in keeping with Douglas Robinson's argument that the 'strategic awkwardness' of a 'foreignizing' translation can be counterproductive, producing a 'quaint' diction that can, in contrast to a more 'liberal' assimilative translation, flatten the aesthetic nuances of the original text and even make the source text 'seem childish, backward, primitive, precisely the reaction foreignism is supposed to counteract' (Robinson, 1997: 111). However, the plurilingualism of Spitz's

---

[21] See, for example, a passage from the prologue: 'Vahine Maòhi à la peau dorée | Fille du soleil | Fille de la lune | Longs cheveux noirs déroulés | Comme les cascades dévalant les montagnes' (1991: 21), which is translated thus: 'Vahine Mā'ohi, golden-skinned woman | Daughter of the sun | Daughter of the moon | Your long black hair tumbling down | Like waterfalls cascading down the mountain' (2007: 15).

text, and her deliberate use of unconventional and estranging syntactical patterns, demand a more complex form of analysis: as Samia Mehrez points out, texts written by 'postcolonial bilingual subjects' problematize the assumption (within traditional translation theory) of a transaction between discrete, clearly defined source and target languages, instead creating a hybrid 'in-between' language that demands a mode of evaluation beyond 'conventional notions of linguistic equivalence or ideas of loss and gain' (Mehrez, 1992: 121).

Furthermore, the sections of poetry in Spitz's text – both source text and translation – produce complex layers of metaphorical and metonymic signification, underscoring central images and issues within the main narrative (particularly the link between the human body and the natural world), while simultaneously inviting comparisons with contiguous poetic traditions in other parts of the 'postcolonial' world. Spitz's vehement anticolonial rhetoric (for example), expressed through metaphors of heat and cold, invites comparisons with Francophone poets such as Aimé Césaire (suggesting that the notion of a 'world literature in French' has some relevance to her work in spite of her opposition to such a concept), but also with Anglophone Pacific poets such as John Kasaipwalova of Papua New Guinea.[22] More specifically, however, the translation appears targeted towards a Pacific readership: Huia is an Indigenous publishing company committed to the publication of works by Māori and 'our cousins from the Pacific' ('The Story of Huia'), and Anderson's reference to Māʻohi as 'another Pacific culture' in her introduction signals an implied readership likely to make links between Māʻohi myths and values and those of their Polynesian 'cousins'. Spitz's exploration of the inimical consequences of French colonialism across generations of Māʻohi, and her excoriating attack upon French nuclear testing as the inverse of Māʻohi environmental conservationism, resonate with the work of New Zealand Māori writers and poets such as Patricia Grace, Witi Ihimaera and Hone Tuwhare, as well as native Hawaiʻian poets such as Haunani-Kay Trask (see Keown, 2007). Such affinities arguably reduce the need for detailed supplementary contextual information, but also, as Anderson acknowledges (2009), create the risk that some of the unique cultural specificities of the source text may be obscured.

A slightly different situation pertains to the bilingual edition of Gorodé's poetry. *Sharing as Custom Provides*, like *The Kanak Apple Season*, is (in Kwame Anthony Appiah's terms) a 'thick translation', containing a lengthy introduction and a range of footnotes designed to assist a (scholarly) reader

---

[22] See, in particular, Césaire's *Cahier d'un retour au pays natal* (1956) and John Kasaipwalova's *Reluctant Flame* (1971).

in situating Gorodé's work within a specifically Kanak literary-cultural context (Appiah, 1993). The introduction, written by Peter Brown (who translated and edited *The Kanak Apple Season*), elaborates primarily upon the politico-cultural context of Gorodé's writing, but the footnotes (prepared by Raylene Ramsay and Deborah Walker, who translated the poetry) are often more specifically attuned to linguistic features that might escape a monolingual reader. A footnote to the poem 'Word of Struggle' [Parole de Lutte], for example, explains that the term *parole* is closely associated with the Kanak oral tradition, and this – as is the case in Anderson's translation – signals the importance of orality in Gorodé's work as a challenge to the discursive restrictions of standard (written) French (Gorodé, 2004b: 6). Most of the other footnotes, however, are translations of words from Gorodé's native language Paicî (used sparingly throughout the collection), or explanations of Kanak cultural practices and values. In an interview, Ramsay and Walker (2009) indicated that they would have liked to include their own translators' introduction explaining their method (a request refused by their publisher), but, to some degree, this omission is offset by the fact that the text is a bilingual edition that allows readers who understand both French and English to compare the translation directly with the original.

Such a comparison can reveal the difficulties of translating poetry that relies on aural effects in the source language. In the poem 'écouter', for example, Gorodé makes widespread use of assonance and alliteration to emphasize the aural theme of the poem: 'Écouter | une note | un mot | un son [...] un cri [...] une rime | un rythme' (Gorodé, 2004b: 102). In their translation, Ramsey and Walker are able to preserve the repeated vowels as a *visual* phenomenon ('Listen | to | a note | a word | a sound [...] a cry [...] a rhyme | a rhythm'), but due to the wide variety of vowel phonemes in English, the aural patterning is lost to some degree. However, the footnote to the earlier poem 'Word of Struggle' alerts even a monolingual Anglophone reader to the fact that the word 'utterance' ('parole' in the source text) combines with other aural signifiers in the poem to posit the Kanak oral tradition as a means by which to break the 'silence' imposed by colonial epistemic and linguistic violence (Gorodé, 2004b: 101). 'Word of Struggle' thus makes the point that a 'word' from the ancestral language can become 'the word that dares make a stand' in a 'radical poetics' which articulates 'a politics of struggle' (Gorodé, 2004b: 6).[23] Significantly (as is the case with Spitz's use of Māʻohi), the Paicî words remain intact and untranslated within the main body of both source

---

[23] This claim is particularly significant given that Gorodé herself was involved in setting up specialist schools in the 1980s which educated Kanak children about their cultures and in their own Kanak languages (which number around

text and translation, with any explanatory matter relegated to a secondary level. In this sense, Gorodé's native language (like Spitz's) remains the only constant between source text and translation, acquiring a transcendental quality that poses a challenge to the dominance of the two 'metropolitan' languages. In this context – and in keeping with Samia Mehrez's arguments on plurilingualism – the process of translation can serve to underscore, rather than dilute, the counterdiscursive aspects of both Gorodé's and Spitz's writing.

Conclusion

As I have maintained in this chapter, the argument for a 'world literature in French' is problematic when considered with reference to the Indigenous Pacific, where writers appear more committed to fostering links with Anglophone Pacific writers than with Francophone writers in other parts of the world. As I have suggested above, the argument for a *littérature-monde* is perhaps more relevant to the work of French settlers and their descendants in New Caledonia, as many of these writers have maintained strong links with metropolitan French literary culture, but within the 'postcolonial' Pacific, emerging translingual dialogues between Indigenous Pacific Islanders are best evaluated within a regional rather than global framework. As I have demonstrated with reference to the work of Déwé Gorodé and Chantal Spitz, there are potential pitfalls associated with the translation of Francophone Pacific texts into English, as some of the specificities of the source texts – including their counterdiscursive responses to French linguistic and literary culture – may be lost to a new audience more concerned with identifying politico-cultural connections between Francophone and other Indigenous Pacific cultures. However, as I have argued with reference to the dialectic between orality and writing in Spitz's and Gorodé's work, the process of translation can preserve and even intensify the counterdiscursive aspects of Francophone Pacific writing, and is viewed by Spitz and others as a crucial means by which to reach a sympathetic readership beyond what has often proved to be an indifferent Francophone literary-critical community.

---

28). In the 1990s, she also collected and transcribed various Melanesian stories and mythological narratives for use in schools.

Works Cited

Anderson, Jean. 2009. Unpublished interview with Michelle Keown. 24 February.

Appiah, Kwame Anthony. 1993. 'Thick Translation'. *Callaloo* 16: 808–19.

Au vent des îles. <*www.auventdesiles.pf*>. Consulted on 5 June 2010.

Brown, Peter. 2004. 'Introduction'. In Déwé Gorodé, *The Kanak Apple Season: Selected Short Fiction of Déwé Gorodé*. Trans. by Peter Brown. Canberra, ACT: Pandanus: pp. ix–xxxix.

—. 2006. 'Books, Writing and Cultural Politics in the Pacific: The New Caledonian *Salon du Livre*, October 2003–October 2005'. *International Journal of Francophone Studies* 9.2: 239–56.

Césaire, Aimé. 1956. *Cahier d'un retour au pays natal*. Paris: Présence Africaine.

Damrosch, David. 2003. *What is World Literature?* Princeton, NJ and Oxford: Princeton University Press.

De Souza, Pascale. 2009. 'Francophone Island Cultures: Comparing Discourses of Identity in "Is-land" Literatures'. In Charles Forsdick and David Murphy (eds), *Postcolonial Thought in the French-Speaking World*. Liverpool: Liverpool University Press, 2009: 238–47.

Forsdick, Charles, and David Murphy (eds). 2003. *Francophone Postcolonial Studies: A Critical Introduction*. London: Arnold.

Gorodé, Déwé. 2004a. *The Kanak Apple Season: Selected Short Fiction of Déwé Gorodé*. Trans. by Peter Brown. Canberra, ACT: Pandanus.

—. 2004b. *Sharing as Custom Provides: Selected Poems of Déwé Gorodé*. Trans. by Raylene Ramsay and Deborah Walker. Canberra, ACT: Pandanus.

Hau'ofa, Epeli. 1998. 'The Ocean in Us'. *The Contemporary Pacific* 10.2: 392–410.

Herrnstein Smith, Barbara. 1998. *Contingencies of Value*. Cambridge, MA and London: Harvard University Press.

Huggan, Graham. 2001. *The Postcolonial Exotic: Marketing the Margins*. London and New York: Routledge.

Kasaipwalova, John. 1971. *Reluctant Flame*. Port Moresby: Papua Pocket Poets.

Keown, Michelle. 2007. *Pacific Islands Writing: The Postcolonial Literatures of Aotearoa/New Zealand and Oceania*. Oxford: Oxford University Press.

Lynch, John. 1998. *Pacific Languages: An Introduction*. Honolulu: University of Hawai'i Press.

Mabanckou, Alain. 2007. 'Le chant de l'oiseau migrateur'. In Michel Le Bris and Jean Rouaud (eds), *Pour une littérature-monde*. Paris: Gallimard: 55–66.

Mateata-Allain, Kareva. 2008. *Bridging Our Sea of Islands: French Polynesian Literature within an Oceanic Context*. Saarbrücken: Verlag Dr. Müller.

Mehrez, Samia. 1992. 'Translation and the Postcolonial Experience: The Francophone North African Text'. In Lawrence Venuti (ed.), *Rethinking Translation: Discourse, Subjectivity, Ideology*. London: Routledge: 120–38.

Molisa, Grace Mera. 1997. *Pierre Noire*. Trans. by Déwé Gorodé. Nouméa: Grain de Sable.

Nicole, Robert. 1999. 'Resisting Orientalism: Pacific Literature in French'. In Vilsoni Hereniko and Rob Wilson (eds), *Inside Out: Literature, Cultural Politics, and Identity in the New Pacific*. Lanham, MD: Rowman & Littlefield: 265–90.

—. 2001. *The Word, the Pen and the Pistol: Literature and Power in Tahiti*. Albany, NY: SUNY Press.

'Pour une "littérature-monde" en français'. 2007. *Le Monde* 16 March.

Ramsay, Raylene, and Deborah Walker. 2009. Unpublished interview with Michelle Keown. 13 March.

Robinson, Douglas. 2007. *Translation and Empire*. Manchester: St Jerome.

Sharrad, Paul. 2009. Review of *Island of Shattered Dreams*, by Chantal Spitz. Trans. by Jean Anderson. *The Contemporary Pacific* 21.1: 190–92.

Spitz, Chantal. 1991. *L'Île des rêves écrasés*. Tahiti: Au vent des îles.

—. 2002a. 'Identité Comment'. *Révue Littérama'ohi* 1: 110–13.

—. 2002b. 'Francophonie'. *Révue Littérama'ohi* 2: 120–22. <http://www.lehman.cuny.edu/ile.en.ile/litteramaohi/02/francophonie.html>. Consulted on 4 August 2009.

—. 2003. 'Écrire Colonisé'. Unpublished paper.

—. 2004. 'Introduction aux rencontres océaniennes'. *Révue Littérama'ohi* 5: 44–45.

—. 2007. *Island of Shattered Dreams*. Trans. by Jean Anderson. Wellington: Huia.

Stewart, Frank, Kareva Mateata-Allain and Alexander Dale Mawyer (eds). 2006. *Vārua Tupu: New Writing and Art from French Polynesia*. Honolulu: University of Hawai'i Press.

'The Story of Huia'. Huia Publishers. <http://www.huia.co.nz/about-us/the-story-of-huia/>. Consulted on 19 August 2009.

'Toward a "World-Literature" in French'. 2009. Trans. by Daniel Simon. *World Literature Today* (March–April): 54–56.

The World and the Mirror
in Two Twenty-First-Century Manifestos:
'Pour une "littérature-monde" en français'
and 'Qui fait la France?'

Laura Reeck

So I am ashamed for the black poet who says, 'I want to be a poet, not a Negro poet', as though his own racial world were not as interesting as any other world. I am ashamed, too, for the colored artist who runs from the painting of Negro faces to the painting of sunsets after the manner of the academicians because he fears the strange unwhiteness in his own features. An artist must be free to choose what he does, certainly, but he must also never be afraid to do what he must choose.

> Langston Hughes, 'The Negro Artist and the Racial Mountain',
> Encyclopædia Britannica's Guide to Black History (1926)

The 'Pour une "littérature-monde" en français' manifesto appeared in *Le Monde* in March 2007 only months before a group of authors mainly born of immigrant parents released their own literary manifesto, 'Qui fait la France?', to *Les Inrockuptibles* and *Le Nouvel Observateur*. Given the temporal proximity of these two manifestos, it is hard not to ask how their projects might compare, especially since both declarations are of considerable pertinence to debates on postcolonial authorship. In much the same vocabulary, both groups of authors – the first led by Michel Le Bris and the second by Mohamed Razane – issue a challenge to the concentration of political and publishing capital around Paris, and ultimately the social and literary reproduction that locks people and texts into categories of the past. But, whereas Le Bris's group framed its declaration with respect to the literary prize season of 2006 that attributed five of France's most prestigious literary awards to authors of non-French origin (two of whom signed the manifesto), the manifesto crafted by the Collectif Qui fait la France? was triggered in many ways by the riots of 2005 and the long-standing marginalization suffered by authors from within France's *banlieues défavorisées*. The dissimilar moments by which the two manifestos are framed point to the fact that the signatories initiated their literary movements from decidedly different locations and situations. While Le Bris and his group may now be seen quite justifiably to occupy a new centre of French letters, Razane and his group have never been the recipients of comparable awards and are not in circulation – be it in the press or in academic circles – in the same way that the *littérature-monde* signatories are.

Drawing on interviews I conducted with Michel Le Bris and Mohamed Razane in December 2008, this chapter reads the 'Qui fait la France?' manifesto alongside the 'Pour une "littérature-monde" en français' manifesto. Although they are both built around a spatial opposition between centre and periphery, the groups highlight two different peripheries: on the one hand, the *external* French-speaking periphery largely located in France's ex-colonies; on the other, the *internal* periphery on the edge of France's largest cities. In what follows, I argue that it is in fact the internal periphery – familiar and indigenous – that garners the most resistance from the centre, and in this way has the most to tell us about the dynamics of publication and reception as well as the changing nature of the French language and cultural expression.

The 'Qui fait la France?' Manifesto:
Its Nowness and Againstness

In September 2007, the Collectif Qui fait la France? released its manifesto on-line ('Qui fait la France?', 2007) and as part of a *livre manifeste* published by Stock, *Chroniques d'une société annoncée*. Some of the signatories had already entered the literary stage – Thomté Ryam, Faïza Guène, Jean-Eric Boulin, Mohamed Razane – while others awaited their literary debut. Most of the authors are the children of immigrants, but this is not a condition for inclusion. Rather, it is a commitment to the *banlieue* specifically, and to a plural vision of France generally, that unites the authors.

The manifesto consists of nine affirmations beginning with 'Parce que', followed by eight beginning with 'Nous', all leading up to a final declaration: 'Ensemble, nous existons' [Together, we exist] ('Qui fait la France?', 2007). Its organization is enumerative and gathers authority through repetition; it does not seek to establish a dialogue. Indeed the manifesto does not ask questions, but rather offers responses: the moment into which the manifesto inscribes itself is not one for debate and discussion. That time has passed. This 'now' inaugurates a time of action, which connects explicitly to the signatories' call for a committed literature for its place and times. In its temporal markers ('moderne', 'actuelle', 'aujourd'hui plus que jamais', 'avenir', 'redevenir', 'non tel qu'il fut', 'demain', 'en devenir', 'aujourd'hui')[1] there is no way to deny the 'nowness' (Caws, 2001: p. xix) of the manifesto.

Throughout the manifesto, but most obviously with the insistent refrain of 'nous', the signatories position themselves as an 'us' against 'them', one of the defining conditions of the literary manifesto as outlined by Mary Ann Caws in her *Manifesto: A Century of Isms* (2001: p. xx). In fact, Razane and his cosignatories readily assume the notion of anger in response to the 'them' against which they set themselves. It finds visual representation in the group's black-and-white photo on their website, which has Razane glaring at the viewer from his central position in the group. The same photo has been used widely, for instance in promotional materials for their collective publication featuring the manifesto and a short story by each of the signatories. According to Razane, the group explicitly chose to appear austere, at a distance:

> On considère qu'effectivement la Marche des Beurs, qui va bientôt dater de 30 ans, a été un soulèvement qui a interpellé les gens sur les réalités sociales. Ils [les Beurs] ont usé de toutes les ficelles qu'on pourrait inclure dans la notion du débat. La situation d'aujourd'hui s'est dégradée. Et la photo c'était véritablement pour dire que on n'est pas là pour discuter, on est là pour demander des comptes, et nous fâcher.[2] (Razane, 2008)

Razane explains that the previous generation, symbolized by the Beur Marchers of 1983, did what they could to engage a social dialogue. However, since that non-violent demonstration, social conditions in the *banlieues défavorisées* have deteriorated to the point where anger is legitimate. 'Nowness' thus relates to change that must come both to the world of letters and to the social world.

While the tone of the declaration is critical, it is mild compared to that adopted by the group in response to a critique of the manifesto by *Nouvel Observateur* journalist Fabrice Pliskin. Two magazines, *Le Nouvel*

---

[1] 'modern', 'present-day', 'now more than ever', 'future', 'become anew', 'not as it was', 'tomorrow, 'changing', 'today'. Unless otherwise indicated, all translations from French into English are by the author of this chapter.

[2] 'We believe that the Beur March of some thirty years ago was an uprising that led people to question social reality. They [the Beurs] used every means imaginable to begin a public debate. Today the situation has worsened. And the photograph is really to say that we are not here to debate; we are here to ask for accountability, and to be angry'.

Observateur and *Les Inrockuptibles,* asked for rights to publish the manifesto. The latter published the full text of the manifesto as promised; the former did not. Fabrice Pliskin of *Le Nouvel Observateur* positions his article with an apostrophe, 'O diversité comment tu es monotone. Comme tu manques de diversité' [O diversity, how monotonous you are. How you lack diversity.] (Pliskin, 2007). Perhaps it is because Pliskin charges that the language of the manifesto is nothing more than the very wooden and official speech against which the authors position themselves that the members of the Collectif opted to use a different tone in response to his article. They posted their September 2007 open letter to Pliskin on their website:

> C'est à cette France [la France lointaine] que nous parlons, que nous nous adressons, pas à la France flétrie de l'intelligentsia parisienne, celle qui officie dans les couloirs mornes et blancs des salles de rédaction. Nous parlons de France diverse, oui, fièrement, parce que c'est celle-ci que nous aimons et qui est éternelle, et non ce parti de la peur, arc-bouté sur ses privilèges et sa noblesse d'âme, que vous incarnez. Quelle tristesse, lorsqu'on y pense, qu'un journal comme le Nouvel Observateur, naguère si courageux, au temps de la guerre d'Algérie, soit aujourd'hui encalminé, rabougri dans le mépris de l'autre, du faible, de l'opprimé.[3] (Qui fait la France?, 12 September 2007)

They conclude with an uncompromising warning – 'promis, la prochaine fois, on vous niquera votre race!' [it's a promise, next time, we'll fuck you all up!] (Qui fait la France?, 12 September 2007) – an outburst that might well have cost them the contract for their sequel publication with Stock. In response to the probability that Stock will not renew their contract, Razane mentioned that the group will probably publish their second collective volume, a set of stories in which the authors are required to make allusion to the same fictional current event, on their website.

The Collectif has already developed its website as a medium for broadcasting its message through a variety of genres including journalism, essays, images,

---

[3] 'We are talking to another France [peripheral France], not to the withered France of the Parisian intelligentsia cooking up its wares in lifeless editorial rooms. We are talking about a France that is diverse, yes, with pride, because this other France is the one we love and is undying. We are not talking about the France that you symbolize – devoured by fear, clinging to its privileges and lofty sentiments. What a shame, when one thinks of it, that a newspaper like *Le Nouvel Observateur*, once so courageous at the time of the Algerian War of Independence, is today stymied in its scorn for others, those who are weakened and oppressed'.

open letters and travelogue entries, and Razane imagines it as an appropriate place for making the stories they write accessible to a large audience at no cost. Qui fait la France? wants to ensure that its writing reaches the largest and broadest audience in the most democratic form possible. Its members have not set their sights on integrating the Parisian literary milieu, since they consider it is a 'petit milieu' [inner circle] based on social reproduction, 'Ils [the members of this 'petit milieu'] sont entre eux: il y a quelques familles qui transmettent leur pouvoir de père en fils' (Razane, 2008).[4] By contrast, members of the collective opt out of established publication and distribution networks in favour of protecting their message and not compromising their agenda, about which they make no excuses.

To Commit or Not to Commit?

Along with 'nowness' and its 'againstness', another imperative of the literary manifesto is its 'newness' (Caws, 2001: p. xx): the signatories must believe that they are marking a new beginning and doing something new. The *littérature-monde* manifesto captures this in its introduction, referring to the moment as a literary watershed and a historical turning point. It is harder to identify the same thrust of 'newness' in the language of the 'Qui fait la France?' manifesto. In fact, when I asked Razane about the group's literary influences, he indicated that the only genealogy into which he and his peers willingly inscribe themselves dates back to the realist genealogy of nineteenth-century France – Zola, Balzac, Flaubert, Stendhal. There is nothing obviously new in extending one of France's most well-known literary traditions. Perhaps it is awareness of the power of genealogy, inheritance and reproduction in French letters that prompts the authors of 'Qui fait la France?' to situate themselves as 'héritiers' [inheritors] (Razane, 2007) in this way. They position themselves as a natural extension of certain historical French literary movements to show that they are not on the outside, but on the inside. Put otherwise, instead of being 'les enfants issus de l'immigration' [the descendants of immigrants] they become 'héritiers' [inheritors] with the same rights and privileges held by those who reside on the 'Place de Paris' (Razane, 2007).

When asked if his group constitutes a new wave of postcolonial literature by second-generation ethnic minority writers and how the group locates itself with respect to longer-established 'Beur' authors such as Mehdi Charef or Azouz Begag, Razane preferred adamantly to return to classic authors of 'la littérature au miroir' [literature as mirror] and also evoked what his

---

[4] 'They keep to themselves as families who hand down power from father to son'.

group sees as the primary function of literature, to question the workings of the world. Although Razane denies a shared genealogy with 'Beur' authors of the 1980s, it is hard not to probe this assertion, especially since the Collectif members use the word 'Beur' as a point of reference in interviews and in their 2007 open letter to the *Petit Robert*, in which they contested the pejorative connotation ascribed to the word 'Rebeu' – a possible origin and now derivative of the word 'Beur'.[5] It seems that ultimately they want to imagine themselves outside of how they have been imagined, which may be felt effectively to augur their newness. At the same time, however, they position themselves in continuity with what are arguably France's most 'French' literary traditions. And so, they in effect create newness within continuity: they are adjusting the definition of Frenchness and extending the reach of the French literary tradition to include *them*.

They also go beyond realism to argue for a form of committed literature – 'engagée, combattante, féroce' [committed, combative, ferocious] ('Qui fait la France?', 2007) – that serves as an antidote to the same autofiction that the *littérature-monde* signatories decry. In fact, both groups condemn introverted fiction that artificially seals off the world as if the subject lives and breathes in a social vacuum. But, in contrast to Razane's group, which makes commitment the centrepiece of its manifesto, Le Bris leaves no place for committed literature in his definition of *littérature-monde*. In fact, he dismisses it along with autofiction as the two traditions that have most dulled the literary field: 'Nous savions alors, d'expérience vécue, de quoi peut mourir la littérature, écrivais-je: de s'être fait la servante des idéologies, sous le prétexte de l'engagement [...]' (Le Bris, 2007: 28).[6] However, in making reference to the particular form of committed literature of the 1960s characterized by a clear Marxist agenda, Le Bris arguably seems to be reacting against a past that is indeed past.

While the foremost concern of the signatories of the *littérature monde* manifesto may well relate to an aesthetic project, denial of an ideological

---

5 In their open letter to the *Petit Robert* (Qui fait la France? website, 25 September 2007), the 'Qui fait la France?' signatories first explore the register of the word 'Rebeu', indicating that familiar language does not translate to a pejorative denotation. The signatories refer to the March for Equality and Against Racism of 1983 as well as to the word 'Beur'. They accordingly situate the two words and the two 'generations' on a linguistic and conceptual continuum. It is also obvious from their interventions that the Collectif authors feel an affinity and a respect for the 'Beur' generation that preceded them.

6 'I wrote that we knew then, from having witnessed it, what can kill literature – becoming the servant to ideology under the guise of commitment'.

project rings false. The reader expects the manifesto to commit itself. Indeed, the manifesto form essentially requires it: 'The manifesto was from the beginning, and has remained, a deliberate manipulation of the public view. Setting out the terms of the faith toward which the listening public is to be swayed, it is a document of an ideology, crafted to convince and convert' (Caws, 2001: p. xix). There is no way to deny that the centre-periphery opposition that frames the manifesto – with its signature of the death certificate of *Francophonie* – has political resonance, and the signatories do not stay away from politicized vocabulary when they reference France's cultural imperialism and the undoing of the colonial pact, which the signatories make an explicit consequence of the 'révolution copernicienne' [Copernican revolution] announced at the beginning of their declaration. In the literary world order proposed in the *littérature-monde* manifesto, the French do not own the French language and may no longer dictate its rules: French is a world language, not a national language. It is in this vein that Michel Le Bris claims that all French-speakers should consider themselves Francophones (Le Bris, 2008), or the category should disappear altogether. While little thought was apparently given to the political dimensions of *Francophonie*, by referencing it, the signatories necessarily placed their manifesto in the political sphere and even elicited a response from Abdou Diouf, the president of the Organisation Internationale de la Francophonie. When asked if the literary prize of Le Grand Prix de la Francophonie should be eliminated in light of their manifesto, Le Bris indicated he had never thought in those terms because here *Francophonie* refers to the political entity: 'Non, on est écrivains, ce qu'on défend c'est une idée de la littérature, surtout. Ce n'était pas un souci politique qu'on avait' (2008).[7] Yet nothing better symbolizes the conflation of the literary and the political than Le Grand Prix de la Francophonie.

On Peripheries and Prizes

Here we should return to the beginning of the *littérature-monde* manifesto, where the signatories declare that the sweep of France's major literary prizes by authors of non-French origin marked a watershed moment.[8] It is a

---

[7] 'No, we are writers, and we are defending a certain type of literature above all else. Our aim was not political'.

[8] In reality, there are more than two subsets of signatories: metropolitan French authors, writers of French expression originating from former colonies, and authors from other countries who have chosen to write in French. Despite this, most of the critical attention has focused on the postcolonial signatories.

purposefully dramatic claim, but it may be worth noting that in his essay 'In Defense of the Novel, Yet Again' (Rushdie, 1996), Salman Rushdie cautions against precisely such excitement. Responding to George Steiner's argument that novels originating in the European capitals have lost ground to novels coming from 'the far rim, from India, from the Caribbean, from Latin America' (Rushdie, 1996: 51), Rushdie suggests that the opposition between 'an exhausted center and a vital periphery' (Rushdie, 1996: 51) is a dangerous and Eurocentric one, and also false since the centre has never stopped producing great novels. Moreover, he points out that India produced great literature long before the West began to read its English-language variant, which is to say that the vitality of this periphery existed long before the West discovered it. By insisting that the periphery will save the centre, Steiner only reverses the terms of the imperial era. And, as Rushdie points out, the 'discovery' of the far rim and its likes resonates in a way that is comparable to the beginning of that very same imperial era.

Rushdie, who serves as a reference both in the *littérature-monde* manifesto and in Le Bris's contribution to the Gallimard collection, looks towards a novel that is 'de-centred, transnational, interlingual, cross-cultural' (Rushdie, 1996: 52), one that erodes the very need to talk about the centre and the periphery. He favours more porous and moveable relationships. The signatories of the *littérature-monde* manifesto do not seem to have fully grasped what is involved here. Instead, they appear to have displaced the centre to the periphery without disabling the operating principles of the opposition.

In our interview, I asked Michel Le Bris if the starting point of the *littérature-monde* manifesto was not a *fait accompli*. By winning or being nominated to France's most prestigious literary prizes, couldn't we say that his group now reflects a norm? And, by publishing with France's foremost presses, wasn't this another sign that the group has successfully integrated the literary scene? This line of questioning elicited a refrain from Le Bris across our interview to the effect that the doors are not yet open wide enough and that he has had to work intensively for more than thirty years, primarily with the Etonnants Voyageurs literary festival, to open these doors.[9] But, as Graham Huggan points out in his *The Postcolonial Exotic*,

---

[9] It is certainly the case that Le Bris has provided a unique forum for new authors, minor genres, and also postcolonial authors in his long-standing and growing literary festival. It is also worth pointing out here that two members of the Collectif have been invited to the festival in recent years, Faïza Guène and Thomté Ryam. Although Le Bris had no knowledge of Razane's group before our interview, he proved very interested in the group and its manifesto. He responded positively to the manifesto and was eager to talk about it: 'C'est bien

literary prizes not only confer notoriety and infer canonization; they often also have an 'unannounced ideological agenda – a hidden politics' (Huggan, 2001: 119). Although Huggan is discussing a history of the Booker Prize, much of what he says translates to literary prizing generally. He suggests that the Booker's apparent openness to postcolonial authors has had the effect of at once introducing the reading public to a set of postcolonial authors and delimiting this very same set. Huggan thus describes the postcolonial recipients of the prize as belonging to an established postcolonial canon, adding 'these writers comprise by and large a list of international figures whose names circulate freely within the media and on school/university curricula and examination lists' (Huggan, 2001: 119). Very much the same thing could be said of the postcolonial signatories of the *littérature-monde* manifesto: there is no denying their name-recognition, the fact that they figure on most 'Francophone' reading lists, and their visibility in the media. Consecration by literary prizes further solidifies their position within the postcolonial canon in French. And in the French-language context they are open to a criticism voiced in the Anglophone world by Huggan, in line with Timothy Brennan, according to which 'the privileging of a certain kind of highly aestheticised "political writing" under the sign of the postcolonial has had the ironic effect of shutting down, or at least deflecting public attention away from, more radically unorthodox alternatives' (Huggan, 2001: 120). In effect, the literary establishment – through the instrument of literary prizes – succeeds in containing more challenging or contestatory postcolonial literatures, specifically those with an obvious and aggressive political agenda.

Whereas the *littérature-monde* signatories may now be as Le Bris puts it 'au sein des seins' [at the middle of the centre] (2008), the 'Qui fait la France?' signatories continue to find that their literature has virtually no *droit de cité* within France's literary borders. On this note, a 13 February 2006 post to Alain Mabanckou's blog incorporates an article by a Swedish journalist, Thomas Lundquist, whose article appeared under the banner of an issue of *Le Courrier International* headed 'Des écrivains déconnectés de la réalité' [Writers cut off from reality]: 'Les émeutes des banlieues françaises

---

trousse', Le Bris told me. 'On peut discuter d'un petit terme par-ci par-là. Mais ça n'a aucune importance, ce qui compte, c'est le sens général et cette prise de parole qui m'importe beaucoup. Il ne faudrait pas qu'elle soit sur idéologisée ou qu'elle soit pénalisée' [One or two terms are open to question here and there. But that doesn't matter. What matters is the overall thrust, and I think the way the manifesto speaks out is really important. It shouldn't be regarded as overly ideological or somehow at fault.] (2008).

ont précisément coïncidé avec la période des remises des prix littéraires, et les jeunes des cités auraient eu toutes les raisons d'être mécontents du palmarès. La littérature française persiste en effet à ignorer l'existence des banlieues défavorisées' (cited in Mabanckou, 2006).[10] Part of the journalist's investigation involved asking French authors about the existence of such a *banlieue* literature. By and large, he found that the idea they had of *banlieue* literature was shapeless and ill-informed.

Perhaps the Academician Frédéric Vitoux spoke most tellingly on behalf of the literary establishment in France when he cited Céline as a '*banlieue* writer' (cited in Mabanckou, 2006), in response to which Mabanckou, one of the most high-profile signatories of the *littérature-monde* manifesto, suggests that Vitoux should get himself up to date. Mabanckou also points out that had the journalist asked so-called Francophone authors like himself for a bibliography, they would have been able to provide him with one. Notwithstanding Mabanckou's position as evidenced in this remark, the postcolonial writers of the *littérature-monde* manifesto and the '*banlieue* writers' of the 'Qui fait la France?' manifesto seem more often than not strangely indifferent to or unaware of one another: they appear to work and write in concentric circles that do not overlap. Perhaps the fact that the first set is a highly mobile group, whose members often live outside of France, whereas the latter was mainly born in and continues to reside in hexagonal France determines this lack of communication. It also reflects what is ultimately the privileged situation of the postcolonial *littérature-monde* signatories: most of them are world travellers, migrant intellectuals and not uncommonly tenured members of foreign academic institutions.

What's in a Missing Analogy?

What the *littérature-monde* and 'Qui fait la France?' manifestos make plain is that France effectively has two peripheries with which to reckon and reconcile itself. As Le Bris acknowledged in our interview, it is the interior periphery that garners the greatest resistance from the centre: 'Mais, oui, parce que francophones, à la limite, s'ils restent à la porte, ça va. Ceux-là [i.e., *banlieue* writers] ils sont Français. S'il y a un problème avec les banlieues, c'est d'abord l'acceptation du fait qu'ils sont Français et qu'il faut apprendre à vivre ensemble et que c'est la France de demain qui est

---

[10] 'The riots in the French *banlieues* coincided exactly with the literary prize season, and the young inhabitants of the *cités* would have every reason to feel unhappy about the list of winners, for French literature continues to ignore the country's disadvantaged *banlieues*'.

là' (Le Bris, 2008).[11] But bringing the France of the past into contact with the France of tomorrow almost invariably involves some form of conflict or contest, as the riots of 2005 demonstrated. I asked Le Bris if the riots had been a source of concern for the signatories of the *littérature-monde* manifesto. He reported a conversation he had with Serge July, founder of *Libération*, during the riots: '[...] on parlait par ailleurs du fait de la similitude de situations, c'était que quand apparaît Salman Rushdie, c'était juste après les émeutes dans les banlieues ouvrières des villes anglaises que la deuxième ou troisième génération des écrivains issus de l'immigration sont arrivés dans cette foulée' (2008).[12] This analogy between the France of today and the England of almost thirty years ago warrants close examination as it proves to be nettlesome and ambiguous. What it skips over is a more directly accurate analogy with the France of the 1980s. Here Le Bris correlates the riots in and around England's industrial and metropolitan centres (i.e., Bristol, Birmingham, Brixton, Manchester) in the early 1980s to the simultaneous emergence in Britain of a new literature by 'la deuxième ou la troisième génération d'écrivains issus de l'immigration' [the second or third generation of writers born to immigrant parents]. As Azouz Begag, one of the lone second-generation North African authors to have interacted with the *littérature-monde* group, demonstrated in *Ecarts d'identité* (1990) and *Quartiers sensibles* (1994), the 1980s in France was similarly an era of social unrest during which, most notably, the children of North African immigrants came of age. And as they protested, they also produced 'Beur' literature, which has come to be the largest ethnic minority literature in France.

Moreover, what Le Bris presents as literary production by second-generation members of ethnic minority groups is in reality almost exclusively the work of authors who emigrated to England – Salman Rushdie, Kazuo Ishiguro, Michael Ondaatje, Ben Okri. Among the authors mentioned in Le Bris's manifesto, Hanif Kureishi is the only one to have been born in England. As Rushdie, who coined the expression, points out, 'Having been borne across the world, we are translated men' (Rushdie, 1991: 17): it is the

---

[11] 'Of course, if the Francophones only knock at the door, that's okay. But they [*banlieue* writers] are French. If there is a problem with the *banlieues*, it is in accepting that they are French and we have to learn to live together, and that it is the France of tomorrow that lives there'.

[12] '[...] we also talked about the similarity of situations – that Salman Rushdie appeared just after the riots in run-down areas of England's industrial centres. The second or third generation of writers born to immigrant parents came onto the scene in that same moment'.

condition of transplantation that informs the experience of Rushdie's cohort. What is puzzling is the slippage that takes place between the original use of 'translated men' and the signatories' use of it in the *littérature-monde* manifesto. In its evocation of these 'translated men', the manifesto declares: 'ceux-là, nés en Angleterre, ne vivaient plus dans la nostalgie d'un pays d'origine à jamais perdu, mais, s'éprouvant entre deux mondes, entre deux chaises, tentaient vaille que vaille de faire de ce télescopage l'ébauche d'un monde nouveau'.[13] This description evokes the second-generation members of ethnic minority groups rather than migrants. Le Bris speaks in very similar terms in his Gallimard essay, referring to the urban riots of the 1980s in Britain as the 'première prise de parole, en forme de cri, des jeunes certes d'origine indienne, pakistanaise, jamaïquaine, mais qui se revendiquaient anglais tout autant, d'une Angleterre nouvelle, désormais multiculturelle' (2007: 32).[14] If indeed the urban riots in England in the 1980s foreshadowed new cultural and linguistic expression as well as changing views of selfhood, then the same can be said of the urban riots and rodeos that were taking place in France as 'Beur' literature took shape during the 1980s, but Le Bris again fails to draw the analogy.

Part of Michel Le Bris's response to my question about the 2005 riots was particularly revealing as it pointed to a critical blind spot. Describing the

---

[13] 'these translated men, born in England, were not living with nostalgia for a lost homeland, but rather were living between two cultures, between two stools. They were trying as best they could to use their stereoscopic vision to draft a new world order'. The signatories' suggestion that these writers were torn 'between two stools' sounds strangely outdated. Early 'Beur' authors such as Nacer Kettane were quick to point out that the metaphor of being torn between two stools – nowhere, unlocalized – was a negative one. He argued in this direction in *Droit de réponse à la démocratie française* (1987) and in his début novel, *Le Sourire de Brahim* (1985), about the beginnings of a young 'Beur''s political activism. In one passage, Kettane debunks the 'being between two stools' metaphor: Brahim's friend Said evokes the all-knowing talk of the media that depicts the 'Beurs' as being 'tiraillés entre deux cultures' [torn between two cultures] (Kettane, 1985: 166). Immediately, Brahim intervenes: 'Ils ne comprennent pas que nous, on n'a pas le cul entre deux chaises et qu'il est assez gros pour s'asseoir sur les deux. Ils ont peur de nous quelque part. Nous, on a une richesse qu'eux ils n'ont pas [...]' [They don't understand that we don't have our arse stuck between two stools, it's big enough to fit on two. They're scared of us. We have depth they don't have] (Kettane, 1985: 166).

[14] 'the first expression, in the form of a cry, of young people of Indian, Pakistani, and Jamaican origin, but who claimed also to be every bit as much English, and who above all wanted a new, multicultural England'.

way in which signatories of his manifesto viewed the riots, Le Bris said: 'Ce n'était pas leur aventure. Ça c'est l'aventure des gens qui sont là.' [It wasn't their affair. The riots concerned people who live there] (2008). Here Le Bris suggests more difference than similarity between the foreign-born signatories of the manifesto and the ethnic minority authors born in France associated with the *banlieues* despite their common relationship to postcoloniality. He also appears detached from any responsibility for what was happening on the periphery of his own country since he chose to answer the question by highlighting only the response of the postcolonial signatories originating outside France. In reality, according to his own logic, there seems no reason for his postcolonial co-signatories to be any more implicated than Le Bris, or Jean Rouaud, since in many cases they live in the United States or other European countries. In the end, Le Bris makes it sounds as if none of the signatories was paying particular attention to the 'prise de parole' coming from the *banlieues défavorisées* in France.

No one sees the second-generation ethnic minority authors in France as their own. When they are not overlooked, they are misrepresented, ghettoized, or oversimplified. Razane's first novel, *Dit violent*, was published in 2006. In its editorial work-up, the author struggled with editors to find a way to present *Dit violent*: 'Je leur disais, mais pourquoi chercher un qualificatif? Pourquoi ne pas parler de littérature?' (Razane, 2008).[15] Razane wanted the beginning of the novel to appear on the back cover, nothing more. Gallimard prevailed in its marketing strategy, and Razane says of the back cover, 'on me l'a imposé' [they forced it on me] (2008). The back cover reads: 'Ici la nouveauté réside dans le ton, l'invention verbale qui font passer avec un grand naturel la vivacité du parler "beur" dans la langue écrite, la littérature'.[16] It is absurd to suggest that more than thirty years of 'Beur' literature had not provided a single example of novelistic language with oral texture and pugnacious tone – one need only think of Mehdi Charef, Azouz Begag, Farida Belghoul, Rachid Djaïdani or Mohand Mounsi. In sum, the writers of the internal periphery remain a lacuna not only in the *littérature-monde* manifesto but also for the French literary establishment in general.

---

[15] 'I asked them why they were looking for a label. Why not just call it literature?'

[16] 'Here newness comes from the tone and the linguistic invention that translate so effortlessly "Beur" speech to written language, literature'.

Conclusion

According to Jean-Marc Roberts, the head of the Stock publishing house, in the wake of the 2005 riots two in five manuscripts submitted to them came from the *banlieues défavorisées* (Berthod, 2007). It is not a new idea that a society's growing pains often find expression in artistic coming-of-ages. Such moments attest to a process at work, one that is often ineluctable and also not at all straightforward. Yet Le Bris's unequal analogy between England and France, like Gallimard's marketing of Razane, bear witness to the extraordinary *décalage* separating mainstream French writing from the nation's diversity. Razane and his peers believe there is no time to lose: they are interested in recording what they see, sending what they see outward and showing how that reflection concerns everyone. Theirs is not an introverted mirror; it is an extroverted one that recalls what Mohand Mounsi has said in the context of the 'Beur' generation about the mirror effect: 'Ils renvoient à la société française une image réfléchie d'elle-même' [They hold up to French society a mirror of itself] (Mounsi, 1995: 96). There is thus meaningful tension in the 'littérature au miroir' that the Collectif authors propose, suggesting a local identity that always already expresses something well beyond and outside of itself.

The committed realism that the 'Qui fait la France?' authors embrace does not give rise to 'highly aestheticized' writing, but rather mobilizes in a profound way the French vernacular and the register of the French language.[17] This *'banlieue* writing' is anti-lyrical and seemingly more mundane than the writing of the *littérature-monde* signatories. In this respect, it meets up squarely with the sort of literature and authorship that Langston Hughes defended in his 1926 essay-turned-manifesto 'The Negro Artist and the

---

[17] In the wake of the riots, Denis Duclos (2006) argued that the rioters challenged cultural forms as much as the economic and environmental factors that have led to disintegration in the *banlieues défavorisées*. He pointed to their 'vulgarized' but increasingly standardized language to say that French ways of speaking and being are being challenged at present: 'ce sont les jeunes des plus lointains cantons ruraux qui – imitant les accents "caillera", comme autrefois les Parisiens imitaient les accents "prolo" – écoutent désormais sur la radio locale les malheurs des Diam's, les leçons de Doc Gyneco, etc.' [now young people in the most far-off parts of the countryside – imitating the accents of *banlieue* youth as once Parisians imitated the 'working class' accents – listen on their local radio stations to the misadventures of Diam's, the lessons of Doc Gyneco, etc.] (Duclos, 2006). Duclos suggests that the re-written and re-articulated cultural forms coming from the *banlieue* periphery (verlan, slam, hip-hop) are in fact more democratic and representative ('partageables') than those coming from the Parisian centre.

Racial Mountain'. Hughes opens by unpacking what he sees to be a racialized statement: 'One of the most promising of the young Negro poets said to me once, "I want to be a poet – not a Negro poet," meaning, I believe, "I want to write like a white poet," meaning subconsciously, "I would like to be a white poet"; meaning behind that, "I would like to be white"' (Hughes, 1926). He contrasts this poet with the poet who comes from the 'common people' about whom he writes: 'They furnish a wealth of colorful, distinctive material for any artist because they still hold their own individuality in the face of American standardizations'. In the charged racialized context of the America of the 1920s, Hughes sees nothing wrong with writing about the common people – in this instance, people of colour, focusing on themes of everyday life, and bringing new rhythms to literature. These are the very things for which the 'Qui fait la France?' signatories will make no excuses. They are not afraid to choose what they must do as no one else will do it for them – to represent their world as they see and know it.

Works Cited

Berthod, Anne. 2007. 'La bauliene a du style'. *L'Express*. <http://www.lexpress.fr/culture/livre/du-reve-puor-les-outs-pieds-blancs-le-poids-d-une-ame-desinte-gration-cites-a-comparaitre_821691.html>. Consulted on 12 January 2007.

Caws, Mary Ann. (ed.) 2001. *Manifesto: A Century of Isms*. Lincoln and London: University of Nebraska Press.

Collectif Qui fait la France?. 2007. *Chroniques d'une société annoncée*. Paris: Stock.

Duclos, Denis. 2006. 'Retour sur la grande révolte des banlieues françaises'. *Le Monde diplomatique* (August): 12–13. <http://www.monde-diplomatique.fr/2006/08/DUCLOS/13741>. Consulted on 11 August 2007.

Huggan, Graham. 2001. *The Postcolonial Exotic: Marketing the Margins*. London and New York: Routledge.

Hughes, Langston. 1926. 'The Negro Artist and the Racial Mountain'. Encyclopædia Britannica's Guide to Black History. <http://www.britannica.com/blackhistory/article-9399832>. Consulted on 10 March 2009. [First published in *The Nation* 23 June 1926.]

Kettane, Nacer. 1985. *Le Sourire de Brahim*. Paris: Denoël.

Le Bris, Michel. 2007. 'Pour une littérature-monde en français'. In Michel Le Bris and Jean Rouaud (eds), *Pour une littérature-monde*. Paris: Gallimard: 23–53.

—. 2008. Unpublished interview with Laura Reeck. 11 December.

Mabanckou, Alain. 2006. 'Où sont les banlieues dans la littérature française'. Blog. d'Alain Mabanckou. 13 February. <http://www.congopage.com/rubrique217.html>. Consulted on 11 August 2007.

Mounsi, Mohand. 1995. *Territoire d'outre ville*. Paris: Stock.

Pliskin, Fabrice. 2007. 'Un nouveau mouvement littéraire, Qui fait la France? Nous'. *Le Nouvel Observateur*. 6 September. <http://hebdo.nouvelobs.com/hebdo/parution/p2235/articles/a353760-.html?xtmc=chroniquesdunesocietea nnoncee&xtcr=3>. Consulted on 13 September 2007.

Qui fait la France?. <http://www.quifaitlafrance.com/>. Consulted on 13 January 2009.

'Qui fait la France?'. 2007. Qui fait la France?. 17 September. <http://www.quifait-lafrance.com/content/view/45/59/>. Consulted on 26 May 2010.

Razane, Mohamed. 2006. *Dit violent*. Paris: Gallimard.

—. 2007. Interview with Vitraulle Mboungou. Afrik. 8 June. <http://www.afrik.com/article11886.html>. Consulted on 11 August 2007.

—. 2008. Unpublished interview with Laura Reeck. 13 December.

Rushdie, Salman. 1991. *Imaginary Homelands*. London: Granta.

—. 1996. 'Onward and Upward with the Arts, "In Defense of the Novel, Yet Again"'. *New Yorker* 24 June: 49–57.

The Post-Genocidal African Subject: Patrice Nganang, Achille Mbembe and the Worldliness of Contemporary African Literature in French

Michael Syrotinski

The 2007 *littérature-monde* manifesto made a series of bold claims to break with the enduring Francocentrism of *Francophonie*, and thereby to open the way for a radically decentred and transnational French-language literature, which might share the same globalized perspectives and concerns as Anglophone World Literature. Around the same time, the Francophone Cameroonian novelist, Patrice Nganang, wrote an equally radical manifesto, *Manifeste d'une nouvelle littérature africaine: Pour une écriture pré-emptive* (2007), which stands in a contrapuntal negative relation to the affirmative, celebratory tone of the *littérature-monde* manifesto. Nganang's manifesto is in effect a rather provocative indirect challenge to the latter's bold 'transnationalism', and a rallying cry for a new (what he calls 'pre-emptive') French-language African literature, in which he makes a claim to a certain worldliness: for him, a long tradition of African thinking died with the Rwandan genocide, and the only hope for its rebirth is literature, but literature as essentially, profoundly, necessarily dissident. According to Nganang, contemporary African writing and philosophy have not yet truly confronted the implications of what happened in Rwanda, with the notable exception of Achille Mbembe, whose work marks a profound rupture with ideologies and prevalent African philosophies of subjectivity. Nganang occupies the same theoretical ground as the writers of the *littérature-monde* manifesto when they make the case for a triumphal return of a number of categories which had been widely critiqued and discredited over the last few decades, namely the *subject, meaning, history* and the *world*. I would like to look more closely at Nganang's manifesto in this light, in particular the place he accords to a differently conceived 'worldliness', and test it against a few examples of what he refers to as 'post-genocide' African writing (including his own novels), in order to assess his claim to initiate a radically new African subjectivity.

Morbid Thinking

Patrice Nganang's central thesis is that the Rwandan genocide has to be read as a metonymy for a wider *self-destruction* in the context of the history of Francophone Africa. Rather than being a socio-political or historical analysis of the Rwandan genocide, the conditions which made it possible, and its aftermath, Nganang implicates not only the West, but, more importantly, what had gone under the name of African philosophy until that point. He begins with a critique of Africa's belated response to the genocide, which he calls 'un rituel à retardement qui trouve son origine dans la profonde culpabilité de la pensée africaine, sommeilleuse au moment de la catastrophe' (Nganang, 2007: 25).[1] The most immediate consequence of this is that African thinking and writing now have to define themselves 'comme nécessairement post-génocide' [as necessarily post-genocide] (Nganang, 2007: 27). However, the drama (and 'truth') of the genocide for Nganang lies precisely in the fact that it was not exceptional: not only was it the logical culmination of a series of earlier 'smaller' episodes of genocidal violence that scarred the history of Rwanda, which was merely the latest in a long history of barbaric post-Independence political regimes in Africa – what he calls 'le temps de l'exception devenue règle' [the time of the exception which has become the rule] (Nganang, 2007: 29) – but in global historical terms it could hardly compete with far larger-scale crimes against humanity (the systematic slaughter of American Indians, the Holocaust, Cambodia, and so on). Through a cruel irony, the Rwandan genocide, insofar as it becomes part of this broader history of world barbarism, marks the moment when Africa becomes, as Nganang puts it, 'fully human': 'Le génocide rend pleinement humain l'Africain, voilà le tragique paradoxe' (Nganang, 2007: 30).[2] The myth of Africa as different, extraordinary, other (whether positively or negatively conceived) no longer holds: instead the genocide is the moment of 'l'entrée fracassante de [l'Africain] dans l'humanité simple, c'est-à-dire fautive' (Nganang, 2007: 30).[3]

---

[1] 'a belated ritual that has its origins in the deep-seated guilt of African thinking, which fell asleep at the moment of the catastrophe'. Unless otherwise indicated, all translations from French into English are by the author of this chapter.

[2] 'the tragic paradox is that the genocide makes the African fully human'.

[3] 'the violent entry of (Africa) into simple, that is to say flawed, humanity'.

The Kantian or Hegelian subject around which most humanist discourses are constructed is thus replaced by the figure of the survivor: 'Au fond ne sommes-nous pas tous des survivants du génocide rwandais?' [Are we not basically all survivors of the Rwandan genocide?] (Nganang, 2007: 33). So this is, according to Nganang, a foundational moment for African philosophy. As he puts it: 'penser négativement pour survivre, voilà la nouvelle geste qui s'impose à la philosophie après le génocide, qui fonde une nouvelle humanité, une nouvelle subjectivité' (Nganang, 2007: 36).[4] In this sense, Rwanda would effectively render obsolete the philosophy of a thinker like Valentin Mudimbe, whose patient archaeological uncovering of the historically determined misrepresentations, or 'inventions' of Africa, allied with the promise of founding an African subject anew as a moment of Fanonian revolutionary rupture, would appear to have been leading African thinking up a blind alley all along. Naming him explicitly, Nganang implicates Mudimbe when he says: 'le philosophe africain, même le plus patient, était endormi quand les cadavres fleurissaient dans sa cour' (Nganang, 2007: 40).[5] For him, this underlines 'l'incapacité de [la philosophie africaine] à avoir été pré-visionnaire de la catastrophe, et l'irruption en son cœur du domaine de l'impensé' (Nganang, 2007: 40).[6] By contrast, however, the Cameroonian social theorist Achille Mbembe is said to be the one writer who has taken the risk of thinking Africa 'à partir du lieu morbide' (Nganang, 2007: 41).[7]

---

[4] 'thinking negatively in order to survive: this is the new gesture which becomes an imperative for philosophy after the genocide, which founds a new humanity, a new subjectivity'.

[5] 'even the most patient of African philosophers fell asleep while the dead bodies were adorning his back yard'.

[6] 'the inability of [African philosophy] to have foreseen the catastrophe of the genocide, and the sudden appearance of the unthought at its very heart'. In my view, Nganang's dismissal of Mudimbe is harsh and unjustified, and needs to be at the very least nuanced. Like Mbembe, Mudimbe is also critical of both indigenism (or what he would describe as the derivative nature of Africanist discourse, including its theologians like Mbiti, its linguists like Alexis Kagamé, its ethnophilosophers such as Placide Tempels, and its historians like Cheikh Anta Diop and Joseph Ki-Zerbo), as well as of the 'philosopher kings' of the early independence years, such as Nkrumah, Nyerere, Cabral, and so on), and of Marxism, which he sees as yet one more version of a universalizing 'will to truth'. Mudimbe notes that the limits of Marxist-inspired political radicalism were clearly seen in the African countries that adopted Socialist programmes following Independence, and he states bluntly: 'African socialisms were a mystification and everyone knows it' (Mudimbe, 1991: 183).

[7] 'as a morbid place', serving as a starting point for thinking Africa.

This is because Mbembe reads the genocide as *symptomatic* of 'le temps du malheur' [time of misery], that is, 'moins celui du rituel du deuil, que du réveil après la catastrophe: de la vie après la mort' (Nganang, 2007: 41),[8] whereas for other writers, the genocide was considered to be an 'epiphenomenon', a kind of exceptional and uncharacteristic madness.

It is certainly true that Mbembe's analysis takes this violence as inextricably bound up with the very ontology of the subject in contemporary Africa. In the chapter 'Of *Commandement*' in his best-known text, *On the Postcolony* (2001), Mbembe traces the corruption and violence that is at the heart of many African postcolonial regimes back to the 'founding violence' of the act of imperial conquest. This domination of *commandement* works by a kind of grotesque parody of citizenship, and is economic in its many corrupt and repressive forms, but Mbembe argues that it functions perhaps even more powerfully at a sensual and imaginary level, and, to this extent, his insistence on bringing the body back into the question of the subject is a radical reconceptualization of the mind/body dualism of Cartesian subjectivity and its subsequent philosophical reformulations. Under colonialism, and the humanism which gave it its moral justification and ideological underpinning, the native African was explicitly excluded from the realm of the human, and belonged to what Mbembe terms 'the grammar of animality' (Mbembe, 2001: 236). In terms of the broader sweep of African history, he distinguishes the imperial relationship of domination (which was geared towards the creation of obedient subjects) from the postcolonial *commandement* (which relies upon the dominated to sustain the relationship of subordination through a powerful imaginary complicity), and this sensualized coercion is elsewhere described, in the chapter 'The Aesthetics of Vulgarity', as the 'banality of power' (Mbembe, 2001: 102–41). In other words, the same dynamics that structured the African as a colonial 'animal' still determine the power relations of subjectivity and subjection in the African postcolony, since the African subject is considered ontologically as a 'thing that is nothing', and Mbembe goes on to ask the question: 'What does it mean to do violence to what is nothing?' (Mbembe, 2001: 74).

Nganang's thesis on 'post-genocide writing' is explicitly aligned with Mbembe's rejection of the two traditions which since *négritude* have dominated African thinking, that is Marxism in its various guises and Afrocentrist indigenism (two traditions Mbembe wryly refers to as 'le rouge et le noir' [red and black]!). From the perspective of radical political philosophy, Nganang sees the subject as perpetually stuck in the mode of victimization,

---

[8] 'less a time of the ritual of mourning, than one of waking up after the genocide: of life after death'.

projecting everything negative onto colonialism, and seeing him/herself as Other, in Hegelian terms – 'l'origine externe d'une extermination de masse inscrite dans les dichotomies belges et dans la longue main génocidaire de la France' (Nganang, 2007: 45)[9] – which effectively stymies the possibility of an unconditional responsibility for autonomy. Indigenism or nativism, on the other hand, can only be founded on essentialism – 'elle s'enfonce dans les miasmes de l'essentialisme' [it disappears into the mists of essentialism] – and, as Nganang rightly says, it was precisely this essentialist thinking, 'la pensée identitaire' [identitarian thinking] (Nganang, 2007: 45), which informed the racialism motivating the genocide. It revealed at the same time the profound historical and ideological complicity linking rationalism with racialism: 'c'est le socle même de la rationalité qui en a été secoué. Sans aucun doute, le Rwanda est le cimetière de la négritude ainsi que de tous ses corollaires conceptuels' (Nganang, 2007: 46).[10]

African philosophy was thus asleep, and was helpless to respond to the genocide. Mbembe's unique status as a post-genocide writer comes precisely from his willingness to position himself specifically within the space left as a result of the wreckage of the two traditions of radicalism and nativism. As Nganang says: 'C'est du creux morbide du cimetière de masse [...] que la pensée de Mbembe redécouvre le pouvoir et la souveraineté du sujet africain. C'est dans le monde en miettes qu'elle pose l'autonomie de celui-ci' (Nganang, 2007: 46).[11] And a little later on: 'Nous pouvons donc dire que la pensée de Mbembe, en posant la question de la souveraineté du sujet dans le chaos, découvre pour la philosophie africaine l'origine de la sagesse dans le manque, à proximité du danger, dans la frontière de la mort, certes, mais aussi dans la négation de ceux-ci' (Nganang, 2007: 52).[12]

[9] 'the external origins of a mass extermination predetermined by the dichotomies of Belgian colonialism and the long genocidal hand of France'.

[10] 'it was the very foundation of rationality that was shaken. Rwanda is without a doubt the graveyard of Negritude, as well as of all of its conceptual corollaries'.

[11] 'It is from the morbid hollow of the mass grave that Mbembe's thought rediscovers the power and sovereignty of the African subject. It is within this crumbling world that his thought situates the autonomy of this subject'.

[12] 'We can say then that Mbembe's thought, by asking the question of the sovereignty of the subject in its chaos, discovers the wisdom of African philosophy in its lack, close to danger, on the border with death, for sure, but also in the negation of both of these'.

A Literature of Detritus

This negative foundational moment is what provides Nganang in his *Manifeste* with the impetus for a new (what he calls 'pre-emptive') African literature: a certain African philosophy died in Rwanda, and can only be reborn in literature, but literature considered as essentially, profoundly, necessarily dissident (which would otherwise simply fall back into the same old traps, perpetuating the same old structures and complicities). For him this renewed subjectivity is not to be found in the old discredited philosophies, but by venturing deep into the heart of contemporary urban Africa (for which his shorthand term is 'la rue'). This is not so much the expression of a commitment to write in a populist vein, or to place a finger on an authentically popular 'pulse', but he characterizes this literature as an incessant, urgent, anxious vigilance, informed by a knowing wisdom about what it means to live – most often to survive – in the African postcolony, but also in terms of a particular linguistic inventiveness: 'nous savons la désinvolture linguistique des rues africaines' [we know how offhand, informal and inventive the language of the street is in Africa] (Nganang, 2007: 11). In the second half of his *Manifeste*, he sketches out an aesthetics of contemporary African literature, distancing himself from more conventional textual analysis, or from discussions of literature in terms of its status as sociological or historical document (in its representational or allegorical mode), but sees literature instead as having an unequivocally metaphysical function, as the development of an *idea*, in what he calls a 'lecture idéale de la littérature' [reading literature as idea]: 'nous entendons par l'idée, le lieu à partir duquel le langage de la rue "de chez nous" pose des questions et se fait philosophe' (Nganang, 2007: 16).[13] Nganang outlines some of the formal characteristics of this new 'philosophical' literature (literature as the expression of a 'pre-visionary' kind of truth; that is marked by chiasmic, ironic forms; and is tragic in its dimensions), and then describes a number of broad categories (the literature of dictatorship, the literature of emigration, the literature of 'detritus'), but it is really this last category which is truly the place where Nganang sees the 'post-genocidal African subject' tentatively taking shape. It is within this context that he mentions the novels of the Congolese writer, Alain Mabanckou, along with a number of allusions to his own fiction-writing. Two short examples from their respective texts will enable us to see more clearly just how their writing dramatizes, in different ways, a renewed African subjectivity. The first is Nganang's own *Temps de chien* (2001) and the second is Mabanckou's *Verre Cassé* (2005).

---

[13] 'what we mean by idea is making "our own" street language the place where one begins to ask questions and to philosophize'.

Both novels are very much, as with their other fiction, novels of 'la rue': the language is a rich, earthy, Africanized French (in the manner of Yambo Ouologuem, Ahmadou Kourouma or Sony Labou Tansi), and the characters all seem to be part of the 'detritus' that characterizes the human-as-survivor, but they also both explicitly pose the question of the subject as a kind of *post-human* subject, telling their stories from the point of view of two animal narrators. These narrators are both presented rather as wise, affectionate and forgiving observers of human nature, constantly thinking about the meaning of the human as such, and forever questioning the activities and behaviours of the many different characters they come into contact with in the course of the narrative. In this sense, they function somewhat like the reverse ethnography we find, say, in Bernard Dadié's travel writings, but the chiasmic structure here is between animals and humans, rather than between Africa and the West.[14] Much of the action is centred around local community bars, which are the focal point for the gathering of a number of very colourful and entertaining regulars, who regale us with the stories of their abject lives. These narratives do not, however, work simply as somewhat naive sociological or 'ethnological' recordings, but are acutely self-aware and self-reflexive, all the while being narrated from the point of view of a subject that is 'less than human' or 'other than human'. These figures are also often survivors, outliving repeated attempts to kill them off. In Nganang's *Temps de Chien*, the dog-narrator, Mboudjak, gets brutally mistreated by his master, Massa Yo, and is then hanged and left for dead by his son, Soumi. Mboudjak somehow survives, frees himself, and returns to Massa Yo and his son, who react at first with terror, but who eventually (if still grudgingly) take him back. He spends much of the rest of the novel sitting in a corner in Massa Yo's bar, *Le Client est roi* [The Customer is King], a vantage point from which he observes all the many daily conversations and goings-on.

In one episode a mysterious, taciturn figure called *Corbeau* [Crow] shows up at the bar, and in a typically playful *mise-en-abîme*, we learn that *Corbeau* is a writer who is writing a novel called *Temps de chien*, in which he aims to record the lives and conversations of the characters in the bar. Once the purpose of his visits is discovered, his very presence generates deep suspicion and mistrust, even though he is the only one to intervene during a police raid one day, and to protest at the unwarranted arrest of one of the regulars, *L'ingénieur* [The Engineer]. The following short extract includes one of Mboudjak's characteristic reflections on the treatment *Corbeau* receives from the regulars:

---

[14] For an extended analysis of Dadié's 'reverse ethnography', see Syrotinski, 2002: 66–99.

'On devrait chasser ce hibou du quartier.'

C'est la parole la plus terrible qui fût jamais lancée sur l'écrivain des bas-fonds. Et je me rendis compte ahuri du traitement que l'ingénieur, celui-là même qui venait échapper à sa vie en se lovant dans la cour de mon maître, m'aurait réservé à moi qui non plus n'avais de cesse d'observer et rien qu'observer les hommes, si j'avais été seulement un homme. Même par pure solidarité professionnelle de co-observateur, je sympathisais avec le philosophe. (Nganang, 2001: 157)[15]

Mabanckou's novel, *Verre Cassé*, also features a dog as narrator (just as the sequel to this novel, *Mémoires de porc-épic* [Memoirs of a porcupine] (2006), which is set in the same bar, has another tough animal survivor as its narrator). Like Mboudjak, he is constantly hovering on the borderline between life and death, appears to die, and then to live on after death. His narration, nevertheless, also has an irrepressible inventiveness and verve about it, in spite of its subject matter, in a manner reminiscent of Sony Labou Tansi's 1979 novel, *La Vie et demie* (which is indeed a major point of reference for Mbembe when he talks of the 'life after death' of the African postcolony), and if we are to adopt Nganang's own temporal divisions and epistemological break, Sony's writing very much prefigures the genocide and its aftermath, such that it would not be wrong to call *La Vie et demie* a 'pre-post-genocide' novel. From the outset, *Verre Cassé* clearly figures the 'shattered' subject of contemporary Africa, but is acutely aware of the place it occupies within a certain literary history and tradition, and has a similar critical self-reflexivity to Nganang's text. The opening section is worth quoting more fully:

[...] disons que le patron du bar *Le Crédit a voyagé* m'a remis un cahier que je dois remplir, et il croit dur comme fer que moi, Verre Cassé, je peux pondre un livre parce que, en plaisantant, je lui avais raconté un jour l'histoire d'un écrivain célèbre qui buvait comme une éponge, un écrivain qu'on allait même ramasser dans la rue quand il était ivre, faut donc pas plaisanter avec le patron parce qu'il prend tout au premier degré, et lorsqu'il m'avait remis ce cahier, il avait tout de suite précisé que c'était pour lui, pour lui tout seul, que personne d'autre ne le lirait, et alors, j'ai

---

[15] '"We should get this owl out of the neighbourhood." These were the most dreadful words ever uttered about the writer of our miserable lives. And I suddenly realized, in a state of shock, the treatment that the engineer, the very person who had escaped with his life by curling up and hiding away in my master's yard, would have given to me, who also spent all my time simply observing humans, if I had been human. Simply out of pure professional solidarity as a co-observer, I sympathized with the philosopher'.

voulu savoir pourquoi il tenait tant à ce cahier, il a répondu qu'il ne voulait pas que *Le Crédit a voyagé* disparaisse un jour comme ça, il a ajouté que les gens de ce pays n'avaient pas le sens de la conservation de la mémoire, que l'époque des histoires que racontait la grand-mère grabataire était finie, que l'heure était désormais à l'écrit parce que c'est ce qui reste, la parole c'est de la fumée noire, du pipi de chat sauvage, le patron du *Le Crédit a voyagé* n'aime pas les formules toutes faites du genre *'en Afrique quand un vieillard meurt, c'est une bibliothèque qui brûle'*, et lorsqu'il entend ce cliché bien développé, il est plus que vexé et lance aussitôt *'ça dépend de quel vieillard, arrêtez donc vos conneries, je n'ai confiance qu'en ce qui est écrit'* [...]. (Mabanckou, 2005: 11–12)[16]

The phrase 'quand un vieillard meurt, c'est une bibliothèque qui brûle' [whenever an old person dies, a library burns], is of course a reference to the famous saying by Ahmadou Hampâté Ba, representing the continuing attachment to the indigenous culture and oral tradition from which many Africanist philosophies are inspired. Mabanckou's novel, like Nganang's, is playfully critical of this tradition, and is in fact full of knowing intertextual allusions to many classic French and Francophone African texts.

Literature and What is Left Over

Literature, or at least a particular mode of dissident literature that takes its theoretical cue from Mbembe's analyses of postcolonial Africa, seems thus to have taken over from African philosophy post-genocide, according to Nganang. It is no accident that Mbembe's own writing both describes in

---

16 '[...] let's say the boss of the bar *Credit Gone West* gave me this notebook to fill, he's convinced that I – Broken Glass – can turn out a book, because one day, for a laugh, I told him about this famous writer who drank like a fish, and had to be picked up off the street when he got drunk, which shows you should never joke with the boss, he takes everything literally, when he gave me this notebook he said from the start it was only for him, no one else would read it, and when I asked why he was so set on this notebook, he said he didn't want *Credit Gone West* just to vanish one day, and added that people in this country have no sense of the importance of memory, that the days when grandmothers reminisced from their deathbeds was gone now, this is the age of the written word, that's all that is left, the spoken word's just black smoke, wild cat's piss, the boss of *Credit Gone West* doesn't like ready-made phrases like "in Africa, whenever an old person dies, a library burns", every time he hears that worn-out cliché he gets mad, he'll say "depends which old person, don't talk crap, I only trust what's written down" [...]' (Mabanckou, 2009: 1–2).

extensive and painful detail the 'life after death' of the African postcolony but also enacts it as a kind of spectral self-inscription within a history and a tradition. Mbembe's own ghostly or spectral other is the figure of Ruben Um Nyobè, the Cameroonian political militant and journalist and founder of the nationalist, anti-colonial UPC (Union des Populations du Cameroun), who was assassinated by the French in 1958, and who has been most famously commemorated by his compatriot Mongo Beti in his 1974 novel *Remember Ruben*, among others. In his essay 'Écrire l'Afrique à partir d'une faille' (1993), Mbembe states his avowed debt to Ruben Um Nyobè. Mbembe had written on Ruben when he first went to France in 1984, as a way of honouring his memory in the face of attempts to censor his work and destroy his memory in his native Cameroon. In this largely autobiographical essay by Mbembe, Ruben serves as the focus for the double contradictory imperative of the essay to both remember and forget, honour a bond by writing the necessity of its dissolution, and indeed Ruben could be said to figure Mbembe's mourning of the irretrievable 'object' that Africa has become for him. He is described as a kind of ghost, neither present nor absent, neither here nor there, a trace of the 'night-of-the-postcolonial-African-world' who is at the very source of Mbembe's writing, or of Mbembe as a writer. He is the gap, the *faille*, in which, or from which, Mbembe's 'writing Africa' can emerge, a writing that can only begin once it has dispelled the myths both of authenticity and of the promises of radical politics, with which Mbembe was quickly disillusioned. This 'writing Africa' is described as a kind of responsibility that goes beyond the responsibility of *representation*, whether in terms of accurate depiction or faithful factual narration, or in terms of speaking 'for' one's people, or one's country, or one's place of origin.

Nganang is no doubt right to point to Mbembe as the most important commentator of the African postcolony, and one can now more readily understand the influence on him not only of Mbembe's critical position with respect to the two broad traditions of African philosophy, but also of Mbembe's practice of 'writing Africa', and the radically new subjective space he is attempting to clear the way for. The 'worldliness' this implies – more Heideggerian in its ontological commitment – is perhaps a world away from the more assertive optimism of the *littérature-monde* manifesto. Nganang's characterization of 'post-genocide' literature is a controversial one, though, which has already been the subject of some fierce criticism, although its most significant gesture is perhaps in according literature – whether African, Francophone or global, however this is conceived – a far more central philosophical importance than it has hitherto had. A number of questions remain, though, and in conclusion I would simply like to pose these questions as paths (again, in a Heideggerian sense) that have, to my mind, been very usefully opened up by Nganang.

(i) Why privilege literature as the site of a re-emergent philosophy and, specifically, a philosophy of subjectivity over other modes of cultural production (for example, music, art, photography, film)? Can these artistic forms not offer equivalent dissident practices?

(ii) Is there not a danger, despite all of the irony and playful invention (as we have seen with Nganang and Mabanckou, for example), that in allowing the street, 'la rue', to speak, one is giving back to the subjective voice it embodies the kind of existential authority it claims to be going beyond, in its post-human dissidence? In other words, is 'pre-emptive' vigilance *enough*?

(iii) In taking the West out of the equation in the Rwandan genocide (that is, a will to autonomy that means taking responsibility for the genocide, insofar as this is how Africa has joined the universal barbarism of humanity), and in making this a story that has to do essentially with Africa's self-destruction, the failure and collapse of African philosophy (and how it moves beyond the 'temps du malheur'), is there not a very grave danger in exculpating the West in the desire to get away from a syndrome of victimization?

(iv) As a corollary to this we might wonder, given the importance of the *writing* of a new dissident literature as the site of a 'post-genocide' African subjectivity and the re-emergence of a new mode of philosophizing within this literature of dissidence, whether there is then a need for a comparable (dissident?) *reading* practice. That is, if we are indeed dealing with a radically new form of being in the world (nothing can ever be the same post-genocide), then we can no longer read as we once did. What would that new mode of reading consist of?

(v) Alongside literature, and given that Nganang uses the insistent question of one woman survivor of the genocide as a constant refrain and a question to those who failed to respond to the genocide ('Vous étiez où?' [Where were you?]), one would need to consider trauma testimony (written or spoken) and the temporal and narrative complexities that inform such testimony.

(vi) Would this then perhaps enable us to regard more sympathetically the texts of the Francophone African *Devoir de mémoire* writers, which are in effect dismissed by Nganang as 'too little, too late'? (He does argue, it should be said, that maybe we are all, inevitably, too late.)

(vii) The question 'How does one live on?', or survive, is of course far more than a philosophical question, or even the privileged question of philosophy as a new literary (or aesthetic) form, but it also has to do profoundly and fundamentally with questions of truth and reconciliation. How does one heal? One cannot simply break with the past, and especially not with a traumatic past, and one might look here to the South African Truth and Reconciliation Commission as a model process for separating out the question of amnesty – as the political and juridical social mechanism by which the transition is made from the apartheid era – from the moral (and psychological) dimension of forgiveness (that is, although political amnesty is granted with full disclosure of crimes, victims are not obliged to forgive or forget).[17]

(viii) Finally, one might ask, from the perspective of gender theory, and since Mbembe's reading of *commandement* is explicitly masculinized, whether we are still within the realm of phallocracy (which is certainly the 'world' of the narratives of Sony Labou Tansi, Nganang and Mabanckou). Is this also ultimately another kind of phallogocentrism, and would this then become a *disabling* element in the claim to philosophical dissidence?

One might be led to conclude that Nganang's diagnosis of the current state, and prognosis of the future 'life after death', of African literature in French is ultimately one of many such examples of the 'vaste ensemble polyphonique' [vast polyphonic ensemble] which emerges out of the *Littérature-monde* manifesto's breaking of the Francophone 'pact' with the nation, and it would thus appear to be entirely consistent with an approach to globalization which welcomes a heterogeneity of specific, or rather singular, sites ('Pour une "littérature-monde" en français', 2007; 'Toward a "World Literature" in French', 2009: 56). What Nganang's text does, though, for all of the rather problematic implications around its edges, is to force us into a more sober, sustained and philosophically serious engagement with each of the key terms in the *littérature-monde* debate – most notably the status of 'literature' and of the 'world' and the relation between the two – and to ensure that the question of the possibilities and continuing limits of subjective reaffirmation, at least within an African context, is still a long way from being adequately resolved.

---

[17] For an insightful, philosophically informed discussion of this question, see Barbara Cassin (2006). For Cassin, the question of narrative truth is marked by an important shift away from a focus on disclosure as a 'revelation' of what was hidden, to a more finely tuned attentiveness to language as performative (reparative) act.

Works Cited

Cassin, Barbara. 2006. '"Removing the Perpetuity of Hatred": On South Africa as a Model Example'. *International Review of the Red Cross* 88.862: 235–44.

Mabanckou, Alain. 2005. *Verre Cassé*. Paris: Éditions du Seuil.

—. 2009. *Broken Glass*. Trans. by Helen Stevenson. London: Serpent's Tail.

Mbembe, Achille. 1993. 'Écrire l'Afrique à partir d'une faille'. *Politique Africaine* 51: 69–97.

—. 2001. *On the Postcolony*. Berkeley: University of California Press.

Mudimbe, V. Y. 1991. 'Anthropology and Marxist Discourse'. *Parables and Fables: Exegesis, Textuality and Politics in Central Africa*. Madison: University of Wisconsin Press: 166–91.

Nganang, Patrice. 2001. *Temps de chien*. Paris: Le Serpent à plumes.

—. 2007. *Manifeste d'une nouvelle littérature africaine: Pour une écriture préemptive*. Paris: Éditions Homnisphères.

'Pour une "littérature-monde" en français'. 2007. *Le Monde* 16 March.

Syrotinski, Michael. 2002. *Singular Performances: Reinscribing the Subject in Francophone African Writing*. Charlottesville: University of Virginia Press.

'Toward a "World-Literature" in French'. 2009. Trans. by Daniel Simon. *World Literature Today* (March–April): 54–56.

Afterword:
The 'World' in World Literature

Emily Apter

Perusing the multiple essays in *Transnational French Studies: Postcolonialism and Littérature-monde* alongside those twenty-seven included in *Pour une littérature-monde* one is swept into the mental ping-pong of 'pro' versus 'con' on the question of whether there should be a 'World Literature in French' positioned to answer to the widely validated, postcolonially inflected model of Anglophone World Lit. Notable arguments in favour of such a construct touch many bases. *Littérature-monde en français* replaces the outmoded term 'Francophone', a carrier of neo-colonial, orientalist baggage, a ghettoizing, divisive, exclusionary term in publishing and academia, and a tautology, since all speakers of French are Francophone. The 'world' can no longer be excluded from literature in French and should be taken fully on board by the Paris-oriented French literary establishment (Michel Le Bris's argument). The strongest literature in French is arguably being produced by extra-hexagonal writers (the manifesto was indeed partly occasioned by their high percentage of literary prizes in 2007). The World Literature perspective brings attention to less internationally exposed writers, putting them into dialogue with each other in an expanded comparative frame. The appellation 'World Literature' in institutional academia abolishes the ontologically objectionable 'us–them' dichotomy between national and 'foreign' language departments. Global literary markets generate new consumers of literature with tastes, interests and cultural literacies no longer satisfied by writing authored by or aimed principally at *les Français de France*. Regional, translingual affiliations (the connection, say, between Indigenous francophone and Anglophone Pacific cultures or the circum-Atlantic cultural contacts inaugurated by the slave trade) appear in sharper relief through a worldly viewfinder. The practice of creolization extends beyond language to 'platforms' (curator Okui Enwezor's coinage) of the aesthetic, putting French literature into colloquy with greater world-systems and non-literary media. The Glissantian *Tout-monde* has provided a poetic and philosophical framework for thinking 'World' as an anti-exoticist francophone *nomos*. World Literature is suited to an era in which the electronic dissemination of information, even in countries with restricted Internet and Web access, has transformed the economics of literary distribution and editorial gatekeeping. Secular criticism, marked by Edward Said's practice of contrapuntal reading and the politics of empire, warrants a more developed counterpart in French studies.

Arguments contra *littérature-monde en français* cover a comparable gamut. It is criticized for being too quick to ape an Anglo-American-style Comparative Literature in French studies, reinforcing an Anglocentric (or, worse, Globish) tendency in the human sciences worldwide, and defeating the purpose of defining a French-based praxis differently. World Lit cartography obscures important divergences in the French-speaking context between postcolonial, extra-hexagonal and continental *banlieue/Beur* writing, while at the same time lumping together wildly discrepant postcolonial literatures. Ambassadorial efforts to support French culture in formerly colonized territories belie attitudes of cultural imperialism, curatorial patronage and salvage rather than commitment to the veritable renewal of French-language expression (as Alain Mabanckou has intimated). The fantasy of a decommercialized literature without borders must perforce remain oblivious to the way market capitalism works. Any French version of World Literature respectful of the Goethean/Auerbachian heritage in the humanities will perpetuate Eurocentric humanist universalism as well as a static lexicon of style, periodization and genre defined largely by Western classics. World Literature is a cosmopolitan project better suited to privileged emigrés than to immigrant, second-generation minority cultures. World fiction uses *métissage* as yet another occidental foil for inattention to cultural and historical particularism. World Literature inadequately takes stock of the impact of colonialism and decolonization on literary history. *Littérature-monde*, like World Literature paradigms in general, either reinforces old national, regional and ethnic literary alignments, or projects a denationalized planetary screen that ignores the deep structures of national belonging and economic interest contouring the international culture industry. World Literature remains oblivious to the systematic critique of globalized literary studies contained in Gayatri Chakravorty Spivak's concept of 'planetarity' (in *Death of a Discipline*). In their rush to franchise 'global' campus outposts all over the world, universities seize on World Literature as a catch-all rubric for flimsy programmes in the humanities that ignore rather than deepen local knowledge. World Literature is all too conducive to the downsizing of 'foreign' language departments, and furthers monolingual coverage of literatures and area studies in other languages. Even the most recent and intellectually creative attempts to remake World Literature for a future-oriented, planetary pedagogy often end in a pluralist critical practice of comparison that massages neoliberalism (the regime of post-political or post-ideological aesthetics, in Christopher Bongie's ascription).

While there are clearly valid points on both sides of the aisle, and important stakes for the study and redistribution of 'Frenches' within the future of Comparative Literature, it strikes me that the polemics summarized and played out in *Transnational French Studies* insufficiently address two concerns. First, in seeking to comparatize French literary criticism and theory, *Litt-monde* partisans and detractors alike assume translatability as both a given and heuristic good, thereby devaluing the importance of non-translation and untranslatability for the politics of cultural relationality. And second, the term 'world' in *littérature-monde* remains curiously undertheorized as a reserve of philosophical untranslatability and conceptual density. In fairness, Typhaine Leservot in her chapter 'From *Weltliteratur* to World Literature to *Littérature-monde*: The History of a Controversial Concept' offers a compelling genealogy casting *littérature-monde* as a 'view of the world' in contrast to earlier models of World Lit that emphasize the fomenting of international canons. Mounia Benalil notes the untapped potential of Antoine Volodine's notion of what it means to 'faire monde' [render the world] (Ruffel, 2007: 99) and calls for 'a formal-thematic axis that could identify a literary grouping displaying qualities worthy of a "world-poetics"'. And Jeanne Garane problematizes the location of 'world' in *littérature-monde* (taking her cue from Christophe Pradeau and Tiphaine Samoyoult's title *Où est la littérature mondiale?*). Pondering whether Le Bris's use of the term implies a generalized *tiermondialisation* of the hexagon, Garane notes that 'the relationship between *littérature-monde, littérature mondiale*, and its German and English counterparts *Weltliteratur* and world literature is made explicit neither in the manifesto, [...] nor in the introductory essays by Jean Rouaud and Michel Le Bris'. These observations notwithstanding, few interventions question what a world is. The shifting definitions of 'world' from language to language and context to context contribute, I would submit, theoretical substance to the paradigm of *littérature-monde*.

In Barbara Cassin's edited volume *Le Vocabulaire européen des philosophies: Dictionnaire des intraduisibles* the word 'world' and its proximate equivalents in other European languages – *kosmos, mundus, Welt, monde, mir, olam, svet,* etc. – emerges as a premier philosophical 'Untranslatable'. Cassin defines the Untranslatable not so much as a philosopheme that fails to translate, but rather as a term that, through continual translation, demonstrates the aliveness of philosophy; the embeddedness of philosophy in living language. Building on this idea, we could say that (philosophical) Untranslatables are key-words with a distinct symptomology: they appear as neologisms or loan words conserved in the original as they pass from one tongue to the next; they are continuously being retranslated or mistranslated, and they signal translational incommensurability (as in *esprit* to *mind* or *Geist*).

Anthony Grafton (2009) has emphasized the world-making power of words in his analysis of the *Respublica literarum* in the early modern period. Cassin, by contrast, maps worlds through philosophical philology. In the *Vocabulaire* the German term *Welt* makes a real incursion into Greek and Roman intellectual estates. Of course, *Ur*-cognates in Greek (*kosmos*), Latin (*mundus*) and Hebrew (*olam*) are duly represented in the modern languages – a trinity comparable to the three monotheisms. But after Kant (whose dissertation written in Latin in 1770 dealt with 'the notion of the world in general'), and in a line leading through Hegel and Schelling to Heidegger, *Welt* gathers momentum to the point where it would seem that German is truly the language in which 'world' is most fully philosophized. The only other language that comes close in claiming philosophical territory is Russian, buoyed perhaps by the movements of folk revival, Slavophilia, nationalism, socialist Utopia, and communism. Generally speaking, the Russian terms are sutured to a vision of society, as in *mir* (world, peace, village community), *svet* (world), *obscina* (primordial communism), *sobernost'* (uni-totality), *narodnost'* (adhesion of the people), *svoboda* (liberty, collective will), *samost'* (human nature) and *vseedinstvo* (uni-totality). Russian aside, what we perceive most clearly in the *Vocabulaire* is the extent to which *Welt* becomes the centre of a substantial concordance comprising *Weltalter* (ages of the world), *Weltgeist* (world spirit), *Weltanschauung* (world view), *Weltlauf* (way of the world), *Welten* (to make to the measure of the world), *Weltkenntnis* (knowledge of the world), *Mitwelt* (contemporaries), *Weltbürger* (citizen of the world), *Umwelt* (environment), *Umweltschutz* (environmental protection), *Umweltverschmutzung* (pollution), *Verweltlichung* (secularization) and *Weltliteratur*, so indelibly marked by Goethe. As strings of apposite meanings are generated, *Welt* annexes semantic approximations like *Leben* (life) or *Heimat* (homeland). The land-grab is consolidated by the success of *Welt* in drawing off earlier French usages of *monde* whose gamut covered diplomatic and courtly codes of conduct, success in society (*mondanité*), and the idea of plural or possible worlds associated with the seventeenth- and eighteenth-century ascriptions of Fontanelle and Rousseau.

Pascal David tracks the way in which this 'German adventure of world' chronicles a gradual ontologization of the term:

> Is there something like a predisposition to phenomenology or even to existentialism in the 'Germanic' concept of the world? One that should be properly separated out from any strictly cosmological conception? If such is actually the case, it is nonetheless the semantic trajectory of the ancient Greek *kosmos* [κόσμος] (from Heraclitus to Saint Paul and Saint John, passing through Plato), which seems to have prefigured the splitting of meaning, to be clearly found in Kant, between a cosmological sense corresponding to the universe and a cosmo-political, anthropological, or existential sense referring to a way of relating to both the universe and the community of men. Paradoxically, Kant himself emphasized, in an anthropological perspective, how the French word *monde* had rubbed off some of its connotations on the German word *Welt* in its cosmopolitan acceptations. *Welt* is further enriched, in the philosophical vocabulary of the twentieth century, through an impersonal verb, *welten, es weltet*, a word coined by Heidegger or at least endowed with new meaning by him. [...]
>
> It has been possible to detect a 'Germanic' concept of the world underlying Heidegger's thought on the subject 'because the sense in which it is to be understood is suggested by the etymology of the terms' in Germanic languages, including the German *Welt*, the English *world*, the Dutch *wereld*, Swedish *vårld*, the Danish *verden, verdensalt*, etc. The Germanic etymon is a compound word which combines an element signifying 'man' (from the Latin *vir*) and a second element signifying 'age' (cf. English 'old'). The resulting meaning would be something like 'where man finds himself as long as he is alive' ('*ce dans quoi l'homme se trouve tant qu'il est en vie*', R. Brague, *Aristote et la question du monde*, 27–28, n.37). We can note in passing that the (17th century) German word *Weltalter* 'age(s) of the world' is essentially redundant, since it can be taken apart as: Ger. *wer-alt* (= 'epoch', 'world', 'generation') + Ger. *Alter*, 'age', whence: *age of ages of man*! As opposed to the cosmological concept of the world which defines a whole of whom I am but a tiny part, there is then perhaps a predisposition in the Germanic etymon leading in the direction of its phenomeno-logical conception; that within which the human being deploys his being, according to a triple determination: cosmological, anthropological, and ontological. (David, 2004: 1390)

Welt's superimposition of temporality, existence and anthropocentrism comes into focus as Enlightenment modernity's counterpart to the Hebrew word *olam* (whose synonyms include *Welt, aiôn*, humanity, life). Rémi Brague (forthcoming) stresses the ontological provisionality of *olam*; its emphasis on the subject's entrance onto and exit from the scene of life:[1]

> Among the words designating the world certain designate the order of things, as with the Greek *Kosmos* (κόσμος) and the Latin *mundus*, and others accentuate the living presence of the subject. The world is that into which we are born and leave upon dying. Such is the case with the English *world*, the German *Welt*, and the Dutch *vereld*, which are etymologically the most legible in connoting the duration of the life (cf. Eng, old) of man (lat. vir; ger. wer- in Werewolf, 'wolf-man', fr. '*loup-garou*'). The Hebraic word for world is '*olam* (עוֹלָם) and although it features in the Bible, it is not used in this particular sense, even in a late text such as *Qohelet* 3, 11. Rather, another temporal sense is communicated in which an undetermined duration informs expressions such as *le-'olam* (לְעוֹלָם), 'an undetermined future', from where we have 'for always', or *më-'olam* (מֵעוֹלָם) 'since a period where the beginning has been ignored' from where we have 'since always'.

---

[1] Pascal David, in a complementary vein to Brague, emphasizes 'the co-belonging of the world and time' in the German Romantic conception of *Welt* put forth by F. W. Schelling:

Etymologically, *Welt* maintains an optional relationship with time. This relationship is underscored by Schelling, the author of the *Weltalter* (Ages of the World), by means of a debatable, if not outright fantasmagorical, albeit illuminating, etymological link between *Welt* and *währen* (to endure), at the end of lesson XIV of the *Philosophy of Revelation*, in order to maintain the speculative equivalence of world and time (the cosmic eon):

True time itself consist of a series of times, and inversely, the world is only one element of true time, and is in this respect itself a time, as the very name *Welt* indicates, which derives from *währen* (to endure) and thus indicates a *duration*, which the Greek *aiôn* reveals even more directly, as it also designates a time of the world. [*wie schon das Wort, das von* währen *herkommt und eigentlich eine* Währung, *eine Dauer, anzeigt, und noch unmittelbarer das griechische* aiôn *beweist, das ebsensowhol eine* Zeit *als die* Welt *bedeutet*] *Schellings Werke*, Vol. 6, addendum, p. 308.

Even if *Welt* does not come from *währen*, which is itself a term related to *wesen* and to the third root in the etymology of the verb 'to be': Sanskrit *vasami*, Germanic *wesan* ('to dwell, remain, to live') (cf. Heidegger, *Introduction* ... , fr. trans. p. 81), Schelling has nonetheless instinctively sensed the essential co-belonging of the world and time in his reference to the Greek *aiôn* [αἰών], 'cosmic eon', even if in an essentially Paulist sense (I Corinthians 7, 31: 'the form of this world [κόσμος] will pass away') (David, 2004: 1390–91; translation by Christian Hubert in Apter, Lezra and Wood, forthcoming).

While the study of *Welt* as an Untranslatable shows how bound up it is conceptually with biblical and Enlightenment notions of time, it also sheds light on an interesting tension, registered in Kant's *Anthropology*, between 'having' and 'knowing' the world: 'Noch sind die Ausdrücke: die Welt *kennen* und Welt *haben* in ihrer Bedeutung zeimlich weit auseinander: indem der Eine nur das Spiel versteht, dem er zugesehen hat, der Andere aber mitgespielt hat' (Kant, 1900: 120).[2] Michel Foucault, in his translation of this passage, would render *Welt kennen* as *connaître le monde* and *Welt haben* as *avoir du monde*, the latter translation recalling the fact that German *Welt haben* was originally a translation of the French import (Kant, 1984: 11–12). David wants to modify Foucault's translation with the French *avoir les usages du monde* (which takes it away from the everyday meaning of 'having company' and closer to the very French notion of *savoir vivre*, or knowing the ways of the world). In English, we enter new thickets of untranslatability. As Christian Hubert, the English translator of David's entry queries: 'What does "having the world" mean in English, especially when it is being contrasted with "knowing the world?"'[3]

'Having the world', or the variation, 'having world', one could say, actually names something that doesn't exist in English or, for that matter, German or French. It coins the idea of a property-drive harnessed to the mastery and the acquisition of resources, information, technology, know-how and symbolic capital. 'Master of the universe' might be the closest colloquial 'translation' of *Welt haben* following this gist. 'Not having world' could lead philosophically in the direction of Peter Singer, whose 'just enough' notion of distributive justice encourages a non-extractive approach to the earth, or a de-propertied way of existence. Alternatively, 'having world' could be ascribed to Edward Said's notion of worldliness; a terrestrial humanism forged by the politics of the Palestinian right to return, and aesthetically attuned to Erich Auerbach's Dantean understanding of earthly (*irdisch*) humanism in the 1929 classic *Dante als Dichter der irdischen Welt* (translated by Ralph Mannheim as *Dante, Poet of the Secular World*). One could also extend the English neologism to Édouard Glissant's *Tout-monde*, where to be in possession of place or possessed by a spirit of place (*genius loci*) corresponds to apprehending the translated worlds of place names.

Consider in this regard how Glissant performs an incantatory operation

---

[2] 'In addition, the expressions "to *know* the world" and "to *have* the world" are rather far from each other in their meaning, since one only *understands* the play that one has watched, while the other has *participated* in it' (Kant, 2006: 4).

[3] Christian Hubert in a note appended to his translation of *Welt* in Apter, Lezra and Wood, forthcoming.

on the name of an American state in *Faulkner, Mississippi*. Sounded out, in the manner of school children reciting its orthography (MISS-ISS-IPPI), the French ear produces *émailless, èssailless, èssaill-pi, pi-aille* (Glissant, 1996: 21). We hear echoes of *émail* (enamel), *émmailler* (to glaze, to sprinkle, to speckle), *emmailloter* (to swaddle or to bind a limb), *essaimer* (to swarm, to hive off, to emigrate), and *pi-aille*: proximate to the verb *piauler* (to whimper, to whine), or *piailler* (to squall, to squeal, to chirp), or *chialer* (to blubber). Out of the proper name springs an entire accursed history of the slaves' bondage, forced emigration, cries of pain and tears as well as the white south's social crack-up, documented mythically in Faulkner's sagas of malediction, secessionism, hereditary finalism and familial dysfunction among the Compsons, Sartoris and Snopes. Homonymic names are magical, like translation, because they show how one language world divides into two. In *Faulkner, Mississippi* one of these homonyms is the name of a plantation manor on the outskirts of Baton Rouge. It is called *Nottoway*. 'Nous nous suggérions pourtant que *"Nottoway"* avait sans doute voulu dire: "pas un chemin", *not a way*, pas une voie, pas un moyen, sous-entendu: d'échapper au lieu. Pas une seule possibilité de marronner' (Glissant, 1996: 24).[4] Housing a curator's dream of soiled antebellum frippery that doubles as a reliquary of slave labour, 'Nottoway' sits in its present-day industrialized surround as an anachronistic redoubt of tourism. What matters here though is not just the familiar *frisson* of southern gothic, but the way in which this monument to past decadence enters the lives of slaves into the temporal world of *durée*. Glissant discovers this Bergsonian register of time in his translation of Faulkner's phrase 'Ils enduraient. Ils endurèrent' [They endured] (Glissant, 1996: 87). The declension leads him to ponder what it means to endure from within, 'duraient dans', to stand, in a kind of civil disobedient posture, like the proverbial cats whose immobility and somnolence allow them to conquer eternity (Glissant, 1996: 87). If Faulkner's blacks escape death, it is because they have found durability within duration. By simply being – obstinately and obdurately – they have built a *Tout-monde* that outlasts time.

Another philosophical cartography for 'world' would have appeared if the *Vocabulaire* had extended its mandate to creolized or exogamous forms of French, not to mention non-European languages. Discussions of the difference between Arabic: مﻻﻋ *a'lam* (which is used to refer to countries of the world) and اﻳﻧد *dunya* (the world we live in now as opposed to the world

---

[4] 'It occurred to us that Nottoway must certainly have signified "not a way", not a path or means of egress, not a single possibility of evasion'. The verb *marroner*, a creole Untranslatable, refers to the slave's fugue. Translation by the author of this Afterword.

after death); between the Swahili *dunia* (world) and *Ulimwengu* (universe) or the Mandarin compound: 世 *shì* (life; age, generation, era, world, lifetime) plus 界 *jiè* (boundary, scope, extent, circles, group, kingdom) would have added worldliness to the definition of world. Ideally, future theories of the 'world' in World Literature and *littérature-monde* will work through this greater lexicon in charting the territory of philosophical Untranslatables; in pondering the terms by which we figure what a world is; and in placing where in the world the literatures of the world might be.

Works Cited

Apter, Emily, Jacques Lezra and Michael Wood (eds). forthcoming. *Dictionary of Untranslatables: A Philosophical Lexicon*. Princeton, NJ: Princeton University Press. [First published as Barbara Cassin (ed.), *Le Vocabulaire européen des philosophies: Dictionnaire des intraduisibles*. Paris: Seuil (2004).]

Brague, Rémi. 2004. 'Olam'. In Barbara Cassin (ed.), *Le Vocabulaire européen des philosophies: Dictionnaire des intraduisibles*. Paris: Seuil: 876–77.

—. forthcoming. 'Olam'. Trans. by Christian Hubert. In Emily Apter, Jacques Lezra and Michael Wood (eds). *Dictionary of Untranslatables: A Philosophical Lexicon*. Princeton, NJ: Princeton University Press.

Cassin, Barbara (ed.). 2004. *Le Vocabulaire européen des philosophies: Dictionnaire des intraduisibles*. Paris: Seuil.

David, Pascal. 2004. 'Welt'. In Barbara Cassin (ed.), *Le Vocabulaire européen des philosophies: Dictionnaire des intraduisibles*. Paris: Seuil: 1390–96.

—. forthcoming. 'Welt'. Trans. by Christian Hubert. In Emily Apter, Jacques Lezra, and Michael Wood (eds). *Dictionary of Untranslatables: A Philosophical Lexicon*. Princeton, NJ: Princeton University Press.

Glissant, Édouard. 1996. *Faulkner, Mississippi*. Paris: Stock.

Grafton, Anthony. 2009. *Worlds Made by Words: Scholarship and Community in the Modern West*. Cambridge, MA: Harvard University Press.

Kant, Immanuel. 1900–. *Anthropologie in pragmatischer Hinsicht*. In *Akademieausgabe* 7. Berlin: de Gruyter.

—. 1984. *Anthropologie du point de vue pragmatique*. Trans. by Michel Foucault. Paris: Vrin.

—. 2006. *Anthropology from a Pragmatic Point of View*. Trans. by Robert B. Louden. Cambridge: Cambridge University Press.

Ruffel, Lionel. 2007. *Volodine post-exotique*. Nantes: Éditions Cécile Defaut.

Appendix:
Toward a 'World-Literature' in French

In a manifesto published in Le Monde *in 2007, forty-four writers – among them Tahar Ben Jelloun, Maryse Condé, Édouard Glissant, and J.-M. G. Le Clézio – declared the death of Francophone literature and the birth of 'world literature in French'. In February 2009, at an international conference ('Littérature-monde: New Wave or New Hype?') held at Florida State University, Azouz Begag and several of the original signatories – Michel Le Bris, Alain Mabanckou, Anna Moï, Jean Rouaud and Abdourahman Waberi – continued the debate.*

In due course, it will perhaps be said that this was a historic moment: in autumn 2006, five of the seven French literary prizes – the Goncourt, the Grand Prize for Novels of the Académie Française, the Renaudot, the Femina and the Goncourt for High School Students – were awarded to foreign-born writers. A random coincidence, among publishers' fall catalogs, uniquely concentrating talent from the 'peripheries,' a random detour before the channel returns to the riverbed? A Copernican revolution, rather, in our opinion. Copernican because it reveals what the literary milieu already knew without admitting it: the center, from which supposedly radiated a franco-French literature, is no longer the center. Until now, the center, although less and less frequently, had this absorptive capacity that forced authors who came from elsewhere to rid themselves of their foreign trappings before melting in the crucible of the French language and its national history: the center, these fall prizes tell us, is henceforth everywhere, at the four corners of the world. The result? The end of 'francophone' literature – and the birth of a world literature in French.

296

The world is returning – and it's the best of news. Wasn't the world always conspicuous by its absence in French literature? The world, the subject, meaning, history, the 'referent': for decades, these have been bracketed off by the masterminds, inventors of a literature with no other object than itself, creating, as it was called at the time, 'its own critique in the very movement of its enunciation.' The novel was too serious an affair to be left to the novelists alone, who were guilty of a 'naïve use of language' and encouraged to repeat themselves in complaisant linguistic exercises. While these texts went along merely referring to other texts in a game of endless combinations, there came a time when the author found himself – and with it the very idea of creation – effectively emptied out in order to make room for the commentators, the exegetes. Rather than rub up against the world in order to capture its essence and vital energies, the novel, in the end, could merely watch itself being written.

That writers were able to survive in such an intellectual atmosphere inspires in us an optimism about the novel's capacity to resist everything that would conspire to negate or subjugate it.

This renewed desire to rejoin the world's routes, this return to literature's powers of incandescence, this felt urgency of a 'world literature,' has a unique historical origin: namely, the return on the world scene ... of the subject, meaning, History, concomitant with the staggering blows that brought about the dissolution of the grand ideologies – that is, from the effervescence of anti-totalitarian movements, in the West as well as the East, that would eventually tear down the Berlin Wall.

This return, one must realize, came about on the intersecting routes of random paths – even as such a path was resisted with extreme force! As if, with their chains cast off, each person had to learn how to walk again. With the desire, first of all, to savor the dust from the roads, the allure of the outdoors, the encounter of a stranger's glance. The tales of these astonishing voyagers, who appeared in the mid-1970s, would turn out to be the world's sumptuous entryways into fiction. Some, concerned with describing the world where they lived – like Raymond Chandler or Dashiell Hammett once described the American city – turned, in the wake of Jean-Patrick Manchette, toward fictional noir. Others, meanwhile, turned to a pastiche of crime fiction or the novel of adventure, skillful or prudent ways in which to recapture narrative, all the while flirting with the 'novel of the forbidden.' Still others, storytellers, staked their claim in comics, in the company of Hugo Pratt, Moebius, and a few others. And 'francophone' literatures were receiving renewed attention, particularly in the Caribbean, as if, far away from vitiated French models, a novelistic and poetic effervescence – inherited from Saint-John Perse and Aimé Césaire – was being affirmed there. And this in spite of the blinders on a literary milieu that professed to be waiting for merely a few new pigments, ancient or creole words (so picturesque, indeed), ready to refresh a gruel that had become exceedingly thin. The years 1976–77: the diverted paths of a return to fiction.

At the same time, a new wind was picking up from across the Channel, imposing evidence of a new English-language literature, uniquely harmonized with a world in the process of being born. In an England given over to its third generation of Woolfian novels – that is to say in the air that was barely palpable which circulated around them – a handful of young dissenters were turning toward the vast world, in order to breathe it in more deeply. Bruce Chatwin departed for Patagonia, and his narrative took on the allure of a manifesto for a generation of travel writers ('I apply to reality narrative techniques of the novel, to restore the novelistic dimension of reality'). Next came clamoring, in an impressive hubbub, a series of noisy, versicolored, métis novels that proclaimed, with a rare force and new vocabulary, the din of these exponential foreign cities where the cultures of all the continents collided, reshuffled, and mingled with one another. At the heart of this effervescence were Kazuo Ishiguro, Ben Okri, Hanif Kureishi, Michael Ondaatje – and Salman Rushdie, who explored with acuity the upsurge of what he called 'translated men': those who, born in England, no longer lived in the nostalgia of a homeland forever lost but, finding themselves between two worlds, astride a chasm, valiantly attempted to draft a new world out of this telescoping condition. For the first time, then, a generation of emigrant writers, instead of melting into their adopted culture, set out to create by drawing on the source of their plural identity, in the ambiguous and shifting territory in which they rubbed up against each other. In this regard, Carlos Fuentes insisted, they were less the products of decolonization than the heralds of the twenty-first century.

How many writers in the French language, themselves caught between two or several cultures, mulled this strange disparity that relegated them to the margins, themselves 'francophones,' an exotic hybrid barely tolerated, while the children of the former British empire were, with complete legitimacy, taking possession of English letters? For the inheritors of the French colonial empire, perhaps they possessed some sort of congenital flaw in comparison to writers of the British empire? Or shouldn't we recognize, rather, that the problem existed in the literary milieu itself, in its strange *ars poetica* turning like a whirling dervish upon itself, and in this vision of a francophone world upon which a maternal France, 'patron of the arts, arms, and laws,' continued to dispense its radiance, like a universal benefactor eager to bring civilization to people living in the shadows? Those writers from the Antilles, Haiti, Africa who had confidence in their project had no reason to envy their counterparts in the English language. The concept of 'creolization' that united them then, and by which they affirmed their singularity, was nothing less than a language in search of an autonomous self – one had to have been deaf and blind, only searching for an echo of oneself in others, not to understand it as such.

Let's be clear: the emergence of a consciously affirmed, transnational world-literature in the French language, open to the world, signs the death certificate of so-called francophone literature. No one speaks or writes 'francophone.' Francophone literature is a light from a dying star. How could the world be concerned with the language of a virtual country? Yet it was the world that invited itself to the fall prize banquets, and we now understand that it was time for a revolution.

It might have come about earlier, this revolution. How was it possible to ignore for decades a Nicolas Bouvier and his aptly named *L'Usage du monde* (1985; Eng. *The Way of the World*, 1992)? Because at that time, the world was forbidden to dwell there. How was it possible not to recognize in Réjean Ducharme one of our greatest contemporary authors, whose *L'hiver de force* (1973; Eng. *Wild to Mild*, 1980), carried along by an extraordinary poetic inspiration, came to overshadow everything that has since been written on the society of consumption and libertarian foolishness? Because the 'Picturesque Provinces' were so highly regarded back then, of which a charming accent was all that was expected, with words that evoked the fragrance of archaic France. And one could pick and choose among African or Antillean writers, similarly marginalized: Why be surprised when the concept of creolization found itself reduced to its opposite, mistaken for a United Colors of Benetton slogan? Why be surprised if some stubbornly clung to an exclusive flesh-and-blood connection between nation and language that expressed a singular genius – since in a strict sense the 'francophone' concept presents itself as the last avatar of colonialism? What these fall prizes confirm is the inverse notion: that the colonial pact is broken, that language thus liberated has become everyone's concern, and that, if one firmly subscribes to it, the era of contempt and adequacy has ended. The end, then, of 'francophone' literature, and the birth of a world-literature in French: such are the stakes, to the extent that these writers accept them.

'World-literature' because literatures in French around the world today are demonstrably multiple, diverse, forming a vast ensemble, the ramifications of which link together several continents. But 'world-literature' also because all around us these literatures depict the world that is emerging in front of us, and by doing so recover, after several decades, from what was 'forbidden in fiction' what has always been the province of artists, novelists, creators: the task of giving a voice and a visage to the global unknown – and to the unknown in us. In the end, if we perceive everywhere this creative effervescence, it's because something in France itself has recommenced, in which the young generation, having shed itself of the era of suspicion, seizes without hesitation the ingredients of fiction in order to open up new novelistic paths – to the extent that it looks to us like we're in the midst of a renaissance, a dialogue in a vast polyphonic ensemble, without concern for any battle for or against the preeminence of one language over the other or any sort of 'cultural imperialism' whatsoever. With the center placed on an equal plane with other centers, we're witnessing the birth of a new constellation, in which language freed from its exclusive pact with the nation, free from every other power hereafter but the powers of poetry and the imaginary, will have no other frontiers but those of the spirit.

Paris
Muriel Barbery, Tahar Ben Jelloun, Alain Borer, Roland Brival, Maryse Condé, Didier Daeninckx, Ananda Devi, Alain Dugrand, Édouard Glissant, Jacques Godbout, Nancy Huston, Koffi Kwahulé, Dany Laferrière, Gilles Lapouge, Jean-Marie Laclavetine, Michel Layaz, Michel Le Bris, J.-M. G. Le Clézio, Yvon Le Men, Amin Maalouf, Alain Mabanckou, Anna Moï, Wajdi Mouawad, Nimrod, Wilfried N'Sondé, Esther Orner, Erik Orsenna, Benoît Peeters, Patrick Rambaud, Gisèle Pineau, Jean-Claude Pirotte, Grégoire Polet, Patrick Raynal, Jean-Luc V. Raharimanana, Jean Rouaud, Boualem Sansal, Dai Sitje, Brina Svit, Lyonel Trouillot, Anne Vallaeys, Jean Vautrin, André Velter, Gary Victor, Abdourahman A. Waberi

Translated by Daniel Simon.

Editorial note: From 'Pour une 'littérature-monde' en français,' *Le Monde*, 16 March 2007. Copyright © 2007 by *Le Monde*. This English translation first appeared in *World Literature Today* 83.2 (March–April 2009), 54–56. English translation copyright © 2009 by *World Literature Today*.

Notes on Contributors

Emily Apter is Professor of French, English, and Comparative Literature at New York University. Her books include: *The Translation Zone: A New Comparative Literature* (Princeton University Press, 2006), *Continental Drift: From National Characters to Virtual Subjects* (Chicago University Press, 1999), as well as studies of fetishism and a monograph on André Gide. Since 1998 she has edited the book series, Translation/Transnation for Princeton University Press. She is currently co-editing (with Jacques Lezra and Michael Wood) the English edition of *Le Vocabulaire européen des philosophies: Dictionnaire des intraduisibles* [Dictionary of Untranslatables: A Philosophical Lexicon], as well as an English edition of Alain Badiou's literary writings (with Bruno Bosteels). Recent essays have focused on authorial property and the creative commons, rethinking world literature around 'the untranslatable,' and the 'untiming' of periodization. She has been the recipient of fellowships from the Guggenheim and Rockefeller foundations.

Mounia Benalil is a postdoctoral researcher on *francophonie* and globalization at the University of Montreal. She is attached to the CRILCQ (Le Centre de recherche interuniversitaire sur la littérature et la culture québécoises) and to the SAIC (Secrétariat aux Affaires Intergouvernementales Canadiennes). She is the editor of *L'Orient dans le roman de la Caraïbe* (CIDIHCA, 2007), co-editor of *Identités hybrides: Orient et orientalisme au Québec* (Presses de l'Université de Montréal, 2006) and the author of numerous articles published in a range of journals including *Protée: Revue internationale de théories et de pratiques sémiotiques*, *Voix et images*, *Nouvelles Francographies: Revue de la société des professeurs français et francophones d'Amérique*, *Expressions maghrébines: Revue de la coordination internationale des chercheurs sur les littératures maghrébines* and *Studies in Canadian Literature/études en littérature canadienne*.

Chris Bongie is Full Professor and Queen's National Scholar in the English Department at Queen's University in Canada. He is the author of two monographs published with Stanford University Press: *Exotic Memories: Literature, Colonialism and the Fin de siècle* (1991) and *Islands and Exiles: The Creole Identities of Post/Colonial Literature* (1998). He has translated Victor Hugo's novel *Bug-Jargal* into English (Broadview Press, 2004), and produced an edition of the first two novels about the Haitian Revolution: Jean-Baptiste Picquenard's *Adonis* and *Zoflora* (L'Harmattan, 2006). His latest book is *Friends and Enemies: The Scribal Politics of Post/Colonial Literature* (Liverpool University Press, 2008) and he is currently working on a translation/edition of the early nineteenth-century Haitian writer Baron de Vastey's pioneering critique of colonialism, *Le système colonial dévoilé*.

Teresa Bridgeman is a professional translator. She was previously a Senior Lecturer in French at the University of Bristol, where she taught translation, among other subjects, and published widely on narratology, the poetics of time and space, stylistics, the French novel and *bande dessinée*. She is on the consultative committee of *European Comic Art* and is a member of the translation division of the Chartered Institute of Linguists. She received her doctorate from the University of Oxford. Her translations include works by the historian Jean-Paul Bled and members of the ACHAC research group, as well as texts on photography, fine art and the history of printing.

Jacqueline Dutton is Senior Lecturer and Convenor of French Studies at the University of Melbourne. She has published widely on utopianism in French literature and thought, including a monograph in French on the utopian writings of the 2008 Nobel Laureate in Literature, *Le Chercheur d'or et d'ailleurs: L'Utopie de J. M. G. Le Clézio* (L'Harmattan, 2003). Her research interests range from travel writing and contemporary world literature in French to comparative utopias and Japanese imaginaries of the ideal. She contributed a chapter on 'Non-western' utopian traditions to the *Cambridge Companion to Utopian Literature* (Cambridge University Press, 2010) and is completing a book-length study of French visions of Australia as Utopia. Her current projects include editing volumes on representations of time in postcolonial and Francophone travel writing and on comparative utopian studies. She is the creator and director of the Australian Festival of Travel Writing (www.aftw.com.au).

Charles Forsdick is James Barrow Professor of French and Head of the School of Cultures, Languages and Area Studies at the University of Liverpool. He is the author of *Victor Segalen and the Aesthetics of Diversity* (Oxford

University Press, 2000), *Travel in Twentieth-Century French and Francophone Cultures* (Oxford University Press, 2005) and *Ella Maillart, 'Oasis interdites'* (Zoé, 2008); and co-author of *New Approaches to Twentieth-Century Travel Literature in French: Genre, Theory, History* (Peter Lang, 2006). He is also editor and co-editor of a number of collections, including *Francophone Postcolonial Studies* (Arnold, 2003), *Human Zoos: Science and Spectacle in the Age of Colonial Empire* (Liverpool University Press, 2008) and *Postcolonial Thought in the French-Speaking World* (Liverpool University Press, 2009).

Jeanne Garane is Associate Professor of French and Comparative Literature at the University of South Carolina, where she teaches courses on Francophone literature and film, postcolonial theory, translation and comparative literary studies. She translated Abdourahman Waberi's *Pays sans ombre* (*The Shadowless Land*) (CARAF books, University of Virgina Press, 2006) and spearheaded the re-edition of Ken Bugul's *Abandoned Baobab* (University of Virginia Press, 2008). She has published articles, introductions and interviews on Francophone literature and film as well as an edited volume, *Discursive Geographies: Writing Space in French/Géographies Discursives: L'écriture de l'espace en français* (Rodopi, 2006) and a co-edited volume with James Day, *Translation in/and French and Francophone Literature and Film* (*French Literature Series*, vol. 39, 2009). She is currently completing a book on Francophone literatures and translation.

Alec G. Hargreaves is Director of the Winthrop-King Institute for Contemporary French and Francophone Studies at Florida State University. A specialist on postcolonial minorities in France, he has authored and edited numerous publications including *The Colonial Experience in French Fiction* (Macmillan, 1981), *Voices from the North African Immigrant Community in France: Immigration and Identity in Beur Fiction* (Berg, 1991), *Immigration, 'Race' and Ethnicity in Contemporary France* (Routledge, 1995), *Post-Colonial Cultures in France* (Routledge, 1997), *Memory, Empire and Postcolonialism: Legacies of French Colonialism* (Lexington, 2005) and *Multi-Ethnic France: Immigration, Politics, Culture and Society* (Routledge, 2007).

Jane Hiddleston is Lecturer in French at the University of Oxford and a Fellow of Exeter College, Oxford. She has published three books: *Reinventing Community: Identity and Difference in Late Twentieth-Century Philosophy and Literature in French* (Legenda, 2005), *Assia Djebar: Out of Algeria* (Liverpool University Press, 2006) and *Understanding Postcolonialism* (Acumen, 2009). Her latest monograph, *Poststructuralism and Postcoloniality: The Anxiety of Theory*, will be published by Liverpool University Press in 2010. She is now working together with Patrick Crowley on an edited volume for the Liverpool series on Francophone Postcolonial Studies entitled *Postcolonial Poetics: Genre and Form*. Her latest research revolves around Francophone intellectuals at the time of decolonization, with a particular focus on their versions of humanism, and on the relation between literature and politics.

Deborah Jenson is Professor of French Studies at Duke University. Her forthcoming book *Beyond the Slave Narrative: Politics, Sex, and Manuscripts in the Haitian Revolution* (Liverpool University Press) introduces the Haitian literary traditions that emerged from the Haitian Revolution itself. Jenson has published numerous articles on political texts produced by revolutionary leaders Toussaint Louverture and Jean-Jacques Dessalines, popular Creole poetry representing the voices of Haiti's libertine courtesans or sex workers, tropes of kidnapping and disaster in Haitian letters, Haitian 'bovarysm' and other subjects; she is also the editor of the 'Haiti Issue' of *Yale French Studies* (2005). In the field of nineteenth-century French studies, Jenson has published the book *Trauma and its Representations: The Social Life of Mimesis in Post-Revolutionary France* (Johns Hopkins University Press, 2001), editions of Desbordes-Valmore's colonial novella *Sarah*, and articles on topics such as Marx against mimesis, and mirror revolutions. With Warwick Anderson and Richard Keller, she is publishing a volume on psychoanalysis and colonialism, *Unconscious Dominions*, forthcoming with Duke University Press. Jenson has developed and co-taught a series of Creole studies courses at Duke, and is co-director of the Duke Franklin Humanities Institute 'Haiti Lab' with Laurent Dubois.

Michelle Keown is Senior Lecturer in English Literature at the University of Edinburgh, where she teaches postcolonial literature and theory. She has published widely on Maori, New Zealand and Pacific writing and is the author of *Postcolonial Pacific Writing: Representations of the Body* (Routledge, 2005) and *Pacific Islands Writing: The Postcolonial Literatures of Aotearoa / New Zealand and Oceania* (Oxford University Press, 2007). She has also published on diaspora theory and culture and is co-editor (with David Murphy and James Procter) of *Comparing Postcolonial Diasporas* (Palgrave, 2009). Current research projects are focused upon translation and multilingualism in indigenous Pacific literature and the literatures of British settler diasporas in Australia, Canada and New Zealand.

Typhaine Leservot is Associate Professor in the Romance Languages and Literatures Department (French) and College of Letters at Wesleyan University.

She specializes in the intersection of globalization and Francophone postcolonial studies. Her book *Le Corps mondialisé: Marie Redonnet, Maryse Condé, Assia Djebar* was published by L'Harmattan in 2007. She has published articles in *Women in French Studies*, *L'Harmattan* and *Contemporary French and Francophone Studies* (SITES) on Maryse Condé, Assia Djebar and the Muslim veil in Quebec. Her article on Occidentalism in Marjane Satrapi is forthcoming in *French Forum*.

Lydie Moudileno is Professor of French and Francophone Literatures at the University of Pennsylvania. Her general area of research is postcolonial literature, with a focus on Sub-saharan Africa and the Caribbbean, contemporary fiction from the 1980s to the present and popular genres. She is the author of *L'Ecrivain antillais au miroir de sa littérature* (Karthala, 1997), *Littératures africaines: 1980–1990* (Codesria Publications, 2003) and *Parades Postcoloniales* (Karthala, 2006).

David Murphy is Professor of French and Postcolonial Studies at the University of Stirling. He has published widely on African – particularly Senegalese – culture and on the relationship between Francophone and Postcolonial Studies. He is the author of two monographs, *Sembene: Imagining Alternatives in Film and Fiction* (James Currey, 2000) and (with Patrick Williams) *Postcolonial African Cinema: Ten Directors* (Manchester University Press, 2007). He is also co-editor of several collections of essays, including two with Charles Forsdick, *Francophone Postcolonial Studies: A Critical Introduction* (Arnold, 2003) and *Postcolonial Thought in the French-Speaking World* (Liverpool University Press, 2009).

Aedín Ní Loingsigh is a Research Assistant at the University of Liverpool. Her specialist interest is travel and mobility in Francophone African literature. She has published several articles on this subject as well as a monograph: *Postcolonial Eyes: Intercontinental Travel in Francophone African Literature* (Liverpool University Press, 2009).

Laura K. Reeck is Associate Professor of French at Allegheny College where she teaches twentieth- and twenty-first-century postcolonial French literature. Her first book, *Writerly Identities in Beur Fiction and Beyond* (Lexington Books, forthcoming), examines the struggles of author-characters to attain self-identity and a place in the world through *writing* and *authorship*, and engages this literary theme with a range of socio-cultural challenges facing contemporary France. She has previously published essays on translation, Mohamed Razane's *Dit violent*, Rachid Djaïdani's *Boumkoeur* and the harkis in literature in journals such as *Expressions maghrébines*, *Romance Quarterly* and the *Journal of North African Studies*.

Jean-Xavier Ridon is a Reader of contemporary French and Francophone studies at the University of Nottingham. His research focuses on contemporary travel narratives and postcolonial studies. His publications include *L'exil des mots* (Kimé, 1995), *Le Voyage en son miroir* (Kimé, 2005) and *Le Poisson-Scorpion de Nicolas Bouvier* (Zoé, 2007), and he has edited collections of essays about exoticism and Europe.

Daniel Simon is Assistant Director and Editor-in-Chief of *World Literature Today* (the University of Oklahoma's bimonthly magazine of international literature and culture, currently in its eighty-fourth year of continuous publication). He joined the *World Literature Today* staff in 2002, after previous editorial positions at the University of Oklahoma Press and University of Nebraska Press. Simon received his doctorate in comparative literature – with an emphasis in translation studies – from Indiana University in 2000. At the University of Oklahoma, in addition to his work at *World Literature Today*, he serves as an adjunct assistant professor in the English department and affiliate faculty member in the School of International & Area Studies. He is also a member of the Council of Editors of Learned Journals and PEN American Center, the US branch of the world's oldest international literary and human rights organization. His previous translations include texts by Tahar Ben Jelloun, Christine Montalbetti, Assia Djebar and Claude Michel Cluny.

Thomas C. Spear is Professor of French at Lehman College and the Graduate Center of the City University of New York (CUNY). Co-editor of *Céline and the Politics of Difference* (University Press of New England, 1995), he is editor of *La Culture française vue d'ici et d'ailleurs* (Karthala, 2002) and *Une journée haïtienne* (Présence africaine, 2007), and has written especially on forms of autobiography in the contemporary Francophone novel. Since 1998, he is the editor of *Île en île*, a database (including an extensive audio and video archive) featuring some 250 authors from French-speaking islands. Projected publications include a collection of essays (edited with Colette Boucher) on the work of Marie-Célie Agnant, a volume of original fiction by New Caledonian authors and a *sidafiction*, a chapter of which was published in *l'Atelier d'écriture* in January 2010.

Michael Syrotinski is Professor of French and Francophone Studies at the University of Aberdeen, and has published widely on Francophone Africa and twentieth-century French literature and theory. His books include *Defying Gravity: Jean Paulhan's Interventions in Twentieth Century French Intellectual History* (State University of New York Press, 1998), *Singular Performances: Reinscribing the Subject in Francophone African Writing* (University of Virginia Press, 2002), *The Flowers of Tarbes, or Terror in Literature* (translation and critical edition of Jean Paulhan's *Les Fleurs de Tarbes, ou la Terreur dans les Lettres*, University of Illinois Press, 2006) and *Deconstruction and the Postcolonial: At the Limits of Theory* (Liverpool University Press, 2007). He is one of a team of five translators who are preparing an English edition of the *Vocabulaire européen des philosophies* (Princeton University Press, forthcoming) and is currently working on a study provisionally entitled *Trauma, Reading and Attachment Theory*.

Dominic Thomas currently chairs the departments of French and Francophone Studies and Italian at the University of California Los Angeles. He has been an invited professor at the École des hautes études en sciences sociales, the Musée Quai Branly, and Humboldt Universität Berlin, and a Research Fellow at the Centre for Research in the Arts, Social Sciences, and Humanities at Cambridge University, the Society for the Humanities at Cornell University, and the Program in African Studies at Northwestern University. He is the author of *Nation-Building, Propaganda and Literature in Francophone Africa* (Indiana University Press, 2002) and *Black France: Colonialism, Immigration and Transnationalism* (Indiana University Press, 2007). As editor, he has published 'Francophone Studies: New Landscapes' (with Françoise Lionnet, *Modern Language Notes*, 2003), 'Textual Ownership in Francophone African Literature' (with Alec G. Hargreaves and Nicki Hitchcott, *Research in African Literatures*, 2006), 'Global Francophone Africa' (*Forum for Modern Language Studies*, 2009), and *Museums in Postcolonial Europe* (Routledge, 2009). Forthcoming editorial projects include *A Companion to Comparative Literature* (with Ali Behdad, Blackwell Publishers, 2010), 'Francophone sub-Saharan African Literature in Global Contexts' (with Alain Mabanckou, *Yale French Studies*, 2011) and 'The Francophone Documentary' (with Philippe Met, *French Forum*, 2011). He is also the editor of the fiction in translation series 'Global African Voices' at Indiana University Press.